INSTRVMENTA PATRISTICA ET MEDIAEVALIA

Research on the Inheritance of Early and Medieval Christianity

97

SVBSIDIA MAXIMIANA 3

Ambiguum 10 of Maximus the
Confessor in Modern Study

Ambiguum 10 of Maximus the Confessor in Modern Study

Papers Collected on the Occasion of the Budapest
Colloquium on Saint Maximus, 3–4 February 2021

Edited by

Alexis Léonas
Vladimir Cvetković

with the collaboration of

Daniel Heide

TURNHOUT
BREPOLS
2025

INSTRVMENTA PATRISTICA ET MEDIAEVALIA

Research on the Inheritance of Early and Medieval Christianity

Founded by Dom Eligius Dekkers († 1998)

SVBSIDIA MAXIMIANA

Editorial responsibility

ISBN 978-2-503-61126-6
E-ISBN 978-2-503-61127-3
DOI 10.1484/M.IPM-EB.5.137207
ISSN 1379-9878
E-ISSN 2294-8457

Printed in the EU on acid-free paper.
D/2025/0095/215

Table of Contents

III. St. Maximus the Christian Philosopher

Abbreviations used in this volume for Maximus' works and *Maximiana*

Add.	*Additamenta e variis codicibus* [CPG 7707]
Amb.Ioh.	*Ambigua ad Iohannem* [CPG 7705.2]
Amb.Thom.	*Ambigua ad Thomam* [CPG 7705.1]
Anim.	*Opusculum de anima* [CPG 7717]
Cap.alia	*Capita alia* [CPG 7716]
Cap.X	*Capita X* [CPG 7694a]
Cap.XV	*Capita XV* [CPG 7695]
Car.	*Capita de caritate* [CPG 7693]
Comp.	*Computus ecclesiasticus* [CPG 7706]
Contra Const.	*Contra Constantinopolitanos* [CPG 7740]
D.B.	*Disputatio Bizyae sive Acta in primo exsilio seu dialogus Maximi cum Theodosio episcopo Caesareae in Bithynia* [CPG 7735]
Div.Cap.	*Diversa capita ad theologiam et oeconomiam spectantia deque virtute et vitio* [CPG 7715]
D.P.	*Disputatio cum Pyrrho* [CPG 7698]
E.O.D.	*Expositio orationis dominicae* [CPG 7691]
E.ps.59	*Expositio in Psalmum LIX* [CPG 7690]
Ep.	*Epistulae XLV* [CPG 7699]
Ep.Max.	*Epistula ad Anastasium monachum discipulum* [CPG 7701]
Ep.Sec.Th.	*Epistola Secunda ad Thomam* [CPG 7700]
L.A.	*Liber asceticus* [CPG 7692]

Myst.	*Mystagogia* [CPG 7704]
Op.	*Opuscula theologica et polemica* [CPG 7697]
Q.D.	*Quaestiones et dubia* [CPG 7689]
Q.Thal.	*Quaestiones ad Thalassium* [CPG 7688]
Q.Theop.	*Quaestiones ad Theopemptum*
R.M.	*Relatio Motionis inter Maximum et principes [CPG 7736]*
Th.Oec.	*Capita theologica et oeconomica* [CPG 7694]
T.S.	*Testimonia et syllogismi*

Critical Editions and Reference Works

AB 91 S. Brock (ed. and trans.), "An Early Syriac Life of Maximus the Confessor", *Analecta Bollandiana* 91 (1973): 302–319. Reprinted in S. BROCK, *Syriac Perspectives on Late Antiquity*, Collected Studies Series 199 (London, 1992).

CAG *Commentaria in Aristotelem Graeca*

CCSG *Corpus Christianorum Series Graeca*

CCSG 7 C. LAGA & C. STEEL (eds), *Quaestiones ad Thalassium I, Quaestiones I–LV, una cum latina interpretatione Ioannis Scotti Eriugenae*, *CCSG* 7 (Turnhout, 1980).

CCSG 10 J. DECLERCK (ed.), *Quaestiones et dubia*, *CCSG* 10 (Turnhout, 1982).

CCSG 18 E. JEAUNEAU (ed.), *Ambigua ad Iohannem iuxta Iohannis Scoti Eriugenae latinam interpretationem*, *CCSG* 18 (Turnhout, 1988).

CCSG 22 C. LAGA & C. STEEL (eds), *Quaestiones ad Thalassium II, Quaestiones LVI–LXV, una cum latina interpretatione Ioannis ScottiEriugenae*, *CCSG* 22 (Turnhout, 1990).

CCSG 23 P. VAN DEUN (ed.), *Opuscula exegetica duo*, *CCSG* 23 (Turnhout, 1991).

CCSG 39 P. ALLEN & B. NEIL (eds), *Scripta Saeculi VII vitam Maximi Confessoris illustrantia cum Latina interpretatione Anastasii Bibliothecarii iuxtaposita*, *CCSG* 39 (Turnhout – Leuven, 1999).

CCSG 40 P. VAN DEUN (ed.), *Liber asceticus*, *CCSG* 40 (Turnhout, 2000).

CCSG 48 B. JANSSENS (ed.), *Ambigua ad Thomam una cum Epistula secunda ad eundem*, *CCSG* 48 (Turnhout, 2002).

CCSG 69 C. BOUDIGNON (ed.), *Mystagogia*, *CCSG* 69 (Turnhout, 2011).

CCSG 89   K. Levrie, *Maximi Confessoris Capita de duabus Christi naturis...*, *CCSG* 89 (Turnhout, 2017).

CCSL   *Corpus Christianorum Series Latina*

Constas, 2014 (1 & 2)   N. Constas (trans.), *Maximos the Confessor, The Ambigua*, Dumbarton Oaks Medieval Library 28, 2 vols (Cambridge, MA, 2014).

Constas, 2018   N. Constas (trans.), *St. Maximos the Confessor, On Difficulties in Sacred Scripture: The Responses to Thalassios*, Fathers of the Church Patristic Series 136 (Washington DC, 2018).

CPG   *Clavis Patrum Graecorum*

CPG Supp.   *Clavis Patrum Graecorum Supplementum*

CSCO   *Corpus Scriptorum Christianorum Orientalium*

ECS 6   B. Neil & P. Allen (ed. and trans.), *The Life of Maximus the Confessor – Recension 3*, Early Christian Studies 6 (Strathfield, 2003).

GNO   *Gregorii Nysseni Opera*

GCS   *Die Griechischen Christlichen Schriftsteller*

Lampe   G.W.H. Lampe, *A Patristic Greek Lexicon* (Oxford, 1961).

LCL   *Loeb Classical Library*

Lectio 11   *Questioning the World. Greek Patristic and Byzantine Question-and-Answer Literature*, by B. Demulder & P. Van Deun, Lectio 11 (Turnhout, 2021), 229–267.

Louth, Maximus   A. Louth, *Maximus the Confessor* (The Early Church Fathers), London-NewYork, 1996.

OECT 2002 P. Allen & B. Neil (eds and trans.), *Maximus the Confessor and his Companions: Documents from Exile*, Oxford Early Christian Texts (Oxford, 2002).

OHMC   P. Allen & B. Neil (eds), *The Oxford Handbook on Maximus the Confessor* (Oxford, 2002).

PG   J.-P. Migne (ed.), *Patrologiae cursus completus. Series Graeca*, 161 vols (Paris, 1857–1866).

PL　　　　J.-P. MIGNE (ed.), *Patrologiae cursus completus. Series Latina*, 221 vols (Paris, 1844–1865).

PTS 33　　B. SUCHLA (ed.), *Corpus Dionysiacum 1: Pseudo-Dionysius Areopagita. De divinis nominibus*, PTS 33 (Berlin-New York, 1990).

PTS 36　　G. HEIL & A. M. RITTER (eds), *Corpus Dionysiacum II: Pseudo-Dionysius Areopagita, De Coelesti Hierarchia, De Ecclesiastica Hierarchia, De Mystica Theologia, Epistulae*, PTS 36 (Berlin, 1991).

SAA 2　　B. NEIL (ed. and trans.), *Seventh-Century Popes and Martyrs: The Political Hagiography of Anastasius Bibliothecarius*, Studia Antiqua Australiensia 2 (Turnhout-Sydney, 2006).

SC　　　　*Sources Chrétiennes*

SP　　　　*Studia Patristica*

Introduction[*]

Vladimir Cvetković and Alex Léonas
(Belgrade and Budapest)

This volume centers on *Ambiguum* 10, the most extensive and philo-sophically diverse *Ambiguum* of St. Maximus the Confessor. While this writing is part of a larger collection referred to as *Ambigua to John*, *Ambiguum* 10, due to its length and distinct subject matter, may be regard-ed as a separate work within this compilation. *Ambiguum* 10 is not only the longest work in Maximus' *Ambigua to John*, it is also a text address-ing the most fundamental issues of the Christian religious itinerary. In this regard, *Ambiguum* 10 explores a diverse array of topics, encom-passing Trinitarian theology, Christology, the doctrine of creation and providence, the interplay between contemplation and asceticism, the connection between the Old and New Testaments, the essence of the soul, and the classification of beings. Andrew Louth has characterized this work as an exemplary demonstration of Maximus' "lateral think-ing"; namely, the Confessor's unique capacity to intuit the most diverse facets of reality while weaving them into a cohesive image.[1] The solu-tions he comes up with have lost none of their validity and relevance. The winding path of thought in Maximus' *Ambiguum* 10 provides a blueprint of live metaphysical reflection.

While *Ambiguum* 10 delves into profound Christian mysteries, it is important to note that certain aspects of this work, as well as *Ambi-gua to John* as a whole, remain shrouded in secrecy and unresolved questions. In 1955, when Polycarp Sherwood released his work *Earlier Ambigua of St. Maximus the Confessor*, it appeared to resolve many of those. In response to Hans Urs von Balthasar's assertion that Maximus

[*] This research was supported by the Science Fund of the Republic of Serbia, #GRANT No 1554, *Assessing Neoplatonism in the 14th and 15th century Balkans – ANEB*.

[1] A. Louth, *Maximus*, pp. 45, 91.

experienced an Origenist crisis,[2] Sherwood put forth the argument
that the first of the two *Ambigua*, specifically the one directed to John,
serves as Maximus' systematic rebuttal of Origenism.[3] It was created
at the behest of Archbishop John of Cyzicus, who held authority over
Maximus during his time as a monk at the St. George Monastery in
Cyzicus.[4] This work was finalized when Maximus relocated to Africa,
likely between 628 and 630. It comprises the dialogues that Maximus
engaged in with Archbishop John while he was still in Cyzicus prior to
his departure.[5] This narrative aligns seamlessly with Maximus' Greek
vita, which narrates how Maximus, originally from Constantinople,
initially pursued a political career as Emperor Heraclius' first secretary
before ultimately opting for a monastic lifestyle.

Sherwood's interpretation faced its initial challenge with the publication of Maximus' Syriac *vita* in English translation by Sebastian
Brock in 1973.[6] Scholars were already aware of the existence of a Syriac
vita, though it had not previously garnered much attention.[7] This was
largely due to the fact that this text was a pamphlet penned by Maximus'
adversary, a certain George of Resh'aina. As such, its primarily aim was
to discredit Maximus. Despite Maximus being depicted as "wicked"
and labeled an Origenist blasphemer by his opponent, Sherwood's perspective regarding Maximus as a staunch anti-Origenist went largely
unchallenged by most scholars. The commonly accepted explanations
for the negative epithets ascribed to Maximus point to their Monothe-
lite origin[8] and not to an anti-Origenist stance of the Syriac author.
During the 1990s, scholars delving into Maximus' work typically con-

---

[2] H. U. VON BALTHASAR, *Die "gnostischen" Centurien des Maximus Confessor*, Freiburg, 1941, pp. 8, 155.

[3] P. SHERWOOD, *Earlier Ambigua of St. Maximus the Confessor*, Rome, 1955,
pp. viii–ix.

[4] SHERWOOD, *Earlier Ambigua*, pp. 6–7.

[5] P. SHERWOOD, *An Annotated Date-list of the Works of Maximus the Confessor*, Rome, 1952, pp. 3–5. See also M. JANKOWIACK & P. BOOTH, "A New
Date-List of the Works of Maximus the Confessor", in *OHMC*, 19–83: 28.

[6] S. BROCK, "An Early Syriac Life of Maximus the Confessor", *Analecta
Bollandiana* 91 (1973), pp. 299–346.

[7] А. Бриллиантовъ, *О мѣстѣ кончины и погребенія св. Максима
Исповѣдника*, Петроградъ, 1918 [offprint from: Христіанскій Востокъ
VI.1 (1917)].

[8] BROCK, "An Early Syriac Life of Maximus the Confessor", p. 301.

sulted both of his *vitas*, while also acknowledging the inconsistencies and limitations within them.

Previous studies had already hinted at seventh century Origenism's inclination to narrow theology down to the concept of the consummation of everything in Christ, and its tendency towards an intellectually complex Platonism, rather than following the orthodox Origenism of the earlier period.[9] In the 2000s a significant shift in the understanding of Maximus' anti-Origenist position emerged. As researchers delved into the intellectual landscape of the early seventh century, it became evident that the doctrine of the soul's dormancy, in direct opposition to Origenist beliefs regarding the soul's pre- and post-existence, had gained traction and spread throughout the Byzantine world.[10] Certain scholars have raised doubts regarding the assertion made by Sherwood half a century ago, suggesting that the *Ambigua to John* might not have been aimed at combating Origenism as Sherwood claimed, but rather directed against those who held radical or vulgar anti-Origenist views.[11]

Historical studies have also yielded fresh insights. It has come to light that the previously unquestioned identity of Archbishop John of Cyzicus was, in fact, a construct within a scholarly discourse. Philip Booth has recently corroborated the suspicions of Sherwood and Jean-Claude Larchet,[12] asserting that "John Cyzicenus" is, in reality, an academic

---

[9] SHERWOOD, *The Earlier Ambigua*, pp. 223–224. M. SIMONETTI, "La controversia origeniana: Caratteri e significato", *Augustinianum* 26 (1986), pp. 7–31: 29. See also V. CVETKOVIĆ, "Maximus the Confessor"s Reading of Origen between Origenism and Anti-Origenism', in *Origeniana Undecima: Origen and Origenism in the History of Western Tradition*, ed. by A.-C. JACOBSEN, Leuven, 2016, pp. 747–758.

[10] D. KRAUSMÜLLER, "Conflicting Anthropologies in the Christological Discourse at the End of the Late Antiquity. The Case of Leontius of Jerusalem"s Nestorian Adversary', *Journal of Theologica Studies. N.S.*, 56/2 (2005), pp. 115–149: 118; N. CONSTAS, "'To Sleep, Perchance to Dream': The Middle State of Souls in Patristic and Byzantine Literature," *Dumbarton Oaks Papers* 55 (2001), pp. 91–24.

[11] A. LEVY, *Le créé et l'incréé: Maxime le confesseur et Thomas d'Aquin*, Paris, 2006, pp. 130–205; G. BENEVICH, "Maximus the Confessor"s Polemics against Anti-Origenism: *Epistula* 6 and 7 as a Context for the *Ambigua ad Iohannem*", *Revue d'histoire ecclésiastique* 104 (2009), pp. 5–15.

[12] SHERWOOD, *An Annotated Date-list*, 22; J.-C. LARCHET, "Introduc-

distortion of the name "Kurisikios", an obscure figure who was the recipient of one of Maximus' letters.[13] According to Booth, Maximus' fascination with Origenism and his enthusiasm for Dionysius the Areopagite align more coherently with the intellectual context of Palestine and Syria than with Constantinople.[14] As Krausmeuller elucidates, the anti-Origenist sentiment in the early seventh century was so intense that even topics like the soul's self-sufficiency in the afterlife, extensively examined in *Ambiguum* 10, were labelled as Origenism.[15] Thus, it becomes easier to comprehend why George of Resh'aina characterized Maximus as a "wicked Origenist".

Given the newly proposed anti-Origenist context, what approach should be taken to comprehend the material found in *Ambiguum* 10? Using the passage from Gregory the Theologian's oration on Saint Athanasius (*Sermon* 21.2)[16] as a springboard, Maximus addresses the problem of the role of the ascetic struggle in the ascent to God. The difficulty in this instance lies in Gregory's reference to reason and contemplation while omitting any mention of ascetic practice.[17] In defense of Gregory's position, Maximus highlights the significance of the terms "cloud" and "veil", which symbolize bodily sensations and passions that require appropriate guidance and can be conquered through dedicated ascetic practices.

The entire *Ambiguum* represents a blend of philosophical contemplation and deep reflection on Scripture. The contemplations of Scripture primarily involve anagogical interpretations of Old Testament texts, including the Pentateuch, Joshua, the Books of Kings,

---

tion", in *Saint Maxime le Confesseur: Lettres 7–62*, ed. by J.-C. LARCHET & E. PONSOYE, Paris, 1998, pp. 41–45.

[13] P. BOOTH, *Crisis of Empire: Doctrine and Dissent at the End of Late Antiquity*, Los Angeles, p. 147.

[14] BOOTH, *Crisis of Empire*, p. 149.

[15] D. KRAUSMÜLLER, "Origenism and Anti-Origenism in the Late Sixth and Seventh Centuries", in *Evagrius and his Legacy, ed. by* J. KALVESMAKI & R. DARLING YOUNG, Notre Dame 2015, pp. 288–316: 307. V. CVETKOVIĆ, "Maximus the Confessor's View on Soul and Body in the Context of Five Divisions", in *The Unity of Body and Soul in Patristic and Byzantine Thought*, ed. by A. USACHEVA, J. ULRICH & S. BHAYRO, Leiden, 2021, pp. 245–276.

[16] *PG* 35, 1084C.

[17] *PG* 35, 1084C.

and the Psalms. The pivotal scriptural interpretation within this context, however, pertains to the Gospel account of the transfiguration, where the presence of Moses and Elijah serves as a bridge connecting the Old and New Testaments to the Kingdom of God. The remaining sections offer highly valuable philosophical reflections concerning various subjects, including the interplay between the soul and the body, the dynamics of the soul, contemplative methods, the origins and ultimate purpose of the world, the cycles of contraction and expansion in creation, divine providence, as well as the concepts of the monad, dyad, and triad. Throughout the entire *Ambiguum*, one discerns a wealth of reflections and allusions to Origenism. In his critique of the intellectualism associated with Origen's adherents, Maximus intriguingly draws upon the ascetical theology of Evagrius.[18] It becomes evident that Maximus exhibits a greater degree of criticism towards Origen himself than towards Origenism, which had been influenced by Evagrius and had been condemned a century earlier.[19]

By emphasizing Evagrian πρακτική, Maximus offers a response to the intellectually inclined Origenists who prioritized contemplation at the expense of rigorous ascetic effort. While Maximus endeavors to disassociate Gregory's passage from any connection to Origenian intellectualism, he does not entirely separate Gregory from the influence of Evagrian Origenism. Maximus interprets Gregory's position in accordance with the Evagrian model of the soul's three-stage ascent towards God. Utilizing the Evagrian concept of practical, physical, and theological contemplation, Maximus elucidates the spiritual progression of individuals across three distinct stages. In interpreting Gregory's references to "cloud" and "veil" as allusions to ascetic endeavor, Maximus supplements Gregory's assertion that union with God can be achieved through "reason and contemplation" by emphasizing the necessity of ascetical struggle as a prerequisite.[20]

Maximus, like Origen and his followers, engages in scriptural interpretation, with its pinnacle being the interpretation of the trans-

---

[18] LOUTH, *Maximus*, p. 66.

[19] LOUTH, *Maximus*, p. 202, n. 9.

[20] A. LOUTH, "St Gregory the Theologian and St. Maximus the Confessor: The Shaping of Tradition", in *The Making and Remaking of Christian Doctrine: Essays in Honour of Maurice Wiles*, ed. by S. COAKLEY & D. A. PAILIN, Oxford, 1993, pp. 117–130: 119.

figuration event. In his analysis of the transfiguration, Maximus frequently adheres to Origen's *Commentary on Matthew*, sometimes even using Origen's words *verbatim*.[21] Maximus interprets the biblical narrative of Christ's transfiguration on Mount Tabor within the framework of a three-stage ascent. He aligns the initial stage of ascetic discipline with the person of Elijah, the second stage of contemplation with Moses,[22] and the third stage of mystical theology with Jesus Christ, conceived as a symbol of Himself.

While Maximus' interpretation employs Origenian terminology, it introduces at least two elements that diverge from Origenism, particularly in relation to the incarnation and the transfiguration. In Origen's perspective, the incarnation of the Logos serves as an exemplar of how the mind of Jesus, despite being confined within a soul and a body, can sustain uninterrupted contemplation of its Creator.[23] As a result, the incarnation is not seen as the ultimate reality but rather as a transitional phase leading to a higher state of divine revelation. In Maximus' interpretation of mystical theology, Christ's historical incarnation is not viewed as merely a moment within the ongoing narrative of His perpetual Theophany. Maximus repurposes Origen's Logos theology to support his Christology, where the divine incarnation takes centre stage as the core of what Maximus refers to as the Mystery of the Logos, or the Mystery of Christ. Therefore, Jesus Christ represents the zenith of the three-stage ascent, rather than being merely a step in the journey toward the divine. Through His transfiguration, Christ becomes the very figure of Himself, the incomprehensible divine Logos. He illustrates that there is no higher expression of divine revelation than that which is manifested through the transfiguration.

The incarnation plays a pivotal role in Maximus' reconfiguration of Evagrius' spiritual doctrine. Much like Evagrius, Maximus introduces five forms or modes of natural contemplation. However, Maximus reinterprets Evagrius' modes of contemplation, specifically those related to divine providence and judgment. He transforms them from being seen as "corrective" and "retributive" divine expressions, into divine

---

[21] E. KLOSTERMANN (ed.), *Origenes Matthäuserklärung I: Die griechisch erhaltenen tomoi*, Leipzig, 1935 (Origenes Werke, 10; *GCS* 40), XII, pp. 37–43.

[22] *Ambig.Ioh.* 10,31a (CONSTAS 2014, I, pp. 254–258, 268).

[23] C. STANG, "Flesh and Fire: Incarnation and Deification in Origen of Alexandria", *Adamantius* 25 (2019), pp. 123–132: 127.

powers that maintain the order of the universe through wisdom, and which ensure the unchanging identity of each being. The incarnation is depicted as the epitome of divine providence because it ensures the highest achievable unity in the universe while also preserving the unalterable natural identity (logos) of every being.[24] Furthermore, the two modes of natural contemplation, "mixture" and "position", emerge as outcomes of both contemplation and ascetic endeavor. "Mixture" denotes the blending of the disposition of the mind with virtues achieved through ascetic discipline, while "position" relates to the ability to firmly establish the mind in the realm of the Good, an achievement made possible through prior ascetic practice. Despite Maximus' use of the terminology and conceptual structure of both orthodox and Evagrian Origenism, he suggests significant revisions of these teachings, akin to the way he revised the Neoplatonic doctrines of Dionysius the Areopagite in order to align them with Christian orthodoxy.

Conventional wisdom asserts that "there is no shortcut to enlightenment" and this is what St. Maximus questions in *Ambiguum* 10. If there is no "shortcut", then the whole concept of Grace – of *Gratia gratis data* – fundamental to monotheist religions, must be thrown overboard. But the opposite is equally problematic: if Grace does all the work, what becomes of human effort? Not just ascetic effort – dear to the Confessor – but any ethical, intellectual, or even esthetical effort? Navigating between this Scylla and Charybdis, St. Maximus draws into the scope of his reflection a whole range of important oppositions: faith *versus* works, form *versus* content, mind *versus* body, faith *versus* knowledge and time *versus* space/nature. It is remarkable that so many of these oppositions have sooner or later re/emerged in the European intellectual space and acquired a defining role.

Faithful to its title, the present volume unites the major achievements of modern scholarship on St. Maximus the Confessor's *Ambiguum* 10. It opens with the critical edition of the Greek text of this work. This

---

[24] M. HARRINGTON, "Creation and Natural Contemplation in Maximus the Confessor"s *Ambiguum* 10:19', in *Divine creation in ancient, medieval, and early modern thought: essays presented to the Rev'd Dr Robert D. Crouse*, ed. by M. TRESCHOW, W. OTTEN & W. HANNAM, Leiden-Boston, 2007, pp. 191–212; V. CVETKOVIĆ, "Wisdom in Maximus the Confessor Reconsidered", in *Proceedings of the Conference "St. Emperor Constantine and Christianity"*, ed. by D. BOJOVIĆ, Niš, 2013, vol. 2, pp. 197–215.

edition was prepared by Carl Laga ahead of the publication of the text of all the *Ambigua to John* in volume 84 of the *Series Graeca* of the *Corpus Christianorum* (*CCSG*). It is worth mentioning here that Professor Laga has already co-edited, in collaboration with Carlos Steel, an important body of Maximus' works viz. the two volumes of the Latin and Greek edition of the *Quaestiones ad Thalassium* (*CC SG* 7 & 22). Besides the original version, this volume contains a new English translation of *Ambiguum* 10 by Dr. Joshua Lollar.[25] Dr. Lollar has already published a translation of *Ambigua to Thomas* in the *CC Translations* series. Apart from this translation, Lollar has done important research on *Ambiguum* 10, which formed the subject of his PhD thesis. This led him to publish *To See into the Life of Things: The Contemplation of Nature in Maximus the Confessor and his Predecessors*.[26] This background amply qualifies Lollar for the difficult endeavour of matching the two existing translations of *Ambiguum* 10 by Fr. Andrew Louth and by Fr. Maximos Constas, both of which are established works of scholarship. The daring aspect of this enterprise stems particularly from the at times unconventional lexical choices of Lollar's translation. A short translator's note included in this volume provides an account of Lollar's translation technique. Dr. Lollar's English translation of the entire corpus of *Ambigua to John* has been published as *CCT* volume 45 in 2024.

Apart from the critical edition and translation of *Ambiguum* 10, this volume offers a series of studies of this work by leading Maximian scholars. These studies were collected on the occasion of the IInd International Colloquium on St. Maximus the Confessor held in Budapest on 3–4 February 2021. This was a memorable time when travel became impossible due to the Covid-19 pandemic, forcing all conferences to go online. Despite this impediment, the conference on *Ambiguum* 10 was an inspiring and lively event. Moreover, we were able to collect several additional papers by colleagues who did not attend the conference but were willing to contribute their research on the *Ambiguum* 10 of St. Maximus.

---

[25] The editors owe many thanks to Bram Roosen who first suggested to include these two texts in this volume and later greatly helped to implement this idea.

[26] J. LOLLAR, *To See into the Life of Things: The Contemplation of Nature in Maximus the Confessor and his Predecessors*, Turnhout, 2013.

The papers in this volume have been divided into two groups. The first group focuses on the intellectual background to St. Maximus' *Ambiguum* 10; the second contains studies of Maximus' religious philosophy, ranging from the concept of creation to that of the ultimate divinization of man. This division is in many ways artificial, given the broad philosophical and religious culture of the Confessor and the originality of his input. Yet it is hoped that this structure will contribute to making this volume more transparent and accessible.

St. Maximus is a highly original thinker. Nevertheless, as Pascal Mueller-Jourdan argues in his study, it is often possible to establish parallels between his ideas and various currents of ancient philosophy. This is particularly evident in the Confessor's treatment of the motif of time in *Ambiguum* 10, where time is famously represented by the figure of Moses at the transfiguration scene. Maximus' discussion of time shows his familiarity with the Neoplatonic tradition, stretching back to *Timaeus* 28–38. Proclus' *Commentary on Timaeus* provides a valuable link to the Platonic tradition and reveals the background issues involved in St. Maximus' reflections.

Maximus' indebtedness to his philosophical predecessors emerges even more clearly in Torstein Tollefsen's study of the function of Aristotelian categories in *Ambiguum* 10. In Maximus' time, Aristotle was viewed through the lens of Porphyry. While aware of the Porphyrian contribution, Maximus proves himself capable of turning directly to the Stagirite when it better suits his logic. Maximus' creative reworking of ancient philosophy is thought-provoking since the Confessor manages – to put it anachronistically – to unite science and spirituality. The concept of categories thus becomes the means of natural contemplation, transforming thought and leading man to self-fulfillment and ultimately towards God.

Dionysius the Areopagite is yet another important source of inspiration for St. Maximus. Lubomira Stefanova demonstrates the presence of Dionysian thinking in St. Maximus' treatment of the contractive and expansive manifestations of Divinity. Her examination centers on St. Maximus' exploration of the notion of contemplation in the context of both philosophy and biblical interpretation, with a particular emphasis on his analysis of texts of *Ambigua to John*, notably *Ambiguum* 10 and 67. Stefanova contends that these texts serve as prime illustrations of a distinct numerical theology. They clarify how creation originates from God as the Monad and then follows a structured numerical sequence, moving from the Monad to the Triad, Pentad, Heptad, and Duodecad, before ultimately returning to the Monad, signifying a cyclical pattern of creation and return to unity. The numbers featured in this philosophical contemplation within *Ambiguum* 10 and the biblical exegesis in *Ambiguum* 67 (such as the five loaves, seven fish, and the twelve baskets) carry profound symbolic meaning, representing various facets of contemplation.

Probably the most daring in this section is the paper by Fr. Aleksandar Djakovac discussing the possible echoes of the *Corpus Hermeticum* in *Ambiguum* 10. After careful methodological preparation, Fr. Djakovac launches his quest to prove that certain formulations in *Ambiguum* 10 may have been due to hermetic inspiration. The question is a difficult one, given St. Maximus' extensive circle of reading. Besides direct influence of the *Corpus Hermeticum*, one can easily imagine numerous intermediators and purveyors of Hermetic ideas to St. Maximus. Djakovac is well aware of the pitfalls of his subject matter and prudently dedicates a long section to the question of *loci communes*. His study has the merit of presenting both the yield and the limitations of this type of search.

Turning now to more general aspects of the Confessor's teaching in *Ambiguum* 10, the idea of creation looms large on the horizon. The study of Daniel Heide offers a clear and careful outline of the Maximian approach to this subject matter. The author scrutinizes the philosophical pitfalls implicated even in the most familiar formulations, such as *creatio ex nihilo*, *creatio ex Deo* (ἐκ Θεοῦ), and creation out of non-existence (ἐκ τοῦ μὴ ὄντος). Heide suggests that St. Maximus' interpretation of creation must be read on multiple levels. These levels are distinct, although related and include a polemic level, aimed at combatting ontological dualism and emanationism, a philosophical level, where creation appears as passage from potentiality to actuality and a theological level where creation appears bound to the phenomenon of time. This structure helps to account for Maximus' statements in various contexts, which might otherwise seem contradictory.

The infinity of God may seem a theological commonplace and yet – as Miklós Vassányi argues in his paper – St. Maximus' approach to this subject is deeply original. Vassányi's study focuses on sections 35 to 42 of *Ambiguum* 10, which the author considers a metaphysical "treatise-within-a-treatise" in its own right. For St. Maximus, the notion of infinity is closely connected to the idea of indivisible oneness, both ideas obviously steeped in Platonic and Neoplatonic philosophy. This philosophical heritage transpires in Maximus' assertion of the exclusivity of infiniteness and in his rejection of the idea of infinite matter. However, unlike his Platonic and Peripatetic predecessors, Maximus' thinking is largely oriented by his Christology. This suggests to him an entirely different view of transcendence – a transcendence willingly condescending to immanence.

The insightful paper by Vukašin Milićević tackles the issues of temporality and incarnation in St. Maximus. The treatment of Melchizedek in *Ambiguum* 10 blurs the boundary between the Old and New Testaments. What is more, it raises the question whether the Confessor regarded the incarnation as an historical event at all. St. Maximus' strong insistence on the atemporal reality of the incarnation seems to give support to this view. However, Milićević contends that every manifestation of God in the created world "implies some kind of incarnation". By this logic every single word of the Bible can be regarded as the incarnation of the Word. By means of subtle theological analysis Milićević demonstrates that, for St. Maximus, creation and salvation are simultaneous events, which do not exclude historicity but rather enrich it with a new spiritual dimension.

Vladimir Cvetković and Ivan Nišavić's paper investigates the significance of wisdom in *Ambiguum* 10.19. The paper embarks on an examination of three prominent interpretations of wisdom as seen in contemporary Maximian studies. Within the broader landscape of existing research on wisdom, the authors delve into the origins, significance, and objectives underlying Maximus' five modes of contemplation found in *Ambiguum* 10.19, namely, being, movement, difference, mixture, and position. The paper offers a comparative analysis of two pyramid-like thought structures, in which wisdom plays a central role. One of these structures is derived from *Ambiguum* 10.19, while the other is from *Mystagogia* 1–5, with a particular focus on *Mystagogia* 5.

Dionysios Skliris' paper on the divinization of man provides a worthy finale to this sequence of studies. Maximian thinking about divinisation, Skliris maintains, achieves a subtle synthesis between metaphysics and biblical theology. The idea of divinization has several aspects: it is the ultimate end of the contemplative path, but also has an ontological dimension, being the ultimate goal of creation in general. Moreover, divinization is an outcome of the act of divine adoption and divine choice, which reveals an intensely personal dimension of this event. In St. Maximus, this personal aspect is firmly rooted in his trini-tarian theology by the same logic that makes his anthropology steeped in the idea of incarnation.

Alex Leonas and Vladimir Cvetković

Editors' Note
Referencing *Ambiguum* 10

As explained in the Introduction, this volume consists of confer-ence proceedings accompanied by an edition of the forthcoming Greek text edited by Carl Laga with a new English translation by Joshua Lollar. While preparing the conference papers for publication, we invited the contributors to use this new text and translation whenever possible. Their use, however, was not mandatory. The outcome is a collection where some authors use Laga's new text and/or Lollar's new English translation of *Am-biguum* 10, included in the present volume, while others rely on the editions by Öhler (*PG*) and Constas, or earlier translations by Constas and Louth. Our main purpose was to ensure that all *Ambiguum* 10 quotations could be traced to the texts in the present edition. This is achieved in two ways: papers using Carl Laga's critical edition and/or Joshua Lollar's translation of *Am-biguum* 10 simply mention the page number within this volume. Others provide the *Ambiguum* 10 division numbers (chapter, paragraph) or the *Patrologia Graeca* column numbers, which also figure in the margins of the present work. Thus, the reader can easily verify any reference to *Ambiguum* 10, relying solely on the book at hand.

I.

The text of *Ambiguum* 10

Critical edition
by
Carl LAGA

with an English translation
by
Joshua LOLLAR

Ambiguum *10 of Maximus the Confessor in Modern Study: Papers Collected on the Occasion of the Budapest Colloquium on Saint Maximus, 3–4 February 2021*, ed. by Alexis LÉONAS & Vladimir CVETKOVIĆ, with the collaboration of Daniel HEIDE, Turnhout, 2025 (IPM 97), pp. 25–193
10.1484/M.IPM-EB.5.141859

Maximus Confessor, *Ambigua ad Iohannem*
Ambiguum V (10)

Critical Edition by Prof. Carl Laga

(Forthcoming in CCSG)

V Ἐκ τοῦ αὐτοῦ λόγου, εἰς τὸ Ὧιτινι μὲν οὖν
ἐξεγένετο διὰ λόγου καὶ θεωρίας διασχόντι τὴν ὕλην
καὶ τὸ σαρκικὸν τοῦτο, εἴτε νέφος χρὴ λέγειν εἴτε
προκάλυμμα, θεῷ συγγενέσθαι καὶ τῷ ἀκραιφνεστάτῳ
φωτὶ κραθῆναι, καθ᾽ὅσον ἐφικτὸν ἀνθρωπίνῃ φύσει,
μακάριος οὗτος τῆς ἐντεῦθεν ἀναβάσεως καὶ τῆς
ἐκεῖσε θεώσεως, ἣν τὸ γνησίως φιλοσοφῆσαι χαρίζεται καὶ τὸ ὑπὲρ τὴν ὑλικὴν δυάδα γενέσθαι διὰ τὴν
ἐν τῇ τριάδι νοουμένην ἑνότητα

Ἐγὼ μὲν οὐκ οἶμαι ἐλλειπῶς ἔχειν τὸν ἀποδο|θέντα
περὶ τῆς ἀρετῆς τῶν ἁγίων τοῦ διδασκάλου λόγον, κἄν
τινες, ὡς γεγράφατε, τοῦτο νομίζωσιν διὰ τοῦ λόγῳ
καὶ θεωρίᾳ μόνον, πρακτικῆς δίχα, τὴν κατὰ θεὸν
τῶν μετελθόντων αὐτὴν φιλοσοφίαν εἰπεῖν, τουναν-
τίον δὲ διῃρημένην τῇ πράξει τὴν ἀληθῆ περὶ τὰ ὄντα
κρίσιν αὐτῶν καὶ ἐνέργειαν, ἣν δὴ φιλοσοφίαν ὄντως
πληρεστάτην ἔγωγε τολμήσας μόνην ὁρίζομαι. Μάλα
σαφῶς εἰσηγεῖσθαι αὐτὸν ὑπολαμβάνω λόγῳ καὶ θεωρίᾳ κατορθοῦσθαι αὐτὴν ἀποφηνάμενον, ὡς τῷ λόγῳ
συνημμένης πάντως τῆς πράξεως καὶ τῆς ἐπ᾽αὐτῇ κρίσεως τῇ θεωρίᾳ περιεχομένης, εἴπερ λόγου μὲν τὸ τάσ-
σειν τὴν τοῦ σώματος κίνησιν, οἷον χαλινῷ τινι, τῷ
ὀρθῷ λογισμῷ τῆς πρὸς ἀτοπίαν φορᾶς ἐπιστημόνως
ἀναχαιτίζοντος, θεωρίας δὲ τὸ τὰ καλῶς νοηθέντα τε
καὶ κριθέντα ἐμφρόνως αἱρεῖσθαι ψηφίζεσθαι, οἱονεὶ

Maximus the Confessor, *Ambigua to John*
Ambiguum V (10)

Translation by Dr. Joshua Lollar
(Published in CCT 45, 2024)

V (10): From the oration *On Saint Athanasius*: "Therefore, anyone to whom it is granted to attain kinship with God and to be mixed with the purest light, as far as this is attainable by human nature, by parting materiality, this fleshly cloud or D veil – whatever we should call it – with reason and contemplation, such a person has the blessing of ascent from here below and of deification there above; this is the gift of genuine 45 philosophy and of transcending material duality through the unity in the Trinity as it is known by the mind."[1]

Introduction: Practical and Contemplative Life

I myself do not think the teacher's statement here about the 1108A saints' virtue is missing anything, even if there are some, as you have written, who think it is because it speaks of the saints' pursuit of divine philosophy with the phrase "reason and contemplation" alone, without making any reference to practical philosophy at all, when, in fact, the truth of their judgments and actions in the world, which I myself firmly define as the only truly complete philosophy, is seen precisely in the practical life. As I understand him, he is actually explaining things very clearly when he shows that philosophy is pursued rightly by "reason and contemplation," because the practical life is always joined to reason, and discernment, which is grounded in the practical life, is included within contemplation. Indeed, it is reason's task to order the movement

---

1   Greg. Naz., Or. 21.2. p. 112.1–114.8.

φῶς παμφαέστατον δι'ἀληθοῦς γνώσεως τὴν ἀλήθειαν
αὐτὴν δεικνυούσης. Οἷς ἀμφοτέροις μάλιστα καὶ δημιουργεῖται πᾶσα φιλόσοφος ἀρετὴ καὶ φυλάττεται·
ὑφ'ὧν καὶ ἐκφαίνεται διὰ σώματος οὐχ'ὅλη – οὐ γὰρ
χωρεῖται σώματι, χαρακτὴρ ὑπάρχουσα θείας δυνάμεως –, ἀλλά τινα τῶν αὐτῆς σκιάσματα, καὶ τοῦτο οὐ
δι'ἑαυτήν, διὰ δὲ τὸ τοὺς γυμνοὺς τῆς κατ'αὐτὴν χάριτος
εἰς μίμησιν ἐλθεῖν τῆς θεοειδοῦς τῶν φιλοθέων ἀνδρῶν
ἀναστροφῆς, ἐφ'ᾧ τῇ μετοχῇ τοῦ καλοῦ καὶ αὐτούς, τὸ
τῆς κακίας αἶσχος ἀποθεμένους, τῆς τῶν ἀξίων θεοῦ
γενέσθαι μοίρας, ἢ τοὺς δεομένους ἐπικουρίας τινὸς
ὑπὸ τῶν δυναμένων τυχεῖν, ἐφ'ᾧ τὴν κρυπτομένην τῷ
βάθει τῆς ψυχῆς τῶν ἐναρέτων διάθεσιν διὰ τοῦ σώματος κατὰ τὴν πρᾶξιν φανεῖσαν ἀποδεξαμένους τὴν πᾶσι
πάντα γινομένην καὶ διὰ πάντων πᾶσι παροῦσαν τοῦ
θεοῦ πρόνοιαν καὶ αὐτοὺς ἀνυμνῆσαι· ὡς, εἴγε μηδεὶς
ἦν ὁ εὖ παθεῖν δεόμενος ἢ ὁ πρὸς ἀρετὴν παραδείγματι
τυπωθῆναι ὀφείλων, αὐτὸν ἕκαστον ἀρκεῖν ἑαυτῷ πάντως, ταῖς κατὰ ψυχὴν τῶν ἀρετῶν χάρισιν ἀβρυνόμε-
νον, καὶ δίχα τῆς τούτων διὰ τοῦ σώματος πρὸς τὸ ἐμφανὲς ἀποδείξεως λέγειν οὐκ ἄτοπον.

Ὁ τοίνυν εὐσεβῶς διὰ θεωρίας κατανοήσας ὡς ἔχει
τὰ ὄντα καὶ διὰ βουλῆς λογικῆς ἐστοχασμένως τε καὶ

of the body, skillfully checking it with clear reasoning, as if
with a bit and bridle, to keep it from wandering off the path,   B
and it is the task of contemplation to choose to take hold of
what must be thought and judged in a beautiful and intelligent way, where true knowledge shows forth the truth itself
as if it were a most radiant light. Most striking of all, all
philosophical virtue is fashioned and preserved by both reason and contemplation and is also made manifest by them
through the body, though not entirely, for it is the distinctive mark of divine power and is thus not confined to the
body; rather, only shadows of what belongs to it are made
manifest. This manifestation is not for the sake of virtue itself but so that those who are stripped of the gift of virtue
may come to the imitation of the God-like way of life that
belongs to those who love God. Then, by participation in   46
beauty, they also may take their place among those who are
worthy of God by putting off the shamefulness of wickedness. Or, those in need of aid may attain it from those who
are able to give it, such that, when they have received an
understanding of the disposition that is hidden in the depth   C
of the souls of the virtuous and is made manifest through the
body in practical life, which becomes all things for all,[2] they
themselves also praise the providence of God, which is present to all through all things.[3] Indeed, if there were no one in
need of beneficial experience or who required an example in
order to be formed in virtue, then each person would clearly
be sufficient in himself and able to boast in the gifts of the
virtues of his soul. In that case, it would not be out of place
to speak with no reference to virtues being shown through
the body and becoming manifest.

Accordingly, one who has piously come to understand the intellectual structure of reality through contemplation and has

---

2   Cf. I Cor 9.22.
3   Cf. Eph 4.6.

ὀρθῶς τὸν περὶ αὐτῶν ὁρισάμενος λόγον καὶ φυλάττων
ἑαυτῷ τὴν κρίσιν, μᾶλλον δὲ ἑαυτὸν τῇ κρίσει ἀπαρ-
έγκλιτον, πᾶσαν ὁμοῦ συλλαβὼν ἔχει τὴν ἀρετήν, πρὸς οὐδὲν ἄλλο μετὰ τὴν ἐγνωσμένην ἀλήθειαν ἔτι κινούμενος,
καὶ πάντα παρῆλθε διὰ σπουδῆς, οὐδενὸς τὸ παράπαν
λόγον ποιούμενος τῶν ὅσα σαρκὸς καὶ κόσμου ἐστὶ καὶ
λέγεται, ἐνδιαθέτως ἔχων ἤδη τῷ λόγῳ περιεχομένην
ἀμάχως τὴν πρᾶξιν, οἷα τοῦ ἐφ'ἡμῖν πάντας ἑαυτῷ τοῦ
διανοητικοῦ τοὺς κρατίστους ἀπαθεῖς ἐπικομιζομένου
λόγους, καθ'οὓς πᾶσα ἀρετὴ καὶ γνῶσίς ἐστι καὶ ὑφέστηκεν, ὡς δυνάμεις ὄντας ψυχῆς λογικῆς, πρὸς μὲν τὸ
εἶναι σώματος οὐδόλως χρήζοντας, πρὸς δὲ τὸ φανῆναι
| διὰ τὰς εἰρημένας αἰτίας κατὰ καιρὸν αὐτῷ χρῆσθαι   1109
οὐκ ἀναινομένους. **Φασὶ γὰρ** τοῦ διανοητικοῦ εἶναι ἰδικῶς
μὲν τὰς νοήσεις τῶν νοητῶν τὰς ἀρετὰς τὰς ἐπιστήμας τοὺς
τῶν τεχνῶν λόγους τὸ προαιρετικὸν καὶ τὸ βουλευτικόν, γε-
νικῶς δὲ τὰς κρίσεις τὰς συγκαταθέσεις τὰς ἀποφυγὰς τὰς
ὁρμάς, **καὶ τὰς μὲν εἶναι μόνης τῆς κατὰ νοῦν θεωρίας,
τὰς δὲ τῆς κατὰ τὸν λόγον ἐπιστημονικῆς δυνάμεως. Εἰ
δὲ τούτοις φρουρουμένην** οἱ ἅγιοι **τὴν ἰδίαν ζωὴν συν-
ετήρησαν,** ἄρα περιληπτικῶς διὰ τοῦ λόγου καὶ τῆς
θεωρίας ὁ **μακάριος οὗτος ἀνὴρ πάντας τοὺς κατ'ἀρετὴν καὶ γνῶσιν εἰσηγήσατο λόγους τοῖς ἁγίοις συνει-
λημμένους, δι'ὧν τῇ κατανοήσει τοῦ θεοῦ κατὰ θεωρίαν
γνωστικῶς προσανέχοντες ἐμφρόνως κατὰ λόγον διὰ**

come accurately and rightly to define through rational deliberation the essential idea that holds things together, who preserves discernment in himself, or rather, preserves himself upright by discernment, such a person "possesses all the virtue he has gathered"[4] together. Because he is no longer moved D by anything other than the truth after the truth has come to be known, he has also fervently passed beyond all things, uttering not a word regarding things that are and are said to be of the flesh and the world, because he already inherently possesses a practice effortlessly embraced by reason, seeing as our faculty of thought brings along with itself all the exceedingly strong and unshakeable aspects of reason, which itself grounds the essence and actual existence of all virtue and knowledge. Because these aspects of reason are the powers of the rational soul, they do not at all need the 47 body for their existence, though they do not refuse to make 1109A use of the body at appropriate times to manifest themselves for the reasons already mentioned. For they say that "the thoughts about intellectual reality, the virtues, the different kinds of understanding, the essential ideas of the arts, the faculty of choice, and the faculty of deliberation are the specific aspects of the thinking faculty, and these fall into the general classes of judgments, assents, refusals, and desires."[5] The first group belong to intellectual contemplation alone and the second belong to the power for knowing things rationally with understanding. If the saints have kept their own lives secure by these, then this blessed man was including all the essential ideas of virtue and knowledge that come together in the saints when he spoke of "reason" and "contemplation." We can be sure that the saints themselves, by devoting themselves with knowledge to the intellectual understanding of God in contemplation, wisely received upon themselves the stamp of the divine form through virtue in accordance with

---

4   GREG. NAZ., Or. 21.1, p. 110.2–3.
5   NEM. EMES., Nat. hom. 12, p. 68.6–9.

τῶν ἀρετῶν τὴν θείαν ἑαυτοῖς μορφὴν ἐνετυπώσαντο
πάντως, οὐκ εἶναι ἀναγκαῖον οἰηθεὶς τὴν διὰ τοῦ σώματος ὀνομάσαι πρᾶξιν, γινώσκων μὴ ἀρετῆς αὐτὴν εἶναι
ποιητικήν, ἀλλ'ἐκφαντικὴν καὶ μόνων τῶν θείων νοημάτων τε καὶ λογισμῶν ὑπουργόν.

Ὡς ἂν δὲ καὶ δι'ἑτέρου τρόπου φανερὸν γένηται τὸ
λεγόμενον· φασὶν οἱ τῶν καθ'ἡμᾶς πραγμάτων δι'ἀκρι-
βείας μετελθόντες τοὺς λόγους τοῦ λογικοῦ τὸ μὲν εἶναι
θεωρητικόν, τὸ δὲ πρακτικόν, καὶ θεωρητικὸν μὲν τὸ κατα-
νοοῦν ὡς ἔχει τὰ ὄντα, πρακτικὸν δὲ τὸ βουλευτικόν, τὸ ὁρί-
ζον τοῖς πρακτοῖς τὸν ὀρθὸν λόγον· καὶ καλοῦσι τὸ μὲν θεωρητικὸν νοῦν, τὸ δὲ πρακτικὸν λόγον, καὶ τὸ μὲν σοφίαν, τὸ
δὲ φρόνησιν. Εἰ δὲ τοῦτο ἀληθές, ἐκ τῆς αἰτίας ἄρα τὴν
πρᾶξιν κατὰ τὸ εἰκός, ἀλλ'οὐκ ἐκ τῆς ὕλης ὠνόμασεν
ὁ διδάσκαλος, λόγον τὴν μηδὲν ἔχουσαν ἀντικείμενον
ἕξιν προσαγορεύσας· λογικῶς γὰρ καὶ γνωστικῶς, ἀλ-
λ'οὐ πολεμικῶς καὶ ἀγωνιστικῶς, ἐμμένει τοῖς ἀληθέ-
σιν ὁ θεωρητικὸς καὶ πλὴν αὐτῶν ἄλλο τι ὁρᾶν διὰ τὴν
πρὸς αὐτὰ ἡδονὴν οὐκ ἀνέχεται.

Εἰ δὲ χρὴ καὶ ἄλλως σαφέστερον τοῦτο ποιήσασθαι
πάλιν· οἱ τῆς κατ'ἀρετὴν τελειότητος τοὺς λόγους γυ-
μνάσαντές φασι τοὺς μήπω τῆς πρὸς τὴν ὕλην κατὰ τὴν
σχέσιν κοινωνίας καθαροὺς γεγονότας περὶ τὰ πρακτὰ
καταγίνεσθαι, μικτῆς οὔσης αὐτοῖς ἔτι τῆς περὶ τὰ ὄντα
κρίσεως, καί εἰσι τρεπτοί, μήπω τὴν περὶ τὰ τρεπτὰ
σχέσιν ἀποθέμενοι, τοὺς δὲ δι'ἀρετῆς ἀκρότητα τῷ θεῷ

reason.   St Gregory did not consider it necessary to mention B
bodily practice, because he knew that it does not produce virtue but rather makes it manifest and is in the service of divine
thoughts and reasoning alone.

Let me approach this in a different way to try to clarify the
point. Those who have rigorously pursued the essential ideas
governing human reality say "there is both a contemplative
and a practical aspect of our rational faculty": "that which
perceives the intellectual structure of beings as they are is
the contemplative aspect, whereas the faculty of deliberation,
which determines the correct idea for practices, is the practical aspect. They call the contemplative faculty 'intellect' and
the practical faculty 'reason;' they also call the contemplative
faculty 'wisdom' and the practical faulty 'mindfulness.'"[6] If
this is true, the teacher very sensibly named the practical life
in terms of its causes but not in terms of its material concerns C
when he used the word "reason" to refer to that habitual
way of being that has nothing set in opposition to it,   for 48
the contemplative person abides in truth with reason and
knowledge but without a battle or struggle, nor does he allow
himself to see anything but truth because of the pleasure
that attends it.

If it is necessary to make this still clearer in a different way,
here is another explanation. Those who are well versed in the
principles of perfection in virtue say that those who have not
yet become purified of the "communion" with "materiality"
that results from their habitual relationship to it "are occupied with practical affairs" in such a way that the process
of making judgments about reality is still complex for them,
and "they are changeable" in that they have not yet put off
their "habitual relationship" to changeable things. By contrast, those "who are closely related to God through the very

---

6   NEM. EMES., *Nat. hom.*, 41, p. 117.17–20.

κατὰ σχέσιν πλησιάζοντας καὶ τῇ τούτου κατανοήσει τὸ
μακάριον καρπουμένους, πρὸς ἑαυτοὺς μόνον καὶ τὸν θεὸν
ἐστραμμένους **τῷ ῥῆξαι γνησίως τῆς ὑλικῆς σχέσεως τὰ
δεσμά, τῶν μὲν πρακτῶν** καὶ τῆς ὕλης **παντελῶς ἠλλοτριῶσθαι,** τῇ δὲ θεωρίᾳ **καὶ τῷ θεῷ προσῳκειῶσθαι. Διό,
φασί,** καὶ μένουσιν ἄτρεπτοι, **μὴ ἔχοντες ἔτι τὴν πρὸς
τὴν ὕλην σχέσιν, καθ'ἢν τῇ ὕλῃ φυσικῶς ἀλλοιουμένῃ
παρὰ φύσιν συναλλοιοῦσθαι ἐξ ἀνάγκης πέφυκεν ὁ τῇ
ὕλῃ κατὰ τὴν σχέσιν κεκρατημένος. Καὶ μεγίστης εἰ-
δὼς δεῖσθαι δυνάμεως** | πρὸς ἀπόθεσιν τῆς ὑλικῆς προ-   1112
σπαθείας τὸν αὐτῆς ἐλευθερωθῆναι βουλόμενόν φησιν
ὁ διδάσκαλος· ᾧτινι μὲν οὖν ἐξεγένετο διὰ λόγου
καὶ θεωρίας διασχόντι τὴν ὕλην καὶ τὸ σαρκικὸν τοῦτο, εἴτε νέφος χρὴ λέγειν εἴτε προκάλυμμα, θεῷ συγγενέσθαι **καὶ τὰ ἑξῆς.**

*

Διὰ τί δὲ νέφος **εἶναι καὶ** προκάλυμμα **τὴν σάρκα φησὶν ὁ διδάσκαλος; Ὡς εἰδὼς ὅτι πᾶς ἀνθρώπινος
νοῦς, πλανώμενος καὶ τῆς κατὰ φύσιν ἀπονεύων κινήσεως, περὶ πάθος καὶ αἴσθησιν καὶ αἰσθητὰ ποιεῖται τὴν
κίνησιν, οὐκ ἔχων ἄλλοθί ποι κινηθῆναι, τῆς πρὸς θεὸν
φυσικῶς φερούσης κινήσεως διαμαρτήσας, καὶ διεῖλε
τὴν σάρκα εἰς πάθος καὶ αἴσθησιν – σαρκὸς γὰρ ἐμψύ-
χου ἀμφότερα –, διὰ τοῦ** νέφους **καὶ τοῦ** προκαλύμ-
ματος **ταῦτα δηλώσας. Νέφος γάρ ἐστι τῷ ἡγεμονικῷ**

highest virtue and bear the fruit of blessedness by perceiving Him intellectually, who have turned toward themselves and God alone" by utterly breaking the bonds of their relation D to materiality, have estranged themselves entirely from practical affairs and "from materiality," and have "come to be at home in contemplation" and "with God." Therefore, they say, "they also remain unchangeable,"[7] since they no longer possess their habitual relationship to matter, for it is a natural consequence that one who is controlled by materiality in his relation to it should necessarily undergo alteration along with matter, which is alterable by nature, in a way that distorts his own nature. And knowing that the one who wants to be freed of passionate materialism needs the greatest power in 1112A order to cast it away, the teacher says, "anyone to whom it is granted to attain kinship with God...by parting this material and fleshly cloud or veil – whatever we should call it – with reason and contemplation" and the rest.

49

Flesh and Soul

Why[8] does the teacher say that the flesh is a "cloud" and a "veil"? He knew that every human mind, by wandering and inclining away from its natural motion, produces a motion that revolves around passion, sensuality, and sensual objects and is unable to be moved anywhere else, because it B has gone completely astray from the motion that naturally carries it towards God. On the basis of this knowledge, he made a distinction between passion and sense-perception in the concept of "flesh" – for both belong to flesh endowed with soul – indicating these with the terms "cloud" and "veil." For fleshly passion, which casts a shadow over the ruling facul-

---

7   NEM. EMES., *Nat. hom.*, 41, p. 118.11–19.

8   *1. How the flesh is a "cloud" and "veil"*

τῆς ψυχῆς ἐπισκοτοῦν τὸ σαρκικὸν πάθος, καὶ προ-
κάλυμμά ἐστιν ἡ κατ᾽αἴσθησιν ἀπάτη, ταῖς ἐπιφανείαις
τῶν αἰσθητῶν αὐτὴν ἐπερείδουσα καὶ τῆς πρὸς τὰ νοητὰ διαβάσεως ἀποτειχίζουσα· δι᾽ὧν, λήθην τῶν φυσικῶν ἀγαθῶν λαμβάνουσα, περὶ τὰ αἰσθητὰ τὴν ὅλην
αὐτῆς ἐνέργειαν καταστρέφει, θυμοὺς καὶ ἐπιθυμίας
καὶ ἡδονὰς διὰ τῶν εἰρημένων ἀπρεπεῖς ἐφευρίσκουσα.
* Πᾶσα γὰρ ἡδονὴ τῶν ἀπηγορευμένων ἐκ πάθους διὰ
μέσης αἰσθήσεως πρός τι πάντως γίνεσθαι πέφυκεν αἰ-
σθητόν· οὐδὲ γὰρ ἄλλο τί ἐστιν ἡδονὴ ἢ εἶδος αἰσθήσεως ἐν τῷ αἰσθητικῷ διά τινος αἰσθητοῦ μορφουμένης
ἢ τρόπος αἰσθητικῆς ἐνεργείας κατ᾽ἐπιθυμίαν ἄλογον
συνιστάμενος· ἐπιθυμία γὰρ αἰσθήσει προστεθεῖσα εἰς
ἡδονὴν μεταπίπτει, εἶδος αὐτῇ ἐπάγουσα, καὶ αἴσθησις
κατ᾽ἐπιθυμίαν κινηθεῖσα ἡδονὴν ἀπεργάζεται, τὸ αἰσθητὸν προσλαβοῦσα. Γνόντες οὖν οἱ ἅγιοι ὅτι διὰ μέσης
σαρκὸς πρὸς τὴν ὕλην ἡ ψυχὴ παρὰ φύσιν κινουμένη
τὴν χοϊκὴν μορφὴν ὑποδύεται, διὰ μέσης μᾶλλον ψυχῆς κατὰ φύσιν αὐτοὶ πρὸς τὸν θεὸν κινουμένης καὶ
τὴν σάρκα τῷ θεῷ πρεπόντως οἰκειῶσαι διενοήθησαν,
δι᾽ἀσκήσεως ἀρετῶν ἐνδεχομένως αὐτὴν ταῖς θείαις ἐμ-
φάσεσι καλλωπίσαντες.

* Τρεῖς γὰρ καθολικὰς κινήσεις ἔχουσαν τὴν ψυχὴν εἰς μίαν συναγομένας ὑπὸ τῆς χάριτος φωτι-
σθέντες, τὴν κατὰ νοῦν τὴν κατὰ λόγον τὴν κατ᾽αἴ-
σθησιν, καὶ τὴν μὲν ἁπλῆν καὶ ἀνερμήνευτον, καθ᾽ἣν
ἀγνώστως περὶ θεὸν κινουμένη κατ᾽οὐδένα τρόπον | 1113
ἐξ οὐδενὸς τῶν ὄντων αὐτὸν διὰ τὴν ὑπεροχὴν ἐπιγι-
νώσκει, τὴν δὲ κατ᾽αἰτίαν ὁριστικὴν τοῦ ἀγνώστου,

ty of the soul, is a "cloud," and the misleading character of
sense-perception, which assaults the soul with the appearances of sensual objects and obstructs its path to the realm of
thought, is a "veil." When the soul forgets what is naturally
good as a result of these, it directs the whole of its natural activity to sensual realities and so discovers unseemly instances
of aggression, appetite, and pleasure through them. For[9] all   C
pleasure that comes from what is forbidden must naturally
arise from passion through the mediation of sense-perception
as it is directed towards a sensual object. Indeed, pleasure is
nothing other than either the form of a sense-perception being
shaped in the sense faculty by a sensual object or the way in
which sensual activity proceeds by way of irrational appetite,
for when appetite has been provoked by sense-perception it
changes into pleasure, bringing sense-perception a form, and
when sense-perception has been moved by the appetite it ful-
fills the pleasure when it has received the sensual object itself
in addition. Accordingly, since the saints knew that the soul
puts on an earthly form when it is moved contrary to nature
towards materiality through the mediation of the flesh, they
were determined to make the flesh at home with God in a fitting way through the mediation of the soul's natural motion   D
towards God by making the flesh beautiful, as much as was   50
in their power, reflecting the divine through the exercise of
the virtues.

For[10] these saints were enlightened by grace to understand
that the soul possesses three general movements, which are
reducible to one: the movements of intellect, reason, and
sense-perception. First, intellectual motion is simple and inexplicable, and when the soul moves intellectually around
God without the mediation of knowledge, it recognizes Him   1113A
in a way that is completely unrelated to existing things be-

---

9   *2. How pleasure comes to be*
10   *3. The functioning and quantity of the motions of the soul*

καθ'ἣν φυσικῶς κινουμένη τοὺς ἐπ'αὐτῇ φυσικοὺς πάντας λόγους, τοῦ κατ'αἰτίαν μόνον ἐγνωσμένου μορφω-
τικοὺς ὄντας, ἑαυτῇ δι'ἐνεργείας κατ'ἐπιστήμην ἐντίθε-
ται, τὴν δὲ σύνθετον, καθ'ἣν τῶν ἐκτὸς ἐφαπτομένη, ὡς
ἔκ τινων συμβόλων, τῶν ὁρατῶν τοὺς λόγους πρὸς ἑαυτὴν ἀναμάσσεται, μεγαλοφυῶς διὰ τούτων κατὰ τὸν
ἀληθῆ καὶ ἄπταιστον τῆς κατὰ φύσιν κινήσεως τρόπον
τὸν παρόντα τῶν σκαμμάτων αἰῶνα διέβησαν, τὴν μὲν
αἴσθησιν, ἁπλοῦς διὰ μέσου τοῦ λόγου πρὸς τὸν νοῦν
τοὺς τῶν αἰσθητῶν πνευματικοὺς λόγους ἔχουσαν μό-
νους, ἀναβιβάσαντες, τὸν δὲ λόγον ἑνοειδῶς κατὰ μίαν
ἁπλῆν τε καὶ ἀδιαίρετον φρόνησιν πρὸς τὸν νοῦν, τοὺς
τῶν ὄντων ἔχοντα λόγους, ἑνώσαντες, τὸν δὲ νοῦν, τῆς
περὶ τὰ ὄντα πάντα κινήσεως καθαρῶς ἀπολυθέντα καὶ
αὐτῆς τῆς καθ'αὑτὸν φυσικῆς ἐνεργείας ἠρεμοῦντα, τῷ
θεῷ προσκομίσαντες, καθ'ὃν ὁλικῶς πρὸς θεὸν συνα-
χθέντες, ὅλοι ὅλῳ θεῷ ἐγκραθῆναι διὰ τοῦ πνεύματος
ἠξιώθησαν, ὅλην τοῦ ἐπουρανίου κατὰ τὸ δυνατὸν ἀνθρώποις τὴν εἰκόνα φορέσαντες καὶ τοσοῦτον ἕλξαντες
τῆς θείας ἐμφάσεως – εἰ θέμις τοῦτο εἰπεῖν –, ὅσον ἑλ-
χθέντες αὐτοὶ τῷ θεῷ ἐνετέθησαν.

Φασὶ γὰρ ἀλλήλων εἶναι παραδείγματα τὸν θεὸν καὶ
τὸν ἄνθρωπον, καὶ τοσοῦτον τῷ ἀνθρώπῳ τὸν θεὸν διὰ
φιλανθρωπίαν ἀνθρωπίζεσθαι, ὅσον ὁ ἄνθρωπος ἑαυτὸν τῷ θεῷ δι'ἀγάπης δυνηθεὶς ἀπεθέωσε, καὶ τοσοῦτον

cause of His transcendent superiority. Second, rational motion serves to define the unknowable one in terms of causal explanation, and as the soul is naturally moved in this way, it places within itself, through its activity of acquiring understanding, all the natural essential ideas within its scope, which allow the one who is known only as cause to appear to reason. Third, the motion of sense-perception is a mixed motion, and when the soul moves in this way, in laying hold of what is outside itself, it receives the impression of the essential ideas of visible things into itself, as though symbols were being stamped upon it. Having been enlightened in this, the saints brilliantly passed beyond the present treacherous age by means of these three movements in accordance with the true and unfailing way that the soul naturally moves. They did so first, by elevating sense-perceptionto the intellect by making it to possess only the simple spiritual essential ideas of sensual reality through the mediation of reason in; second, by unifying reason, making it to possess the essential ideas of beings in one simple and undivided act of mindfulness thereby becoming one with the intellect; and finally, by conveying the B intellect to God, freeing it completely from its motion in the midst of all of reality and by quieting even its own natural activity. Having been gathered in intellect entirely to God, then, they were deemed worthy to be blended fully with God in His fullness through the Spirit, having come *to bear* the full *image of the heavenly man* (I Cor. 15.49), as far as it is possible for human beings to do so. They were, moreover, given to 51 have their place in God insofar as they had drawn the divine reflection to themselves – if it is permissible to say this – even as they had been drawn to Him in the very same way.

For they say that God and man are paradigms of each other. God becomes human because of His love for humanity to the degree that man, when he has been empowered by God through love, makes himself God. And man is seized intel-

ὑπὸ θεοῦ τὸν ἄνθρωπον κατὰ νοῦν ἁρπάζεσθαι πρὸς τὸ
ἄγνωστον, ὅσον ὁ ἄνθρωπος τὸν ἀόρατον φύσει θεὸν
διὰ τῶν ἀρετῶν ἐφανέρωσεν. Ὑπὸ ταύτης τοίνυν τῆς
κατὰ λόγον καὶ θεωρίαν συνισταμένης φιλοσοφίας,
καθ᾽ἣν καὶ ἡ τοῦ σώματος ἐξ ἀνάγκης εὐγενίζεται φύσις, ἀπλανῶς πρὸς τὸν τοῦ θεοῦ πόθον τρωθέντες οἱ
ἅγιοι διὰ τῶν ἐνουσῶν αὐτοῖς πρὸς τὰ θεῖα φυσικῶν
ἐμφάσεων ἀξιοπρεπῶς πρὸς θεὸν παρεγένοντο, σῶμα
καὶ κόσμον ἀθλητικῶς διασχόντες, ἀλλήλοις ταῦτα
περιεχόμενα θεώμενοι, τὸν μὲν φύσει, τὸ δὲ αἰσθήσει,
καὶ θατέρῳ θάτερον ὑποπίπτον τῇ κατ᾽ἐπαλλαγὴν θατέρου πρὸς τὸ ἕτερον ποιᾷ ἰδιότητι, καὶ μηδὲν τούτων
τῷ καθ᾽ἑαυτὸν λόγῳ περιγραφῆς ὑπάρχον ἐλεύθερον·
καὶ αἰσχρὸν ἡγησάμενοι τοῖς θνητοῖς καὶ περιγραπτοῖς
ἐμφθείρεσθαί τε καὶ περιγράφεσθαι τῆς ψυχῆς ἐᾶν τὸ
ἀθάνατον καὶ ἀεικίνητον, μόνῳ θεῷ τῷ ἀθανάτῳ καὶ
πάσης ἀπειρίας ἀνωτέρῳ ἀλύτως ἑαυτοὺς ἐνέδησαν,
οὐδαμῶς ταῖς κόσμου καὶ σαρκὸς ἀνθολκαῖς ἐνδιδόν-
τες· ὅπερ ἐστὶ πάσης ἀρετῆς τε καὶ γνώσεως πλήρωσις,
οἶμαι δὲ ὅτι καὶ τέλος.

Ἀλλὰ κἂν εἴ ποτε περὶ τὰ τῶν ὄντων θεάματα
κεκίνηνται οἱ ἅγιοι, οὐκ ἐπὶ τῷ αὐτὰ ἐκεῖνα προηγουμένως θεάσασθαί τε καὶ γνῶναι καθ᾽ἡμᾶς ὑλικῶς
κεκίνηνται, ἀλλ᾽ἵνα τὸν διὰ | πάντων καὶ ἐν πᾶσιν   1116
ὄντα τε καὶ φαινόμενον θεὸν πολυτρόπως ὑμνήσω-
σι καὶ πολλὴν ἑαυτοῖς συναγείρωσι θαύματος δύναμιν καὶ δοξολογίας ὑπόθεσιν. Ψυχὴν γὰρ εἰληφότες
παρὰ θεοῦ νοῦν καὶ λόγον καὶ αἴσθησιν ἔχουσαν, πρὸς
τῇ νοητῇ καὶ ταύτην τὴν αἰσθητήν, ὥσπερ καὶ λόγον
πρὸς τῷ ἐνδιαθέτῳ τὸν κατὰ προφοράν, καὶ νοῦν πρὸς
τῷ νοητῷ τὸν παθητικόν, ὃν καὶ φαντασίαν καλοῦ-

lectually by God so that he is brought before the unknown, C
insofar as it is man that manifests God, who is invisible by
nature, through the virtues. Accordingly, it was by means of
this philosophy, which is composed of "reason and contemplation" and by which even the nature of the body is necessarily
ennobled, that the saints, who had been pierced to the heart
with longing for God, came near to God in a worthy manner
through the natural reflections of divine reality that were in
them. They "parted" body and world with the skill of elite
athletes by seeing that body and world are enveloped by each
other – the world by nature, the body by sense-perception –
and that each is subject to the other by the fact that the indi-
viduating quality of the one is directly related to the other in
that each is interwoven inseparably with the other, and that
no aspect of either of these exists free of the enclosure of its
own essential idea. They came, moreover, to understand that
it is shameful for the immortal and ever-moving reality of the
soul to undergo corruption and enclosure among mortal and
enclosed things. Thus, they bound themselves inseparably to D
God alone who is immortal and beyond all infinity, in no way
giving in to the allurements of world and flesh. This is the
fulfilment of all virtue and knowledge, and it is also, I think,
their final end.

But even if the saints ever have been moved to concern 52
themselves with the spectacle of existing things, they have
not been concerned materialistically like we are, for we principally want to see and know those things themselves. Rather,
they are moved that they might praise God, who exists and is 1116A
made manifest in many ways *through all and in all* (Eph 4.6),
and that they might gather to themselves the great power of
wonder and the purpose of glorification. For they have received from God a soul that possesses intellect, reason, and
sense-perception. This soul is sensual as well as intellectual,
just as it possesses articulate rationality in addition to its in-

σι τοῦ ζῴου, καθ᾽ὃν καὶ τὰ λοιπὰ ζῷα καὶ ἄλληλα καὶ
ἡμᾶς καὶ τοὺς τόπους οὓς διώδευσαν ἐπιγινώσκουσι,
περὶ ἣν συνίστασθαι τὴν αἴσθησίν φασιν οἱ σοφοὶ τὰ
τοιαῦτα, ὄργανον αὐτῆς οὖσαν ἀντιληπτικὸν τῶν αὐτῇ
φαντασθέντων, δεῖν ᾠήθησαν τούτων τὰς ἐνεργείας
εἰκότως οὐχ᾽ἑαυτοῖς, ἀλλὰ τῷ δεδωκότι θεῷ, δι᾽ὃν καὶ
ἐξ οὗ πάντα, προσενέγκαι.

Τρεῖς γὰρ ὄντας καθολικοὺς τρόπους, ὡς ἀνθρώποις
ἐστὶν ἐφικτόν, ἐκ τῆς περὶ τὰ ὄντα ἀκριβοῦς κατανοήσεως παιδευθέντες, ἐφ᾽οἷς ὁ θεὸς τὰ πάντα πεποίηκεν,
ἐφ᾽ᾧ τε γὰρ εἶναι καὶ εὖ εἶναι καὶ ἀεὶ εἶναι οὐσιώσας
ἡμᾶς ὑπεστήσατο, καὶ τοὺς μὲν δύο ἄκρους ὄντας καὶ
μόνου θεοῦ ἐχομένους ὡς αἰτίου, τὸν δὲ ἕτερον μέσον
καὶ τῆς ἡμετέρας ἠρτημένον γνώμης τε καὶ κινήσεως,
καὶ δι᾽ἑαυτοῦ τοῖς ἄκροις τὸ κυρίως λέγεσθαι παρέχον-
τα, καὶ οὗ μὴ παρόντος ἄχρηστος αὐτοῖς καὶ ἡ προση-
γορία καθίσταται, τὸ εὖ συνημμένον οὐκ ἔχουσι, οὐκ
ἄλλως δύνασθαι καὶ προσγίνεσθαι αὐτοῖς καὶ φυλαχθῆ-
ναι τὴν ἐν τοῖς ἄκροις ἀλήθειαν, ἣν ποιεῖν πέφυκε τὸ
εὖ εἶναι κατὰ τὸ μέσον τοῖς ἄκροις ἐπικιρνώμενον, ἢ τῇ
πρὸς θεὸν ἀεικινησίᾳ διενοήθησαν.

Καὶ λοιπὸν τῷ κατὰ φύσιν ἐντεῦθεν τὸ ὀπτικὸν τῆς
ψυχῆς συνεπιτείναντες λόγῳ, καὶ τρόπον τινὰ μὴ δεῖν
ἀντιστρόφως χρῆσθαι ταῖς φυσικαῖς ἐνεργείαις διὰ τὴν
ἐξ ἀνάγκης ἐπισυμβαίνουσαν ταῖς φυσικαῖς δυνάμεσιν

herent rationality, and a passive mode of intellect in addition
to the conceptual aspect of the mind. They call this passive
mode "animal imagination," the faculty by which the rest
of the animals recognize each other and us and the various
places through which they go. Those who are wise in such
matters say that the activity of sense-perception constitutes
the content of animal imagination, since sense-perception is
the organ by which the imagination takes hold of the things
that are imagined by it. In light of all this, they thought it
necessary to direct the activities of these aspects of the soul
not to themselves but to God who has given them, by whom
and *from whom are all things* (I Cor 8.6).   B

For they were instructed through the rigorous examination of
the intellectual structure of reality, as much as this is possible
for human beings, that God has made all things in accordance
with three general modes: having endowed us with an essence,
God has made us actually to exist, to exist in the good, and
to exist forever. They were instructed, moreover, that the first
and last terms belong to God alone as their cause, whereas
the other, middle term also depends upon our mentality and
motion. It provides through itself the proper way to speak
about the first and last, and when it is not present even the
mere mention of them is useless, since they would not then
have "good" joined to them. In light of this, they came to   53
understand that the truth in the first and last terms, which
existence in the good naturally produces when the middle
term is mixed with the first and last, can only be realized
and preserved for them when their motion is always directed
towards God.

What is more, on this basis they sharpened the vision of the   C
soul with their natural reason and heard, in a sense, from reason's own explicit crying out that we must not use the natural activities in a disordered way, because corruption comes

ἐκ τοῦ κατὰ παράχρησιν τρόπου φθοράν, αὐτοῦ βοῶντος τοῦ λόγου διαρρήδην ἀκούσαντες, ὁμαλῶς κατὰ
τὸν πρέποντα λόγον τῆς φύσεως πρὸς τὸν αὐτῆς αἴτιον
φέρεσθαι ἐδιδάχθησαν, ἵν᾽ὅθεν ἁπλῶς αὐτοῖς ἐστι τὸ εἶναι, καὶ τὸ ὄντως εἶναί ποτε προστεθὲν ὑποδέξωνται.
Τί γὰρ ἂν καὶ ἔσται τῷ μὴ ἑαυτοῦ κατὰ τὸ εἶναι αἰτίῳ,
πρὸς ἑαυτοὺς ἴσως λογισάμενοι εἶπον, πρὸς ἑαυτὸν ἢ
ἄλλο τι παρὰ τὸν θεὸν κινουμένῳ, τὸ κέρδος, ὁπότε εἰς
τὸν τοῦ εἶναι λόγον οὐδὲν ἑαυτῷ ἀφ᾽ἑαυτοῦ ἢ ἄλλου τινὸς παρὰ τὸν θεὸν περιποιῆσαι δυνήσεται; Διατοῦτο τὸν
μὲν νοῦν περὶ μόνου θεοῦ καὶ τῶν αὐτοῦ ἀρετῶν δια-
νοεῖσθαι καὶ τῇ ἀρρήτῳ δόξῃ τῆς αὐτοῦ μακαριότητος
ἀγνώστως ἐπιβάλλειν, τὸν δὲ λόγον ἑρμηνευτὴν τῶν
νοηθέντων γίνεσθαι καὶ ὑμνῳδὸν καὶ τοὺς πρὸς αὐτὰ
ἑνοποιοὺς ὀρθῶς διαλέγεσθαι τρόπους, τὴν δὲ αἴσθησιν
κατὰ λόγον εὐγενισθεῖσαν, τὰς ἐν τῷ παντὶ διαφόρους
δυνάμεις τε καὶ ἐνεργείας φαντασιουμένην, τοὺς ἐν
τοῖς οὖσιν, ὡς ἐφικτὸν τῇ ψυχῇ, διαγγέλλειν λόγους
διδάξαντες καὶ διὰ τοῦ νοῦ καὶ τοῦ λόγου, ὥσπερ ναῦν,
σοφῶς τὴν ψυχὴν οἰακίσαντες, τὴν ὑγρὰν ταύτην καὶ
ἄστατον καὶ ἄλλοτε ἄλλως φερομένην καὶ τὴν αἴσθησιν ἐπικλύζουσαν τοῦ βίου κέλευθον ἀβρόχοις διώδευ-
σαν ἴχνεσιν. |

* Οὕτω τάχα καὶ Μωϋσῆς ἐκεῖνος ὁ μέγας τῇ πλη-   1117
γῇ τοῦ παντοδυνάμου λόγου, οὗ σύμβολον ἦν ἴσως ἡ
ῥάβδος, θαλάσσης τρόπον τῶν αἰσθητῶν διελὼν τὴν
ἀπάτην, ἢ περιελὼν εἰπεῖν οἰκειότερον, στερρὰν καὶ
ἀσάλευτον τῷ πρὸς τὰς θείας ἐπαγγελίας ἐπειγομένῳ
λαῷ τὴν ὑπίχνιον παρέσχετο γῆν, τὴν ὑπὸ αἴσθησιν

necessarily upon the natural powers when they are misused. Thus were they taught how to be moved along evenly, in accordance with the essential idea that clearly reveals nature, to the cause of nature, so that they may receive the addition of substantial existence from the one from whom they have bare existence. When they had thought all this through, they said something like this to themselves: Indeed, what benefit could there be for that which is not self-caused to be moved towards itself or towards anything other than God, when it would be unable to keep secure for itself any idea of existence from itself or from anything other than God? Because of this, they D taught the intellect to think only of God and of the virtues that come from Him and to devote itself, without knowledge, to the ineffable glory of His blessedness. They taught reason to become the interpreter and hymnist of intellectual reality and to reason accurately about the ways it is unified. Finally, they taught sense-perception to be ennobled by appropriating it to reason when sense-perception receives the images of the diverse powers and activities in the universe to make known the essential ideas in beings, as far as this is accessible to the soul. They wisely guided the soul, as if it were a ship, by means of the intellect and reason, and in this way they passed 54 through this fluid, unstable, and unevenly moving journey of life, where sensuality floods everything, without getting their feet wet.

Figures of Passage

Perhaps[11] this is how Moses, that great man, provided firm 1117A and stable land underfoot – I mean the nature subject to sense-perception – for the people who were being driven on to the divine promises, with the stroke of all-powerful reason – his staff was possibly a symbol of this – when he separated,

---

11   4. Contemplating the passage through the sea in the figure of Moses

φημὶ φύσιν, ὀρθῷ λόγῳ εἶναι θεατὴν καὶ εὐπερίγραπτον
καὶ βίῳ ἀρεταῖς ἠγλαϊσμένῳ βατὴν δείξας καὶ εὐπαρό-
δευτον καὶ μηδένα κίνδυνον ἐκ τῆς ἑκατέρωθεν παφλα-
ζούσης τῶν διακριθέντων ὑδάτων, οἷς τέως κεκάλυ-
πτο, ὁρμῆς τοῖς οὕτως αὐτὴν διαπερῶσιν ἐπάγουσαν,
εἴπερ τῷ κατ᾽ἀναγωγὴν λόγῳ διάκρισις ὑδάτων νοητῆς
θαλάττης ἐστὶν ἡ τῶν κατ᾽ἔλλειψιν καὶ πλεονασμὸν
ἀντικειμένων ταῖς ἀρεταῖς κακιῶν τῆς πρὸς ἄλληλα
συνεχείας διάστασις, ἣν πέφυκε λόγος ποιεῖν, καιρίως
αὐτῶν καθαψάμενος καὶ τοῖς ἐπὶ θεὸν προτροπάδην
ἐπειγομένοις οὐδαμῶς ἀλλήλαις αὐτὰς συναφθῆναι
συγχωρῶν.

* Οὕτω πάλιν, τῷ καλοῦντι ἑπόμενος θεῷ, ὑπερ-
σχὼν τὰ τῇδε πάντα, εἰς τὸν γνόφον εἰσῆλθεν, οὗ ἦν ὁ
θεός, τουτέστιν εἰς τὴν ἀειδῆ καὶ ἀόρατον καὶ ἀσώματον διατριβήν, νῷ πάσης ἐλευθέρῳ τῆς πρὸς ὁτιοῦν
πάρεξ θεοῦ σχέσεως· ἐν ᾗ γενόμενος, ὡς ἐνῆν μάλιστα
ἀνθρωπίνην ἀξιωθῆναι φύσιν, οἷον ἔπαθλον τῆς μακαρίας ἐκείνης ἀναβάσεως ἄξιον, τὴν χρόνου καὶ φύσεως τὴν γένεσιν περιγράφουσαν κομίζεται γνῶσιν,
καὶ τύπον καὶ παράδειγμα τῶν ἀρετῶν αὐτὸν ποιησάμενος τὸν θεόν, πρὸς ὅν, καθάπερ γραφὴν εὐφυῶς τοῦ
ἀρχετύπου τὴν μίμησιν σώζουσαν, ἑαυτὸν ἀποτυπώσας
κάτεισι τοῦ ὄρους, ἧς μετείληφε δόξης κατὰ τὸ πρό-
σωπον ἐπισημαίνων τὴν χάριν καὶ τοῖς ἄλλοις ἀνθρώποις ὥσπερ θεοειδοῦς τύπου τύπον ἑαυτὸν γενόμενον
ἀφθόνως διδοὺς καὶ προτιθέμενος· καὶ δηλοῖ, τοῦτο
ποιῶν, περὶ ὧν εἶδέ τε καὶ ἤκουσε, τῷ λαῷ ἐξηγούμε-

or, to speak more appropriately, when he stripped away the deceit of sensual objects, as he did the sea. He showed thereby that the nature perceived by the senses can be surveyed and easily comprehended by rightly exercised reason, that it is traversable for the life adorned with virtues and admits of easy passage, and that there is no danger from the desire seething on either side of the divided waters, by which sensual nature is still covered, for those who pass through it, even as this desire threatens them. Indeed, to take the imagery of the passage as referring to spiritual concepts, the separation of the waters of the sea represents, with respect to the mind, the interruption of the continuous sequence of evils resulting from the oscillation of deficiency and excess, which are set against the virtues. Reason naturally produces this interruption when   B
it is violently set upon by evil things, effectively hindering them from being joined to each other in those who are pressing on urgently toward God.

This[12] also applies to when God called to Moses and Moses followed Him, rose above everything here in this world, and *entered the darkness where God was* (Ex 20.21) – that is, the eternal, invisible, and bodiless manner of life – with a mind   55
free of every habitual relationship to anything other than God. Having taken on this way of life, he acquired the knowledge that comprehends the becoming of time and nature as a prize given to honor that blessed ascent, since it was in this way of life that human nature is most honored. Then, when   C
he had composed the account of how God Himself is the very model and paradigm of the virtues and had shaped himself in accordance with His form, as when a well-executed painting renders an accurate depiction of his model, he descended the mountain. He showed in his face the sign of the grace of the glory of which he had partaken and generously gave and offered himself to others, having become the representation of

12   *5. Contemplating Moses's ascent up the mountain*

νος καὶ γραφῇ τοῖς μετ᾽αὐτὸν οἷόν τινα κλῆρον θεόσδο-
τον, παραδιδούς, τοῦ θεοῦ τὰ μυστήρια.

* Οὕτως ὁ λαὸς ὁ τῆς Αἰγύπτου δι᾽αὐτοῦ ἐξαγόμενος,
τοῖς ἐσθήμασιν ἐνδεδεμένον τὸ σταῖς κομιζόμενος κατὰ
τὴν ἔρημον, τὸ δεῖν, ὡς οἶμαι, τυχὸν τὴν τοῦ ἐν ἡμῖν λόγου δύναμιν τῆς πρὸς τὰ αἰσθητὰ φυλάττειν ἐπιπλοκῆς
καθαρὰν καὶ ἀνέπαφον τοὺς τὸν μὲν αἰσθητὸν φεύγον-
τας, πρὸς δὲ τὸν νοητὸν κόσμον ὁδεύοντας, μυστικῶς
ἐδιδάσκετο, ἵνα δι᾽ἀρετῆς καὶ γνώσεως ἐντεῦθεν ἤδη
γένωνται κατὰ τὴν γνώμην, ὅπερ δι᾽ἐλπίδος γενήσεσθαι
κατὰ τὸν ἄφθαρτον αἰῶνα τοὺς ἀξίους πιστεύομεν.

* Οὕτως Ἰησοῦς ὁ Μωϋσέως διάδοχος, ἵνα τὰ πολλὰ τῶν περὶ αὐτοῦ ἱστορουμένων παραλείψω διὰ τὸ
πλῆθος, παραλαβὼν τὸν λαὸν πολλοῖς πρότερον πρὸς
εὐσέβειαν παιδευθέντα κατὰ τὴν ἔρημον τρόποις μετὰ
τὴν ἐν τῷ ὄρει Μωϋσέως τελευτὴν καὶ ξένῳ περιτομῆς
εἴδει καθαγνίσας αὐτὸν ταῖς ἐκ πέτρας μαχαίραις καὶ
τὸν Ἰορδάνην ξηρανθέντα τῇ προπομπῇ τῆς θείας κι-
βωτοῦ τοὺς τοῦ λαοῦ πάντας | ἀτεγγεῖς διαβιβάσας,   1120
τὸν δι᾽αὐτοῦ τυπικῶς μηνυόμενον σωτῆρα λόγον τοῦ
θεοῦ παρεδήλου, μετὰ τὴν τελευτὴν τοῦ γράμματος
τῶν νομικῶν διατάξεων τὴν ἐν τῷ ὕψει τῶν νοημάτων
γινομένην τοῦ ἀληθινοῦ Ἰσραὴλ καὶ ὁρῶντος θεὸν τὴν
ἡγεμονίαν παραλαμβάνοντα καὶ παντὸς μὲν ψυχῆς καὶ
σώματος μολυσμοῦ τῷ τομωτάτῳ λόγῳ τῆς εἰς αὐτὸν
πίστεως περιτέμνοντα, παντὸς δὲ ὀνειδισμοῦ τῶν πρὸς
ἁμαρτίαν ἐρεθιζόντων ἐλευθεροῦντα καὶ τὴν ῥέουσαν
τοῦ χρόνου φύσιν καὶ τῶν κινουμένων διαβιβάζοντα
πρὸς τὴν τῶν ἀσωμάτων κατάστασιν τοὺς ὤμοις ἀρε-

the divine form. He indicates, in doing this, the things he saw and heard, explaining directly to the people the mysteries of God and handing them down in writing as an inheritance for those who would come after him.

The[13] people who were led out of Egypt by him, in carrying away *the dough* that was *bound up* (Ex 12.34) in their clothes when they were in the desert, may, I think, have been taught mystically in these terms as well that it is necessary for those fleeing sensuality to keep the power of reason within us pure from and untouched by entanglement with sensual things as they make their way to the intellectual world, so that through   56 virtue and knowledge they might thereby become, in inclination now, what we believe the worthy will become through hope in the incorruptible age.

This[14] also applies to Joshua the successor of Moses,[15] and here   D I will skip most of his story because there is so much in it. After Moses's death on the mountain, Joshua inherited the people who had previously been instructed in piety in many ways in the desert, and he made them ritually pure with the unusual form of circumcision with knives of stone. He then led the whole people carrying the ark in procession through the Jordan without getting wet, for it had been dried up. In doing all this, he represented the Savior Word of God, who was revealed through him as in a type. The Savior inherited   1120A authority over the true Israel who sees God[16] after the death of the letter of the legal commandments, which takes place

---

13   *6. Contemplating the unwetted mixture of the unleavened bread. This section is omitted in PG*

14   *7. Contemplating the authority of Joshua, and the passage of the Jordan, and the second circumcision with blades of stone that was performed through him*

15   Cf. Joshua 3.3–17, 5.1–9.

16   MAXIMUS here refers to an ancient etymology of the Hebrew name Israel as "He who sees God." Cf. PHIL. ALEX., *Alleg. Leg.*, II.34, GREG. NAZ., Or. 30, 19 (p. 264, 11-12)..

τῶν ἐπαιωρουμένην ἔχοντας τὴν δεκτικὴν τῶν θείων μυστηρίων γνῶσιν.

* Οὕτω πάλιν, περιόδοις ἑπτὰ καὶ σάλπιγξι το-σαύταις σὺν ἀλαλαγμῷ μυστικῷ τὴν δυσάλωτον ἢ καὶ ἀνάλωτον εἶναι δόξασαν πόλιν Ἱεριχὼ κατασείσας, τὸν αὐτὸν τοῦ θεοῦ λόγον μυστικῶς ἐνέφαινεν ὡς νι-κητὴν τοῦ κόσμου καὶ συντελεστὴν τοῦ αἰῶνος καὶ νῷ καὶ λόγῳ, ἤτοι γνώσει καὶ ἀρετῇ, ὧν ἡ κιβωτὸς καὶ αἱ σάλπιγγες τύπος ὑπῆρχον, τοῖς ἑπομένοις αὐτῷ τὸν αἰσθητὸν αἰῶνα εὐάλωτον δεικνύοντα καὶ εὐκα-θαίρετον καὶ μηδὲν τῶν ἐν αὐτῷ πρὸς ἀπόλαυσιν ἐπι-τήδειον τοῖς τῶν θείων ἐρασταῖς ἀγαθῶν, ὡς θανάτῳ καὶ φθορᾷ συνημμένον καὶ θείας ἀγανακτήσεως αἴτιον· καὶ δηλοῖ Ἄχαρ ὁ τοῦ Χαρμῆ, ὅπερ ἐστὶν ὁ ταραχώδης καὶ φιλόϋλος λογισμός, ὑπὲρ τοῦ εἰσοικίσασθαί τι τῶν αἰσθητῶν τὸν οἴκτιστον ἐκεῖνον κατὰ θείαν ψῆφον ἀπ-ενεγκάμενος θάνατον, ὃν ἐργάζεται λόγος, τῷ βάθει τῆς πονηρᾶς συνειδήσεως ἐναποπνίγων τὸν οὕτω τιμω-ρηθῆναι ἄξιον.

in the height of intellectual reality, and he cuts away from him every defilement of soul and body with the sharply cutting word of faith in Him. He also frees those who possess the knowledge that contains divine mysteries, which rests upon the shoulders of the virtues, from every reproach of those who incite to sin, and He leads them through the flowing nature of time and of things subject to change toward the state of the bodiless ones.

57

This[17] also applies to when Joshua shook the city of Jericho to the ground with seven circumambulations and seven blasts of the trumpet together with a mystical shout, and this a city that had thought itself to be difficult or even impossible to conquer.[18] In so doing, he mystically showed that the same Word of God both conquers the world[19] and *completes the age* (Matt 28.20) with intellect and reason, that is, with knowledge and virtue, which the ark and the trumpets represent. He showed thereby that the age of sensuality is easy to conquer and subdue for those who follow Him, and that not one of the goods in this age is suitable for the enjoyment of those who are in love with divine goodness, since it is bound to death and corruption and is the cause of divine wrath. Achar the son of Charmi shows what the disordered and materialistic way of thinking looks like, since, in accordance with the divine decree, he received that most pitiable death for taking possession of some of the sensual goods, a death that reason accomplishes by suffocating the one who deserves to receive retaliation in this way for the baseness of his wicked crime.[20]

B

C

---

17   8. *Contemplating Jericho and the seven circumambulations; and also the ark, the trumpets, and the curse*

18   Cf. Joshua 6.8–21.

19   Cf. John 16.33.

20   Cf. Joshua 7.1, 17–26. The people stoned Achar and buried him beneath a heap of stones.

* Οὕτω πάλιν, καθὼς γέγραπται· ἐν τῷ καιρῷ ἐκείνῳ
καταλαβόμενος τὴν Ἀσσὼρ καὶ τὸν βασιλέα αὐτῆς ἀποκτείνας ἐν ῥομφαίᾳ, καὶ πᾶν ἐμπνέον ἐξολοθρεύσας ἐν
αὐτῇ, ἥτις ἦν πρότερον ἄρχουσα πασῶν τῶν χωρῶν,
ἐδιδάσκετο ὧν μυστηρίων τύπος προεβέβλητο τοὺς
λόγους, ὅτι ὁ ἀληθινὸς σωτὴρ ἡμῶν Ἰησοῦς Χριστός,
ὁ υἱὸς τοῦ θεοῦ, ὁ τῶν πονηρῶν καθαιρέτης δυνάμεων
καὶ κληροδότης τῶν ἀξίων τῆς χάριτος, κατὰ τὸν καιρὸν τῆς αὐτοῦ ἐνανθρωπήσεως διὰ σταυροῦ καταλαβόμενος τὴν ἁμαρτίαν καὶ τὸν βασιλέα αὐτῆς, τὸν διάβο-
λον – ἦρχε γὰρ πάντων ποτὲ *βασιλεύουσα ἡ ἁμαρτία*
–, ἀπέκτεινε τῷ ῥήματι τῆς δυνάμεως αὐτοῦ καὶ ἐξω-
λόθρευσεν αὐτῆς πᾶν ἐμπνέον, τουτέστι τὰ πάθη τὰ ἐν
ἡμῖν καὶ τὰ ἐπ'αὐτοῖς αἰσχρὰ καὶ πονηρὰ ἐνθυμήματα,
ἵνα μὴ δὲ τὸ ὁπωσοῦν ἐν τοῖς τοῦ Χριστοῦ καὶ κατὰ
Χριστὸν ζῶσιν, ἐμπνέοντος δίκην, καθ'ὁτιοῦν ἔχῃ λοι-
πὸν τὸ κινεῖσθαι καὶ ζῆν ἡ ἁμαρτία.|

* Οὕτω Δαυίδ, ὁ μετ'ἐκείνους μὲν τῷ χρόνῳ, κα-   1121
τ'ἐκείνους δὲ τῷ πνεύματι, ἵνα τοὺς **Κριτὰς** παραδραμῶ
πολλὰ ἔχοντας ἐν τῷ βίῳ μυστήρια, τὴν δόξαν τοῦ
θεοῦ διηγουμένων τῶν οὐρανῶν ἀκούων καὶ τὴν ποίη-
σιν τῶν χειρῶν αὐτοῦ ἀναγγέλλοντος τοῦ στερεώμα-
τος, τὸ θαυμάσιον, οἷς ψυχὴν ὁ δημιουργὸς οὐκ ἐνέθηκε, τοὺς περὶ θεολογίας νόος ἀκοαῖς παρὰ τῶν ἀψύχων
ὑπεδέχετο λόγους καὶ τοὺς τῆς προνοίας καὶ κρίσεως
ἐξ ἀποτελέσματος κατὰ τὸ ἀνθρώποις ἐφικτὸν ἐδιδάσκετο τρόπους, τῶν οἷς δηλονότι κατὰ μέρος ποικίλλε-
ται ἡ τοῦ παντὸς διεξαγωγὴ οὐκ ἐφικνούμενος λόγων.
* Οὕτω πάλιν ὁ πατήρ μου καὶ ἡ μήτηρ μου ἐγκατέλι-
πόν με, ὁ δὲ κύριος προσελάβετό με φάσκων, τὴν τοῦ
κατὰ φύσιν τῆς σαρκὸς περὶ γένεσιν καὶ φθορὰν νόμου,
καθ'ὃν πάντες διὰ τὴν παράβασιν καὶ γεννώμεθα καὶ
συνιστάμεθα, καὶ τῆς τιθηνούσης ἡμᾶς, μητρὸς δίκην,
αἰσθήσεως ἀπόλειψίν τε καὶ ἀποφυγὴν ἀναγκαίαν εἶναι

We[21] can consider the following scriptural passage in the same way: *At that time, having taken Assor, and having killed its king with the broad sword, and having utterly destroyed everything breathing, which previously had ruled all the regions...*(Joshua 11.10–11). We learn from these "regions" that a type of the mysteries motivatedthese words, for our true Savior Jesus   58
Christ the Son of God, the purifier of evil powers and the one who distributes inheritance to those who are worthy of grace, *having taken* sin and its king the devil by means of the cross when He became human – for the devil ruled all things while *sin was reigning* (Rom 5.21) –, killed and *utterly destroyed*   D
everything breathing that belonged to sin *with the word of His power* (Heb 1.3). That is, He killed the passions in us and the shameful and evil patterns of thought that depend upon them, so that sin would not be left with anything that moves and lives in any way, like something breathing, in those who have life from Christ and live according to Christ.

The[22] same applies to David, who comes after these figures   1121A
in time but is like them in spirit (and here I shall pass over the book of Judges, which contains many mysteries of life). When David heard *the heavens declaring the glory of God and the firmament announcing the work of His hands* (Ps 18.2) – an amazing thing, since the fashioner did not place a soul within them – he received from soulless creatures the essential ideas of theology in what he heard with his mind and thoroughly learned the ways that providence and judgment proceed, as far as these are accessible to human beings. However, he clearly did not reach the essential ideas by which the arrangement of the universe is elaborated in its various parts. Similarly,[23]   B
when he said, *My father and mother forsook me, but the Lord*   59

---

21   *9. Contemplating Tyre, its king, and its capture*

22   *10. Contemplating the passage, "The heavens declare the glory of God" (Ps 18.2)*

23   *11. Contemplating the passage, "My father and mother forsook me" (Ps 26.10)*

τοῖς τῶν ἀφθάρτων ἐπιθυμηταῖς ἐπικεκρυμμένως οἶμαι διηγόρευε, δι'ὧν ὁ μὲν ὁρώμενος κόσμος ἀφίεται καὶ ἀφίησιν, ὁ δὲ κύριος προσλαμβάνεται καὶ τῷ πνευματικῷ υἱοθετῶν νόμῳ τοὺς ἀξίους καὶ τοῖς ἀξίοις πατροθετούμενος δι'ἀρετῆς καὶ γνώσεως ὅλον ἑαυτὸν ὅλοις αὐτοῖς καθ'ὁμοίωσιν, ὡς ἀγαθός, ἐνδίδωσιν· ἢ τάχα διὰ τοῦ πατρὸς καὶ τῆς μητρὸς τὸν γραπτὸν νόμον καὶ τὴν κατ'αὐτὸν σωματικὴν λατρείαν αἰνίττεται, ὧν τῇ ὑποχωρήσει τὸ φῶς τοῦ πνευματικοῦ νόμου ταῖς καρδίαις τῶν ἀξίων ἀνατέλλειν πέφυκε καὶ τῆς κατὰ σάρκα δουλείας ἐλευθερίαν χαρίζεσθαι.

* Οὕτως Ἠλίας ὁ περιβόητος μετὰ τὸ πῦρ ἐκεῖνο, μετὰ τὸν συσσεισμόν, μετὰ τὸ μέγα καὶ κραταιὸν πνεῦμα τὸ διαλῦον ὄρη, ἃ δὴ ζῆλον καὶ διάκρισιν εἶναι καὶ τὴν ἐν πληροφορίᾳ πρόθυμον πίστιν ὑπολαμβάνω – ἡ μὲν γὰρ διάκρισις, ὥσπερ σεισμὸς τὰ συνεχῆ, τὴν μοχθηρίᾳ πυκνωθεῖσαν ἕξιν διὰ τῆς ἀρετῆς ἐπισείουσα, τῆς κακίας ἐξίστησι· ὁ δὲ ζῆλος, πυρὸς δίκην, ἀνάπτων τοὺς ἔχοντας τῇ *ζέσει τοῦ πνεύματος* παιδεύειν πείθει τοὺς ἀσεβεῖς· ἡ δὲ πίστις, πνεύματος βιαίου τρόπον, δόξης ἕνεκεν θεοῦ πρὸς καθαίρεσιν ὀχυρωμάτων δι-'ἐπιδείξεως θαυμάτων ὠθοῦσα τοὺς ἀπαθεῖς, ὕδατος γνωστικοῦ καὶ πυρὸς θεοποιοῦ χορηγὸν τὸν ὄντως πιστὸν ἄνθρωπον καθίστησι, καὶ τῷ μὲν τὸν δι'ἀγνοίας λιμὸν θεραπεύ|ουσα, τῷ δὲ τοῖς θύουσι δι'οἰκειότητος   1124 τὸν θεὸν εὐμενίζουσα καὶ τοὺς τῆς κακίας διδασκάλους λογισμούς τε καὶ δαίμονας λόγῳ σοφίας κτιννῦσα, τῆς τῶν παθῶν δουλείας τοὺς κεκρατημένους ἐλευθεροῖ –,

took me to Himself (Ps 26.10), I think he was secretly declaring that those who desire what cannot be destroyed must endure the abandonment and flight of the natural law of the flesh, its coming to be and destruction, which determines our birth and constitution because of the transgression, as well as the abandonment and flight of sense-perception, like a mother who nurses us. The visible world is sent away by indestructible reality and departs, and the Lord takes to Himself those who are worthy by adopting them through the spiritual law, and in becoming a father to the worthy through virtue and knowledge, He gives the whole of Himself to them fully by conferring His likeness upon them since He is good. Or perhaps David is speaking enigmatically about the written law C and the bodily worship it prescribes in the figures of *father* and *mother*. When they withdraw, the light of the spiritual law naturally arises in the hearts of the worthy, and freedom from fleshly service is given.

We[24] may consider the renowned Elijah in the same way, in the passage *after the fire, after the earthquake*, after the *great and strong wind* that *split the mountains* (III Ki 19.11–12). I take "fire," "earthquake," and "wind" to refer to zeal, discernment, and eager, certain faith. Discernment displaces evil by shaking with virtue the habitual state bound tightly to depravity, like an earthquake shaking things held securely together. Zeal, enflaming like fire those who possess it, prevails upon D them to instruct the impious with "fervor of spirit."[25] And |60 faith, pushing those who have attained freedom from passion like a *mighty wind* (Acts 2.2) *to the pulling down of strongholds* (II Cor 10.4) through the demonstration of wondrous things for the glory of God, establishes the truly faithful person as a benefactor who provides the waters of knowledge and deifying

---

24   *12. Contemplating the vision of Elijah, which he saw in the cave at Choreb*

25   Greg. Naz., Or. 17.1, PG 35.965B1, etc.; cf. Rom 12.11.

μετὰ ταῦτα πάντα, φωνῆς τῆς ἐν ᾗ ὁ θεὸς ὑπῆρχε λε-
πτῆς αὔρας αἰσθόμενος, τὴν προφορᾷ λόγου καὶ τρόποις βίου καὶ ἤθεσι θείαν καὶ ἀτάραχον καὶ εἰρηνικὴν
καὶ παντελῶς ἄϋλον καὶ ἁπλῆν καὶ παντὸς εἴδους ἐλευ-
θέραν καὶ σχήματος κατάστασιν λεχθῆναι ἢ δειχθῆναι
μὴ δυναμένην μυστικῶς ἐδιδάσκετο·

ἧς καταπλαγείς τε τὴν δόξαν καὶ τῷ κάλλει τρωθείς,
τοῦ ζηλωτὴς εἶναι τὸ πρὸς αὐτὴν εἶναι μᾶλλον ποθήσας, τουτέστι τοῦ ὑπὲρ ἀληθείας μάχεσθαι τὸ μετὰ τῆς
ἀληθείας διόλου γενέσθαι, καὶ μηδὲν ἀντικείμενον ὁρᾶν
ἢ γινώσκειν τῷ μόνον τὸν θεὸν ὅλον διόλου ἐν πᾶσιν
ὄντα ἐπίστασθαι πολλῷ τιμιώτερον κρίνας, ἔτι ὢν ἐν
σαρκὶ πρὸς αὐτὴν ὑπάρχων φυλάττεται, θείῳ ἀρετῶν
ἅρματι τὴν ὕλην διαπεράσας, ὡς προκάλυμμα τῆς κα-
θαρᾶς τοῦ νοῦ πρὸς τὰ νοητὰ διαβάσεως, καὶ τῆς σαρκὸς τὸ νέφος, τὸ ἐπισκοτοῦν τῷ ἡγεμονικῷ τῆς ψυχῆς
διὰ τῶν αὐτῆς παθημάτων, ἵνα καὶ αὐτὸς ὢν ἐπόθησεν
ἀρρήτων ἀγαθῶν μέτοχος γένηται, ὡς ἐφικτὸν τῷ ἔτι
μετὰ σαρκὸς τῆς ὑπὸ φθοράν, καὶ ἡμῖν τάχα τῶν ἐπηγ-
γελμένων βεβαία γένηται πίστωσις· τοῦτο γὰρ αὐτῷ
καὶ ὁ θεὸς ὑπετίθετο, διὰ τῶν οὕτω μυστικῶς δεδραμα-
τουργημένων ἀλαλήτως βοῶν ὅτι παντὸς ἄλλου ἀγα-
θοῦ τὸ μετὰ θεοῦ μόνου διὰ τῆς εἰρήνης εἶναι λυσιτελέ-
στερον.

fire. Moreover, faith frees those who have been overwhelmed by servitude to the passions by relieving the hunger that comes from ignorance, by supplicating God on behalf of those 1124A who offer sacrifices merely through custom, and by killing the structures of thinking and the demons that are the teachers of evil, all with the word of wisdom. After all these things, when he sensed the *sound* of the *light breeze* (III Ki 19.12) in which God was, he mystically learned a stability in speaking and in ways and practices of life that was divine, unperturbed, peaceful, completely unbound by materiality, simple, and free from all form and definite shape, a stability that cannot be reckoned or explained.

He was struck with amazement by the glory of this stability and was wounded by its beauty. He desired to be close to it rather than to be a zealot for it, that is, to come to be with the truth in every way rather than to fight on its behalf, for he judged it to be much more valuable to see and to know nothing in opposition to his understanding that God alone in His fullness is wholly in all things. Thus, even though he was B still in the flesh, he guarded himself by staying close to this |61 stability, for he had passed through material reality on the divine chariot of virtues, as through the "veil" of the intellect's pure passage to the intellectual realm, and through the "cloud" of the flesh, which darkens the soul's guiding power through its passions. This he did that he might become a partaker of the ineffable good things he desired, as far as this is possible for someone who is still in flesh subject to corruption, and also perhaps so that we might be assured of what has been promised. For it was God who had this purpose for him, proclaiming without words in the actions of this mystical drama that being with God alone in peace is more profitable than any other good thing.

* Οὕτως ὁ τούτου μαθητὴς καὶ κληρονόμος τοῦ πνεύματος Ἐλισσαῖος, μηκέτι ταῖς ὑλικαῖς φαντασίαις ἐνεχομένην ἔχων δι'ἐνεργείας τὴν αἴσθησιν, ἅτε διαβαθεῖσαν ἤδη ταῖς κατὰ νοῦν τοῦ πνεύματος χάρισι, τὰς ταῖς πονηραῖς ἀντιθέτους θείας δυνάμεις περὶ αὐτὸν οὔσας δι'ἄλλης ὀμμάτων ἐνεργείας αὐτός τε ὁρῶν καὶ τῷ φοιτητῇ τὸ ὁρᾶν χαριζόμενος, ἰσχυροτέραν τῆς ἀσθενείας τὴν δύναμιν, λέγω δὴ τῆς σαρκός, περὶ ἣν τῆς πονηρίας τὰ πνεύματα τὸν διορατικὸν νοῦν ἐνεδρεύουσι, πλέον ἔχειν τὴν ψυχήν, περὶ ἣν τῶν ἀγγέλων αἱ φάλαγγες παρεμβάλλουσιν οἷον βασιλικὴν εἰκόνα περιϊστάμενοι, καὶ ἐδιδάσκετο καὶ ἐδίδασκεν.

* Οὕτω καὶ ἡ μακαρία Ἄννα, ἡ τοῦ μεγάλου μήτηρ Σαμουήλ, στεῖρα οὖσα καὶ ἄτεκνος, παρὰ τοῦ θεοῦ καρπὸν αἰτησαμένη κοιλίας καὶ ἀντιδώσειν καὶ ἀντιχαρίζεσθαι τὸ δοθησόμενον τῷ διδόντι καὶ χαριζομένῳ θεῷ διὰ τῆς ἐν τῷ ναῷ προσεδρείας θερμῶς ὑποσχομένη, ἐδίδασκε μυστικῶς τὸ δεῖν πᾶσαν ψυχήν, ἡδονῶν σαρκικῶν στειρεύουσαν διὰ τῆς κατὰ τὴν σχέσιν τῶν ὑλικῶν ἀφαιρέσεως, αἰτεῖσθαι παρὰ θεοῦ τῶν ἀρετῶν τὰ σπέρματα, ἵνα τὸν βλέπειν τὰ ἔμπροσθεν γνωστικῶς δυνάμενον κατὰ διάνοιαν συλλαβοῦσα ὑπήκοον τοῦ θεοῦ λόγον καὶ τεκοῦσα προσ|ενέγκαι θεῷ δυνηθῇ διὰ τῆς κατὰ τὴν θεωρίαν εὐσεβοῦς προσεδρείας, ὡς μέγα χρέος καὶ τίμιον μηδὲν ἴδιον ἔχειν κρίνουσα, ὥστε δεῖξαι τὸν θεὸν μόνον διδόντα τε καὶ δεχόμενον, καθάπου φησὶ ὁ νόμος· τὰ δῶρά μου δόματά μου, καρπώματά μου διατηρήσετε προσφέρειν μοι, ὡς ἐξ αὐτοῦ τε καὶ εἰς αὐτὸν παντὸς ἀγαθοῦ καὶ ἀρχομένου καὶ λήγοντος· πέφυκε γὰρ ὁ τοῦ θεοῦ λόγος οἷς ἂν ἐγγένηται τῆς τε σαρκὸς ἀθετεῖν τὰ κινήματα καὶ τῆς πρὸς αὐτὰ τὴν ψυχὴν ἀναστέλλειν ῥοπῆς καὶ πάσης πληροῦν ἀληθοῦς διαγνώσεως.

1125

Elisha,[26] the disciple and heir of the spirit of Elijah, did   C
something similar. When his senses were no longer actively
bound up with the material imagination, when they had already passed through it by means of the intellectual gifts of
the Spirit, and he himself saw, with a different activity of
his eyes, divine powers surrounding him and set against evil
powers, as it was also given to his follower likewise to see,
he was taught, and he also taught others, that the soul has a
power much stronger than weakness (by "weakness" I mean
the flesh), around which the spirits of evil lie in wait to attack
the clear-sighted intellect, for the ranks of angels are arrayed
around the soul, stationed, as it were, around a royal image.[27]

The[28] blessed Hannah, the mother of the great Samuel, gave   62
a similar teaching. She was barren and without child and had | D
asked for the fruit of the womb from God, and she readily consented to give back and return the child she had been given
to God, who gives and grants gifts, so that he would attend in
the temple. In this she taught mystically that it is necessary
for every soul, in being barren of fleshly pleasures through the
putting off of its habitual relation to material things, to ask
God for the seeds of the virtues, so that, when it has conceived
in the mind and given birth to reason, which is obedient to
God and is able to see with knowledge what is before it, it may
be able to offer it to God with pious attention in contemplation, for such a soul does not think it possesses anything of   1125A
its own as a great recompense and reward. This shows that
God alone gives and receives – as the law says somewhere, *you
shall be diligent in offering unto me my gifts, my donations, and
my offerings* (Num 28.2), because every good thing takes its
beginning *from Him* and comes to an end *in Him* (Rom 11.36).
For should reason from God be born in them it naturally ren-

---

26   *13. Contemplating Elisha his disciple*
27   Cf. IV Ki 6.15–17.
28   *14. Contemplating Hannah and Samuel*

* **Καὶ** γὰρ τὸν ἱερέα κατὰ τὴν νομικὴν διαταγὴν εἰσιόντα εἰς τὴν καθοντιναοῦν τρόπον ἀκάθαρτον οἰκίαν
καὶ ἀφορίζοντα αὐτὴν καὶ τὰ πρὸς κάθαρσιν διαστέλ-
λοντα τοῖς κεκτημένοις ἀκούων τὸν ἀρχιερέα λόγον
δι᾽αὐτοῦ παραδηλοῦσθαι νοῶ, φωτὸς δίκην καθαρωτάτου
εἰσιόντα εἰς τὴν ψυχὴν καὶ τὰ ἐναγῆ βουλεύματα καὶ
διανοήματα μετὰ τῶν ὑπαιτίων πράξεων ἐκκαλύπτον-
τα καὶ τοὺς τῆς ἐπιστροφῆς καὶ καθάρσεως τρόπους
σοφῶς ὑποτιθέμενον. Ὅπερ οἶμαι σαφέστερον ἢ τὸν
μέγαν Ἠλίαν τὸν προφήτην ὑποδεξαμένη παραδηλοῦ-
σα ἔλεγεν· *ἄνθρωπε τοῦ θεοῦ εἰσῆλθες πρὸς ἐμὲ τοῦ
ἀναμνῆσαί με τὰς ἀδικίας μου·* * πᾶσα γὰρ ψυχὴ χη-
ρεύουσά τε καλῶν καὶ ἀρετῆς ἔρημος καὶ γνώσεως
θεοῦ, ἐπειδὰν τὸν θεῖον καὶ διαγνωστικὸν ὑποδέξηται
λόγον, εἰς μνήμην ἐρχομένη τῶν αὐτῆς ἁμαρτημάτων,
διδάσκεται πως ἀρετῶν ἄρτοις τὸν διατρέφοντα τρέ-
φειν λόγον καὶ ποτίζειν ἀληθείας δόγμασι τὴν πηγὴν
τῆς ζωῆς, καὶ αὐτῆς τῆς φύσεως τὴν εἰς αὐτὸν προκρί-
νειν θεραπείαν, δι᾽ἧς ἥ τε ὑδρία σὰρξ τὴν ἐπὶ ταῖς ἀρεταῖς πρακτικὴν συντονίαν χορηγήσει, καὶ ὁ καμψάκης
νοῦς τὴν τὸ φῶς συντηροῦσαν τῆς γνώσεως θεωρίαν
διηνεκῶς πηγάσειε, καὶ ὁ ἔμφυτος λογισμός, ὥσπερ
ἐκεῖ τῆς χήρας ὁ υἱός, τὴν ἐμπαθῆ προτέραν ἀποθέμενος ζωήν, τῆς παρὰ τοῦ λόγου διδομένης θείας καὶ ἀπα-
θοῦς γενέσθαι μέτοχος ἀξιωθήσεται ζωῆς.

ders the movements of the flesh of no effect and restrains the soul from inclining towards them and fills it with knowledge for true discernment in every circumstance.

For[29] when I hear about the priest who, according to the legal decree, enters into a house that is unclean in some way, B makes a determination about it, and makes a pronouncement |63 to those who own it concerning what is required for its purification,[30] I think that high-priestly reason is indicated through him, for it enters the soul like the purest light, uncovers its polluted intentions and thoughts along with its blameworthy actions, and wisely instructs it in the ways of conversion and purification. I[31] think that the woman who received the great prophet Elijah indicated this idea very clearly when she said, *man of God, have you come to me to remind me of my unrighteousness?* (III Ki 17.18). For whenever the widowed soul, C bereft of beauty, virtue, and the knowledge of God, receives divine and discerning reason and comes to the remembrance of its sins, it is taught that reason sustains it by nourishing it with the bread of virtues and that the fountain of life gives drink with the teachings of truth. It is also taught to take care of reason first, before its own nature, where the *water pot* flesh will supply practical exertion in service of the virtues, and the *cruse* intellect (III Ki 17.12) will continuously pour forth a stream of contemplation, preserving the light of knowledge. The thinking born in the mind, then, just like the son of the widow in the scriptural passage, will be made worthy, when it has put away its former life filled with passion, to become a partaker of the divine life, which is given by reason and free of passion.[32]

---

29   *15. Contemplating the one who makes determinations about an unclean house*
30   Cf. Lev 14.34–48.
31   *16. Contemplating the holy Elijah and the widow of Zarephath*
32   Cf. III Ki 17.8–24.

* Οὕτω καὶ τῶν Χριστοῦ μαθητῶν πρὸς τοῖς εἰρη-
μένοις τινές, οἷς συναναβῆναί τε καὶ συνεπαρθῆναι
αὐτῷ πρὸς τὸ ὄρος τῆς αὐτοῦ φανερώσεως δι'ἀρετῆς
ἐπιμέλειαν ἐξεγένετο, μεταμορφωθέντα θεασάμενοι
τῷ τε φωτὶ τοῦ προσώπου ἀπρόσιτον καὶ τῇ τῶν ἐσθημάτων λαμπρότητι κατάπληκτον, καὶ τῇ τῶν ἑκατέρωθεν συνόντων τιμῇ Μωσέως καὶ Ἠλίου γεγενημένον
αἰδεσιμώτερον ἐπεγνωκότες, ἀπὸ τῆς | σαρκὸς εἰς τὸ   1128
πνεῦμα μετέβησαν πρὶν τὴν διὰ σαρκὸς ἀποθέσθαι ζωὴν
τῇ ἐναλλαγῇ τῶν κατ'αἴσθησιν ἐνεργειῶν, ἣν αὐτοὺς τὸ
πνεῦμα ἐνήργησε, περιελὸν τῆς ἐν αὐτοῖς νοερᾶς δυνάμεως τῶν παθῶν τὰ καλύμματα· δι'οὗ καθαρθέντες τὰ
ψυχῆς καὶ σώματος αἰσθητήρια, τῶν παραδειχθέντων
αὐτοῖς μυστηρίων τοὺς πνευματικοὺς ἐκπαιδεύονται
λόγους·

τὴν μὲν ἀκτινοφανῶς ἐκλάμπουσαν τοῦ προσώπου πανόλβιον αἴγλην, ὡς πᾶσαν ὀφθαλμῶν νικῶσαν
ἐνέργειαν, τῆς ὑπὲρ νοῦν καὶ αἴσθησιν καὶ οὐσίαν καὶ
γνῶσιν θεότητος αὐτοῦ σύμβολον εἶναι μυστικῶς ἐδιδάσκοντο, ἀπὸ τοῦ μὴ ἔχειν αὐτὸν εἶδος μήτε κάλλος
καὶ τοῦ σάρκα τὸν λόγον γεγενημένον γινώσκειν ἐπὶ
τὴν ὡραῖον κάλλει παρὰ τοὺς υἱοὺς τῶν ἀνθρώπων καὶ
τὴν ἐν ἀρχῇ αὐτὸν εἶναι καὶ πρὸς τὸν θεὸν εἶναι καὶ
θεὸν εἶναι ἔννοιαν χειραγωγούμενοι καὶ πρὸς τὴν ὡς
μονογενοῦς παρὰ Πατρὸς πλήρη χάριτος καὶ ἀληθείας
δόξαν διὰ τῆς παντελῶς πᾶσιν ἀχώρητον αὐτὸν ἀνυ-
μνούσης θεολογικῆς ἀποφάσεως γνωστικῶς ἀναγόμε-
νοι, τὰ δὲ λευκαθέντα ἱμάτια τῶν ῥημάτων τῆς ἁγίας
γραφῆς φέρειν σύμβολον, ὡς τηνικαῦτα λαμπρῶν καὶ

The Transfiguration of Perception: Scripture and Nature

In[33] addition to the figures that have already been mentioned, 64
we may consider in this same way those disciples of Christ who |D
were permitted to ascend and be lifted up together with Him to
the mountain of His manifestation because of their diligence
in virtue. They saw Him transfigured, but they could not
approach Him because of the light of His countenance and
were stunned by the radiance of His clothing. They also witnessed an exceedingly awesome event in the honor paid Him
by Moses and Elijah, who were with Him on either side. In   1128A
so doing, they passed over from flesh to spirit, before life in
the flesh had been put aside, by a change in the activities of
their senses, which the Spirit made active in them by removing the veils of the passions from their intellectual power.
Having been purified in the perceptual faculties of both soul
and body through this, they were thoroughly instructed in
the spiritual ideas of the mysteries presented to them.

The disciples were mystically taught that the blessed splendor
radiantly shining forth from Christ's countenance, because it
completely overwhelms the activity of the eyes, is the symbol
is the symbol of His divinity, which is beyond all intellect,
sense-perception, being, and knowledge. They were led in this
from knowing Him as *having neither form nor beauty* (Is 53.2)
and as *the Word that had become flesh* (Jn 1.14) to the concept
that He is *fair in beauty beyond the sons of men* (Ps 44.3) and
that He is *in the beginning* and is both *with God* and *is God* B
(Jn 1.1). They were then led on with knowledge by theolog-
ical negation, which praises the One who is utterly unattain- |65
able for all, to the *glory as of the only-begotten of the Father*
full of grace and truth (Jn 1.14). Then, they were taught that

---

33   17. *Contemplating the Transfiguration of the Lord*

τρανῶν καὶ σαφῶν αὐτοῖς γενομένων καί, παντὸς γρι-
φώδους αἰνίγματος καὶ συμβολικοῦ σκιάσματος χωρίς,
νοουμένων καὶ τὸν ἐν αὐτοῖς ὄντα τε καὶ καλυπτόμενον
παραδηλούντων λόγον, ὁπηνίκα τὴν τελείαν καὶ ὀρθὴν
περὶ θεοῦ γνῶσιν ἔλαβον καὶ τῆς πρὸς τὸν κόσμον καὶ
τὴν σάρκα προσπαθείας ἠλευθερώθησαν ἢ τῆς κτίσεως
αὐτῆς, κατὰ περιαίρεσιν τῆς δοκούσης τέως ἐμφαίνεσ-
θαι αὐτῇ τῶν ἠπατημένων καὶ μόνῃ αἰσθήσει προσ-
δεδεμένων ῥυπαρᾶς, ὑπολήψεως, διὰ τῆς τῶν αὐτὴν
συμπληρούντων διαφόρων εἰδῶν σοφῆς ποικιλίας,
ἀναλόγως ἱματίου τρόπον, τὴν ἀξίαν τοῦ φοροῦντος
τὴν τοῦ γενεσιουργοῦ λόγου δύναμιν μηνυούσης· ἄμφω
γὰρ ἐπὶ τοῦ λόγου ἁρμόσει λεγόμενα, ἐπεὶ καὶ ἀμφοῖν
δι' ἀσαφείας κεκάλυπται, δι' ἡμᾶς εἰκότως, πρὸς τὸ μὴ
τολμᾶν τοῖς ἀχωρήτοις ἀναξίως προσβάλλειν, τῷ μὲν
ῥητῷ τῆς ἁγίας γραφῆς, ὡς λόγος, τῇ δὲ κτίσει, ὡς κτί-
στης καὶ ποιητὴς καὶ τεχνίτης.

Ὅθεν ἀναγκαίως ἀμφοτέρων ἐπιδεῖσθαί φημι τὸν
πρὸς θεὸν ἀμέμπτως εὐθυπορεῖν βουλόμενον, τῆς τε
γραφικῆς ἐν πνεύματι γνώσεως καὶ τῆς τῶν ὄντων
κατὰ πνεῦμα φυσικῆς θεωρίας, ὥστε ἰσοτίμους καὶ τὰ
αὐτὰ ἀλλήλοις παιδεύοντας τοὺς δύο νόμους, τόν τε φυσικὸν καὶ τὸν γραπτόν, καὶ μὴ δ' ἕτερον θατέρου ἔχοντα
πλέον ἢ ἔλαττον δύνασθαι δεῖξαι, ὡς εἰκός, τὸν τελείας
ἐραστὴν γενέσθαι τῆς σοφίας τέλειον ἐπιθυμοῦντα, *
τὸν μὲν ὁμαλῶς ὅτι μάλιστα κατὰ λόγον διευθυνόμε-
νον, διὰ τῶν ἐν αὐτῷ συμφυῶν θεαμάτων, βίβλου τρό-
πον, τὸ ἐναρμόνιον τοῦ παντὸς ὕφασμα | ἔχοντα, γράμ-   1129
ματα μὲν καὶ συλλαβὰς ἐχούσης τὰ πρὸς ἡμᾶς πρῶτα
προσεχῆ τε καὶ μερικὰ καὶ πολλαῖς παχυνόμενα κατὰ
σύνοδον ποιότησι σώματα, ῥήματα δὲ τὰ τούτων καθο-

the *whitened clothes* (Matt 17.2; Mk 9.3; Lk 9.29) are a symbol
of the sayings of holy scripture, since it was then that they
became bright and clear and distinct for the disciples. The
disciples received complete and genuine knowledge concerning
God at that time, for the sayings of scripture were understood
without any riddling enigma or symbolic shadow and pointed
directly to the Word that is both in them and hidden in them.
They were freed, moreover, from passionate attachment to the
world and the flesh, or from creation itself, by the removal of
the base assumptions about the world that seem to have been
reflected up to that time in those who had been deceived and
bound exclusively to sense-perception, for the wise adornment   C
of the different forms, which, as though wrapped in a coat, fill
creation, revealed the worthiness of one who was able to bear
the power of the creative Word. Indeed, both explanations
apply to the Word because He has been hidden obscurely in
both, and appropriately so given our state, for we dare not
approach unworthily those things that cannot be contained,
neither the language of holy scripture, since He is the Word,
nor creation, since He is creator, maker, and artificer.

For this reason I say that one who wishes to be blameless as
he goes straight to God necessarily needs both the spiritual
knowledge of scripture and the spiritual contemplation of the
nature of reality. The result is that one who desires to become
a perfect lover of perfect wisdom is able, rightly, to show that
the two laws, the natural and the written, are equal in honor   66
and teach the same things as each other and that one cannot   D
possess more or less than the other. The[34] natural law, since it
is arranged in an exceedingly rational way, coherently holds
together the harmonious web of the universe like a book by
means of the visible realities that naturally arise in it. For   1129A
letters and syllables, the contemplation of nature has bodies,

---

34   18. *Contemplating the natural and written law and how they coherently
fit with each other*

λικώτερα πόρρω τε ὄντα καὶ λεπτότερα, ἐξ ὧν σοφῶς ὁ
διαχαράξας καὶ ἀρρήτως αὐτοῖς ἐγκεχαραγμένος λόγος
ἀναγινωσκόμενος ἀπαρτίζεται, τὴν ὅτι μόνον ἔστιν, οὐ-
χ᾽ὅ,τι ποτὲ δέ ἐστιν, οἱανοῦν παρεχόμενος ἔννοιαν καὶ
διὰ τῆς εὐσεβοῦς τῶν διαφόρων φαντασιῶν συλλογῆς
εἰς μίαν τοῦ ἀληθοῦς εἰκασίαν ἐνάγων, ἀναλόγως ἑαυτὸν διὰ τῶν ὁρατῶν ὡς γενεσιουργὸς ἐνορᾶσθαι διδούς,
τὸν δέ, μαθήσει κατορθούμενον διὰ τῶν αὐτῷ σοφῶς
ὑπηγορευμένων, ὥσπερ κόσμον ἄλλον ἐξ οὐρανοῦ καὶ
γῆς καὶ τῶν ἐν μέσῳ, τῆς ἠθικῆς φημι καὶ φυσικῆς καὶ
θεολογικῆς φιλοσοφίας, συνιστάμενον, τὴν ἄφατον
καταμηνύειν τοῦ ὑπαγορεύσαντος δύναμιν καὶ ταυτὸν
ἀλλήλοις κατ᾽ἐπαλλαγὴν ὄντας δεικνύοντα, τὸν μὲν
γραπτὸν τῷ φυσικῷ κατὰ τὴν δύναμιν, τὸν δὲ φυσικὸν
ἔμπαλιν τῷ γραπτῷ κατὰ τὴν ἕξιν, καὶ τὸν αὐτὸν μη-
νύοντας καὶ καλύπτοντας λόγον, τὸ μὲν τῇ λέξει καὶ τῷ
φαινομένῳ, τὸ δὲ τῇ νοήσει καὶ τῷ κρυπτομένῳ.

Ὡς γὰρ τῆς ἁγίας γραφῆς τὰ ῥήματα ἱμάτια λέγοντες, τὰ δὲ νοήματα σάρκας τοῦ λόγου νοοῦντες, τοῖς
μὲν καλύπτομεν, τοῖς δὲ ἀποκαλύπτομεν, οὕτω καὶ
τῶν γεγονότων τὰ πρὸς τὸ ὁρᾶσθαι προβεβλημένα εἴδη
τε καὶ σχήματα ἱμάτια λέγοντες, τοὺς δὲ καθ᾽οὓς ἔκτι-
σται ταῦτα λόγους σάρκας νοοῦντες, ὡσαύτως τοῖς μὲν
καλύπτομεν, τοῖς δὲ ἀποκαλύπτομεν· κρύπτεται γὰρ
φαινόμενος ὁ τοῦ παντὸς δημιουργὸς καὶ νομοθέτης
λόγος, κατὰ φύσιν ὑπάρχων ἀόρατος, καὶ ἐκφαίνεται

which are the first things most proximate and particular to us and are condensed by the conjunction of their many qualities; for words it has realities that are far more integrative and refined than bodies. The Word, who wisely shaped them and was ineffably engraved in them, corresponds to them as He is read, though He provides only the concept that He is, not what He is, whatever He may be, and He leads the way to a single likeness of truth through the pious gathering of different mental images, giving Himself to be seen *in a way that is ideally suited* to vision by means of visible reality as the *one who brings creation into being* (Wis 13.5). The scriptural law is ordered for learning through what has been wisely dictated in it, as if it were another world composed of heaven, earth and what is in the midst of them, which refer to ethical, natural, and theological philosophy. Thus it reveals the ineffable power of the one who gave this dictation and shows that the scriptural and natural law are equivalent to each other on account of how they fit together. The scriptural law is equivalent to the natural in that it is possible to discern the natural law in it, and, from the other side, the natural law is equivalent to the scriptural law in that it already possesses all the content of the scriptural law within itself. Moreover, they both reveal and conceal the same Word, revealing by language and appearance, concealing with respect to meaning and hiddenness.

For in calling the words of holy scripture "clothes," and in understanding the meanings to be the "flesh" of the Word, we cover Him with words and uncover Him with meaning. Likewise, in using "clothes" for the forms and shapes of things that have come into being and have become visible, and in understanding the essential ideas according to which these things have been created to be "flesh," we also cover the Word with forms and shapes and uncover Him with the essential ideas. For the Word who fashions the universe and

κρυπτόμενος, μὴ ληπτὸς εἶναι φύσει τοῖς σοφοῖς πι-
στευόμενος. Εἴη δὲ ἡμῖν τοῦ διἀποφάσεως ἐκφαίνειν
κρυπτόμενον καὶ πᾶσαν σχημάτων τε καὶ αἰνιγμάτων
τὸ ἀληθὲς εἰκονίζουσαν δύναμιν παρελθεῖν μᾶλλον καὶ
πρὸς αὐτὸν τὸν λόγον ἀπὸ τοῦ γράμματος καὶ τῶν φαινομένων κατὰ τὴν τοῦ πνεύματος δύναμιν ἀρρήτως ἀνα-
βιβάζεσθαι ἢ τοῦ φαινόμενον κρύπτειν διὰ τῆς θέσεως
γίνεσθαι, ἵνα μὴ καὶ ἡμεῖς, φονευταὶ τοῦ λόγου γενόμε-
νοι, ἑλληνικῶς τῇ κτίσει λατρεύσωμεν παρὰ τὸν κτίσα-
ντα, μηδὲν ἀνώτερον τῶν ὁρωμένων εἶναι πιστεύοντες
καὶ τῶν αἰσθητῶν μεγαλοπρεπέστερον, ἢ μέχρι μόνου
τοῦ γράμματος διαβλέποντες, τὸ σῶμα μόνον ἰουδαϊκῶς
περὶ πολλοῦ ποιησώμεθα, τὴν κοιλίαν θεοποιήσαντες
καὶ τὴν αἰσχύνην ἡγησάμενοι δόξαν, τὸν αὐτὸν τοῖς
θεοκτόνοις κλῆρον ἀπενεγκώμεθα, ὡς τὸν καθ'ἡμᾶς δι'ἡ-
μᾶς πρὸς ἡμᾶς γενόμενον διὰ σώματος, καὶ συλλαβαῖς
καὶ γράμμασι παχυνθέντα διὰ τὴν αἴσθησιν, ὅλην τοῦ
ἐν ἡμῖν νοεροῦ τὴν δύναμιν πρὸς ἑαυτὴν ἐπικλίνασαν,
οὐ διαγινώσκοντες λόγον.

Φησὶ γὰρ ὁ θεῖος ἀπόστολος· τὸ γράμμα ἀποκτένει,
τὸ δὲ πνεῦμα ζωοποιεῖ – καὶ γὰρ καθ'ἑαυτὸ μόνον τὸ
γράμμα στεργόμενον τὸν ἐν αὐτῷ ἀποκτένειν λόγον
τοῖς στέργουσιν εἴωθεν, ὥσπερ καὶ τὸ κάλλος τῶν κτι-
σμάτων μὴ πρὸς δόξαν τοῦ πεποιηκότος | ὁρώμενον   1132
τῆς κατὰ λόγον εὐσεβείας ἀποστερεῖν τοὺς θεωμένους
πέφυκε –, καὶ πάλιν τὸ εὐαγγέλιον· εἰ μὴ ἐκολοβώθη-
σαν αἱ ἡμέραι ἐκεῖναι δηλαδὴ τῆς κακίας, οὐκ ἂν ἐσώθη
πᾶσα σάρξ, τουτέστι πᾶσα περὶ θεοῦ εὐσεβὴς ἔννοια.
Κολοβοῦνται γὰρ κακίας ἡμέραι τῆς κατ'αἴσθησιν δη-
μιουργούσης αὐτὰς ἐσφαλμένης κρίσεως, τῷ λόγῳ πε-
ριγραφείσης καὶ τοῦ κατ'αὐτὸν εὐσεβοῦς δικαιώματος
κατόπιν γεγενημένης. Ἀντιχρίστου γὰρ οὐδὲν διενήνο-

establishes the law is hidden when He is made manifest, be- C
cause He is invisible by nature, and He is made manifest when
He is hidden, because He is believed by the wise to be ungraspable by nature. So let the truth become manifest to us by
remaining hidden through negation and so pass beyond every
power for making images with forms and enigmatic figures
and mount up ineffably, away from letter and appearance, to
the Word Himself by the power of the Spirit, and let it not
become hidden by appearing through assertion. Otherwise,
we would become murderers of the Word and would *worship
the creature instead of the creator* (Rom 1.25) like the Greeks,
because we wouldn't believe that there is anything beyond
visible reality and more magnificent than sensual reality. Or,
by seeing only as far as the letter, we would, like the Jews, 68
consider the body alone to be of great value, making *the belly* D
a god. Considering *shame* to be *glory* (Phil 3.19), we would be
born away to the same fate with the God-slayers, because we
would not have discerned the Word who came to us in the
body as one of us and on our behalf and was reduced to syllables and letters to accommodate sense-perception, which had
drawn the power of our intellect entirely to itself.

As the divine apostle says, *the letter kills, but the Spirit gives
life* (II Cor 3.6), for it typically happens that, when the letter
becomes an object of devotion for its own sake alone, it kills
the rational meaning contained within it for those who are
devoted to it, just as the beauty of created things, when it is
not seen relative to the glory of the one who made it, tends
to separate those who gaze upon it from rational piety. Sim- 1132A
ilarly, it also says in the Gospel, *unless those days should be
shortened*, that is, the days of evil, *no flesh*, that is, no pious
concept of God, *would be saved* (Matt 24.22). The days of evil
are shortened when the erring judgment that produces them
by relying upon sense-perception has been enclosed by reason
and is thereafter subject to its divine correction. For the law

χεν ὁ τῆς σαρκὸς νόμος, ἀεὶ παλαίων τῷ πνεύματι καὶ
τῷ αὐτοῦ θείῳ νόμῳ ἀντιτασσόμενος, ἕως ἡ παροῦσα
ζωὴ τοῖς ἡττημένοις αὐτῇ προσφιλής ἐστι καὶ ἐράσμι-
ος, καὶ οὔπω φανεὶς ὁ λόγος τῷ ῥήματι τῆς δυνάμεως ἀνεῖλε, διακρίνας τοῦ ἀθανάτου τὸ θνητὸν καὶ τῆς
ἐλευθερίας τὴν διοχλοῦσαν ἔξω ποιησάμενος δουλείαν
καὶ τὴν ἀλήθειαν αὐτὴν καθ'ἑαυτὴν ψεύδους καθαρὰν
ἀποδείξας καὶ τῶν θείων καὶ αἰωνίων τὰ ὑλικὰ καὶ
πρόσκαιρα ἀποδιορίσας· πρὸς ἃ πέφυκεν ὁ νοῦς, διὰ
τῆς κατ'αἴσθησιν πρὸς αὐτὰ οἰκειότητος πλανώμενος,
ἐπικλίνεσθαι καὶ τῇ ἀλόγῳ θανατοῦσθαι στοργῇ· πρὸς
ὃν μάλιστα προηγουμένως ἡ θεοπρεπὴς τοῦ λόγου κα-
τάβασις γίνεται, τοῦ θανάτου τῆς ἀγνοίας αὐτὸν ἀνε-
γείρουσα καὶ τῆς πρὸς τὰ ὑλικὰ ἐμπαθοῦς διαθέσεως
ἀναστέλλουσα καὶ πρὸς τὸ κατὰ φύσιν ἐραστὸν τὴν
ἔφεσιν αὐτοῦ ἐπανάγουσα. Διὸ ἀναγκαίως οἶμαι δεῖν
τοῦ ὑπὲρ τὰ ἐνδύματα μακρῷ κρείσσονος σώματος,
τουτέστι τῶν θείων καὶ ὑψηλῶν νοημάτων τῆς τε ἁγίας
γραφῆς καὶ τῶν κατὰ τὴν κτίσιν θεαμάτων, φροντίζειν
λογικοὺς ὄντας καὶ διὰ λόγου πρὸς λόγον σπεύδοντας – κα-
θώς φησιν ὁ λόγος αὐτός· *οὐχὶ πλέον ἐστὶν ἡ ψυχὴ τῆς*
τροφῆς καὶ τὸ σῶμα τοῦ ἐνδύματος; –, μήπως ἐν καιρῷ μηδὲν ἔχοντες διελεγχθῶμεν τούτων ἐπειλημμένοι, τοῦ ὑφεστῶτος καὶ ὑφιστῶντος τὰ πάντα λόγου
οὐ περιδραξάμενοι κατὰ τὴν Αἰγυπτίαν ἐκείνην, ἥτις
μόνον τῶν ἱματίων τοῦ Ἰωσὴφ ἐπιλαβομένη τῆς τοῦ

of the flesh is no different from Antichrist: it is always wres-
tling against the Spirit and is arrayed against His divine law,
as long as the present life is dear to and loved by those who
have been overcome by it and the Word has not yet risen
up by being made manifest *by the word of power* (Heb 1.3),
and has not yet separated the mortal from the immortal by   69
expelling wearying servitude from freedom, demonstrating
the very truth in and of itself pure of falsehood , and bind-   B
ing off material and temporal realities from the divine and
eternal realm.

The mind tends to incline towards material and temporal
things when it wanders in its sensual connection to them and
then dies in its irrational devotion. It is, above all, for the
mind that the Word divinely descends; He rouses the mind
from the death of ignorance, removes it from an impassioned
disposition towards material things, and directs its desire back
up towards the one whose nature it is to be loved. Therefore,
I am compelled to think that "those who are rational and who
zealously pursue rationality through rational thought"[35] must
regard the body, that is, the divine and exalted meanings of
both Holy Scripture and of the visible realities of creation, to
be much better than its "clothing," just as the Word Himself   C
says, *Is not life more than food, and the body more than clothing?* (Matt 6.25). Otherwise, we would be exposed as having
nothing in the decisive moment, since we would have failed to
get hold of these meanings, having failed to get into our embrace the actually existing Word who grants actual existence
to all things, like the Egyptian woman who only got hold of
Joseph's garments and completely missed being with the one
she was in love with.[36]

---

35   GREG. NAZ., Or. 25.1, p. 156.7–8.
36   Cf. Gen 39.12.

ἐραστοῦ παντελῶς διήμαρτεν ὁμιλίας. Οὕτω γὰρ ἂν τά
τε ἐνδύματα τοῦ λόγου, φημὶ δὴ τὰ ῥήματα τῆς γραφῆς
καὶ τὰ φαινόμενα κτίσματα, λαμπρά τε καὶ ἐπίδοξα τῇ
ἐναλλαγῇ τῶν περὶ αὐτῶν δογμάτων καὶ τῷ θείῳ λόγῳ
ἐμπρέποντα, διὰ τῆς ὑψηλῆς θεωρίας καὶ ἡμεῖς, ἐπὶ τὸ
ὄρος ἀναβάντες τῆς θείας μεταμορφώσεως, θεασόμε-
θα, οὐδαμῶς πληκτικῶς εἰργόμενοι τῆς μακαρίας τοῦ
λόγου ἁφῆς κατὰ τὴν Μαγδαληνὴν Μαρίαν, *κηπουρὸν*
εἶναι δόξασαν τὸν κύριον Ἰησοῦν καὶ μόνον τῶν ὑπὸ
γένεσιν καὶ φθορὰν δημιουργόν, οὔπω μηδὲν ὑπὲρ τὴν
αἴσθησιν εἶναι νομίζουσαν, ἀλλὰ καὶ ὀψόμεθα καὶ προσ-
κυνήσομεν ζῶντα ἐκ νεκρῶν πρὸς ἡμᾶς τῶν θυρῶν
κεκλεισμένων γενόμενον, τῆς κατ'αἴσθησιν παντελῶς
ἐν ἡμῖν ἐνεργείας ἀποσβεσθείσης, τόν τε λόγον αὐτὸν
καὶ θεὸν *πάντα ἐν πᾶσιν ὄντα* καὶ πάντα ἑαυτοῦ δι'ἀ-
γαθότητα, τὰ μὲν νοητὰ σῶμα, τὰ δὲ αἰσθητὰ ἱμάτιον
πεποιηκότα γνωσόμεθα· περὶ ὧν ἴσως εἰρῆσθαι δοκεῖν
οὐκ ἀπεικὸς τὸ | *πάντες ὡς ἱμάτιον παλαιωθήσονται*   1133
διὰ τὴν ἐπικρατοῦσαν νῦν τῶν ὁρωμένων φθορὰν *καὶ*
ὡσεὶ περιβόλαιον ἑλίξεις αὐτοὺς καὶ ἀλλαγήσονται διὰ
τὴν προσδοκωμένην τῆς ἀφθαρσίας χάριν.

* Πρὸς τούτοις δὲ καὶ τοὺς λόγους εἰσόμεθα, τοὺς
τελευταίους δηλαδὴ καὶ ἡμῖν ἐφικτούς, ὧν προβέβλη-
ται ἡ κτίσις διδάσκαλος, καὶ τοὺς αὐτοῖς συνημμένους
πέντε τῆς θεωρίας τρόπους, οἷς διαιροῦντες τὴν κτίσιν οἱ ἅγιοι τοὺς ἐπ'αὐτῇ μυστικοὺς μετ'εὐσεβείας συ-
νελέξαντο λόγους, εἰς οὐσίαν καὶ κίνησιν καὶ διαφορὰν
κρᾶσίν τε καὶ θέσιν αὐτὴν ἐπιμερίσαντες· ὧν τρεῖς μὲν
ἔφασαν εἶναί τε πρὸς ἐπίγνωσιν θεοῦ προηγουμένως
καὶ προβεβλῆσθαι χειραγωγικούς, τὸν κατ'οὐσίαν τὸν
κατὰ κίνησιν τὸν κατὰ διαφοράν, δι'ὧν ὁ θεὸς γνωστὸς

This being so, we hope that, if we have ascended the mountain of divine transfiguration, we shall also see, by means of exalted contemplation, the clothes of the Word, I mean the words of scripture and created phenomena, which are seen clearly in their radiance and glory in virtue of both the interrelation of what is taught about them and of divine reason. We hope we shall not have to endure the shocking refusal of the blessed touch of the Word like Mary Magdalene, who *thought* the Lord Jesus was *the gardener* (Jn 20.15),[37] that is, the fashioner only of those things that are subject to coming to be and corruption, since she did not yet believe that there is anything beyond the realm of sense-perception. We hope, rather, that we shall both see and worship the one who comes to us *living from the dead* (Rom 6.13)[38] when *the doors have been shut* (Jn 20.26), when, that is, the activity of sense-perception in us has been entirely extinguished. If we attain to these, then we shall also know the Word Himself as *God* who is *all in all* (1 Cor 15.28) and has in His goodness made everything His own, intellectual reality His body and sensual reality His clothing. In light of this, it seems not inappropriate to cite the passages *all of them will grow old like clothing*, which refers to the corruption of visible things that now holds sway, and *as a covering You will fold them up and they will be changed* (Ps 101.27; Heb 1.11–12), referring to the grace of incorruption for which we hope.

In[39] addition to these,[40] we shall now attempt to approach the essential ideas, which are clearly the furthest extreme of what is attainable for us. Creation has emerged as the teacher, along with the five modes of contemplation joined to them, of the

---

37   Cf. John 20.11–17.

38   Cf. Lk 24.5.

39   *19. A brief explication of the five modes of natural contemplation*

40   I.e. the words of scripture and created phenomena.

τοῖς ἀνθρώποις γίνεται, ἐκ τῶν ὄντων τὰς περὶ αὐτοῦ
ἐμφάσεις συλλεγομένοις, ὡς δημιουργοῦ καὶ προνοη-
τοῦ καὶ κριτοῦ, δύο δὲ παιδαγωγικοὺς πρὸς ἀρετὴν καὶ
τὴν πρὸς θεὸν οἰκείωσιν, τὸν κατὰ κρᾶσιν καὶ τὸν κατὰ
θέσιν, δι'ὧν τυπούμενος ὁ ἄνθρωπος θεὸς γίνεται, τὸ
θεὸς εἶναι παθών, ἐκ τῶν ὄντων ὅλην τοῦ θεοῦ τὴν κατ'ἀ-
γαθότητα ἔμφασιν κατὰ νοῦν ὥσπερ ὁρῶν καὶ ἑαυτῷ
κατὰ λόγον ταύτην εἰλικρινεστάτην μορφούμενος.

Ὃ γὰρ δι'εὐσεβοῦς γνώσεώς φασιν ὁ καθαρὸς ὁρᾶν
πέφυκε νοῦς, τοῦτο καὶ παθεῖν δύναται, αὐτὸ ἐκεῖνο
κατὰ τὴν ἕξιν δι'ἀρετῆς γινόμενος· οἷον τὴν μὲν οὐσίαν
θεολογίας εἶναι διδάσκαλον, δι'ἧς τῶν ὄντων τὸν αἴτιον
ἐπιζητοῦντες, δι'αὐτῶν ὅτι ἔστι διδασκόμεθα, τὸ τί
ποτε εἶναι τοῦτο κατ'οὐσίαν γνῶναι μὴ ἐπιχειροῦντες,
ὅτι μὴ δὲ ἔστιν ἐμφάσεως ἐν τοῖς οὖσι τούτου προβολή,
δι'ἧς κἂν ποσῶς ὡς δι'αἰτιατοῦ πρὸς τὸ αἴτιον ἀνανεύ-
σωμεν, τὴν δὲ κίνησιν τῆς τῶν ὄντων προνοίας εἶναι
ἐμφαντικήν, δι'ἧς τῶν γεγονότων τὴν κατ'οὐσίαν ἑκάστου κατ'εἶδος ἀπαράλλακτον ταυτότητα καὶ ὡσαύτως
ἀπαρεγχείρητον διεξαγωγὴν θεωροῦντες, τὸν συνέ-
χοντα καὶ φυλάττοντα καθ'ἕνωσιν ἄρρητον ἀλλήλων
εὐκρινῶς ἀφωρισμένα τὰ πάντα, καθ'οὓς ὑπέστησαν
ἕκαστα λόγους, ἐννοοῦμεν, τὴν διαφορὰν δὲ τῆς κρίσεως εἶναι μηνυτικήν, καθ'ἣν διανομέα σοφὸν ἐκ τῆς
ἐν ἑκάστῳ τῶν ὄντων συμμέτρου τῷ ὑποκειμένῳ τῆς
οὐσίας φυσικῆς δυνάμεως τῶν καθ'ἕκαστα λόγων εἶναι τὸν θεὸν παιδευόμεθα – πρόνοιαν δέ φημι νῦν οὐ
τὴν ἐπιστρεπτικὴν καὶ οἷον οἰκονομικὴν τῆς τῶν προ-

essential ideas. In dividing creation into these five modes, the
saints piously discern the mystical ideas in it, analyzing cre-   71
ation as essence, motion, distinction, mixture, and placement.   B
Of these five, they say that three, those that relate to essence,
motion, and distinction, pertain principally to the knowledge
of God and have been given as guiding ideas. By means of
these three, God becomes known as fashioner, provider, and
judge by men, who discern His reflections in existing things.
The other two, those that relate to mixture and placement,
educate us in virtue and in living familiarly with God. In being
formed by these a person becomes God, for he has experienced
divine existence and sees intellectually the full reflection of
God's goodness coming from beings and rationally gives shape
in himself to this absolutely clear reflection.

For they say that what the pure intellect sees naturally by
means of pious knowledge, it is also able to experience and
becomes that very thing by possessing it through virtue. It   C
is something like this: first, essence is the teacher of theology. When we seek the cause of beings through the concept of
essence, we are taught through them that the cause exists,
though we do not try to know what it is in its own essence,
since it is not as though there is something that comes forward
from its appearance reflected in beings by means of which we
might look upward, even to a certain degree, as though looking through what is caused towards the cause. Second, motion
reflects the providence of existing things. When we see the
essential unwavering formal identity of each thing that has   72
come into being and the inviolable arrangement that holds its
identity together in the midst of its motion, we gain insight
concerning the one who holds all things together and keeps
them clearly defined from each other in their ineffable unity.
It is in accordance with this unwavering identity and inviolable arrangement that each reality has given actual existence
to its essential idea. Third, distinction reveals judgment. With

νοουμένων ἀφ'ὧν οὐ δεῖ ἐφ'ἃ δεῖ ἐπαναγωγῆς, ἀλλὰ
τὴν συνεκτικὴν τοῦ παντὸς καὶ καθ'οὓς τὸ πᾶν προηγουμένως ὑπέστη λόγους συντηρητικήν, καὶ κρίσιν οὐ
τὴν παιδευτικὴν καὶ οἷον κολαστικὴν τῶν ἁμαρτανό-
ντων, ἀλλὰ τὴν σωστικὴν καὶ ἀφοριστικὴν τῶν ὄντων
διαμονήν, καθ'ἣν τῶν γεγονότων ἕκαστα τοῖς καθ'οὓς
γεγένηται συνημμένα λόγοις ἀπαράβατον ἔχει | τὴν ἐν   1136
τῇ φυσικῇ ταυτότητι ἀναλλοίωτον μονιμότητα, καθὼς
ἐξ ἀρχῆς ὁ δημιουργὸς περὶ τοῦ εἶναι καὶ τί εἶναι καὶ
πῶς καὶ ὁποῖον ἕκαστον ἔκρινέ τε καὶ ὑπεστήσατο, ἐπεί
τοιγε ἡ ἄλλως λεγομένη πρόνοια καὶ κρίσις ταῖς ἡμῶν
προαιρετικαῖς ὁρμαῖς παραπεπήγασι, τῶν μὲν φαύλων
πολυτρόπως ἀπείργουσαι, πρὸς δὲ τὰ καλὰ σοφῶς ἐπι-
στρέφουσαι καὶ τῷ διευθύνειν τὰ οὐκ ἐφ'ἡμῖν ἐναντίως
τοῖς ἐφ'ἡμῖν καὶ παροῦσαν καὶ μέλλουσαν καὶ παρελ-
θοῦσαν κακίαν ἐκτέμνουσαι (οὐκ ἄλλην δὲ καὶ ἄλλην
πρόνοιαν διὰ τούτων εἶναι λέγω καὶ κρίσιν· μίαν γὰρ
καὶ τὴν αὐτὴν οἶδα κατὰ τὴν δύναμιν, διάφορον δὲ ὡς
πρὸς ἡμᾶς καὶ πολύτροπον τὴν ἐνέργειαν ἔχουσαν) –,
τὴν δὲ κρᾶσιν τῶν ὄντων ἤτοι σύνθεσιν τῆς ἡμετέρας
γνώμης εἶναι σύμβολον – κραθεῖσα γὰρ αὕτη ταῖς ἀρεταῖς καὶ ἑαυτῇ ταύτας κεράσασα τὸν κατὰ διάνοιαν θεο-
πρεπέστατον καὶ αὐτὴ συνίστησι κόσμον –, τὴν δὲ θέσιν
τοῦ κατὰ γνώμην ἤθους εἶναι διδάσκαλον, ὡς παγίως
ἔχειν περὶ τὸ εὖ δόξαν τῷ ῥυθμίζοντι λόγῳ ὀφείλοντος,
ἥκιστα τοῖς συμπίπτουσιν ἐκ τῆς κατὰ λόγον βάσεως
ἀλλοίωσιν τὴν οἱανοῦν δεχομένου.

respect to judgment, we learn from the natural potentiality
of the essence in each being, which coincides with each individual subject, that God is the wise distributor of the essential ideas that pertain to each thing. I mean by this that   D
providence is not something that now returns and, as it were,
restores foreknown realities from being what they should not
be to being what they should be, but is rather constitutive of
the universe and preserves it in accordance with the essential
ideas according to which the universe has been primordial-
ly endowed with actual existence. Moreover, judgment is not
pedagogical and a kind of punishment for sinners but is rather
a salvific and definitive distribution of beings, in accordance
with which each of the things that have come to be possesses
an unchanging constancy in natural identity, grounded in the
essential ideas according to which they have been permanent-
ly bound together . For the fashioner, from the beginning,   1136A
made a judgment and granted each thing actual being in its
existence and in what, how, and what quality each thing is.
This is realized in the fact that what are named alternatively
as "providence" and "judgment" are affixed closely to the inclinations of our desires. They keep us away from base things
in various ways and then wisely turn us towards beautiful
things. They cut off present, future, and past wickedness by
ordering rightly the realities that are not up to us as they
face what is up to us (I mean by this that providence is not
one thing and judgment another, for I see them as one and   73
the same in terms of what they are capable of, though they
work this out differently and in various ways in relation to
us). Fourth, the mixture or synthesis of beings is the symbol
of our mentality, for when it has been mixed with virtues,   B
and has mingled these with itself, it establishes a world of
thought most fitting to the Divine. Fifth, placement is the
teacher of the mental aspect of our moral character, since our
moral character ought to remain fixed to a good way of considering things by the ordering of reason, so that it can avoid,

Συνάψαντες δὲ πάλιν τῇ κινήσει τὴν θέσιν καὶ τὴν κρᾶσιν τῇ διαφορᾷ, εἰς οὐσίαν καὶ διαφορὰν καὶ κίνησιν τὴν τοῦ παντὸς ἀδιαιρέτως διέκριναν ὑπόστασιν, καὶ τῷ κατ’ἐπίνοιαν λόγῳ τεχνικῶς ἐνθεωρεῖσθαι τοῖς αἰτιατοῖς διαφόρως τὸ αἴτιον κατανοήσαντες, καὶ εἶναι καὶ σοφὸν εἶναι καὶ ζῶν εἶναι εὐσεβῶς τοῦτο κατέλαβον, καὶ τὸν περὶ Πατρὸς καὶ Υἱοῦ καὶ ἁγίου Πνεύματος θεοτελῆ καὶ σωτήριον ἐντεῦθεν ἐδιδάχθησαν λόγον, καθ’ὃν οὐ τὸν τοῦ εἶναι μόνον ἁπλῶς τοῦ αἰτίου λόγον μυστικῶς ἐφωτίσθησαν, ἀλλὰ καὶ τὸν τῆς ὑπάρξεως τρόπον εὐσεβῶς ἐμυήθησαν. Καὶ πάλιν κατὰ μόνην τὴν θέσιν πᾶσαν τὴν κτίσιν περιαθρήσαντες, τοὺς εἰρημένους πέντε εἰς τρεῖς συνέστειλαν θεωρίας τρόπους, ἐξ οὐρανοῦ καὶ γῆς καὶ τῶν ἐν μέσῳ, ἠθικῆς καὶ φυσικῆς καὶ θεολογικῆς φιλοσοφίας διδάσκαλον τὴν κτίσιν εἶναι τῷ καθ’αὑτὴν λόγῳ ἐπεγνωκότες. Πάλιν δὲ ἐκ μόνης τῆς διαφορᾶς τὴν κτίσιν θεωρήσαντες, τουτέστιν ἐκ τῶν περιεχόντων καὶ περιεχομένων, λέγω δὲ τοῦ οὐρανοῦ καὶ τῶν ἐντός, εἰς δύο τοὺς τρεῖς συνήγαγον τρόπους, σοφίαν φημὶ καὶ φιλοσοφίαν, τὴν μέν, ὡς περιεκτικὴν καὶ πάντας θεοπρεπῶς τοὺς εὐσεβεῖς ἐπ’αὐτῆς λεγομένους ἐπιδεχομένην τρόπους καὶ τοὺς περὶ τῶν ἄλλων ἐντὸς ἑαυτῆς μυστικούς τε καὶ φυσικοὺς περικλείουσαν λόγους, τὴν δέ, ὡς ἤθους καὶ γνώμης, πράξεώς τε καὶ θεωρίας καὶ ἀρετῆς καὶ γνώσεως συνεκτικὴν καὶ οἰκειότητι σχετικῇ πρὸς τὴν σοφίαν ὡς αἰτίαν ἀναφερομένην. Καὶ πάλιν κατὰ μόνην τὴν κρᾶσιν, ἤτοι τὴν ἐναρμόνιον τοῦ παντὸς σύνθεσιν τὴν κτίσιν κατανοήσαντες καὶ διὰ πάντων τῶν ἀλλήλοις ἀρρήτως εἰς ἑνὸς συμπλήρωσιν κόσμου συνδεδεμένων μόνον τὸν συνδέοντα καὶ ἐπισφίγγοντα τῷ ὅλῳ τὰ μέρη καὶ ἀλλήλοις δημιουργὸν | ἐννοήσαντες λόγον, τοὺς δύο εἰς ἕνα θεωρίας   1137

in this way, all the various deviations that draw off those who fall away from their rational foundation.

Then, in connecting placement to motion and mixture to distinction, they distinguished – without dividing – the actual existence of the universe into essence, distinction, and motion; and having understood how to contemplate systematically, with conceptual reason, the cause that is diversely in its effects, they piously grasped that this cause exists, that it is wise, and that it is living. From this they learned the divinely perfect and saving teaching concerning the Father, Son, and Holy Spirit. They were, in this way, not only illumined   C simply and mystically with respect to the essential idea of the existence of the cause but were also piously initiated into the way it exists. To take this a step further, they thoroughly inspected all of creation in terms of placement alone and then contracted the aforementioned five modes of contemplation into three, for they had come to know creation to be, in virtue of its own essential idea, the teacher of ethical, natural, and   74 theological philosophy, for it contains heaven and earth and what is in the midst them. Further still, they contemplated creation in terms of distinction alone, that is, in terms of what contains and what is contained, I mean heaven and what is in it, and then gathered the three modes into two: wisdom and philosophy. Wisdom, as all-embracing, both receives all the pious ways attributed to it as befits the divine and en-   D closes within itself the mystical and natural essential ideas pertaining to other realities, while philosophy, as constitutive of moral practice and mentality, of practical life and contemplation, and of virtue and knowledge, also refers to wisdom as its cause because of its close affinity with it. Finally, they understood creation in terms of mixture alone, that is, in terms of the harmonizing synthesis of the universe, and reflecting, by means of all the things that have been ineffably bound together with each other to form a complete, single world, upon

συνέκλεισαν τρόπον, καθ'ὃν ἁπλῇ προσβολῇ διὰ τῶν ἐν
τοῖς οὖσι λόγων πρὸς τὸ αἴτιον τὸν νοῦν διαπορθμεύσαν-
τες καὶ μόνῳ αὐτῷ ὡς συναγωγῷ τῶν ἐξ αὐτοῦ πάντων καὶ ἑλκτικῷ προσδήσαντες τοῖς καθ'ἕκαστα τῶν
ὄντων τῷ ὑπερβαθῆναι οὐκέτι διαχεόμενον λόγοις,
διὰ τοῦ πεπεῖσθαι σαφῶς μόνον τὸν θεὸν κυρίως εἶναι
λοιπὸν ἐκ τῆς πρὸς τὰ ὄντα ἀκριβοῦς ἐνατενίσεως καὶ
οὐσίαν τῶν ὄντων καὶ κίνησιν καὶ τῶν διαφερόντων
εὐκρίνειαν καὶ συνοχὴν ἀδιάλυτον τῶν κεκραμένων καὶ
ἵδρυσιν ἀμετάθετον τῶν τεθειμένων καὶ πάσης ἁπλῶς
τῆς ὁπωσοῦν νοουμένης οὐσίας καὶ κινήσεως καὶ διαφορᾶς κράσεώς τε καὶ θέσεως αἴτιον, σοφῶς δι'ἐμφε-
ροῦς ὁμοιότητος τὴν κατὰ τὸν αἰσθητὸν αἰῶνα μυστι-
κὴν θεωρίαν ἐπὶ τὸν κατὰ διάνοιαν ἐν πνεύματι διὰ τῶν
ἀρετῶν συμπληρούμενον κόσμον μετήνεγκαν, καθ'ἣν
τοὺς εἰρημένους τρόπους εἰς ἕνα συναγαγόντες, τὸν
διαφόροις ἀρετῶν εἴδεσι τὴν τοῦ κατὰ διάνοιαν γνω-
μικοῦ κόσμου οὐσίαν ἐκπληροῦντα διόλου λόγον μονώτατον ἑαυτοῖς ὡς ἐφικτὸν ἐναπωμόρξαντο, πάντας
δηλαδὴ περάσαντες τοὺς τῶν ὄντων καὶ αὐτοὺς τοὺς
τῶν ἀρετῶν λόγους, μᾶλλον δὲ μετὰ τούτων πρὸς τὸν
ὑπὲρ τούτους καὶ εἰς ὃν οὗτοι καὶ ἐξ οὗ τὸ εἶναι τούτοις
ἐστὶν ὑπερούσιον καὶ ὑπεράγαθον λόγον ἀγνώστως
ἀναδραμόντες καὶ ὅλοι ὅλῳ κατὰ τὸ ἐφικτὸν τῆς ἐνού-
σης αὐτοῖς φυσικῆς δυνάμεως ἑνωθέντες, τοσοῦτον ἐνδεχομένως ὑπ'αὐτοῦ ἐποιώθησαν, ὥστε καὶ ἀπὸ μόνου
γνωρίζεσθαι, οἷον ἔσοπτρα διειδέστατα, ὅλον τοῦ ἐνορῶν-
τος θεοῦ λόγου τὸ εἶδος ἀπαραλείπτως διὰ τῶν θείων
αὐτοῦ γνωρισμάτων φαινόμενον ἔχοντες τῷ ἐλλειφθῆ-
ναι μηδένα τῶν παλαιῶν χαρακτήρων, οἷς μηνύεσθαι
πέφυκε τὸ ἀνθρώπινον, πάντων εἰξάντων τοῖς ἀμείνο-
σιν, οἷον ἀὴρ ἀφεγγὴς φωτὶ διόλου μετεγκραθείς.

the Word, who alone is the fashioner who joins and binds the
parts tightly to the whole and to each other , they closed the   1137A
gap between the two to form one mode of contemplation. In
this way, they conveyed the intellect to the cause, approaching it simply through the essential ideas in existing things,
and bound the intellect solely to the cause, since it gathers
and attracts everything that comes from it. In this the intellect is no longer dispersed amongst the essential ideas of
individual beings, because it has been taken beyond them by
being utterly convinced, through a rigorous examination of
beings, that God alone truly is and is the essence and motion
of beings, the clear distinction of different things, the insoluble continuity of things that have been mixed together, and
the immovable foundation of what has been established and
that, in His simplicity, He is the cause of every essence, motion, distinction, mixture, and placement that can be thought
in any way whatsoever.

Thus, they wisely transposed their mystical contemplation   75
of the sensual age through a corresponding likeness into a
world that is filled with spiritual thought through the virtues.   B
Having gathered the aforementioned modes into unity by this
mystical contemplation, they imbued themselves, as much as
is possible, with the utterly singular Word who, in the different forms of virtue, gives complete fulness to the essence of
the mental world of thought. In this they clearly passed beyond the limits of all the essential ideas of beings and of the
virtues, or rather, made their way all the way back, without
the intervention of knowledge, by means of the essential ideas, to the Word beyond being and goodness, who is beyond the
essential ideas and is the one toward whom and from whom
they have their existence. When they had been wholly united to the whole, as far as this is attainable for their natural
capability, they received their qualities from the Word to the
degree they were able to do so, so that they are recognized,

* Ὅπερ οἶμαι καὶ γνοὺς καὶ παθὼν ὁ θαυμαστὸς
ἐκεῖνος καὶ μέγας Μελχισεδέκ, περὶ ὂν τὰ μεγάλα καὶ
θαυμαστὰ παρὰ τῇ γραφῇ ὁ θεῖος διεξέρχεται λόγος,
χρόνου καὶ φύσεως ὑπεράνω γενέσθαι καὶ ὁμοιωθῆναι τῷ υἱῷ τοῦ θεοῦ κατηξιώθη, τοιοῦτος ἕξει δηλαδὴ
κατὰ τὴν χάριν ὡς ἐφικτὸν γενόμενος, οἷος αὐτὸς ὁ δο-
τὴρ τῆς χάριτος κατὰ τὴν οὐσίαν ὑπάρχων πιστεύεται.
Τὸ γὰρ ἀπάτωρ καὶ ἀμήτωρ καὶ ἀγενεαλόγητος περὶ
αὐτοῦ λεγόμενον οὐκ ἄλλο μηνύειν ὑπονοῶ ἢ τὴν ἐγ-
γενομένην αὐτῷ ἐκ τῆς κατ᾽ ἀρετὴν ἀκροτάτης χάριτος
τελείαν τῶν φυσικῶν γνωρισμάτων ἀπόθεσιν· τὸ δὲ
μήτε ἀρχὴν ἡμερῶν μήτε ζωῆς τέλος ἔχειν τὴν χρόνου
παντὸς καὶ αἰῶνος ἰδιότητα περιγράφουσαν γνῶσιν |
καὶ πάσης ὑλικῆς καὶ ἀΰλου οὐσίας τὴν ὕπαρξιν ὑπερ-   1140
βαίνουσαν θεωρίαν μαρτυρεῖν, τὸ δὲ ἀφωμοιωμένος τῷ
υἱῷ τοῦ θεοῦ μένει ἱερεὺς εἰς τὸ διηνεκὲς τάχα τὸ μέχρι
τέλους καθ᾽ ἕξιν ἄτρεπτον τῆς θεοειδεστάτης ἀρετῆς καὶ
τῆς θείας καὶ πρὸς τὸν θεὸν ἐνατενίσεως τὸ νοερὸν ὄμμα
ἀνεπίμυστον δυνηθῆναι φυλάξαι παραδηλοῖ. Τῇ φύσει
γὰρ ἡ ἀρετὴ μάχεσθαι πέφυκε, καὶ χρόνῳ καὶ αἰῶνι ἡ
ἀληθὴς θεωρία, ἵνα ἡ μὲν ἀδούλωτος μείνῃ τοῖς ἄλλοις,
ὅσα μετὰ θεὸν εἶναι πιστεύεται, καὶ ἀκράτητος, ὡς θεὸν
μόνον εἰδυῖα γεννήτορα, ἡ δὲ ἀπερίγραφος, οὐδενὶ τῶν
ἀρχὴν ἢ τέλος ἐχόντων ἐναπομένουσα, ὡς θεὸν δι᾽ ἑαυ-

like "a perfectly clear mirror,"[41] from the divine Word alone, C
who beholds their completed form, which appears flawlessly in
the divine realities by which He is recognized. For this form
lacks nothing of His venerable characteristics, by which human reality is naturally revealed and which are superior to
every unstable image, as when unillumined air has been completely infused with light.

The Figure of the Saint

I[42] think that marvelous and great man Melchizedek, concerning whom the divine word has related *great and marvelous*
things (Rev 15.3) in writing, knew this reality and experi- 76
enced it, and was, therefore, deemed worthy to transcend time
and nature and to be made like the Son of God, becoming D
habitually by grace, as far as is possible, what we believe the
giver of grace Himself to be in His essence. For I suppose that
when the phrases *without father* and *without mother* and *without*
descent (Heb 7.3) are said about him, they disclose nothing else
than the complete displacement, which came to him from the
most exalted grace of virtue, of the natural realities by which
he was recognized. The phrase *having neither beginning of days*
nor end of life (Heb 7.3) bears witness to the knowledge that
encloses the property of all time and every age and to the 1140A
contemplation that transcends the existence of every material
and immaterial essence, while the phrase *made like unto the*
Son of God he remains a priest continually (Heb 7.3) perhaps
indicates that the attentive intellectual eye is able to keep
watch until the end because of its sure possession of the most
God-like virtue and divine attention that is fixed on God. For
virtue naturally fights against nature, and true contemplation fights against time and age, so that virtue may remain

---

41   Ps. Dion. Areo., *Div. Nom.* IV.22, p. 170.1–2.
42   *20. Contemplating Melchizedek*

τῆς εἰκονίζουσα, τὸν πάσης ἀρχῆς καὶ τέλους ὁριστικὸν
καὶ πᾶσαν νόησιν τῶν νοούντων κατ'ἔκστασιν ἄρρητον
πρὸς ἑαυτὸν ἕλκοντα· ἐξ ὧν ἡ θεία ὁμοίωσις δείκνυται,
γνώσεώς τέ φημι καὶ ἀρετῆς, καὶ δι'ὧν ἡ εἰς μόνον τὸν
θεὸν ἀκλόνητος ἀγάπη τοῖς ἀξίοις φυλάττεται, καθ'ἣν
τὸ τῆς υἱοθεσίας ἀξίωμα, θεοπρεπῶς διδόμενον, διηνεκῶς ἐντυγχάνειν θεῷ καὶ παρεστάναι χαρίζεται, πρὸς
δυσώπησιν αὐτὴν τοῦ ἐντυγχάνοντος τὴν θείαν ὁμοίωσιν παρεχόμενον. Ὅθεν εἰκότως ὑπολαμβάνω μὴ διὰ
χρόνου καὶ φύσεως, ὑφ'ἃ φυσικῶς ἐτέλει ὁ μέγας Μελχισεδέκ, βίῳ καὶ λόγῳ ὑπερβαθέντων ἤδη καὶ παντελῶς
καταλελειμμένων, προσαγορευθῆναι δεῖν ὁ θεῖος αὐτὸν
ἐδικαίωσε λόγος, ἀλλ'ἐξ ὧν καὶ δι'ὧν ἑαυτὸν μετεποίη-
σε γνωμικῶς, ἀρετῆς λέγω καὶ γνώσεως, ὀνομασθῆναι·
ἐφ'ὧν γὰρ ἡ γνώμη γενναίως διὰ τῶν ἀρετῶν τὸν δυσ-
μαχώτατον τῆς φύσεως κατηγωνίσατο νόμον, καὶ τὴν
χρόνου καὶ αἰῶνος ἰδιότητα διὰ γνώσεως ἀχράντως ἡ
τοῦ νοῦ ὑπερίπταται κίνησις, τούτοις οὐκ ἔστιν ἐπιφη-
μίσαι δίκαιον τῶν ἀπολειφθέντων, ὡς γνώρισμα, τὴν
ἰδιότητα, ἀλλὰ μᾶλλον τὴν τῶν προσληφθέντων με-
γαλοπρέπειαν, ἐξ ὧν καὶ ἐν οἷς μόνον εἰσὶ λοιπὸν καὶ
ἐπιγινώσκονται, ἐπεὶ καὶ ἡμεῖς φυσικῶς τοῖς ὁρατοῖς
ἐπιβάλλοντες ἐκ τῶν χρωμάτων τὰ σώματα καὶ γνωρί-
ζομεν καὶ ὀνομάζομεν, οἷον ὡς φῶς τὸν πεφωτισμένον
ἀέρα καὶ πῦρ τὴν οἱανοῦν πυρὸς ἐξημμένην ὕλην καὶ
λευκὸν τὸ λελευκασμένον σῶμα καὶ ὅσα ἄλλα τοιου-
τότροπα.

unenslaved to other things, inasmuch as it is committed to
pursuing God and not being under anyone's authority, since
it knows God as its only progenitor, and so that true contemplation may remain unenclosed, not remaining within what
has a beginning or end, since through itself it presents the
image of God, who defines every beginning and end and draws
to Himself every thought of those who think in an ineffable
ecstasy. The divine likeness is shown forth from knowledge   B
and virtue, and through these the worthy keep an unshakable |77
love for God alone. In this way, the honor of adoption, which
is given in a way that befits the Divine, is granted so that one
may forever attain to and remain with God, providing the
source of respect for one who attains the divine likeness.

I suspect this is the most likely reason that the divine word
proclaimed it necessary to address the great Melchizedek not
in terms of time and nature, under which he naturally died,
since these had already been transcended and entirely left behind by his life and speech, but rather that he be named in
terms of that from which and through which – I mean virtue
and knowledge – he deliberately transformed himself. For our
mentality relies upon virtue and knowledge when it struggles
valiantly by means of the virtues against the law of nature,
which is so very difficult to fight. The motion of the intellect   C
also relies upon them when it flies clear beyond what is proper to time and age by means of knowledge, for it is not right
to attribute to virtue and knowledge the property of what
has been left behind as the mark by which we recognize it;
rather, we must attribute to them the magnificence of what
has been received, out of which and in which alone they ultimately exist and are recognized. It is like when we come upon
visible things: we naturally recognize and name bodies from
their surface appearance, calling, for example, illumined air
"light" and any kind of matter that is consumed by fire "fire"
and a body that has been whitened "white," and we speak of
other things as well in this same way.

Εἰ τοίνυν γνωμικῶς τὴν ἀρετὴν τῆς φύσεως καὶ
τῶν κατ᾽αὐτὴν ἁπάντων προυτίμησε διὰ τὴν καλὴν τοῦ
ἐφ᾽ἡμῖν ἀξιώματος αἵρεσιν, καὶ πάντα χρόνον καὶ αἰῶνα κατὰ τὴν γνῶσιν ὑπερηκόντισεν, πάντα ὅσα μετὰ
θεὸν κατόπιν ἑαυτοῦ γνωστικῶς κατὰ τὴν θεωρίαν ποιησάμενος, οὐδενὶ τῶν ὄντων ἐμμείνας, ᾧ ἐπιθεωρεῖται
τὸ οἱανοῦν πέρας ὁ θεῖος Μελχισεδέκ, πρὸς δὲ τὰς θείας
καὶ ἀνάρχους καὶ ἀθανάτους τοῦ θεοῦ καὶ Πατρὸς ἀκτῖ-
νας τὸν νοῦν ἀνεπέτασε καὶ ἐκ τοῦ θεοῦ διὰ τοῦ λόγου
κατὰ χάριν ἐν Πνεύματι γεγέννηται καὶ σῶαν καὶ ἀληθῆ ἐν ἑαυτῷ φέρει τοῦ γεννήσαντος θεοῦ τὴν ὁμοίωσιν,
ἐπεὶ καὶ πᾶσα γέννησις ταυτὸν τῷ γεννῶντι πέφυκεν
ἀποτελεῖν τὸ γεννώμενον – τὸ γὰρ γεγεννημένον, φη-
σίν, ἐκ τῆς σαρκὸς σάρξ ἐστι, καὶ τὸ γεγεννημένον ἐκ
τοῦ πνεύματος πνεῦμά ἐστιν –, εἰκότως | οὐκ ἐκ τῶν   1141
φυσικῶν καὶ χρονικῶν ἰδιωμάτων, οἷς πατήρ τε καὶ
μήτηρ καὶ γενεαλογία ἀρχή τε καὶ τέλος ἡμερῶν περιέχεται, ἅπερ φθάσας ἑαυτοῦ παντελῶς ὑπελύσατο, ἀλ-
λ᾽ἐκ τῶν θείων καὶ μακαρίων γνωρισμάτων, οἷς τὸ εἶδος ἑαυτῷ μετεποίησεν, ὠνομάσθη, ὧν οὐκ ἐφικνεῖται
οὐ χρόνος οὐ φύσις οὐ λόγος οὐ νοῦς οὐδ᾽ἄλλο τι, κατὰ
περιγραφὴν φάναι, τῶν ὄντων οὐδέν.

Ἀπάτωρ οὖν καὶ ἀμήτωρ καὶ ἀγενεαλόγητος, μήτε
ἀρχὴν ἡμερῶν μὴ δὲ τέλος ζωῆς ἔχων ἀναγέγραπται ὁ
μέγας Μελχισεδέκ, ὡς ὁ ἀληθὴς τῶν θεοφόρων ἀνδρῶν
τὰ περὶ αὐτοῦ διεσάφησε λόγος, οὐ διὰ τὴν φύσιν τὴν
κτιστὴν καὶ ἐξ οὐκ ὄντων, καθ᾽ἣν τοῦ εἶναι ἤρξατό τε
καὶ ἔληξεν, ἀλλὰ διὰ τὴν χάριν τὴν θείαν καὶ ἄκτιστον
καὶ ἀεὶ οὖσαν ὑπὲρ πᾶσαν φύσιν καὶ πάντα χρόνον ἐκ
τοῦ ἀεὶ ὄντος θεοῦ, καθ᾽ἣν διόλου μόνην ὅλος γνωμικῶς
γεννηθεὶς ἐπιγινώσκεται. Μόνος δὲ τοῦτο ὢν τῇ γραφῇ
τετήρηται, ὡς πρῶτος ἴσως ὑπὲρ τὴν ὕλην καὶ τὸ εἶδος
κατὰ τὴν ἀρετὴν γενόμενος, ἅπερ διὰ τοῦ ἀπάτωρ καὶ
ἀμήτωρ καὶ ἀγενεαλόγητος δηλοῦσθαι δύναται, καὶ ὡς

If therefore the divine Melchizedek willingly preferred virtue
to nature and everything natural by means of the good choice
that belongs to the worthiness we control, he also cast his
knowledge beyond all time and every age. He put every real-   D
ity after God behind himself with knowledge in contemplation
and did not remain near any being in which any sort of limitation is observed, but rather he lay bare his intellect to the
divine, beginningless, immortal splendor of God the Father.   78
Thus, he was *born of God* (I Jn 4.7, 5.1) through the Word by
grace in the Spirit and carries safe and true in himself the likeness of the God who gave birth to him, since every birth-giv-
ing naturally produces an offspring that is the same as the one
who gives birth: *that which is born of the flesh*, it says, *is flesh,
and that which is born of the Spirit is spirit* (Jn 3.6). He was   1141A
appropriately named, therefore, not from natural and temporal characteristics, in which father, mother, and descent,
and beginning and end of days are included, for, when he had
surpassed these, he completely unbound them from himself.
He was named, rather, from the divine and blessed traits by
which he was recognized, by which he altered his own form,
which no existing thing, neither time, nor nature, nor reason,
nor intellect, can reach.

Therefore, the great Melchizedek has been described as *without father* and *without mother* and *without descent, having neither beginning of days nor end of life* (Heb 7.3). As the true
reasoning of the God-bearing men make clear, these qualities
pertain to him, not because of the nature that is created and
was brought from non-being, which determines that he has a
beginning and a cessation of existence, but because of the divine, uncreated grace that always exists beyond all nature and
all time from God who always is. He is made known wholly in   B
accordance with this grace alone in that he was born entirely
as a matter of mental intention. He alone is observed in scripture as existing in this way, since he was likewise the first who

πάντα τὰ ὑπὸ χρόνον καὶ αἰῶνα κατὰ τὴν γνῶσιν παρ-
ελθών, ὧν τὸ εἶναι χρονικῶς τῆς γενέσεως ἤρξατο, τὸ
ποτὲ εἶναι οὐκ ἠρνημένης, οὐδ'ότιοῦν τῷ κατὰ διάνοιαν θείῳ δρόμῳ ἐνσκάσας, ὅπερ σημαίνει τυχὸν τὸ μήτε
ἀρχὴν ἡμερῶν μήτε τέλος ζωῆς ἔχειν, καὶ ὡς ἐξῃρη-
μένως τάχα κρυφίως τε καὶ σεσιγημένως καί, συνελόν-
τα εἰπεῖν, ἀγνώστως μετὰ πᾶσαν τῶν ὄντων ἁπάντων
ἀφαίρεσιν κατὰ νοῦν εἰς αὐτὸν εἰσδὺς τὸν θεὸν καὶ ὅλος
ὅλῳ ποιωθείς τε καὶ μεταποιηθείς, ὅπερ τὸ ἀφωμοιωμένος δὲ τῷ υἱῷ τοῦ θεοῦ μένει ἱερεὺς εἰς τὸ διηνεκὲς
ὑπεμφαίνειν δύναται.

Πᾶς γάρ τις τῶν ἁγίων οὗτινος κατ'ἐξαίρετον ἀπήρ-
ξατο καλοῦ, κατ'αὐτὸ καὶ τύπος εἶναι τοῦ δοτῆρος
θεοῦ ἀνηγόρευται· καθ'ὃ σημαινόμενον καὶ οὗτος ὁ
μέγας Μελχισεδὲκ διὰ τὴν ἐμποιηθεῖσαν αὐτῷ θείαν
ἀρετὴν εἰκὼν εἶναι κατηξίωται Χριστοῦ τοῦ θεοῦ καὶ
τῶν ἀπορρήτων αὐτοῦ μυστηρίων, εἰς ὃν πάντες μὲν
οἱ ἅγιοι συνάγονται ὡς ἀρχέτυπον καὶ τῆς ἐν ἑκάστῳ αὐτῶν τοῦ καλοῦ ἐμφάσεως αἴτιον, μάλιστα δὲ
οὗτος, ὡς τῶν ἄλλων ἁπάντων πλείους ἐν ἑαυτῷ
φέρων τοῦ Χριστοῦ τὰς ὑποτυπώσεις. * Μονώτατος
γὰρ ὁ κύριος ἡμῶν καὶ θεὸς Ἰησοῦς Χριστὸς φύσει καὶ
ἀληθείᾳ ἀπάτωρ ἐστὶ καὶ ἀμήτωρ καὶ ἀγενεαλόγητος
καὶ μήτε ἀρχὴν ἡμερῶν μήτε ζωῆς τέλος ἔχων· ἀμήτωρ
μὲν διὰ τὸ ἄϋλον καὶ ἀσώματον καὶ παντελῶς ἄγνωστον τῆς ἄνω ἐκ τοῦ πατρὸς προαιωνίου γεννήσεως,
ἀπάτωρ δὲ κατὰ τὴν κάτω καὶ χρονικὴν ἐκ τῆς μητρὸς
καὶ ἐνσώματον γέννησιν, ἧς κατὰ τὴν σύλληψιν τὸ διὰ
σπορᾶς εἶδος οὐ καθηγήσατο, ἀγενεαλόγητος δὲ ὡς |
ἐπ'ἀμφοῖν αὐτοῦ τῶν γεννήσεων τὸν τρόπον ἔχων κα-   1144

transcended matter and form by virtue, a fact that can be   79
demonstrated by the phrase *without father* and *without mother*
and *without descent*. This is also because his knowledge passed
beyond everything subject to time and age, whose existence
began temporally by becoming and is not without a "when"
in its existence, and because he did not in any way falter in
the divine course of thought, which is what the phrase, *having neither beginning of days nor end of life*, probably means.
In addition to these, he transcendently, perhaps secretly and
silently and, to put it most strikingly, without the mediation
of knowledge, entered into God Himself after his intellect was
purged of every existing thing, and he fully received His quality and was fully remade by God in the fullness of His presence, which can be indicated by the phrase, *made like unto the*   C
Son of God; remains a priest continually.

For every individual saint offers a certain unique aspect of
that which is beautiful and so is also declared to bear the
mark of God the giver. Here, this means that the great man
Melchizedek was also deemed worthy to be an image of Christ
God and of His ineffable mysteries because of the divine virtue that had been produced in him. All the saints are gathered
to Christ as to the archetype and cause of the beautiful reflection in each of them, but this applies to Melchizedek most of
all, since he bears in himself more patterns of Christ than all   80
the others. For[43] our Lord and God Jesus Christ is unique-   D
ly by nature and in truth *without father, without mother,* and
without descent, having neither beginning of days nor end of life.
He is *without mother* in virtue of the immateriality, bodiless-
ness, and complete unknowability of His pre-temporal birth
above from the Father. He is *without father* with reference to
the temporal, bodily birth below from His mother, which was
not preceded at conception by formation through seed. He is

---

43   *21. An explication of the Lord with reference to what has been said
about Melchizedek*

θόλου τοῖς πᾶσιν ἄβατον καὶ ἀκατάληπτον· τὸ δὲ μήτε
ἀρχὴν ἡμερῶν μήτε ζωῆς τέλος ἔχων ὡς ἄναρχος καὶ
ἀτελεύτητος καὶ παντελῶς ἄπειρος, οἷα φύσει θεός, μένει δὲ ἱερεὺς εἰς τὸ διηνεκὲς ὡς μηδενὶ θανάτῳ κακίας
ἢ φύσεως τοῦ εἶναι παυόμενος, ὅτι θεὸς καὶ πάσης τῆς
κατὰ φύσιν καὶ ἀρετὴν ζωῆς χορηγός.

Μὴ νόμιζε δὲ ταύτης τινὰ ἀμοιρεῖν τῆς χάριτος, ἐπειδὴ περὶ μόνου τοῦ μεγάλου Μελχισεδὲκ ὁ λόγος αὐτὴν
εἶναι διωρίσατο. Πᾶσι γὰρ ἴσως ὁ θεὸς τὴν πρὸς σω-
τηρίαν φυσικῶς ἐνέθηκε δύναμιν, ἵν’ἕκαστος βουλό-
μενος τῆς θείας μεταποιεῖσθαι χάριτος δύνηται καὶ
θέλων Μελχισεδὲκ γενέσθαι καὶ Ἀβραὰμ καὶ Μωϋσῆς
καὶ ἁπλῶς πάντας μεταφέρειν εἰς ἑαυτὸν τοὺς ἁγίους
μὴ κωλύηται, οὐκ ὀνόματα καὶ τόπους ἀμείβων, ἀλλὰ
τρόπους καὶ πολιτείαν μιμούμενος. * Πᾶς τοιγαροῦν
τὰ μέλη νεκρώσας τὰ ἐπὶ τῆς γῆς καὶ ὅλον ἑαυτοῦ τῆς
σαρκὸς ἀποσβέσας τὸ φρόνημα καὶ τὴν πρὸς αὐτὴν διόλου σχέσιν ἀποσεισάμενος, δι’ἧς ἡ τῷ θεῷ μόνῳ χρε-
ωστουμένη παρ’ἡμῶν ἀγάπη μερίζεται, καὶ ἀρνησάμε-
νος πάντα τὰ τῆς σαρκὸς καὶ τοῦ κόσμου γνωρίσματα
τῆς θείας ἕνεκεν χάριτος, ὥστε καὶ λέγειν δύνασθαι
μετὰ τοῦ μακαρίου Παύλου τοῦ ἀποστόλου· τίς ἡμᾶς
χωρίσει ἀπὸ τῆς ἀγάπης τοῦ Χριστοῦ; καὶ τὰ ἑξῆς, ὁ
τοιοῦτος ἀπάτωρ καὶ ἀμήτωρ καὶ ἀγενεαλόγητος κατὰ
τὸν μέγαν Μελχισεδὲκ γέγονεν, οὐκ ἔχων ὅπως ὑπὸ
σαρκὸς κρατηθῇ καὶ φύσεως διὰ τὴν γεγενημένην πρὸς
τὸ πνεῦμα συνάφειαν. * Εἰ δὲ καὶ ἑαυτὸν πρὸς τούτοις
ἠρνήσατο, τὴν ἰδίαν ἀπολέσας ψυχὴν κατὰ τὴν λέγου-
σαν θείαν φωνήν· ὁ ἀπολέσας τὴν ψυχὴν αὐτοῦ ἕνεκεν
ἐμοῦ εὑρήσει αὐτήν, τουτέστι τὴν παροῦσαν ζωὴν μετὰ
τῶν αὐτῆς θελημάτων τῆς κρείττονος ἕνεκεν προέμε-
νος, ζῶντα δὲ καὶ ἐνεργοῦντα μονώτατον τὸν τοῦ θεοῦ

without descent since in both cases the modes of His births are   1144A
completely inaccessible and incomprehensible to all. He has
neither beginning of days nor end of life in that He is without
beginning, without end, and entirely infinite, for God is such
things by nature, and He *remains a priest continually* since He
does not cease to exist because of either a wicked or a natural
death, as God is the patron of all life, both the natural and
the virtuous.

Do not think that no one else has a share of this grace just
because the passage defined it as belonging only to the great
Melchizedek. For God has naturally placed the power for salvation equally in all, so that each person who wants to be
made anew by divine grace can be, and the one who wishes
to become Melchizedek and Abraham and Moses and, to put
it simply, who wishes to transpose all the saints into his own
situation will not be hindered, since he would not thereby be   B
changing name and place, but would be imitating their ways
and manner of life. Accordingly,[44] everyone who has *mortified*
his *members which are upon the earth* (Col 3.5) and has entirely   81
extinguished his own *fleshly way of thinking* (Rom 8.6), who
has thoroughly shaken off his habitual relation to the flesh,
which disperses the love that we owe to God alone, and has
denied all the recognizable marks of the flesh and the world
for the sake of divine grace, so that he is also able to say with
the blessed apostle Paul, *Who shall separate us from the love of
Christ?* (Rom 8.35) and so on, such a person has become *without father, without mother,* and *without descent* like the great
Melchizedek. He does not behave in such a way as to be dominated by flesh or nature because of the connection with the
Spirit he has obtained. And[45] if, in addition to this, he also   C
has denied himself by having lost his own life in accordance

---

44   22. *Contemplating Melchizedek again*
45   23. *Contemplating the phrase, 'having neither beginning of days nor
end of life'*

λόγον κέκτηται, διϊκνούμενον κατ᾽ἀρετὴν καὶ γνῶσιν
ἄχρι μερισμοῦ ψυχῆς καὶ πνεύματος, καὶ μηδὲν τὸ
παράπαν τῆς αὐτοῦ παρουσίας ἄμοιρον ἔχει, γέγονε καὶ
ἄναρχος καὶ ἀτελεύτητος, τὴν χρονικὴν μηκέτι φέρων
ἐν ἑαυτῷ κινουμένην ζωήν, τὴν ἀρχὴν καὶ τέλος ἔχουσαν καὶ πολλοῖς δονουμένην παθήμασι, μόνην δὲ τὴν
θείαν τοῦ ἐνοικήσαντος λόγου καὶ ἀΐδιον καὶ μηδενὶ
θανάτῳ περατουμένην. * Εἰ δὲ καὶ προσοχῇ πολλῇ τῷ
ἰδίῳ ἐπαγρυπνεῖν οἶδε χαρίσματι, διὰ πράξεως καὶ θεωρίας τῶν ὑπὲρ φύσιν καὶ χρόνον ἐπιμελούμενος ἀγα-
θῶν, γέγονε καὶ | ἱερεὺς διηνεκὴς καὶ αἰώνιος, νοερῶς   1145
ἀεὶ τῆς θείας ἀπολαύων ὁμιλίας καὶ διὰ τὸ μιμεῖσθαι
τῇ περὶ τὸ καλὸν κατὰ τὴν γνώμην ἀτρεψίᾳ τὸν κατὰ
φύσιν ἄτρεπτον, μὴ κωλυόμενος Ἰουδαϊκῶς ἁμαρτίας
θανάτῳ εἰς τὸ διηνεκὲς παραμένειν καὶ θυσίαν προσ-
φέρειν αἰνέσεως καὶ ἐξομολογήσεως, ἐνδόξως θεο-
λογῶν ὡς δημιουργὸν τῶν ἁπάντων καὶ εὐγνωμόνως
εὐχαριστῶν ὡς προνοητῇ καὶ κριτῇ τῶν ὅλων δικαίῳ
ἐν τῷ κατὰ διάνοιαν θείῳ θυσιαστηρίῳ, ἐξ οὗ φαγεῖν
οὐκ ἔχουσιν ἐξουσίαν οἱ τῇ σκηνῇ λατρεύοντες· οὐ γὰρ
οἷόν τε μυστικῶν θείας γνώσεως ἄρτων καὶ κρατῆρος
ζωτικοῦ σοφίας μεταλαχεῖν τοὺς μόνῳ στοιχοῦντας
τῷ γράμματι καὶ ἀλόγων θυσίαις παθῶν πρὸς σωτη-
ρίαν ἀρκουμένους καὶ τὸν μὲν θάνατον τοῦ Ἰησοῦ διὰ
τῆς καθ᾽ἁμαρτίαν ἀργίας καταγγέλλοντας, τὴν δὲ ἀνά-
στασιν αὐτοῦ, ὑπὲρ ἧς καὶ δι᾽ἣν ὁ θάνατος γέγονε, διὰ
τῆς κατὰ νοῦν θεωρίας, τῆς ἐν δικαιοσύνῃ ἔργων ἀγαθῶν πεφωτισμένης, οὐχ᾽ὁμολογοῦντας καὶ τὸ μὲν θα-
νατωθῆναι σαρκὶ εὖ μάλα προθύμως ἑλομένους, τὸ δὲ
ζωοποιηθῆναι καὶ πνεύματι οὐδ᾽ὁπωσοῦν ἀνεχομένους
ἔτι τῆς κατ᾽αὐτοὺς σκηνῆς ἐχούσης στάσιν διὰ τὸ μήπω
πεφανερῶσθαι αὐτοῖς τὴν διὰ λόγου καὶ γνώσεως τῶν
ἁγίων ὁδόν, ἥτις ἐστὶν ὁ λόγος τοῦ θεοῦ ὁ εἰπών· ἐγώ
εἰμι ἡ ὁδός, καὶ ἀπὸ τοῦ σάρκα λόγον εἰδέναι διὰ πρακτικῆς τὸν κύριον ἐπὶ τὴν ὡς μονογενοῦς παρὰ Πατρὸς

with the divine utterance that says *whoever has lost his life for my sake will find it* (Lk 9.24), that is, has let go this present life with its wants for the sake of what is better, such a person has acquired the *living and active* unique *Word of God*, who *pierces* with virtue and knowledge *even to the dividing of soul and spirit* (Heb 4.12). Such a person possesses nothing that is altogether without a share of His presence, and has become without beginning and without end, for he no longer bears in himself a form of life that moves temporally, which has a beginning and an end and is disturbed by so many sufferings, but bears only the life of the indwelling Word, which is divine, everlasting, "and unlimited by death."[46] If[47] he also knows how to keep watch over his own proper grace with great attention, and takes care of the good things beyond nature and time through the practical life and contemplation, he has also become a *priest continually* and eternally. He enjoys the divine communion of the mind forever, and by imitating the one who is naturally unchangeable by keeping his mentality unchanged in its relation to beauty, he is not prevented in a sort of Jewish sense by the death that comes from sin from remaining *continually* and offering the *sacrifice of praise* (Heb 13.15) and confession. He glorifies Him as the fashioner of all and sincerely gives thanks to Him as the righteous provider and judge of the universe in the divine altar of thought, *from which those who serve the tabernacle have no right to eat* (Heb 13.10). For there are those who are accustomed only to the letter and are satisfied with the sacrifices of irrational passions for their salvation. These announce the death of Jesus through their lack of sin but do not, through intellectual contemplation, confess His resurrection, which is brought to light in the righteousness of good works, and is the purpose and cause that the death, in fact, occurred. They are very eager indeed to suffer death in the flesh but do not in any

82

D

1145A

B

83

---

46   GREG. NAZ., Or. 20.5, p. 66.18–19.
47   *24. Contemplating the phrase, He 'remains a priest continually'*

δόξαν, τὴν πλήρη χάριτος καὶ ἀληθείας, διὰ θεωρίας ἐλθεῖν οὐκ ἐφιεμένους.

* Καὶ Ἀβραὰμ πάλιν πνευματικὸς γίνεται, τῆς γῆς
καὶ τῆς συγγενείας καὶ τοῦ οἴκου τοῦ πατρὸς ἐξερχόμε-
νος καὶ εἰς τὴν ὑπὸ θεοῦ δεικνυμένην ἐρχόμενος γῆν, ὁ
τῆς σαρκὸς ἑαυτὸν κατὰ διάθεσιν ἀπορρήξας καὶ ἐκτὸς
αὐτῆς γενόμενος τῷ χωρισμῷ τῶν παθῶν καὶ τὰς αἰ-
σθήσεις ἀπολιπὼν καὶ μὴ δὲ μίαν δι' αὐτῶν ἁμαρτίας
ἔτι παραδεχόμενος πλάνην καὶ τὰ αἰσθητὰ πάντα παρ-
ελθών, ἐξ ὧν τῇ ψυχῇ διὰ τῶν αἰσθήσεων τὸ ἀπατᾶ-
σθαι καὶ πταίειν προσγίνεται, καὶ μόνῳ τῷ νῷ παντὸς
ὑλικοῦ ἐλευθέρῳ δεσμοῦ εἰς τὴν θείαν καὶ μακαρίαν
τῆς γνώσεως ἐρχόμενος γῆν καὶ εἰς μῆκος καὶ πλάτος
αὐτὴν μυστικῶς διοδεύων, ἐν ᾗ τὸν κύριον ἡμῶν εὑρήσει καὶ θεὸν Ἰησοῦν Χριστόν, τὴν ἀγαθὴν τῶν φο-
βουμένων αὐτὸν κληρονομίαν, δι' ἑαυτὸν μὲν εἰς μῆκος
ἀνείκαστον ὑπὸ τῶν ἀξίων κατὰ τὸ ἐφικτὸν ἀνθρώποις
θεολογούμενον, δι' ἡμᾶς δὲ εἰς πλάτος δοξολογούμενον
διὰ τῆς συνεκτικῆς τοῦ παντὸς σοφωτάτης αὐτοῦ προνοίας καὶ τῆς ὑπὲρ ἡμῶν μάλιστα θαυμαστῆς καὶ ὑπερ-
αρρήτου οἰκονομίας, καὶ μέτοχος τῶν οἷς γεραίρειν
τὸν κύριον ἐξεπαιδεύθη τρόπων κατὰ πρᾶξιν τέως καὶ
θεωρίαν γενόμενος, δι' ὧν ἡ πρὸς θεὸν βεβαίως κυροῦσ-
θαι πέφυκε φιλία τε καὶ ἀφομοίωσις. Καὶ συντόμως
περὶ τούτων εἰπεῖν· ὁ σάρκα καὶ αἴσθησιν καὶ κόσμον,
περὶ ἃ τοῦ νοῦ ἡ πρὸς τὰ νοητὰ κατὰ | τὴν σχέσιν διάλυ-   1148
σις γίνεται, πρακτικῶς καταπαλαίσας καὶ μόνῃ διανοίᾳ

way consent to being made alive in spirit as well since *the tab-ernacle is yet standing* for them, because *the way* that proceeds through the reasoning and knowledge *of the saints is not yet made manifest* to them (Heb 9.8), the way being the Word of God, who says, *I am the way* (Jn 14.6). Indeed, they do not set out to come to the Lord, proceeding from the knowledge of the Word as flesh through the practical life to the knowledge of the *glory as of the only-begotten of the Father, full of grace and truth* (Jn 1.14) through contemplation.

And[48] he may, in turn, become a spiritual Abraham, who   C
went out of his country and kindred and from his father's house and came *to the land* shown him by God (Gen 12.1). Such a person breaks himself away from his fleshly disposition and transcends it by separating from the passions and leaves be-hind the senses and no longer accepts any error of sin through them and goes beyond all sensuality, from which deception and stumbling approach the soul through the senses. This per-son comes to the divine and blessed land of knowledge with a mind simple and freed from every material bond and *walks* mystically *in the length and in the breadth* (Gen 13.17) of it, where he will find our Lord and God Jesus Christ, the good inheritance of those who fear Him. In Himself, He is ad-   D
dressed theologically to an unattainable "*length*" by those who are worthy, as far as this is possible for human beings, but on account of us, He is praised to the "*breadth*" for His most wise "providence that holds the whole universe together"[49] and for   84
His exceedingly wonderful and ineffable ordering of things for our sake. Such a person has become a partaker of the ways in which Abraham was thoroughly instructed up to that time by practical life and contemplation to honor the Lord, the ways through which friendship with God[50] and likeness to Him are

---

48   *25. Contemplating Abraham*
49   GREG. NAZ., Or. 14.33, PG 35.901C15-D1.
50   Cf. James 2.23.

δι'ἀγάπης θεῷ γνωστικῶς προσχωρήσας, ὁ τοιοῦτος ἄλλος Ἀβραὰμ ὑπάρχει, διὰ τῆς ἴσης χάριτος τὸν αὐτὸν τῷ πατριάρχῃ τῆς ἀρετῆς καὶ τῆς γνώσεως ἔχων χαρακτῆρα δεικνύμενος.

* Καὶ Μωϋσῆς πάλιν ἄλλος ἐκφαίνεται ὁ ἐν τῷ καιρῷ τῆς τῶν παθῶν δυναστείας, ὁπηνίκα, τοῦ διαβόλου τοῦ νοητοῦ Φαραὼ τυραννοῦντος, τὸ χεῖρον ἐπικρατεῖν τοῦ ἀμείνονος καὶ τοῦ πνευματικοῦ τὸ σαρκικὸν ἐπανίστασθαι καὶ πᾶς εὐσεβὴς ἀναιρεῖσθαι πέφυκε λογισμός, κατὰ θεὸν γνωμικῶς γεννώμενος καὶ θῖβι ἀσκήσεως ἀληθοῦς ἐμβληθείς, ἠθικοῖς ἔξωθεν κατὰ σάρκα τρόποις καὶ ἔσωθεν κατὰ ψυχὴν θείοις ἠσφαλισμένος νοήμασι καὶ μέχρι μόνον τῆς ἀναλήψεως τῶν φυσικῶν θεωρημάτων ἀνεχόμενος εἶναι ὑπὸ τὴν αἴσθησιν, τὴν τοῦ νοητοῦ Φαραὼ θυγατέρα, ζήλῳ δὲ γνησίῳ τῶν θείων ἀγαθῶν τὸ αἰγυπτιάζον τῆς σαρκὸς ἀποκτείνας φρόνημα καὶ ὑπὸ τὴν ψάμμον, τὴν τῶν κακῶν ἄγονον ἕξιν φημί, καταθέμενος, ἐν ᾗ, κἂν ὑπὸ τοῦ ἐχθροῦ σπαρῇ, τὸ τῆς κακίας ζιζάνιον οὐ πέφυκε φύεσθαι διὰ τὴν ἐνοῦσαν ἐνδιαθέτως πτωχείαν τοῦ πνεύματος, τὴν τὸ ἀπαθὲς γεννῶσάν τε καὶ φυλάττουσαν καὶ θείῳ προστάγματι τὴν ἀγριουμένην τοῖς πνεύμασι τῆς πονηρίας καὶ τοῖς ἀλλεπαλλήλοις τῶν πειρασμῶν κύμασι δενδρουμένην τῆς πικρᾶς καὶ ὄντως ἁλμώδους κακίας ὁρίζουσαν θάλασσαν, καθὼς γέγραπται· ὁ τιθεὶς ἄμμον ὅριον τῇ θαλάσσῃ καὶ λέγων αὐτῇ· μέχρι τούτου διελεύσῃ καὶ οὐχ ὑπερβήσῃ καὶ ἐν σοὶ συντριβήσονταί σου τὰ κύματα, τοὺς δὲ εἰς γῆν ἔτι κατανεύοντας λογισμοὺς καὶ τὴν ἐξ αὐτῆς ἐπιζητοῦντας ἀπόλαυσιν, ὑπὲρ ἧς τὸ θυμικὸν

naturally firmly attained. To summarize these points: a person
who has overthrown the flesh, sense-perception, and the world
through the conduct of the practical life – these three being
implicated when we free the intellect in its relation to intellectual reality –, and has approached God with knowledge   1148A
through love with single-mindedness, such a person is another
Abraham and is shown to have the same character of virtue
and knowledge as the patriarch, because he possesses an equal
endowment of grace.

Another[51] Moses can appear in turn as well. Such a person
is born according to God's intention in the time of the do-
minion of the passions, when the worse has control over the
better, the fleshly is set up against the spiritual, and every
pious thought tends to be destroyed because Pharaoh, the intellectual devil, rules as a tyrant. He is placed into the bas-
ket of true asceticism and thus is kept safe, externally by the
ethical ways of life that pertain to the flesh and internally by   B
the divine thoughts that pertain to the soul. He consents to
be subject to sense-perception, which is the daughter of the
intellectual Pharaoh, only until he acquires the ability to contemplate nature. He puts to death the Egyptian way of fleshly
thinking with genuine zeal for divine good things and places
it under the sand, which I take to refer to the habitual way
of living that is barren of evil deeds, for even if it should be   85
sown by the enemy, the tare[52] of wickedness does not naturally sprout up in this way of life because of the poverty of spirit
that is innate to it. This poverty of spirit both gives birth to
and protects freedom from passion and, by divine command,
sets a bound to the sea of pungent and truly bitter wickedness
that has grown wild with *the spirits of wickedness* (Eph 6.12)
and has become like a forest in its gathering waves of temptations, as it is written , *The one who* has placed *the sand*   C

---

51   *26. Contemplating Moses*
52   Cf. Matt 13.25.

διαμάχεσθαι καὶ τὸν διαγνωστικὸν τυραννεῖν καὶ ἀπω-
θεῖσθαι πέφυκε λόγον, προβάτων δίκην, διὰ τῆς ἐρήμου
παθῶν καὶ ὑλῶν ἐστερημένης καὶ ἡδονῶν καταστάσεως,
ἄγων ὡς ἐπιστήμων ποιμὴν πρὸς τὸ ὄρος τῆς γνώσεως
τοῦ θεοῦ, τὸ ἐν τῷ ὕψει τῆς διανοίας ὁρώμενον, ᾧ φι-
λοπόνως ἐνδιατρίβων διὰ τῶν προσφυῶν κατὰ πνεῦμα
θεωρημάτων μετὰ τὴν ἀπόλειψιν τῆς κατὰ νοῦν πρὸς
τὰ αἰσθητὰ σχέσεως – τοῦτο γὰρ οἶμαι δηλοῦν τὴν τοῦ
τεσσαρακονταετοῦς χρόνου πάροδον –, καὶ τοῦ ἀρρήτου
καὶ ὑπερφυοῦς, ὥσπερ θάμνῳ, τῇ οὐσίᾳ τῶν ὄντων
ἐνυπάρχοντος θείου πυρὸς κατ᾽ἔννοιαν θεατὴς γενέσθαι
καὶ ἀκροατὴς ἀξιωθήσεται, τοῦ ἐκ τῆς βάτου, τῆς ἁγίας
παρθένου φημί, ἐπ᾽ἐσχάτων τῶν χρόνων ἐκλάμψαντος
καὶ διὰ σαρκὸς ἡμῖν ὁμιλήσαντος θεοῦ λόγου, γυμνὸν τὸ
τῆς διανοίας ἴχνος τῷ τοιούτῳ μυστηρίῳ προσάγων
καὶ λογισμῶν ἀνθρωπίνων, ὡς νεκρῶν ὑποδημάτων,
παντελῶς ἐλεύθερον, καὶ πρὸς μὲν ζήτησιν, ὥσπερ πρό-
σωπον, τὸ τῆς διανοίας ὀπτικὸν ἀποστρέφων, πίστει
δὲ μόνῃ πρὸς ὑποδοχὴν τοῦ μυστηρίου, ἀκοῆς τρόπον,
τὸ τῆς ψυχῆς εὐπειθὲς διανοίγων, παρ᾽οὗ, τὴν ἰσχυρὰν
καὶ ἀήττητον κατὰ τῶν πονηρῶν δυνάμεων | κομισάμε-   1149
νος δύναμιν, τῶν παρὰ φύσιν τὰ κατὰ φύσιν καὶ τῶν
σαρκικῶν τὰ ψυχικὰ καὶ τῶν ὑλικῶν τε καὶ αἰσθητῶν
τὰ νοητὰ καὶ ἄϋλα κατὰ πολλὴν ἀφορίζει ἐξουσίαν, τῆς
δοῦλον ποιεῖν τὸ ἐλεύθερον πειρωμένης πολὺ ὑπερέχων

for the bound of the sea (Jer 5.22) and *says to it, 'up to this point shall you pass and you shall not go beyond it: and in you shall your waves be broken up'* (Job 38.11). As a knowledgeable shepherd, he leads like a flock those thoughts that still incline towards the earth and seek out enjoyment from it, enjoyment which naturally inspires the aggressive faculty to fight against, tyrannize, and cast out discerning reason, and he guides them through the desert state deprived of passions, material things, and pleasures to the mountain of the knowledge of God, which is seen in the height of thought. He ardently devotes much time to this mountain of knowledge with acts of contemplation that are naturally attracted to it spiritually once the mind abandons its habitual relation to sensuality, for I think this is what the wandering of the period of forty years means. Such a person will also be made D worthy to become a seer and hearer of the ineffable and supernatural divine fire that exists conceptually in the essence of things like the fire in the bush. This fire is God the Word, who shone forth at the end of time from the plant, I mean the holy Virgin, and "has held converse with us through 86 the flesh."[53] This person walks a path of thought bare and completely free of human ways of thinking, as of dead sandals,[54] to such a mystery, and with respect to questioning, he *averts* the eye of the mind, like a *face* (Ex 3.6), in order to receive the mystery with faith alone. He opens the soul's ready obedience as a pure listening, and when he has received the strong and unconquerable power against evil powers, he 1149A separates natural things from things contrary to nature, the realities of the soul from the realities of the flesh, and the intellectual and immaterial from the material and sensual with his obedience and with great authority, lifting, in this way, that which is free far above the power trying to enslave it.

---

53   GREG. NAZ., Or. 39.13, p. 176.15–16, etc.
54   Cf. Ex 3.5.

δυνάμεως, * καὶ ἵνα συνελὼν εἴπω· ὁ μὴ ὑπελθὼν τὸν
τῆς ἁμαρτίας ζυγὸν μήτε τῷ θολερῷ τῶν παθῶν ῥεύμα-
τι διὰ τῆς κακῆς ἐπιθυμίας ἑαυτὸν ἐμπνίξας καὶ αἰσθήσει τρέφεσθαι, τῇ πηγῇ τῶν ἡδονῶν, μὴ ἀνασχόμενος,
ἀποκτείνας δὲ μᾶλλον τὸ φρόνημα τῆς σαρκός, τὸ τυ-
ραννοῦν τῆς ψυχῆς τὴν εὐγένειαν, καὶ πάντων τῶν
φθειρομένων ὑπεράνω γενόμενος, τὸν πλάνον τοῦτον
κόσμον, ὥσπερ Αἴγυπτόν τινα, φυγών, τὸν ἐκθλίβοντα
ταῖς σωματικαῖς φροντίσι τὸν διορατικώτατον νοῦν,
καὶ καθ'ἡσυχίαν ἑαυτῷ συγγενόμενος καὶ φιλοπόνῳ
σχολῇ τῆς διεπούσης τὸ πᾶν θείας προνοίας τὴν σοφὴν
οἰκονομίαν διὰ τῆς ἐπιστημονικῆς τῶν ὄντων θεωρίας
ἀρρήτως διδαχθείς, κἀντεῦθεν διὰ μυστικῆς θεολογίας,
ἣν κατ'ἔκστασιν ἄρρητον νοῦς καθαρὸς διὰ προσευχῆς
πιστεύεται μόνος, ὡς ἐν γνόφῳ, τῇ ἀγνωσίᾳ ἀφθέγ-
κτως θεῷ συγγενόμενος καὶ ἑαυτὸν ἔσωθεν κατὰ νοῦν
εὐσεβείας δόγμασι καὶ ἔξωθεν, ὡς τὰς πλάκας ὁ Μωϋσῆς, ἀρετῶν χάρισι δακτύλῳ θεοῦ, τῷ ἁγίῳ Πνεύματι,
ἐγχαράξας ἢ γραφικῶς εἰπεῖν, ὁ ἑλόμενος συγκακου-
χεῖσθαι τῷ λαῷ τοῦ θεοῦ μᾶλλον ἢ πρόσκαιρον ἔχειν
ἁμαρτίας ἀπόλαυσιν καὶ τῶν ἐν Αἰγύπτῳ θησαυρῶν
τὸν ὀνειδισμὸν τοῦ Χριστοῦ τιμιώτερον κρίνας, τουτέστι πλούτου καὶ δόξης τῶν προσκαίρων καὶ φθειρομένων τοὺς ὑπὲρ ἀρετῆς ἑκουσίως ἀνθαιρούμενος πό-
νους, οὗτος Μωϋσῆς πνευματικὸς γέγονεν, οὐχ'ὁρατῷ
διαλεγόμενος Φαραώ, ἀλλ'ἀοράτῳ τυράννῳ καὶ ψυχῶν
φονευτῇ καὶ κακίας ἀρχηγῷ, τῷ διαβόλῳ, καὶ ταῖς ἀμ-
φ'αὐτὸν πονηραῖς δυνάμεσι, μεθ'ἧς διὰ χειρὸς ἐπιφέρε-
ται ῥάβδου, τῆς κατὰ τὸ πρακτικόν φημι τοῦ λόγου δυνάμεως, νοητῶς παρατασσόμενος.

To[55] put this all concisely: Consider someone who has not come under the yoke of sin, who has not choked himself with the muddy stream of the passions through wicked desire, and does not consent to be fed by sense-perception, the font of pleasures, but has rather put to death the *fleshly way of thinking* (Rom 8.6), which tyrannizes the nobility of the soul, and has transcended all of corruptible reality by fleeing this unstable world, which, like Egypt, distresses the most clear-sighted intellect with bodily anxieties. Such a person has come together within himself in silence   and, by his ardent   study   B and systematic contemplation of beings, he has been ineffably |87 taught the ways in which divine providence, which directs the universe, has ordered all things and from this has come wordlessly to be with God without the mediation of knowledge, as in *darkness* (Ex 20.21), through mystical theology, which is entrusted to the pure intellect alone through prayer in ineffable ecstasy. He has, moreover, engraved himself, internally in the intellect with the teachings of piety and externally with the gifts of the virtues, *by the finger of God* (Ex 31.18), which is the Holy Spirit, as Moses did *the tablets*. Or, to speak in the terms of scripture, he *has chosen to suffer affliction with the people of God rather than to obtain the temporary enjoyment of sin*, and has judged the *reproach of Christ* to be more honorable *than the treasures in Egypt* (Heb 11.25–26), that is, he has willingly chosen labors on behalf of virtue over wealth and glory, which are temporary and destructible. It is this one who has become a spiritual Moses, who holds converse not with the C visible Pharaoh, but with the invisible tyrant and murderer of souls and chief of evil, the devil, and who wields a staff in the midst of the evil powers surrounding him, this staff being the power of reason exercised in the practical life, with which his mind stands ready.

---

55   *27. Briefly contemplating Moses again*

* Ὡσαύτως δὲ καὶ πάντας τοὺς ἁγίους ἕκαστος ἡμῶν
θέλων εἰς ἑαυτὸν μεταθεῖναι δύναται, πρὸς ἕκαστον
πνευματικῶς ἐκ τῶν περὶ αὐτοῦ καθ᾽ἱστορίαν τυπικῶς
γεγραμμένων μορφούμενος – συνέβαινε γὰρ ἐκείνοις
τυπικῶς, φησὶν ὁ θεῖος ἀπόστολος, ἐγράφη δὲ πρὸς νου-
θεσίαν ἡμῶν, εἰς οὓς τὰ τέλη τῶν αἰώνων κατήντησε –,
πρὸς μὲν τοὺς πάλαι πρὸ νόμου ἁγίους ἀπὸ μὲν κτίσεως κόσμου τὴν περὶ θεοῦ γνῶσιν εὐσεβῶς ποριζόμενος,
ἀπὸ δὲ τῆς τὸ πᾶν σοφῶς διοικούσης προνοίας τὰς ἀρετὰς κατορθοῦν διδασκόμενος κατ᾽αὐτοὺς ἐκείνους τοὺς
πρὸ νόμου ἁγίους, οἵ, διὰ πάντων φυσικῶς ἐν ἑαυτοῖς
τὸν γραπτὸν ἐν πνεύματι προχαράξαντες νόμον, εὐ|σε- 1152
βείας καὶ ἀρετῆς τοῖς κατὰ νόμον εἰκότως προεβλήθη-
σαν ἐξεμπλάριον – ἐμβλέψατε γάρ φησι πρὸς Ἀβραὰμ
τὸν πατέρα ὑμῶν καὶ Σάρραν τὴν ὠδίνουσαν ὑμᾶς –,
πρὸς δὲ τοὺς κατὰ νόμον διὰ τῶν ἐντολῶν εἰς ἐπίγνωσιν τοῦ ἐν αὐταῖς ὑπηγορευμένου θεοῦ δι᾽εὐσεβοῦς ἐννοίας ἀναγόμενος καὶ τοῖς καθήκουσι τῶν ἀρετῶν τρόποις δι᾽εὐγενοῦς πράξεως καλλωπιζόμενος καὶ ταυτὸν
τῷ γραπτῷ νόμῳ τὸν φυσικὸν ὄντα παιδευόμενος, ὅταν
σοφῶς διὰ συμβόλων κατὰ τὴν πρᾶξιν ποικίλληται,
καὶ ἔμπαλιν τῷ φυσικῷ τὸν γραπτόν, ὅταν ἐνοειδὴς καὶ
ἁπλοῦς καὶ συμβόλων ἐν τοῖς ἀξίοις κατ᾽ἀρετήν τε καὶ
γνῶσιν διὰ λόγου καὶ θεωρίας ἐλεύθερος γένηται, κα-
τ᾽αὐτοὺς ἐκείνους τοὺς ἐν νόμῳ ἁγίους, οἵ, τὸ γράμμα
ὥσπερ κάλυμμα περιελόντες τοῦ πνεύματος, τὸν φυσικὸν μόνον ἔχοντες πνευματικῶς διεδείχθησαν. * Πάντες γὰρ διαρρήδην ἑτέραν παρὰ τὴν νομικὴν ἔσεσθαι
λατρείαν προθεωρήσαντες τὸ κατ᾽αὐτὴν φανησόμενον
τῆς θεοπρεπεστάτης ζωῆς τέλειον προεκήρυξαν καὶ τῇ
φύσει πρόσφορόν τε καὶ οἰκειότατον, ὡς μηδενὸς τῶν
ἐκτὸς πρὸς τελείωσιν ἐπιδεόμενον, καθὼς πᾶσι δῆλον
καθέστηκε τοῖς μὴ ἀγνοοῦσι τὰ διὰ τοῦ νόμου καὶ τῶν
προφητῶν θεῖα θεσπίσματα, ὅπερ μάλιστα Δαυῒδ καὶ
Ἐζεκίας καὶ τῷ καθ᾽ἑαυτὸν πρὸς τοῖς ἄλλοις ἑκάτερος

In[56] the same way, all of us who wish to are also able to trans-
fer all the saints to ourselves, so that we may be spiritually   88
conformed to each one in the terms that are written of each |D
as types in the narrative of scripture: for *these things happened
to them as types*, says the divine apostle, *and they were written
for our admonition, upon whom the ends of the ages have come*
(I Cor 10.11). With the ancient saints who lived before the law,
we piously derive the knowledge of God *from the creation of the
world* (Rom 1.20) and learn, from the providence that wisely
administers the universe, how to establish the virtues success-
fully in ourselves like those very saints who lived before the
law. They spiritually engraved in their nature the written law
in every aspect of their lives and thus were appropriately put   1152A
forth as examples of piety and virtue for those who lived in accordance with the law: *Look unto Abraham your father*, it says,
and unto Sarah who gave birth to you (Is 51.2). With those who
lived in accordance with the law through the commandments,
we lift ourselves up through pious thinking to the knowledge
of God, who is indicated in them, and beautify ourselves with
the virtues that are most appropriate to each given circumstance through the noble pursuit of the practical life. We
learn, moreover, that the natural law is identical to the written law, whenever we wisely adorn ourselves in diverse ways
through the symbolic deeds of the practical life. Conversely,
we learn that the written is identical to the natural, whenever
we become unified and simple and free of symbols with those
who are worthy by virtue and knowledge through reason and
contemplation, like those very saints in the law, who, having
taken away the letter from the spirit like a *veil* (II Cor 3.16),
were clearly shown to have spiritual possession of the natural   89
law alone. For[57] all those who had clearly foreseen that there   B

---

56   28. *Contemplating the question of how someone is able to imi-
tate the saints who came before the law and after the law, and what
the identity of the natural and written laws is in terms of their
mutual transferability*
57   29. *That even the saints who lived in accordance with the law, in re-*

δράματι παρηνίττετο, ὁ μὲν ὑπὲρ τῆς ἁμαρτίας νομικῶς
τὸν θεὸν οὐκ ἐξιλεούμενος, ὁ δὲ προσθήκῃ ζωῆς ἑτέρῳ
παρὰ τὸν νόμον θεσμῷ παρὰ τοῦ θεοῦ σεμνυνόμενος.

* Οὐδὲν δὲ τὸ κωλύον, ὡς οἶμαι, ἐστὶ τὸν ἐν τούτοις
προπαιδευθέντα τοῖς νόμοις, τῷ φυσικῷ τέ φημι καὶ
τῷ γραπτῷ, θεοφιλῶς καὶ ὑπὲρ τούτους γενέσθαι θεοπρεπῶς καὶ τούτων χωρίς, διʼεἰλικρινοῦς πίστεως
μόνῳ τῷ ἐπὶ τὸ ἀκρότατον ἀγαθὸν ἄγοντι λόγῳ γνησίως ἀκολουθήσαντα καὶ μηδενὸς κατʼἔννοιαν τὸ παράπαν ἁπτόμενον πράγματος ἢ λογισμοῦ ἢ νοήματος, οἷς
ἡ ὁπωσοῦν οὖσα παντὸς τοῦ ὁπωσοῦν νοουμένου τε καὶ
ὄντος φύσις τε καὶ γνῶσις ὑποπίπτει καὶ ἐμφαίνεται,
ὥσπερ εἰκὸς τὸν ἕπεσθαι γνησίως προθέμενον τῷ διε-
ληλυθότι τοὺς οὐρανοὺς Ἰησοῦ καὶ τῇ παραδείξει τοῦ
θείου φωτὸς δυνηθῆναι τὴν ἀληθῆ τῶν ὄντων, ὡς ἔστιν
ἀνθρώπῳ δυνατόν, συνεκδοχικῶς ὑποδέξασθαι γνῶσιν. | 1153
* Εἰ γὰρ πᾶσα ἡ τῶν ὄντων φύσις εἰς τὰ νοητὰ καὶ τὰ
αἰσθητὰ διῄρηται, καὶ τὰ μὲν λέγεται καὶ ἔστιν αἰώνια,
ὡς ἐν αἰῶνι τοῦ εἶναι λαβόντα ἀρχήν, τὰ δὲ χρονικά, ὡς
ἐν χρόνῳ πεποιημένα, καὶ τὰ μὲν ὑποπίπτει νοήσει τὰ
δὲ αἰσθήσει διὰ τὴν ταῦτα ἀλλήλοις ἐπισφίγγουσαν τοῦ
κατὰ φύσιν σχετικοῦ ἰδιώματος ἄλυτον δύναμιν – πολ-
λὴ γὰρ ἡ πρὸς τὰ νοούμενα τῶν νοούντων καὶ πρὸς τὰ
αἰσθητὰ τῶν αἰσθανομένων ἡ σχέσις –, ὁ δὲ ἄνθρωπος,
ἐκ ψυχῆς καὶ σώματος τυγχάνων αἰσθητικοῦ, διὰ τῆς

would be an explicitly different form of worship beyond that of the law proclaimed beforehand the perfection of the most divine form of life that would appear with it and is by nature productive and most coherent, since it lacks nothing outside itself for its perfection. This is perfectly clear to all who are not ignorant of the divine oracles given through the law and the prophets. David and Hezekiah in particular amongst all the others hinted at this, each in his own story: David did not appease God for his sin by fulfilling what would have been demanded by the law,[58] and Hezekiah had years added to his life when God decreed something different that went beyond C the law.[59]

There[60] is nothing, to my mind, that can hinder someone who has already been trained in the natural and the written laws from divinely transcending them and from becoming free of them with divine love. Such a person has authentically followed with sincere faith only the Word, who leads the way to the highest good, and he does not connect himself mentally to any object, form of reasoning, or thought that governs and reflects any nature or knowledge of any intellectual reality or being whatsoever. Therefore, the one who sets out to fol- 90 low authentically after *Jesus, who has passed into the heavens* |D (Heb 4.14), is also able, rightly, to receive the whole of the true knowledge of reality from a single existing thing, as far as this is possible for a human being, when it is illumined by the divine light. Indeed,[61] let us take it as given that the 1153A collective nature of existing things has been divided into intellectual and sensual realities. The former are said to be and are

---

ceiving the law spiritually, foresaw the grace that is disclosed by it
58   Cf. II Ki 24.17; Ps 50.18–21.
59   Cf. IV Ki 20.1–11.
60   *30. That the one who genuinely follows Christ in his disposition through the virtues transcends both the written and natural law*
61   *31. Contemplating how the one who has become obedient to God in all things transcends the natural and written laws*

κατ'ἐπαλλαγὴν πρὸς ἑκάτερα τὰ τῆς κτίσεως τμήματα
φυσικῆς σχέσεώς τε καὶ ἰδιότητος καὶ περιγράφεται
καὶ περιγράφει, τὸ μὲν τῇ οὐσίᾳ, τὸ δὲ τῇ δυνάμει, ὡς
τοῖς ἑαυτοῦ πρὸς ταῦτα διαιρούμενος μέρεσι καὶ ταῦτα
διὰ τῶν οἰκείων μερῶν ἑαυτῷ καθ'ἕνωσιν ἐπισπώμε-
νος – περιγράφεσθαι γὰρ τοῖς νοητοῖς καὶ αἰσθητοῖς,
ὡς ψυχὴ τυγχάνων καὶ σῶμα, καὶ περιγράφειν ταῦτα
κατὰ δύναμιν πέφυκεν, ὡς νοῶν καὶ αἰσθανόμενος –, ὁ
δὲ θεὸς ἁπλῶς καὶ ἀορίστως ὑπὲρ πάντα τὰ ὄντα ἐστί,
τὰ περιέχοντά τε καὶ περιεχόμενα καὶ τὴν ὦν οὐκ ἄνευ
ταῦτα, χρόνου φημὶ καὶ αἰῶνος καὶ τόπου φύσιν, οἷς τὸ
πᾶν περικλείεται, ὡς πᾶσι παντελῶς ἄσχετος ὤν, ἄρα
σωφρόνως ὁ διαγνοὺς πῶς ἐρᾶν τοῦ θεοῦ δεῖ, τοῦ ὑπὲρ
λόγον καὶ γνῶσιν καὶ πάσης ἁπλῶς τῆς οἰασδήποτε παντάπασι σχέσεως ἐξῃρημένου καὶ φύσεως, πάντα τὰ
αἰσθητὰ καὶ νοητὰ καὶ πάντα χρόνον καὶ αἰῶνα καὶ τόπον ἀσχέτως παρελεύσεται καί, πάσης τελευταῖον ὅλης
τῆς κατ'αἴσθησιν καὶ λόγον καὶ νοῦν ἐνεργείας ἑαυτὸν
ὑπερφυῶς ἀπογυμνώσας, ἀρρήτως τε καὶ ἀγνώστως
τῆς ὑπὲρ λόγον καὶ νοῦν θείας τερπνότητος ἐπιτεύξε-
ται, καθ'ὃν οἶδε τρόπον τε καὶ λόγον ὁ τὴν τοιαύτην
δωρούμενος χάριν θεὸς καὶ οἱ ταύτην παρὰ θεοῦ λαβεῖν ἀξιωθέντες, οὐκέτι οὐδὲν φυσικὸν ἢ γραπτὸν ἑαυτῷ συνεπικομιζόμενος, πάντων αὐτῷ τῶν λεχθῆναι ἢ
γνωσθῆναι δυναμένων παντελῶς ὑπερβαθέντων τε καὶ
κατασιγασθέντων.

eternal, since they have received the source of their existence
in eternity, while the latter are temporal, since they have been
made in time. The former are subject to thinking while the
latter are subject to sense-perception because of the insoluble
power of the natural relative property that binds these to each
other, for the relation of intellectual beings to intellectual realities and that of beings endowed with sense-perception to
sensual realities is exceedingly strong. Moreover, let us take
it that the human being, existing of soul and sensual body, is
both enclosed by and encloses these facets of creation through
the natural relation and property that make the realities fit
with each other, one with respect to essence, and one with   B
respect to potentiality, since humanity is divided in its own
parts in relation to these and draws these through its own
proper parts to itself in union. Indeed, since it exists of soul
and body, it is natural for it potentially to be enclosed by the
intellectual and the sensual, and, since it thinks and perceives,
it is natural for it potentially to enclose them in turn. Finally,
let us take it that God exists simply and boundlessly beyond
all existing things, beyond things that contain and things that
are contained, and beyond the nature of those realties that
these are never without, I mean time, age, and placement, by
which the universe is confined, since He is entirely without
relation to anything. If all this is so, then the one who has   91
intelligently discerned how one must love God, who is beyond
reason and knowledge and is removed, in His simplicity, from
every kind of relation to anything and from the whole of nature, such a person will pass beyond all sensual and intellectual realities and all time and every age and place in a manner   C
free from all relation. When he has finally stripped himself
supernaturally of every active expression of sense-perception,
reason, and intellect, he will ineffably and without the mediation of knowledge attain to divine delight beyond reason and
intellect. In this he will know the way in which God grants
such grace, and its essential idea, as well as the way and es-

* Καὶ τάχα τοῦτό ἐστι τὸ τοῖς δοθεῖσιν ἐπὶ θερα-
πείᾳ τοῦ λησταῖς περιπεσόντος δυσὶ δηναρίοις ἐν τῷ
πανδοχείῳ παρὰ τοῦ κυρίου τῷ ἐπιμελεῖσθαι κεκελευ-
σμένῳ προσδαπανώμενον, ὅπερ καὶ φιλοτίμως ἐπαν-
ερχόμενος ὁ κύριος δώσειν ὑπέσχετο, ἡ διὰ πίστεως
γινομένη παντελὴς τῶν ὄντων ἐν τοῖς τελείοις ἀφαίρε-
σις – φησὶ γὰρ ὁ κύριος· ὅστις οὐκ ἀποτάσσεται πᾶσι
τοῖς ὑπάρχουσιν αὐτοῦ οὐ δύναταί μου εἶναι μαθητής –,
καθ᾽ἥν, πάνθ᾽ἑαυτοῦ ἢ ἑαυτὸν πάντων ἀφαιρούμενος
εἰπεῖν οἰκειότερον, ὁ τῆς σοφίας ἑαυτὸν ἐραστὴν κα|τα-   1156
στήσας μόνῳ θεῷ συνεῖναι καταξιοῦται, τὴν εὐαγγε-
λικῶς ὑποδειχθεῖσαν υἱοθεσίαν δεξάμενος κατὰ τοὺς
ἁγίους καὶ μακαρίους ἀποστόλους, οἳ τὸ πᾶν ἑαυτῶν
ὁλοσχερῶς περιελόμενοι καὶ μόνῳ διόλου τῷ θεῷ καὶ
λόγῳ προσφύντες – ἰδοὺ πάντα, ἔφασαν, ἀφήκαμεν
καὶ ἠκολουθήσαμέν σοι –, τῷ καὶ τῆς φύσεως ποιητῇ
καὶ δοτῆρι τῆς κατὰ νόμον βοηθείας, καὶ ὅν, ὥσπερ
ἀληθείας φῶς, μονώτατον κτησάμενοι ἀντὶ νόμου καὶ
φύσεως, πάντων εἰκότως τῶν μετὰ θεὸν ἄπταιστον τὴν
γνῶσιν παρέλαβον· αὐτῷ γὰρ πέφυκε συνεκφαίνεσθαι
κυρίως ἡ τῶν ὑπ᾽αὐτοῦ γεγενημένων γνῶσις· ὡς γὰρ
τῷ αἰσθητῷ ἡλίῳ ἀνατέλλοντι πάντα καθαρῶς συνεκ-
φαίνεται τὰ σώματα, οὕτω καὶ θεός, ὁ νοητὸς τῆς δι-
καιοσύνης ἥλιος ἀνατέλλων τῷ νῷ, καθὼς χωρεῖσθαι
ὑπὸ τῆς κτίσεως οἶδεν αὐτός, πάντων ἑαυτῷ νοητῶν
τε καὶ αἰσθητῶν τοὺς ἀληθεῖς βούλεται συνεμφανίζε-
σθαι λόγους. Καὶ δηλοῖ τοῦτο τῆς ἐπὶ τοῦ ὄρους μεταμορφώσεως τοῦ κυρίου ἡ λαμπρὰ τῶν ἐσθημάτων τῷ
φωτὶ τοῦ προσώπου αὐτοῦ γενομένη συνένδειξις, τῷ

sential idea by which those who have been deemed worthy receive this grace from God, and he will no longer carry any natural or scriptural reality along with himself, since all of his powers to reason and to know will have been entirely surmounted and reduced to silence.

Perhaps[62] the complete separation from beings that comes through faith to those who are perfect is the amount that was spent beyond the two denarii that were given for the care of the man who had fallen among thieves to the one in the inn who had been ordered by the Lord to attend to him, which the Lord also readily agreed to give whenever He should return,[63] for the Lord says, Whoever *does not forsake all the things belonging to him cannot be my disciple* (Lk 14.33). In accordance with this, by removing everything from himself, or to speak more appropriately, by removing himself from everything, the one who has established himself as a lover of wisdom is made worthy to be with God alone, for he has received the adoption that is indicated in the Gospel like the holy and blessed apostles. The apostles, who completely stripped everything from themselves and clung thoroughly to God the Word alone – *Behold*, they say, *we have left all and have followed You* (Mk 10.28) – who is both the maker of nature and the giver of help as concerns the law, and who acquired Him alone, instead of the law and nature, as the light of truth, firmly received infallible knowledge of all things that naturally come after God. Indeed, it is natural for the knowledge of things that have come to be by His agency to appear together with Him in the full force of their presence. For as all bodies appear clearly together with the sun that appears to the senses when it rises, thus also God, the intellectual *sun of righteousness* (Mal 4.2), when He rises for the intellect, even as He Himself seems to be contained by

D

92

1156A

B

62   *32. Contemplation of the passage in the Gospel concerning the man who fell among thieves*
63   Cf. Lk 10.30–37; cf. Max. Conf., *Cap. char.* IV.75.

θεῷ τὴν τῶν μετ'αὐτόν, ὡς οἶμαι, καὶ περὶ αὐτὸν συνεισ-
άγουσα γνῶσιν. Οὔτε γὰρ δίχα φωτὸς τῶν αἰσθητῶν
ὀφθαλμὸς ἀντιλαμβάνεσθαι δύναται, οὔτε νοῦς χωρὶς
γνώσεως θεοῦ θεωρίαν δέξασθαι πνευματικήν· ἐκεῖ τε
γὰρ τῇ ὄψει τὸ φῶς τῶν ὁρατῶν τὴν ἀντίληψιν δίδωσι
καὶ ἐνταῦθα τῷ νῷ τὴν γνῶσιν τῶν νοητῶν ἡ τοῦ θεοῦ
ἐπιστήμη χαρίζεται.

* Ἀμέλει τούτῳ μὴ ἐπερείσας τῷ θείῳ φωτὶ τὸν
τῆς ψυχῆς ὀφθαλμὸν ὁ προπάτωρ Ἀδὰμ τυφλοῦ δίκην
εἰκότως ἐν σκότει τῆς ἀγνωσίας ἄμφω τὼ χεῖρε τὸν
τῆς ὕλης φορυτὸν ἑκουσίως ἀφάσσων, μόνῃ αἰσθήσει
ἑαυτὸν ὅλον ἐπικλίνας ἐκδέδωκε, δι'ἧς τοῦ πικροτάτου
θηρὸς τὸν φθαρτικὸν ἰὸν εἰσδεξάμενος οὐδ'αὐτῆς, ὡς
ἠβουλήθη, ἀπέλαυσε τῆς αἰσθήσεως, δίχα θεοῦ καὶ πρὸ
θεοῦ καὶ οὐ κατὰ θεόν, ὡς οὐκ ἔδει, ὅπερ ἀμήχανον ἦν,
τὰ τοῦ θεοῦ ἔχειν ἐπιτηδεύσας· τὴν γὰρ σύμβουλον παραδεξαμένην τὸν ὄφιν θεοῦ πλέον παραδεξάμενος αἴσθησιν καὶ τοῦ ἀπηγορευμένου ξύλου, ᾧ καὶ θάνατον
συνεῖναι προεδιδάχθη, τὸν καρπὸν ὀρέγουσαν, βρώσεως
ἀπαρχὴν ποιησάμενος πρόσφορον τῷ καρπῷ τὴν ζωὴν
μετηλλάξατο, ζῶντα τὸν θάνατον ἑαυτῷ κατὰ πάντα
τὸν χρόνον τοῦ παρόντος καιροῦ δημιουργήσας. Εἰ γὰρ
φθορὰ γενέσεως ὑπάρχει ὁ θάνατος, ἀεὶ δὲ τὸ δι'ἐπιρροῆς τροφῶν γινόμενον φυσικῶς φθείρεται σῶμα τῇ
ῥοῇ διαπνεόμενον, ἀεὶ ἄρα, δι'ὧν εἶναι τὴν ζωὴν ἐπί-
στευσεν, ἀκμάζοντα ἑαυτῷ τε καὶ ἡμῖν τὸν θάνατον ὁ
Ἀδὰμ συνετήρησεν, ὡς, εἴ γε τῷ θεῷ μᾶλλον ἢ τῇ συν-
οίκῳ πεισθεὶς τῷ ξύλῳ τῆς ζωῆς διετράφη, οὐκ ἂν

creation, wills that the true essential ideas of intellectual and sensual beings appear together with Him. And the radiance of the garments that showed forth together with the light of the face of the Lord upon the mountain of His transfiguration shows this, since, in my view, it introduces the knowledge of things that come after God and the knowledge that pertains to God together with God Himself. The eye is unable to grasp sensual realities without light, and the intellect is unable to receive spiritual contemplation without the knowledge of God, for in the realm of sense-perception light grants to sight the ability to grasp visible things, and in the intellectual realm the understanding of God gives knowledge of intellectual realities to the intellect.

For[64] instance, because our forefather Adam did not direct the eye of his soul toward this divine light as he groped about willingly in the darkness of ignorance for the rubbish of material reality with both hands like a blind man, he gave himself exclusively to sense-perception by having inclined himself entirely to it. In having received the noxious poison of the viciously spiteful beast through sense-perception, he did not enjoy his sensuality itself, as he wished, since he tried to possess the things of God without God, instead of God, and not in accordance with God, as though He were unnecessary, though this was actually impossible. For having accepted sense-perception, which is symbolized by the snake and reaches out for the fruit of the forbidden tree and which he had been taught was death's companion, over God, he exchanged his original life for food by producing what befits the fruit: he fashioned a living death for himself, and it has spread itself across the whole duration of the present time. For if death exists as the destruction of becoming, and the body that comes to be through the influx of nourishment is always naturally destroyed by flowing back out in its dissipation, then Ad-

93

C

D

94

---

64   *33. Contemplation of how Adam's transgression took place*

τὴν δοθεῖσαν ἀπέθετο ἀθανασίαν ἀεὶ συντηρουμένην
τῇ μετοχῇ τῆς ζωῆς, | ἐπειδὴ πᾶσα ζωὴ οἰκείᾳ τε καὶ   1157
καταλλήλῳ πέφυκε συντηρεῖσθαι τροφῇ. Τροφὴ δὲ τῆς
μακαρίας ἐκείνης ζωῆς ἐστιν ὁ ἄρτος ὁ ἐκ τοῦ οὐρανοῦ
καταβὰς καὶ ζωὴν διδοὺς τῷ κόσμῳ, καθὼς αὐτὸς περὶ
ἑαυτοῦ ἐν τοῖς εὐαγγελίοις ὁ ἀψευδὴς ἀπεφήνατο λόγος. Ὧι διατραφῆναι μὴ βουληθεὶς ὁ πρῶτος ἄνθρωπος τῆς μὲν θείας εἰκότως ἀπεγένετο ζωῆς, ἄλλης δέ,
θανάτου γεννήτορος, ἐπελάβετο, καθ᾽ἥν, τὴν μὲν ἄλογον ἑαυτῷ μορφὴν ἐπιθέμενος, τῆς θείας δὲ τὸ ἀμήχανον ἀμαυρώσας κάλλος, βορὰν τῷ θανάτῳ τὴν ἅπασαν
φύσιν παρέδωκε, δι᾽ἧς ὁ μὲν θάνατος ζῇ, δι᾽ὅλου τοῦ
χρονικοῦ τούτου διαστήματος ἡμᾶς βρῶσιν ποιούμενος, ἡμεῖς δὲ ζῶμεν οὐδέποτε, ἀεὶ διὰ φθορᾶς ὑπ᾽αὐτοῦ
κατεσθιόμενοι.

*34 Ἧς τὸ ἀδρανὲς καὶ ἀλλεπάλληλον σοφῶς κατα-
νοήσαντες οἱ ἅγιοι τὴν ἀνθρώποις προηγουμένως ἐκ
θεοῦ δεδωρημένην ταύτην μὴ εἶναι τὴν ζωήν, ὡς εἰκός,
ἐπαιδεύθησαν, ἄλλην δὲ θείαν καὶ ὡσαύτως ἔχουσαν,
ἥν μάλιστα δεῖν ὑπέλαβον ἑαυτῷ πρεπόντως, ἀγαθὸν
ὄντα, τὸν θεὸν προηγουμένως δημιουργῆσαι μυστικῶς ἐδιδάχθησαν· πρὸς ἥν διὰ σοφίας κατὰ τὴν χάριν
τοῦ πνεύματος, ὡς ἐφικτὸν ἀνθρώποις τοῖς ὑπὸ θάνατον, τὸ ὄμμα τῆς ψυχῆς ἀνανεύσαντες καὶ ἐνδιαθέτως
τὸν αὐτῆς θεῖον ὑποδεξάμενοι πόθον, ἀποθέσθαι δεῖν
ταύτην τὴν παροῦσαν ζωὴν εἰκότως ᾠήθησαν, εἰ μέλ-
λοιεν καθαρῶς ἐκείνης κατὰ τὸν δέοντα λόγον ἐπιλήψε-
σθαι. Καὶ ἐπειδὴ ζωῆς ἀπόθεσις θανάτου χωρὶς οὐ γίνεται, θάνατον αὐτῆς ἐπενόησαν τὴν ἀποβολὴν τῆς κατὰ

am secured a perpetually flourishing death for himself and
for us through the nourishment which he believed to carry
life. Indeed, if he had obeyed God rather than his companion
and had thus been nourished with *the tree of life* (Gen 2.9),
he would not have set aside the gift of immortality, which is
always preserved by participation in life, since all life is natu-   1157A
rally preserved by its own proper, corresponding form of nourishment. The nourishment of that blessed life is *the bread that
comes down from heaven and gives life to the world* (Jn 6.33),
as the Word Himself, who does not lie, revealed concerning
Himself in the Gospels. The first man, because he did not want
to be fed by the Word, rightly had no part in divine life but
obtained a different form of "life," which was actually the
originator of death. He placed an irrational form upon himself
and defaced the extraordinary beauty of the divine form, and
in this way he handed over his whole nature as food for death.
Death therefore lives on human nature by making us its food
through the course of this whole present time, while we do not
live at all, for we are ever being devoured by it through the
process of destruction.

The[65] saints wisely grasped the feebleness and constant chang-   B
ing of this life with their minds and so are seen to have learned
that this life is not the life that was originally given by God
to man. They have been mystically taught, moreover, that   95
there is a different, divine, and deeply coherent life, which
they understand that God, being good, most certainly must
have originally fashioned in a manner befitting Himself. In
directing themselves towards this life, they renewed the eye of
their soul and received divine desire for this life within themselves, as much as this is possible for human beings who are
subject to death, through the wisdom that comes by the grace
of the Spirit. Thus, they were right to think it necessary to put

---

65   *34. That the saints have been taught from the unstable course of events
that true, divine, and coherent life is different than the present life*

σάρκα στοργῆς, δι'ἧς εἰς τὸν βίον ἡ τοῦ θανάτου γέγονεν εἴσοδος, ἵνα, θανάτῳ θάνατον ἐπινοήσαντες, τοῦ
ζῆν τῷ θανάτῳ παύσωνται, τὸν τίμιον ἐναντίον κυρίου
θάνατον ἀποθανόντες, τὸν ὄντως τοῦ ὄντως θανάτου
θάνατον, τὸν τὴν φθορὰν μὲν φθείρειν δυνάμενον, τῇ δὲ
μακαρίᾳ ζωῇ καὶ ἀφθαρσίᾳ ἐν τοῖς ἀξίοις παρεχόμενον
εἴσοδον. Τὸ γὰρ πέρας τῆς παρούσης ταύτης ζωῆς οὐδὲ
θάνατον οἶμαι δίκαιον ὀνομάζειν, ἀλλὰ θανάτου ἀπαλ-
λαγὴν καὶ φθορᾶς χωρισμὸν καὶ δουλείας ἐλευθερίαν
καὶ ταραχῆς παῦλαν καὶ πολέμων ἀναίρεσιν καὶ συγ-
χύσεως πάροδον καὶ σκότους ὑποχώρησιν καὶ πόνων
ἄνεσιν καὶ βομβήσεως ἀσήμου σιγὴν καὶ βράσματος
ἠρεμίαν καὶ αἰσχύνης συγκάλυμμα καὶ παθῶν ἀποφυγὴν καὶ ἁμαρτίας ἀφανισμὸν καὶ πάντων, ἵνα συνελὼν
εἴπω, τῶν κακῶν περιγραφήν· ἅπερ δι'ἑκουσίου νεκρώ-
σεως οἱ ἅγιοι κατορθώσαντες, ξένους ἑαυτοὺς τοῦ
βίου καὶ παρεπιδήμους παρέστησαν· κόσμῳ τε γὰρ καὶ
σώματι καὶ ταῖς ἐξ αὐτῶν ἐπαναστάσεσι γενναίως μα-
χόμενοι καὶ τὴν ἐξ ἀμφοῖν κατὰ τὴν τῶν αἰσθήσεων
πρὸς τὰ αἰσθητὰ συμπλοκὴν παραγενομένην ἀπάτην
ἀποπνίξαντες ἀδούλωτον ἑαυτοῖς ἐφύλαξαν τῆς ψυχῆς τὸ ἀξίωμα, μάλα γε εἰκότως ἔννομον κρίναντες
εἶναι καὶ δίκαιον τὸ ἧττον ἄγεσθαι | μᾶλλον τῷ κρείτ-   1160
τονι ἢ τὸ κρεῖττον τῷ χείρονι συμποδίζεσθαι, ὥσπερ δὴ
νόμος θεῖος, καὶ τοῖς προαιρουμένοις τὴν λογικοῖς προηγουμένως πρέπουσαν ἀσπάζεσθαι ζωήν, ἐμπεφυκὼς
τὴν ἐμφερῶς δι'ὀλιγαρκίας τὸ ἀπροσδεὲς τῶν ἀγγέλων
μιμουμένην καὶ ἄνετον.

* Ἀλλ'ἐπανελθόντες καθ'εἱρμόν, τὰ λείποντα τῆς μεταμορφώσεως τοῖς προθεωρηθεῖσι κατὰ δύναμιν δια-
σκοπήσαντες προσαρμόσωμεν, ἵνα δειχθῇ τῶν ἁγίων ἡ
ἐν πᾶσιν ἀκρότης καὶ ἡ γνησία πρὸς τὴν σάρκα καὶ τὴν

off this present life, if they would be ready to attain purely   C
to that other life according to this necessary principle. Now,
since the putting off of life does not occur without death, they
have conceived the death of life as the casting off of devotion
to the flesh, through which death has entered life, so that, by
having conceived of a death for death, they can stop living
for death, for they have died the *death* that is *precious in the
sight of the Lord* (Ps 116.15). This is, in fact, the actual death
of death itself, a death that is able to destroy destruction by
opening a way into blessed life and indestructibility for those
who are worthy. For I do not think that the end of this present life is rightly named death. It is rather deliverance from
death, separation from destruction, freedom from slavery, rest
from trouble, escape from warfare, a way past confusion, the   D
withdrawal of darkness, relaxation from labors, the silenc-
ing of meaningless noise, stillness of agitation, the covering
of shame, flight of the passions, and disappearance of sin. In
short, it is the closing off of all evils. By accomplishing this
through voluntary mortification, the saints established them-   96
selves as sojourners and foreigners in life. For by nobly fight-
ing against the world, the body, and the rebellions that originate from them, and by having smothered the trickery that
comes with both when the senses are interwoven with sensual
reality, they have preserved for themselves the dignity of the
soul unenslaved. For they very fittingly indeed judged it to be
right and just for the weaker to be led by the stronger rather   1160A
than for the stronger to be bound by what is worse, just as the
divine law requires. Moreover, they judged it to be right and
just for the life that is most fitting to rational creatures to be
fully embraced by those who choose it, the life that naturally
imitates the self-sufficiency and serene state of the angels by
resembling the angels' contentment with little.

But[66] to return to the sequence of our analysis, let us harmo-
nize the remaining elements of the transfiguration with what

---

66   *35. That the saints practiced neither natural contemplation nor mystical scriptural interpretation in a merely human way*

ὕλην ἀποδιάθεσις καὶ ὅτι μὴ καθ'ἡμᾶς καὶ αὐτοὶ ἢ τὴν
κτίσιν ἢ τὴν ἁγίαν γραφὴν ὑλικῶς τε καὶ χαμερπῶς
ἐθεώρουν, αἰσθήσει μόνον καὶ ἐπιφανείαις καὶ σχήμασι
πρὸς ἀνάληψιν τῆς μακαρίας γνώσεως τοῦ θεοῦ, γράμ-
μασί τε καὶ συλλαβαῖς χρώμενοι, ἐξ ὧν τὸ πταίειν ἐστὶ
περὶ τὴν κρίσιν τῆς ἀληθείας καὶ σφάλλεσθαι, ἀλλὰ νῷ
μόνῳ καθαρωτάτῳ καὶ πάσης ὑλικῆς ἀπηλλαγμένῳ
ἀχλύος. Εἴπερ εὐσεβῶς κρίνειν βουλόμεθα, τοὺς τῶν
αἰσθητῶν νοητῶς διασκοποῦντες λόγους, εἰς τὴν περὶ
θεοῦ καὶ τῶν θείων αὐτοὺς ἄπταιστον γνῶσιν ὀρθῶς
δι'εὐθείας τρίβου βαίνοντας ἰέναι κατίδοιμεν.

    * Εἴρηται τοίνυν ἀνωτέρω ὅτι διὰ μὲν τῆς γενο-
μένης ἐπὶ τοῦ ὄρους τοῦ προσώπου τοῦ κυρίου φωτο-
ειδοῦς λαμπρότητος πρὸς τὴν πᾶσι καθόλου τοῖς οὖσιν
ἄληπτον τοῦ θεοῦ μυστικῶς οἱ τρισμακάριοι ἀπόστο-
λοι κατὰ τὸ ἄρρητόν τε καὶ ἄγνωστον ἐχειραγωγοῦντο
δύναμίν τε καὶ δόξαν, τῆς ἀφανοῦς κρυφιότητος τὸ
φανὲν αὐτοῖς πρὸς τὴν αἴσθησιν φῶς σύμβολον μανθάνοντες – ὡς γὰρ ἐνταῦθα τοῦ γενομένου φωτὸς τὴν
τῶν ὀφθαλμῶν νικᾷ ἐνέργειαν ἡ ἀκτίς, ἀχώρητος αὐτοῖς
διαμένουσα, οὕτω κἀκεῖ θεὸς πᾶσαν νοὸς δύναμιν ὑπερ-
βαίνει καὶ ἐνέργειαν, οὐδ'ὅλως ἐν τῷ νοεῖσθαι τῷ νοεῖν
πειρωμένῳ τὸν οἱονοῦν τύπον ἀφείς –, διὰ δὲ τῶν λευ-
κῶν ἱματίων τήν τε ἐν τοῖς κτίσμασιν, ἀναλόγως τοῖς
καθ'οὓς γεγένηνται λόγοις, μεγαλουργίαν καὶ τὴν ἐν
τοῖς ῥήμασι τῆς ἁγίας γραφῆς κατὰ τὸ νοούμενον μυ-
σταγωγίαν ἐν ταυτῷ τε καὶ ἅμα θεοπρεπῶς ἐδιδάσκον-

has just been considered by examining them as closely as possible, so that the excellence of the saints in all things and their
noble estrangement from flesh and materiality may be shown.
We shall also show that they contemplated neither creation
nor holy scripture materialistically and basely like we do,   B
for when we seek to acquire the blessed knowledge of God,
we are completely dependent upon sense-perception, appearances, shapes, letters and syllables, all of which can make one
stumble and fall when making a judgment about the truth. By
contrast, the saints relied only upon a mind utterly purified   97
and delivered from the haze of all material reality. If we wish
to make pious judgments in our intellectual investigation of
the essential ideas of sensual reality, we must understand that
the saints approach the infallible knowledge of God and divine
reality by proceeding uprightly along a direct path.

The Transfiguration of Knowledge

To[67] continue, then, it was said above that the thrice-blessed
apostles were guided mystically, in an ineffable and unknowable way, through the luminous radiance that came from the
face of the Lord upon the mountain, to the power and glo-   C
ry of God, which are incomprehensible for all existing things.
They learned in this that the light that appeared to their
senses is a symbol of a hiddenness that never appears, for as
the radiance of the light that shone forth there conquers the
activity of the eyes by always resisting being contained by
them, thus also here God transcends every potentiality and
activity of the mind and leaves no mental impression at all
for someone to try to think about Him. Through the bright
garments, they were divinely taught at one and the same time
both the magnificence in created things that is ideally suited
to the ideas that have determined their becoming, and the

---

67   *36. Contemplating the Transfiguration more broadly*

το, οἷα τῇ ἐπιγνώσει τοῦ θεοῦ συναναφαινομένης τῆς
τε γραφικῆς κατὰ τὸ πνεῦμα δυνάμεως καὶ τῆς ἐν τοῖς
κτίσμασι κατ᾽αὐτὸ σοφίας καὶ γνώσεως, δι᾽ὧν πάλιν
αὐτὸς ἀναλόγως ἐκφαίνεται, διὰ δὲ Μωϋσέως καὶ
Ἠλίου τῶν ἑκατέρωθεν αὐτῷ συνόντων – τοῦτο γὰρ
εἰς τὴν ἐξέτασιν τῆς θεωρίας λείπεται – πολλοὺς κατὰ
πολλὰς ἐπινοίας, ὧν τύποι προεβέβληντο μυστηρίων,
δι᾽ἀληθοῦς θεωρίας γνωστικοὺς ὑπεδέχοντο τρόπους. |

* Καὶ πρῶτον μὲν τὴν περὶ τοῦ δεῖν πάντως συνεῖ-   1161
ναι τῷ λόγῳ καὶ θεῷ τόν τε νομικὸν καὶ τὸν προφητικὸν λόγον διὰ Μωϋσέως καὶ Ἠλίου εὐσεβεστάτην
ἐλάμβανον ἔννοιαν, ὡς ἐξ αὐτοῦ καὶ περὶ αὐτοῦ καὶ
ὄντας καὶ ἀναγγέλλοντας καὶ περὶ αὐτὸν ἱδρυμένους·
*εἶτα σοφίαν καὶ χρηστότητα συνούσας αὐτῷ διὰ τῶν
αὐτῶν ἐπαιδεύοντο, τὴν μὲν ὅτι κατ᾽αὐτὴν διαγορευτι-
κός ἐστι τῶν ποιητέων ὁ λόγος καὶ ἀπαγορευτικὸς τῶν
οὐ ποιητέων, ἧς τύπος ὑπῆρχε Μωϋσῆς – σοφίας γὰρ
τὴν τῆς νομοθεσίας χάριν εἶναι πιστεύομεν –, τὴν δὲ ὅτι
κατ᾽αὐτὴν προτρεπτικός ἐστι καὶ ἐπιστρεπτικὸς πρὸς
τὴν θείαν ζωὴν τῶν αὐτῆς ἀπολισθησάντων, ἧς τύπος
ὑπῆρχεν Ἠλίας, δι᾽ἑαυτοῦ ὅλον τὸ προφητικὸν δηλῶν
χάρισμα – χρηστότητος γὰρ θείας ἴδιον γνώρισμα τῶν
πεπλανημένων ἡ μετὰ φιλανθρωπίας ἐπιστροφή, ἧς
κήρυκας τοὺς προφήτας γινώσκομεν –, * ἢ γνῶσιν καὶ
παιδείαν, τὴν μὲν ὅτι καλοῦ τε καὶ κακοῦ τῆς εἰδήσε-
ως τοῖς ἀνθρώποις ὑπάρχει παρεκτικός – δέδωκα γὰρ
φησι, πρὸ προσώπου σου τὴν ζωὴν καὶ τὸν θάνατον,
ἐφ᾽ᾧ τὴν μὲν ἑλεῖν αἱρεῖσθαι, τὸν δὲ φυγεῖν καὶ μὴ ὡς
καλῷ περιπεσεῖν ἐξ ἀγνοίας τῷ χείρονι –, ὅπερ Μωϋσῆς
πεπραχὼς ἀνηγόρευται, προτυπῶν ἐν ἑαυτῷ τῆς ἀλη-

mystical initiation into the words of holy scripture so that
they could see its intellectual meaning. So then, the meaning   D
of scripture appeared together with the knowledge of God by
the Spirit, and wisdom and knowledge appeared together in
creatures by the same Spirit, through which, again, He Himself is made manifest in a way that is ideally suited to them.
Moses and Elijah were also with Him on either side, and this   98
aspect of our contemplation on the Transfiguration still needs
to be examined. The apostles received from them many ways
of thinking that gave them knowledge through true contemplation, and various types of the mysteries have emerged from
these thoughts.

First,[68] they grasped most piously that it was absolutely nec-   1161A
essary for both the legal and the prophetic words to be present
with the Word who is God in the persons of Moses and Elijah, since they come from Him, proclaim tidings about Him,
and are fundamentally about Him. Then[69] they were taught
through them that wisdom and goodness are to be found together with Him. Wisdom is present because the Word, in
accordance with wisdom, declares what has been made and
excludes what has not been made. Moses represents wisdom,
for we believe the grace of the lawgiver to be that of wisdom.
Goodness is present because the Word makes His exhortation
out of goodness and is able to return to divine life those who
have slipped away from it. Elijah represents this goodness, for   B
he shows in himself the entirety of the gift of prophecy, and
we recognize divine goodness most readily when those who
have gone astray turn back again to the right path in response
to human love, and we know the prophets to be heralds of this
conversion. Or,[70] they were taught through them that knowledge and instruction are to be found with Him. Knowledge

---

68   *37. Contemplating Moses and Elijah (a)*
69   *38. Contemplating Moses and Elijah (b)*
70   *39. Contemplating Moses and Elijah (c)*

θείας τὰ σύμβολα, τὴν δὲ ὅτι τῶν τοῖς ἐναντίοις ἀνέ-
δην χρωμένων κατὰ τὸν Ἰσραήλ, οὗ παιδευτὴς Ἠλίας
ὁ μέγας ἐγένετο, καὶ μιγνύντων ἀδιακρίτως τὰ ἄμικτα
τῆς ἀδιαφορίας ἐστὶ κολαστικός καὶ τῶν παντελῶς τῷ
κακῷ προστεθειμένων τὴν ἄνοιαν καὶ τὴν πώρωσιν εἰς
ἔννοιαν ἄγων, ὡς λόγος, καὶ αἴσθησιν, * ἢ πρᾶξιν καὶ
θεωρίαν, τὴν μὲν ὡς κακίας ἀναιρετικὴν καὶ κόσμου δι’ἐ-
πιδείξεως ἀρετῶν τοὺς δι’αὐτῆς ἀγομένους παντελῶς
κατὰ διάθεσιν τέμνουσαν, ὡς Μωϋσῆς τῆς Αἰγύπτου
τὸν Ἰσραήλ, καὶ θείοις νόμοις τοῦ πνεύματος εὐπειθῶς
παιδεύουσαν ἄγεσθαι, τὴν δὲ ὡς εἴδους καὶ ὕλης ἁρπά-
ζουσαν, ὡς τὸν Ἠλίαν τὸ ἐκ πυρὸς ἅρμα, καὶ θεῷ διὰ
γνώσεως προσάγουσάν τε καὶ συνάπτουσαν ὑπὸ σαρκὸς
οὐδ’ὁτιοῦν βαρουμένους διὰ τὴν τοῦ κατ’αὐτὴν νόμου
ἀθέτησιν, ἢ ἐπάρσει καθοτιοῦν ἐπὶ τοῖς κατορθώμασι
φλεγομένους διὰ τὴν συνημμένην ταῖς ὄντως ἀρεταῖς
δρόσον τῆς πτωχείας τοῦ πνεύματος· * ἢ πάλιν τὰ
κατὰ τὸν γάμον καὶ τὴν ἀγαμίαν μυστήρια παρὰ τῷ
λόγῳ εἶναι μανθάνοντες διὰ Μωϋσέως, τοῦ διὰ γάμον
τῆς θείας ἐραστοῦ γενέσθαι δόξης μὴ κωλυθέντος, καὶ
διὰ Ἠλίου, τοῦ παντελῶς γαμικῆς συναφείας καθαροῦ
διαμείναντος, οἷα τοῦ λόγου καὶ θεοῦ τοὺς λόγῳ ταῦτα
ἰθύνοντας κατὰ τοὺς θειωδῶς περὶ αὐτῶν κειμένους
νόμους ἑαυτῷ μυστικῶς εἰσποιεῖσθαι κηρύττοντος· *

is present since He is able to bring about the understanding
of good and evil in men, for He says, *I have set life and death
before your face* (Dt 30.19), so that you would prefer to choose
life, and flee death and not, out of ignorance, fall in with what
is lower as though it were beautiful. Moses proclaimed this   99
by doing it himself and thus prefigured the truth symbolically
in himself. Instruction is present since He corrects those who
conduct themselves freely among the adversaries of Israel,
whose teacher was the great Elijah. These are people who un-
critically and indifferently mix what should remain unmixed
and who have become completely bound up with evil. He   C
achieves this correction by leading their thoughtlessness and
callousness to clear thinking, since He is Reason, and to per-
ceptivity. Or,[71] they were taught through them that practical
life and contemplation are to be found with Him. Practical
life is present since it destroys evil and, by displaying the virtues, cuts off from the world those who are led in their disposition entirely by it, as Moses cut Israel off from Egypt, and
it trains them to be led obediently by the divine *laws of the
Spirit* (Rom 8.2). Contemplation is present since it snatches
away from form and matter, as the *chariot of fire* (II Ki 2.11)
did Elijah, those who are not in any way weighed down by
the flesh – because the law of the flesh has been abolished in
them or inasmuch as they are aflame with elation for upright
deeds because of the dew of poverty of spirit, which is bound
to genuine virtues – and leads them through knowledge and
binds them to God.

From[72] another point of view, they learned that the mysteries   D
of marriage and the unmarried state are both present with
the Word through Moses and Elijah. Moses was not hindered
from becoming a lover of divine glory because he was married,
whereas Elijah remained completely free of the marital bond,

71   *40. Contemplating Moses and Elijah (d)*
72   *41. Contemplating Moses and Elijah (e)*

ἢ ζωῆς καὶ θανάτου διὰ τῶν αὐτῶν κύριον πιστῶς ὄντα
τὸν λόγον πληροφορούμενοι· | * ἢ καὶ τὸ πάντας ζῆν   1164
τῷ θεῷ καὶ μηδένα παντελῶς παρ'αὐτῷ νεκρὸν εἶναι διὰ
τῶν αὐτῶν μανθάνοντες, πλὴν τοῦ ἑαυτὸν τῇ ἁμαρτίᾳ
νεκρώσαντος καὶ τῇ ἑκουσίῳ πρὸς τὰ πάθη ῥοπῇ τοῦ
λόγου ἑαυτὸν ἀποκόψαντος· * ἢ πάλιν πρὸς τὸν λόγον,
ὡς ἀλήθειαν ὄντα, κατ'ἀναφορὰν εἶναί τε καὶ ὑπάρχειν
τοὺς τύπους τῶν μυστηρίων καὶ εἰς αὐτὸν συνάγεσθαι
τῆς τε νομικῆς καὶ τῆς προφητικῆς πραγματείας, ὡς εἰς
ἀρχὴν καὶ τέλος, ἐφωταγωγοῦντο, * ἢ τὰ μετὰ θεὸν
πάντα καὶ ἐκ θεοῦ γεγονότα, τουτέστι τὴν φύσιν τῶν
ὄντων καὶ τὸν χρόνον, παρὰ τῷ θεῷ ὄντα συνεκφαίνεσθαι, ἀληθῶς φαινομένῳ κατὰ τὸ ἐφικτόν, ὡς αἰτίῳ
καὶ ποιητῇ· ὧν τοῦ μὲν χρόνου τύπος ἂν εἴη Μωϋσῆς,
οὐ μόνον ὡς χρόνου καὶ τοῦ κατ'αὐτὸν ἀριθμοῦ διδάσκαλος – οὗτος γὰρ πρῶτος τὸν κατὰ τὴν γένεσιν τοῦ
κόσμου χρόνον ἠρίθμησε – καὶ ὡς χρονικῆς γενόμενος
λατρείας καθηγητής, ἀλλὰ καὶ ὡς μὴ συνεισερχόμενος
ἐκείνοις σωματικῶς εἰς τὴν κατάπαυσιν, ὧν πρὸς τὰς
θείας καθηγήσατο ἐπαγγελίας – τοιοῦτον γὰρ καὶ ὁ
χρόνος, οὐ φθάνων ἢ συνεισερχόμενος κατὰ τὴν κίνησιν ἐκείνοις, οὓς πρὸς τὴν θείαν τοῦ μέλλοντος αἰῶνος
ζωὴν πέφυκε παραπέμπειν ('Ιησοῦν γὰρ ἔχει τὸν παντὸς
ὄντα καὶ χρόνου καὶ αἰῶνος διάδοχον, κἂν εἰ ἄλλως οἱ
λόγοι τοῦ χρόνου ἐν τῷ θεῷ διαμένωσιν, ὡς δηλοῖ μυστικῶς ἡ τοῦ ἐν ἐρήμῳ δοθέντος νόμου διὰ Μωϋσέως
τοῖς τὴν γῆν λαβοῦσι τῆς κατασχέσεως συνείσοδος)·
αἰὼν γάρ ἐστιν ὁ χρόνος, ὅταν στῇ τῆς κινήσεως, καὶ
χρόνος ἐστὶν ὁ αἰών, ὅταν μετρῆται κινήσει φερόμενος,
ὡς εἶναι τὸν μὲν αἰῶνα, ἵνα ὡς ἐν ὅρῳ περιλαβὼν εἴπω,
χρόνον ἐστερημένον κινήσεως, τὸν δὲ χρόνον αἰῶνα κινήσει μετρούμενον –, τῆς δὲ φύσεως 'Ηλίας, οὐ μόνον
ὡς τοὺς καθ'ἑαυτὸν ἀλωβήτους φυλάξας λόγους καὶ τὸ
ἐπ'αὐτοῖς κατὰ γνώμην φρόνημα τροπῆς τῆς ἐκ πάθους
ἐλεύθερον, ἀλλὰ καὶ ὡς ἐν κρίσει παιδεύων, οἷόν τις
φυσικὸς νόμος, τοὺς παρὰ φύσιν τῇ φύσει χρωμένους

for the Word who is God proclaims that those who conduct these modes of life uprightly with reason in accordance with the laws divinely laid down concerning them are mystically   100 adopted by Him. Or[73] they were assured through the presence of Moses and Elijah that the Word is genuinely lord of life and death. Or[74] they learned through them that all things *live with*   1164A *God* (Rom 6.10) and that there is absolutely nothing dead with Him, except the one who has killed himself by sin and has cut himself off from the Word by voluntarily gravitating towards the passions. Or[75] again, we can say that, on the basis of all this, they were enlightened to know that the types of the mysteries are and actually exist in relation to the Word by referring to Him, since He *is the truth*,[76] and are gathered from the content of the law and the prophets to Him as to their *source and final end* (Rev 21.5; 22.13), or[77] that all things after God and that have come into being from God, that is, the nature of beings and time, appear together with God when He truly appears, as far as this is possible, as their cause and maker. Of these, Moses represents time, not only as the one who   B teaches about time and its numbering – for he was the first to number time starting from the beginning of the world – and as the one who became the instructor of temporal worship, but also as one who did not *enter* bodily *into repose* (Ps 94.11; Heb 3.11, 18) with those whom he was leading to the divine promises. For this is also a quality of time: it does not arrive   101 before or enter together in its motion with those whom it naturally escorts to the divine life of the age to come (for he has Joshua as the one who is the successor of all time and every age, even if the essential ideas of time abide otherwise in God, as is mystically shown when the law given in the wilderness

---

73   *42. Contemplating Moses and Elijah (f)*

74   *43. Contemplating Moses and Elijah (g)*

75   *44. Contemplating Moses and Elijah (h)*

76   Cf. John 14.6.

77   *45. Contemplating Moses and Elijah (i)*

– τοιοῦτον γὰρ καὶ ἡ φύσις, τοὺς αὐτὴν παραφθείρειν
ἐπιχειροῦντας τοσοῦτον κολάζουσα, ὅσον τοῦ παρὰ φύσιν ζῆν ἐπιτηδεύουσι, τῷ μὴ ὅλην αὐτῆς φυσικῶς ἔτι
κεκτῆσθαι τῆς φύσεως τὴν δύναμιν μειωθέντας ἤδη
τῆς κατ'αὐτὴν ἀρτιότητος καὶ διατοῦτο κολαζομένους,
ὡς ἑαυτοῖς ἀβούλως τε καὶ ἀφρόνως διὰ τῆς πρὸς τὸ
μὴ ὂν νεύσεως τοῦ εἶναι παρεχομένους τὴν ἔλλειψιν –.

* Ἴσως δὲ καὶ τὴν νοητὴν καὶ τὴν αἰσθητὴν κτίσιν ἔχε-
σθαι τοῦ δημιουργοῦ λόγου τις εἰπὼν διὰ Μωϋσέως καὶ
Ἠλίου, τῆς ἀληθείας οὐ διαμαρτάνει· ὧν τῆς μὲν αἰσθη-
τῆς Μωϋσῆς λόγον ἐπέχει, ὡς ὑπὸ γένεσιν καὶ φθορὰν
γεγενημένος, καθὼς ἡ περὶ αὐτοῦ ἱστορία δηλοῖ, τὴν γένεσιν καὶ τὸν θάνατον αὐτοῦ καταγγέλλουσα – τοιοῦτον
γὰρ καὶ ἡ αἰσθητὴ κτίσις, ἀρχὴν ἐγνωσμένην γενέσεως
ἔχουσα | καὶ διὰ φθορᾶς ὡρισμένον τέλος ἐλπίζουσα –,   1165
τῆς δὲ νοητῆς Ἠλίας, ὡς οὔτε γέννησιν αὐτοῦ τῆς περὶ
αὐτοῦ μηνυούσης ἱστορίας, κἂν εἰ γεγέννηται, οὔτε μὴν
τὴν διὰ θανάτου φθορὰν ἐλπίζεσθαι ὁριζομένης, κἂν
εἰ τεθνήξεται – τοιοῦτον γὰρ καὶ ἡ νοητὴ κτίσις, οὔτε
ἀρχὴν γενέσεως ἀνθρώποις κατάδηλον ἔχουσα, κἂν εἰ
γεγένηται καὶ ἦρκται καὶ ἐκ τοῦ μὴ ὄντος εἰς τὸ εἶναι

through Moses entered in together with those who were taking the land for possession). Time is eternity whenever it stops moving, and eternity is time whenever it is measured while C being moved along in motion, since eternity, to put it comprehensively, as in a definition, is time deprived of motion, and time is eternity measured by motion.[78] Elijah, then, represents nature, not only as one who preserved unharmed the essential ideas that pertain to himself and kept the way of thinking that characterized his mentality and was based upon the essential ideas free from the alteration that comes from passion, but also as one who, as a sort of natural law, trains those who use their nature contrary to nature to have discernment. For this is also a quality of nature: it chastens those who try to distort it precisely insofar as they pursue a life contrary to nature, in that they have already been diminished thereby by not yet having naturally acquired the whole power of nature from it in its integrity. This itself is how they are chastened, since they unwittingly and mindlessly render to themselves a deficiency of existence through their inclination towards what D is not real.

Likewise,[79] anyone who says the intellectual and sensual creation are near the creative Word in the figures of Moses and 102 Elijah has not missed the truth. Of these, Moses presents the idea of sense-perception, since he was subject to becoming and corruption, as the narrative about him shows by reporting his coming into being and his death. For this is also a quality of sensual creation: it has a recognizable beginning when it comes into being and expects a definitive end through 1165A its destruction. Elijah, on the other hand, presents the idea of intellectual reality, since the narrative about him neither discloses his birth, even if he had been born, nor does it de-

---

78   Cf. PLAT., *Timaeus* 37d; PLOT., *Enneads* III.vii.2.20–21; Ps. DION. AREO. *Div. Nom.* X.3.

79   *46. Contemplating Moses and Elijah (j)*

παρῆκται, οὔτε τέλος τοῦ εἶναι διὰ φθορᾶς ὡρισμένον
ἐκδέχεται· τὸ γὰρ ἀνώλεθρον φυσικῶς ἔχει λαβοῦσα
παρὰ θεοῦ, τοῦ οὕτως αὐτὴν δημιουργῆσαι θελήσαν-
τος –.

* Εἰ δέ τῳ μὴ περιεργότερος τοῦ δέοντος εἶναι δοκῶ,
καὶ ἕτερον μέγα τε καὶ θεῖον, ὡς οἶμαι, ἐκ τῆς θείας μεταμορφώσεως μυστήριον ἡμῖν ἀναφαίνεται καὶ τῶν
εἰρημένων λαμπρότερον. Οἶμαι γὰρ τοὺς καθόλου δύο
τῆς θεολογίας τρόπους μυστικῶς ὑφηγεῖσθαι τὰ ἐπὶ
τοῦ ὄρους κατὰ τὴν μεταμόρφωσιν θεοπρεπῆ δραμα-
τουργήματα, τόν τε προηγούμενόν φημι καὶ ἁπλοῦν
καὶ ἀναίτιον καὶ διὰ μόνης καὶ παντελοῦς ἀποφάσεως
τὸ θεῖον ὡς ἀληθῶς καταφάσκοντα καὶ τὴν ὑπεροχὴν
αὐτοῦ διʼἀφασίας δεόντως σεμνύνοντα, καὶ τὸν ἑπόμε-
νον τούτῳ καὶ σύνθετον διὰ καταφάσεως μεγαλοπρεπῶς ἐκ τῶν αἰτιατῶν ὑπογράφοντα· οἷς, κατὰ τὸ δυνατὸν ἀνθρώπους εἰδέναι, ἡ περὶ θεοῦ τε καὶ τῶν θείων
ἐπαιωρουμένη γνῶσις διὰ τῶν προσφυῶν ἡμῖν συμβόλων πρὸς ἀμφοτέρους ἡμᾶς ἄγει τοὺς τρόπους, διʼεὐ-
σεβοῦς τῶν ὄντων κατανοήσεως ἀμφοτέρων ἡμῖν ἐφι-
στῶσα τοὺς λόγους καὶ τοῦ μὲν προτέρου πᾶν τὸ ὑπὲρ
αἴσθησιν σύμβολον εἶναι διδάσκουσα, τοῦ δὲ δευτέρου
τὰ κατʼαἴσθησιν ἀθροιστικὰ εἶναι παιδεύουσα μεγα-
λουργήματα. Ἐκ γὰρ τῶν ὑπὲρ αἴσθησιν συμβόλων τὴν
ὑπὲρ λόγον καὶ νοῦν ἀλήθειαν εἶναι μόνον πιστεύομεν,
περὶ τοῦ τί καὶ πῶς καὶ ὁποίαν εἶναι καὶ ποῦ καὶ πότε
μηδόλως τολμῶντες σκοπεῖν ἢ ἐννοεῖν ἀνεχόμενοι,
τῆς ἐγχειρήσεως τὸ ἀσεβὲς παραιτούμενοι, ἐκ δὲ τῶν
κατʼαἴσθησιν, ὡς ἡμῖν ἐστι δυνατόν, κατʼἔννοιαν μόνον

fine his destruction through death as would be expected,
even if he will have died. For this is also a quality of intellectual creation: the original moment when it came to be is
not observable for human beings, even if it has come to be
and has received a beginning and has been led from non-being into existence; nor does it admit of a definitive end to
its existence through destruction, for it naturally possesses
indestructibility, which it has received from God, who had
willed to fashion it so.

And,[80] at the risk of seeming to go further than is necessary,   B
there is another great and divine mystery, I think, that appears to us from the divine transfiguration and is even more
luminous than what has already been said. For I think that
the divine dramatic accounts of the transfiguration upon the
mountain mystically indicate the two general modes of theology. The first of these is the primary, simple mode, which   103
makes no reference to causality. It truly affirms the divine
through strict and absolute negation and stays within its
bounds by exalting the pre-eminence of the Divine without
saying anything. The second mode follows upon this primary
one and is a complex discourse that magnificently sketches the
Divine in outline through affirmation in terms of the things
that have their cause in Him. With respect to these, given
what is possible for human beings to know, the knowledge of
God and divine things that arises through symbols appropriate to our nature leads us to both modes: it establishes for us   C
the ideas that are essential to both through the pious understanding of reality, it teaches us that every symbol that transcends sense-perception belongs to the first, and it instructs us
that the magnificent deeds that gather together in the realm
of sense-perception belong to the second. For we believe that
the truth beyond reason and intellect is only derived from
symbols beyond sense-perception, and we do not at all dare to

---

80   *47. Concisely contemplating the Transfiguration again (k)*

ἰσχνῶς τῆς περὶ θεοῦ γνώσεως τὰς εἰκασίας λαμβάνον-
τες, πάντα αὐτὸν εἶναι φαμέν, ὅσα ἐκ τῶν αὐτοῦ ποιημάτων, ὡς αἴτιον, ἐγνωρίσαμεν.

* Σκοπήσωμεν δὲ εἰ μὴ καλῶς ἑκάστῳ τῶν εἰρημένων τρόπων κατὰ τὴν θείαν ἐκείνην τοῦ κυρίου μεταμόρφωσιν καὶ σοφῶς ἐνυπάρχει τὸ σύμβολον. Ἔδει
γὰρ αὐτόν, καθ᾽ἡμᾶς ἀτρέπτως κτισθῆναι δι᾽ἄμετρον
φιλανθρωπίαν καταδεξάμενον, ἑαυτοῦ γενέσθαι τύπον
καὶ σύμβολον καὶ παραδεῖξαι ἐξ ἑαυτοῦ συμβολικῶς
ἑαυτὸν καὶ δι᾽ἑαυτοῦ φαινομένου πρὸς ἑαυτόν, ἀφανῶς
πάντη κρυπτόμενον, χειραγωγῆσαι τὴν ἅπασαν κτίσιν
καὶ τῆς ἀφανοῦς καὶ πάντων ἐπέκεινα κρυφιομύστου
καὶ ὑπ᾽οὐδενὸς τῶν ὄντων οὐδενὶ τὸ σύνολον τρόπῳ
νοηθῆναι ἢ λεχθῆναι δυνα|μένης ἀπειρίας τὰς ἐκφανεῖς   1168
διὰ σαρκὸς θεουργίας ἀνθρώποις παρασχεῖν φιλανθρώπως μηνύματα. * Τὸ τοίνυν φῶς τοῦ προσώπου τοῦ
Χριστοῦ, τὸ νικῆσαν τῆς ἀνθρωπίνης αἰσθήσεως τὴν
ἐνέργειαν, τὸν τρόπον διετύπου τοῖς μακαρίοις ἀπο-
στόλοις τῆς κατ᾽ἀπόφασιν μυστικῆς θεολογίας, καθ᾽ὃν
ἡ ἁγία καὶ μακαρία θεότης κατ᾽οὐσίαν ἐστὶν ὑπεράρ-
ρητος καὶ ὑπεράγνωστος καὶ πάσης ἀπειρίας ἀπειράκις
ἐξῃρημένη, οὐδ᾽ἴχνος ὅλως καταλήψεως, κἂν ψιλόν,
τοῖς μετ᾽αὐτὴν καταλείψασα, οὐδὲ τὴν πῶς, κἂν ποσῶς, ἡ αὐτὴ καὶ μονάς ἐστι καὶ τριὰς ἔννοιαν ἐφιεῖσα
τινὶ τῶν ὄντων, ἐπειδὴ μὴ δὲ χωρεῖσθαι κτίσει τὸ ἄκτιστον πέφυκε, μὴ δὲ περινοεῖσθαι τοῖς πεπερασμένοις
τὸ ἄπειρον· * τὸν δὲ καταφατικὸν τρόπον, εἰς τε τὸν
κατ᾽ἐνέργειαν πρόνοιάν τε καὶ κρίσιν διαιρούμενον, τὸν
μὲν κατ᾽ἐνέργειαν, τὸν ἐκ καλλονῆς καὶ μεγέθους τῶν

examine or allow ourselves to consider the questions What?, How?, What quality?, Where?, and When?[81] in relation to it, and we denounce the impiety of the attempt. From sensual symbols, however, as far as it is possible for us who weakly grasp the likenesses of the knowledge of God on the conceptual level only, we say that He is all things, inasmuch as we have recognized Him, as cause, from the things that have been made by Him.

D

Let[82] us examine whether the symbol that conveys beauty in each of the modes mentioned here in reference to the divine transfiguration of the Lord also conveys wisdom. For it was necessary that He, who consented to be created like us without change because of His immeasurable love for humanity, become and symbolically present Himself from Himself and, through being made manifest Himself, lead all of creation to Himself, who is hidden in absolute non-appearance. It was necessary, moreover, in His love for humanity, that he provide to human beings, through His divinely wrought flesh, manifest indications of the non-appearing and mystically hidden infinity that transcends all things and cannot be thought or spoken by anything in any way whatsoever. Therefore,[83] the light of the face of Christ, which surpassed the activity of human sense-perception, represented to the blessed apostles a type for the mode of mystical theology that proceeds by negation and teaches that the holy and blessed Divinity is "beyond ineffable and beyond unknowable"[84] in its essence and forever transcending all infinity, for it has left absolutely no trace, however slight, for those who come after it to grasp it; neither does it yield to any being, even to a minimal degree, any concept of how Unity and Trinity are the same reality,

104

1168A

B

---

81   Cf. Arist., *Cat.* 4.1b26, etc.
82   *48. That the Lord has become a type of Himself according to the economy of His flesh (1)*
83   *49. Contemplating the sudden illumination of the Lord's face*
84   Ps. Dion. Areo., *Div. Nom.* II.4, p. 126.9.

κτισμάτων τὴν περὶ τοῦ δημιουργὸν εἶναι τῶν ὅλων
τὸν θεὸν εἰσηγούμενον δήλωσιν διὰ τῶν λαμπρῶν ἐσθημάτων τοῦ κυρίου δηλοῦσθαι, ἅπερ εἰς τὰ φαινόμενα
κτίσματα προεκλαβὼν ὁ λόγος ἀπέδειξε, * τὸν δὲ κατὰ
πρόνοιαν τρόπον διὰ τοῦ Μωϋσέως σημαίνεσθαι, ὡς
πλάνης φιλανθρώπως ἐξαιρουμένην τοὺς κακίᾳ συνει-
λημμένους καὶ τοὺς τρόπους σοφῶς τοῖς ἀνθρώποις δι-
αποικίλλουσαν τῆς πρὸς τὰ θεῖα καὶ ἄϋλα καὶ ἀσώματα
ἀπὸ τῶν ὑλικῶν καὶ φθαρτῶν καὶ σωματικῶν ἐκδημίας
καὶ θείοις νόμοις ἐπιστημόνως ἐρείδουσαν, * τὸν δὲ
τῆς κρίσεως τρόπον διὰ τοῦ Ἠλίου μηνύεσθαι, ὡς λόγῳ
τε καὶ ἔργῳ τοὺς μὲν κατ’ἀξίαν τιμωρουμένης, τοὺς δὲ
περιεπούσης διὰ τοῦ κατὰ τὴν ὑποκειμένην ὕλην τε καὶ
ποιότητα τῆς ἀρετῆς ἢ τῆς κακίας ἑκάστῳ προσφόρως
αὐτὴν ἁρμόζεσθαι. Ταῦτα γὰρ πάντα τὰ προθεωρηθέν-
τα κατὰ τὸν παρόντα τῆς ἁγίας γραφῆς τόπον Μωϋσῆς
τε καὶ Ἠλίας, ὡς ἐνῆν μάλιστα τοὺς τὰ θεῖα τυπικῶς
δι’ἑαυτῶν ὑπογράφοντας πράγματα, ἐν τοῖς ἑαυτῶν
ἑκάτερος χρόνοις καθ’ἱστορίαν εἰργάσατο, ἐμφερῶς
ἔχοντα πρὸς τὰ εἰρημένα κατὰ τὸν τῆς θεωρίας τρόπον.

* Ἐκ δὲ τοῦ συλλαλεῖν αὐτοὺς τῷ κυρίῳ καὶ τὴν |
ἔξοδον λέγειν ἣν ἔμελλε πληροῦν ἐν Ἱερουσαλὴμ οὐ μό-   1169
νον τὴν ἐπ’αὐτῷ διὰ νόμου καὶ προφητῶν προκεκηρυγ-
μένην τῶν μυστηρίων ἔκβασιν ἐδιδάσκοντο, ἀλλ’ἴσως
καὶ τὸ μὴ ληπτὸν εἶναι μηδενὶ καθόλου τῶν ὄντων τὸ
πέρας τῆς ἀρρήτου περὶ τὸ πᾶν βουλῆς τοῦ θεοῦ καὶ τῶν
ἐπ’αὐτῇ θείων οἰκονομιῶν, πλὴν τῆς μεγάλης αὐτοῦ

since it is not natural for that which is uncreated to be contained by creation, or for the infinite to be comprehensively understood by finite beings. The[85] light also represented the affirmative mode, which is divided into activity, providence, and judgment. As it pertains to activity, the affirmative mode asserts *from the beauty and grandeur of creatures* (Wis 13.5)   105 that the identification of God as the fashioner of the whole of reality is demonstrated through the radiant clothing of the Lord, which the Word displayed to visible creation by having taken them entirely upon Himself. As[86] it pertains to provi-   C dence, the affirmative mode is signified through Moses, since providence lovingly lifts those who have been seized by wickedness out of error and wisely provides paths of departure for human beings toward divine, immaterial, and bodiless reality and away from material, corruptible, and bodily reality and gives the support of understanding through the divine laws. As[87] it pertains to judgment, the affirmative mode is disclosed through Elijah, since judgment aids some according to their merit in word and deed and deals with others by fitting itself appropriately to each person according to the underlying content and quality of each person's virtue or wickedness. For   D Moses and Elijah, in the narrative of their own times, each achieved all the things we have just considered in this passage of holy scripture, inasmuch as it was possible for them to sketch divine realities in outline typologically through their own lives, for their lives bear a resemblance to what has been said in this contemplative mode.

From[88] their *talking* with the Lord and *speaking of His death,*   1169A *which He was about to accomplish at Jerusalem* (Lk 9.30–31),

---

85   *50. Contemplating the bright clothing of the Lord*

86   *51. Contemplating Moses again*

87   *52. Contemplating Elijah again*

88   *53. Contemplating the conversation between Moses and Elijah and the Lord at the Transfiguration*

προνοίας καὶ κρίσεως, δι᾽ ὧν εἰς τὸ μόνῳ τῷ θεῷ προε-
γνωσμένον τέλος τὸ πᾶν εὐτάκτως ἐπείγεται· ὅπερ πάντες μὲν ὁμοίως ἠγνόησαν κατὰ τὸ τί ποτε εἶναι καὶ πῶς
καὶ ποῖον καὶ πότε, μόνοι δὲ ἀληθῶς μόνον ἐπέγνωσαν
ἔσεσθαι οἱ τὴν ψυχὴν ἀρεταῖς ἐκκαθάραντες ἅγιοι καὶ
πρὸς τὰ θεῖα τὴν ῥοπὴν αὐτῆς ὅλην τὴν νοερὰν ὁλικῶς
μετεγκλίναντες, αὐτῆς, ὡς εἰπεῖν, τῆς καθόλου τῶν
ὁρατῶν φύσεως, δι᾽ ὧν συνίστασθαι πέφυκε τρόπων, τὸ
τέλος τῆς παρούσης αὐτῇ εὐκοσμίας μονονουχὶ διαρρήδην βοώσης ἀκούσαντες. * Περιαθρήσαντες γάρ, ὡς
ἐνῆν μάλιστα, ἐπιστημόνως τὸν παρόντα κόσμον καὶ
τῶν ἐν αὐτῷ ποικίλως ἀλλήλοις συνηρμοσμένων σωμάτων τὸν συνεπτυγμένον κατ᾽ ἔννοιαν σοφῶς ἐξαπλώ-
σαντες λόγον, εὗρον τὰ μὲν αὐτῶν αἰσθητά τε καὶ ἀντι-
ληπτὰ καὶ καθολικά, τὰ δὲ αἰσθητικὰ καὶ ἀντιληπτικὰ
καὶ μερικά, πάντα δὲ πᾶσι περιεχόμενά τε καὶ περιτρεπόμενα τῇ ἐπαλλαγῇ τῆς περὶ ἕκαστον ποιᾶς ἰδιότητος·
τοῖς μὲν γὰρ αἰσθητοῖς περιέχεται κατὰ φύσιν τὰ αἰ-
σθητικά, τὰ δὲ αἰσθητὰ τοῖς αἰσθητικοῖς κατ᾽ αἴσθησιν,
ὡς ἀντιληπτά, καὶ πάλιν τὰ μὲν καθόλου τοῖς μερικοῖς
κατ᾽ ἀλλοίωσιν, τὰ δὲ μερικὰ τοῖς καθόλου κατ᾽ ἀνάλυσιν
περιτρεπόμενα φθείρεται· καὶ τῶν μὲν διὰ τῆς τῶν ἄλλων φθορᾶς ἡ γένεσις ἄρχεται, τῶν δὲ διὰ τῆς τῶν ἄλλων γενέσεως ἡ φθορὰ ἐπιγίνεται· τῶν γὰρ καθόλου ἡ
πρὸς ἄλληλα σύνοδος τῶν μερικῶν ποιουμένη τὴν γένεσιν, ἀλλήλων τῇ ἀλλοιώσει ἐστὶ φθορά, καὶ τῶν αὖ μερικῶν ἡ κατὰ διάλυσιν τῆς συνθέσεως πρὸς τὰ καθόλου
ἀνάλυσις, τὴν φθορὰν ἐπεισάγουσα, τῶν καθόλου ἐστὶ

they were not only taught the fulfilment of the mysteries concerning Him, which had been proclaimed through the law and
the prophets, but also that the purpose of the ineffable will of   106
God for the universe and of His divine means of achieving it
cannot be grasped by any being whatsoever, although knowledge of His great providence and judgment, through which
the universe is driven on with good order to the final end that
is foreknown by God alone, is an exception to this. All alike
are ignorant of what this final end essentially is, how it is,
what its quality is, and when it will be achieved. The only
ones who truly recognize what it alone will be are the saints,
who have purified the soul with the virtues and have thoroughly changed the whole of its intellectual inclination and
have directed it towards divine things. They have heard the
general nature of visible things, the means by which nature is
naturally constituted, all but shouting aloud, so to speak, the
final end of the present good order in nature. For,[89] the saints   B
examined the present world in all its aspects to understand it,
as far as was possible, and wisely explained the essential idea
that is inherent to the concept of embodiment, which frames
the diverse joining together of bodies to one another in the
world. In so doing, they discovered those aspects of embodiment that are perceptible and able to be grasped and that pertain to universals, and then also those faculties that perceive
and grasp and particularize. All of these are contained by and
overlap each other in the link that is formed by the specific
property that pertains to each of them. For perceptual faculties are naturally enveloped by their objects of perception,
and the objects of perception are enveloped as impressions
grasped in the moment of perception by the perceptual faculties that perceive them. Again, in overlapping each other,   C
universals are dissolved as universals by being differentiated
into particulars, and particulars are dissolved as particulars

---

89   *54. Contemplating nature with respect to the fact that the world necessarily has an end*

διαμονὴ καὶ γένεσις. Καὶ ταύτην εἶναι μαθόντες τοῦ αἰσθητοῦ κόσμου τὴν σύστασιν, τὴν εἰς ἄλληλα τῶν ἐν αὐτῷ σωμάτων, ἐξ ὧν καὶ ἐν οἷς ὑφέστηκε, δι᾽ἀλλήλων φθορὰν καὶ ἀλλοίωσιν, ἀκολούθως διὰ τῆς κατὰ φύσιν ἀστάτου καὶ ἀλλοιωτῆς καὶ ἄλλοτε ἄλλως φερομένης τε καὶ περιτρεπομένης καθόλου τῶν ἐξ ὧν συνέστηκε σωμάτων ἰδιότητος, τὴν ἐξ ἀνάγκης καθ᾽εἱρμὸν γενησομένην αὐτοῦ συντέλειαν ἐπαιδεύθησαν, οὐκ εἶναι δυνατόν, οὔτε μὴν λογικῆς συνέσεως, ἀΐδιον φάναι τὸ μὴ ὡσαύτως ἔχον ἀεί, δίχα τροπῆς καὶ τῆς οἱασοῦν ἀλλοιώσεως, ἀλλὰ μυρίοις σκεδαννύμενον τρόποις καὶ περιτρεπόμενον ὀρθῶς λογισάμενοι· * ἐντεῦθεν τῶν ὁρωμένων ὑπεράνω γενόμενοι | μεγαλοφυῶς τοῦ πάντως ἐσομένου τῶν ὅλων κατεστοχάσαντο πέρατος, ἐν ᾧ τι τῶν ὄντων οὐκέτι φέρον ἐστὶ καὶ φερόμενον, οὐδέ τις οὐδενὸς τὸ σύνολον κίνησις, παγιότητος ἀρρήτου τὴν τῶν φερομένων τε καὶ κινουμένων φοράν τε ὁρισαμένης καὶ κίνησιν· πρὸς ὃ γενέσθαι κατὰ νοῦν ἐπιθυμήσαντες ἔτι τὴν ὑπὸ φθορὰν περικείμενοι σάρκα ἐμφρόνως τὸ μεταξὺ θεοῦ καὶ ἀνθρώπων χάσμα διέβησαν, σαρκὸς καὶ κόσμου κατὰ τὴν σχέσιν ἑκουσίως ἀπογενόμενοι. Χάσμα γάρ, ὡς ἀληθῶς φοβερόν τε καὶ μέγα, μεταξὺ θεοῦ καὶ ἀνθρώπων ἐστὶν ἡ πρὸς τὸ σῶμα καὶ τὸν κόσμον τοῦτον στοργὴ καὶ διάθεσις· ὧν γενναίως τὴν στέρησιν χαίρων στέρξας ὁ Λάζαρος, ὡς δηλοῖ ἥ τε νόσος καὶ ἡ πενία, ἡ μὲν τὴν πρὸς τὸν κόσμον, ἡ δὲ τὴν πρὸς τὸ σῶμα ποιουμένη αὐτῷ ἀλλοτρίωσιν, τὴν ἐν κόλποις Ἀβραὰμ κατηξιώθη λαβεῖν ἀνάπαυσιν, τὸν τούτοις προστετηκότα πλούσιον ἔξω ἀφεὶς τῆς ἀνέσεως, μηδὲν ἄλλο τῆς διὰ σαρκὸς ὠφεληθέντα ζωῆς, πλὴν τοῦ ἐπ᾽αὐτῇ ἀπεράντως κολάζεσθαι, ὡς οὔτε τὴν

1172

by being reduced again to universals. The one begins just as   107
the other is dissolved, while one dissolves immediately as the
other begins. For as the conjunction of universals with each
other brings particulars into being, we observe the dissolution
of each of them by differentiation, and as we reduce particular
realities into universals by ceasing to think of them as particularly localized things and thus dissolve them, we observe the
continuity of universals as they become present to us. And
having learned that the sensual world's composition just is
this dissolution and differentiation of bodies into each other
and through each other, bodies out of which and in which this
composition is constituted, they have been taught accordingly
through the naturally unstable and changeable general property of the bodily reality out of which the world is established
– the property of "moving about variously and undergoing
change at various times"[90] – that the end of the world will
necessarily come about in due course. They have reasoned   D
correctly that it is not possible, neither does it belong to rational understanding, to assert, that something that is not always self-identical but rather is scattered about and overlaps
other things in all sorts of ways is eternal and without change
or any kind of differentiation.

The[91] saints acquired, in consequence, a brilliant mastery of
the visible, and then set their minds on the final limit of the   1172A
whole of reality that surely will come, in which there is no   108
longer anything that causes spatial movement or is moved
about, in which nothing has any kind of motion at all, for an
ineffable steadfastness will have set a bound to the movement
of things that are moved about in space and to the motion of
things that undergo any kind of motion. Desiring, with the

---

90   GREG. NAZ., *Or.* 14.20, PG 35.884A15-B2.
91   *55. Briefly contemplating the age to come, and what the chasm is between God and human beings, and what Lazarus and the bosom of the patriarch are*

παροῦσαν ἔτι ζωὴν ἔχοντα, ἣν ποθήσας μόνην ἠσπά-
ζετο, ἀκράτητον φύσει κατὰ τὴν ῥεῦσιν ὑπάρχουσαν,
οὔτε τῆς μελλούσης μεταλαχεῖν δυνάμενον, πρὸς ἣν ἀρ-
γὸς παντάπασι διέμεινε καὶ ἀνέραστος, μόνοις ἐκείνοις
συμφύεσθαι τοῖς αὐτὴν ὁλοσχερῶς ἀγαπήσασι πεφυκυ-
ίας καὶ τοῦ πρὸς αὐτὴν εἵνεκα πόθου πάντα τὰ ἀλγεινὰ
προθύμως μεθ'ἡδονῆς ὑπομείνασι.

Κόλπους δὲ Ἀβραὰμ ἀκούοντες τὸν ἐκ σπέρμα-
τος Ἀβραὰμ τὸν κατὰ σάρκα ἡμῖν ἐπιφανέντα νοήσο-
μεν θεόν, τὸν ὄντως πάντων χωρητικὸν καὶ πᾶσι τοῖς
ἀξίοις τῆς χάριτος, ἀναλόγως τῇ κατ'ἀρετὴν ἑκάστου
ποιότητί τε καὶ ποσότητι, οἷόν τινας διαφόρους μονὰς ἀμερῶς ἑαυτὸν ἐπιμερίζοντα καὶ τοῖς μετέχουσιν
οὐδ'ὁπωσοῦν συνδιατεμνόμενον διὰ τὴν κατὰ φύσιν
ἄτμητον ὀντότητα τῆς ἑνότητος, κἂν πάλιν διὰ τὴν
διάφορον ἀξίαν τῶν μετεχόντων ταῖς μετοχαῖς παρα-
δόξως καθ'ἕνωσιν ἄρρητον ἀφοριστικῶς ἐπιφαινόμεν-
νον οἶδεν ὁ λόγος· πρὸς ὃν οὐδεὶς διαβῆναι δυνήσεται

intellect, that this will happen, even while yet wearing flesh subject to dissolution, they have intelligently made the passage through the chasm that is set between God and human beings by willingly forgoing any habitual relation to the flesh and the world, for satisfaction in, and disposition toward, the body and this world form a truly fearful and great chasm between God and human beings. Lazarus[92] was genuinely satisfied with the denial of this satisfaction and disposition to the point of rejoicing, as both his affliction and poverty show, the one producing in him estrangement from the world and the other estrangement from the body. He was, therefore, B accounted worthy to receive rest in the bosom of Abraham when he had forgiven the rich man who had clung to the flesh and the world out of licentiousness. The rich man had received no other benefit from his life in the flesh than being endlessly chastised because of it, since he neither possessed this present life, to which he cleaved with obsessive desire, for it is ungovernable by nature because of its flow; nor was he able to have a share of the life to come, for he remained in a state of abject laziness and had no love for it, whereas the life to come springs forth and becomes the natural life of those who have loved it absolutely and have willingly endured with pleasure every painful experience in their desire for it.

When we hear "bosom of Abraham," we should understand it to mean God, who has appeared to us in the flesh from the seed of Abraham and truly contains all things and parcels Himself out, as it were, as diverse habitations, without dividing Himself into parts, to all those who are worthy of grace, in the way that is ideally suited to the quality and quantity of each one's virtue. Moreover, He is not carved up thereby in any way amongst those who partake of Him because of the naturally indivisible integrity of His unity, even if, on the contrary, the Word would appear to be separated out, para-

109

C

92   Cf. Lk 16.19–31.

θρύψει χαίρων σαρκὸς καὶ τῆς αὐτοῦ μακαρίας δόξης
τῇ τοῦ κόσμου ἀπάτῃ πλέον ἡδόμενος, οὐδὲ στήσεται
μετὰ τοῦ τὸν κόσμον νικήσαντος ὁ τῷ κόσμῳ ἡττηθεὶς
καὶ ἐπ'αὐτῷ κακῶς εἰδὼς ἀγαλλόμενος. Οὐκ εἶναι γὰρ
ἄξιον ἔκρινεν ἡ θεία δικαιοσύνη τοὺς τῇ ζωῇ ταύτῃ
τὰ κατὰ τὸν ἄνθρωπον περιγράφοντας καὶ πλούτῳ καὶ
ὑγείᾳ σώματος καὶ τοῖς ἄλλοις ἀξιώμασιν ἀβρυνομένους
καὶ τοῦτο μόνον μακάριον κρίνοντας, τὰ δὲ τῆς ψυχῆς
ἀγαθὰ παρ'οὐδὲν τιθεμένους, τῶν θείων καὶ αἰωνίων μεταλαχεῖν ἀγαθῶν, ὧν οὐδόλως ἐφρόντισαν, διὰ τὴν
πολλὴν περὶ τὰ ὑλικὰ σπουδὴν ἀγνοήσαντας ὅσον
πλούτου καὶ ὑγείας καὶ τῶν ἄλλων προσκαίρων ἀγαθῶν
αἱ ἀρεταὶ ὑπερέχουσιν. * Μόναι γὰρ καὶ σὺν τοῖς ἄλλοις αἱ ἀρεταὶ μακάριον ποιοῦσιν τὸν ἄνθρωπον, μετὰ μὲν
τῶν ἄλλων κατὰ | πλάτος, ὥς τις ἔφη τῶν τὰ θεῖα σοφῶν,   1173
μόναι δὲ καὶ καθ'ἑαυτὰς κατὰ περιγραφήν. Τῶν γὰρ ὄντων
τὰ μὲν κατὰ περιγραφὴν νοεῖται, ὡς δίπηχυ, τὰ δὲ κατὰ
πλάτος, ὡς σωρός· σωροῦ γὰρ κἂν δύο μεδίμνους ἀφέλῃς,
τὸ λειπόμενον μένει σωρός, καὶ τῆς κατὰ πλάτος μακαριότητος ἂν ἀφέλῃς τὰ τοῦ σώματος καὶ τῶν ἐκτὸς ἀγαθά,
καταλίπῃς δὲ μόνας τὰς ἀρετάς, μένει καὶ οὕτως ἀνελλι-
πὲς τὸ μακάριον· αὐτάρκης γὰρ καὶ καθ'ἑαυτὴν τῷ ἔχοντι
πρὸς εὐδαιμονίαν ἡ ἀρετή. Πᾶς οὖν κακὸς ἄθλιος, κἂν πάντα συλλήβδην ἔχῃ τὰ λεγόμενα τῆς γῆς ἀγαθά, τῶν ἀρετῶν ἐστερημένος· καὶ πᾶς ἀγαθὸς μακάριος, κἂν πάντων
ἐστέρηται τῶν ἐπὶ γῆς ἀγαθῶν, ἔχων τῆς ἀρετῆς τὴν
λαμπρότητα, μεθ'ἧς Λάζαρος τὴν ἐν κόλποις Ἀβραὰμ
ἀνάπαυσιν ἔχων ἀγάλλεται.

doxically so because of His ineffable unity, when those who
participate in Him do so in accordance with their different
degrees of worthiness. No one who rejoices in the wanton-
ness of the flesh and who takes more pleasure in the deceit
of the world than in His blessed glory is able to pass over to
Him, neither will the one who has yielded to the world and
who wickedly and knowingly exults in a worldly way stand
with the one who has overcome the world.[93] For divine righteousness judges those who enclose human reality within this
life and "take excessive pride in wealth," bodily health, "and   D
other things considered valuable," and who judge this alone
to be "blessed", "but who take no care for the goods of the
soul," to be unworthy of sharing in divine and eternal goodness. Indeed, those who are ignorant of just how superior "the
virtues" are to "wealth, health, and other" temporal goods
because of their great striving for material things know absolutely nothing of this goodness. For[94] "only the virtues along
with these other things make a person blessed, though we say
'with other things' in an inexact sense," as someone who is   1173A
wise in divine realities has said, "when the virtues are simply
sufficient in themselves in the strict sense. Indeed, some qualities are understood to belong to things in a strict sense, two
cubits, for example, whereas others are understood inexactly,
like a heap, for even if you remove two measures from the
heap, what is left over is still a heap. So, if you remove the
goods of the body and of what is external from blessedness
conceived inexactly, you would leave behind only virtues,   110
and thus blessedness remains" lacking nothing, "for virtue is
its own source and sufficient in itself for happiness" for the one
who has it. Therefore, every wicked person is wretched even if
he should possess all of the goods of the earth here mentioned
at the same time" yet is deprived of the virtues, and "every

---

93   Cf. Jn 16.33.
94   *56. Contemplating the virtues*

* **Οὕτω μὲν οὖν τὴν κτίσιν κατανοήσαντες οἱ ἅγιοι**   1176
καὶ τὴν εὐκοσμίαν αὐτῆς καὶ τὴν ἀναλογίαν καὶ τὴν
χρείαν, ἣν ἕκαστον παρέχεται τῷ παντί, καὶ ὡς τέλεια
πάντα σοφῶς τε καὶ προνοητικῶς, καθ'ὃν δεδημιούρ-
γηνται λόγον, δεδημιουργημένα, καὶ ὡς οὐχ'οἷόν τε
ἄλλως γε καλῶς ἔχειν τὰ γενόμενα παρ'ὃ νῦν ἔχει,
προσθήκης ἢ ἀφαιρέσεως πρὸς τὸ καλῶς ἄλλως ἔχειν
μὴ δεόμενα, τὸν δημιουργὸν ἐκ τῶν αὐτοῦ ποιημάτων
ἐδιδάχθησαν· οὕτω δὲ τὴν διαμονὴν τήν τε **τάξιν καὶ τὴν**
θέσιν **τῶν γεγονότων καὶ τὴν διεξαγωγήν, καθ'ἣν πάν-**
τα κατὰ τὸ οἰκεῖον ἕκαστα εἶδος ἕστηκεν ἀσύγχυτα
καὶ παντὸς ἐλεύθερα φυρμοῦ, τήν τε τῶν ἄστρων φορὰν
κατὰ τὸν αὐτὸν τρόπον **γινομένην,** μηδὲν μηδέποτε δι-
αλλάττουσαν, καὶ τὸν κύκλον τοῦ ἐνιαυτοῦ **κατὰ** τὴν **τῶν**
αὐτῶν ἀπὸ τοῦ αὐτοῦ εἰς τὸν αὐτὸν τόπον ἀποκατάστα-
σιν **εὐτάκτως** γινόμενον, τῶν τε νυκτῶν καὶ τῶν ἡμερῶν
τὴν κατ'ἔτος ἰσότητα, παρὰ μέρος ἑκατέρας αὐξανομένης
τε καὶ μειουμένης, οὔτε πλείονι οὔτε ἐλάττονι μέτρῳ **τῆς**
αὐξήσεως αὐταῖς ἢ τῆς μειώσεως ἐπιγινομένης, προνο-
ητὴν εἰκότως ἐπίστευσαν εἶναι τῶν ὄντων, ὃν καὶ θεὸν
καὶ δημιουργὸν τῶν ὅλων ἐπέγνωσαν. * **Τίς γάρ, τὸ**
κάλλος καὶ τὸ μέγεθος τῶν τοῦ θεοῦ κτισμάτων θεώ-
μενος, οὐκ εὐθὺς αὐτὸν γενεσιουργὸν ἐννοήσει, ὡς ἀρ-
χὴν καὶ αἰτίαν τῶν ὄντων καὶ ποιητήν, καὶ πρὸς αὐτὸν
μόνον ἀναδραμεῖται τῇ διανοίᾳ, ταῦτα ἀφεὶς κάτω, ὅτι
μὴ δὲ πέφυκε τῆς διανοίας χωρεῖν τὴν ὅλην διάβασιν,
λαβεῖν ποθῶν ἀμέσως ὃν διὰ μέσων τῶν ἔργων ἐγνώρι-

good person is blessed,"[95] even if he has been deprived of all of the goods of the earth yet possesses the radiance of virtue. It is in this radiance that Lazarus fervently rejoices in his rest in the bosom of Abraham.   B

Finitude

In[96] this way, therefore, the saints were taught about the fashioner from the things that have been made by Him as they came to an understanding of the intellectual structure of creation, its good order, ideal proportion, and functioning, which each thing provides to the universe. By understanding that all things have been fashioned complete with wisdom and providence, in line with the essential idea that has governed their fashioning, they were also taught that the things that have come to be are not such that they could exist differently and more beautifully than they do now, for they require nothing more nor less such that they could exist beautifully in some other way. They understood in this way the intellectual structure of "the stability, arrangement, and placement" of the things that have come into being, as well as their comportment, in accordance with which C everything was established in its own form, unmixed and free from all confusion: "the revolution of the stars" proceeding in a uniform way, "never altering in any way, and the cycle of the year" proceeding in an orderly manner with the "restoration" of the stars to the same point from which they started, "the equal number of nights and days in a year, each increasing 111 and decreasing as its portion is determined, with their increase and decrease proceeding on by neither a greater nor a lesser measure."[97] From all this they reasonably believed that there

---

95   NEM. EMES., *Nat. Hom.* 43, p. 129.1–15.
96   *57. Contemplating nature, the means by which the saints learn about God from created things*
97   NEM. EMES., *Nat. Hom.* 42, p. 120.25–121.5.

σε, καὶ τὴν περὶ τοῦ ἄναρχον εἶναι τὸν κόσμον ἑαυτοῦ
πλάνην | ἑτοίμως ἀπώσεται, λογιζόμενος ἀληθῶς ὅτι   1177
πᾶν κινούμενον πάντως καὶ ἤρξατο τῆς κινήσεως, πᾶσα
δὲ κίνησις οὐκ ἄναρχος, ἐπειδὴ οὐδὲ ἀναίτιος – ἀρχὴν
γὰρ ἔχει τὸ κινοῦν καὶ αἰτίαν ἔχει τὸ καλοῦν τε καὶ ἕλ-
κον πρὸς ὃ καὶ κινεῖται τέλος –; Εἰ δὲ πάσης κινήσεως
παντὸς κινουμένου τὸ κινοῦν ἐστιν ἀρχή, καὶ τέλος ἡ
πρὸς ἣν φέρεται τὸ κινούμενον αἰτία – οὐδὲν γὰρ ἀναι-
τίως κινεῖται –, οὐδὲν δὲ τῶν ὄντων ἀκίνητον, εἰ μὴ
τὸ πρώτως κινοῦν – τὸ γὰρ πρώτως κινοῦν πάντως
ἀκίνητον ὅτι καὶ ἄναρχον –, οὐδὲν ἄρα τῶν ὄντων ἐστὶν
ἄναρχον, ὅτι μὴ καὶ ἀκίνητον.

Πάντα γὰρ κινεῖται τὰ ὁπωσοῦν ὄντα, δίχα τῆς μόνης
καὶ ἀκινήτου καὶ ὑπὲρ πάντα αἰτίας, τὰ μὲν νοερά τε καὶ
λογικὰ γνωστικῶς τε καὶ ἐπιστημονικῶς, ὅτι μὴ αὐτο-
γνῶσις ἢ αὐτοεπιστήμη ἐστίν – οὔτε γὰρ οὐσία αὐτῶν
ἡ γνῶσις αὐτῶν ἐστι καὶ ἡ ἐπιστήμη, ἀλλ᾽ ἕξεις, τῇ
αὐτῶν οὐσίᾳ ἐπιθεωρούμεναι, ἐκ τῆς κατὰ νοῦν καὶ λόγον (τὰς συστατικὰς αὐτῶν λέγω δυνάμεις) ὀρθῆς κρίσεως ἐπιγενόμεναι –, * ἀλλὰ καὶ αὐτὴ ἡ ἁπλῶς λεγομένη οὐσία· οὐ μόνον ἡ τῶν ἐν γενέσει καὶ φθορᾷ κατὰ
γένεσιν κινεῖται καὶ φθοράν, ἀλλὰ καὶ ἡ τῶν ὄντων

is one who makes provision for existing things, whom they also recognized to be God, the fashioner of the whole of reality. For[98] who, seeing *the beauty and grandeur of the creations* D of God, will not immediately think of Him as the *originator* (Wis 13.5), source, cause, and maker of what exists, and then run in thought toward Him alone, leaving these things behind, for they do not naturally allow thought to complete its journey, since he desires to receive without mediation what he has come to know through intermediate works? Will he not also readily cast away from himself the error that the world has no source? He will reason accurately that everything that 1177A is in motion must also have had a source of its motion, and that there is no motion that is without a source, since it is not without a cause, for it has as source that which produces motion and it has as cause the final end that calls and attracts it, towards which it is also moved. If that which produces motion is the source of every motion of anything that is moved, and if the cause towards which a moving thing is moved along is its final end – for nothing is moved without a cause – and there is no being that is without motion, except that which produces motion first – for that which produces motion first is obviously unmoved, since it is also without a source[99]– then there is no being that is without a source, since there is also no being that is unmoved.

For all existing things whatsoever are moved, apart from the 112 sole and unmoved cause that is also beyond all things. Intellectual and rational beings are moved with respect to knowledge and understanding, since they are not self-sufficient with respect to either knowledge or understanding – for neither their knowledge nor their understanding is their essence but rather B are habitual states, which are observed as pertaining to their

---

98   58. *Contemplating nature with respect to the fact that the world and everything else after God have a source and a becoming*
99   Cf. Arist., *Physica* VIII.5, 258b4–9.

ἀπάντων καὶ κεκίνηται καὶ κινεῖται τῷ κατὰ διαστολὴν καὶ συστολὴν λόγῳ τε καὶ τρόπῳ. Κινεῖται γὰρ ἀπὸ
τοῦ γενικωτάτου γένους διὰ τῶν γενικωτέρων γενῶν
εἰς τὰ εἴδη, δι'ὧν καὶ εἰς ἃ διαιρεῖσθαι πέφυκε προϊοῦ-
σα, μέχρι τῶν εἰδικωτάτων εἰδῶν, οἷς περατοῦται ἡ
κατ'αὐτὴν διαστολή, τὸ εἶναι αὐτῆς πρὸς τὸ κάτω περι-
γράφουσα, καὶ συνάγεται πάλιν ἀπὸ τῶν εἰδικωτάτων
εἰδῶν, διὰ τῶν γενικωτέρων ἀναποδίζουσα, μέχρι τοῦ
γενικωτάτου γένους, ᾧ περατοῦται ἡ κατ'αὐτὴν συστολή, πρὸς τὸ ἄνω τὸ εἶναι αὐτῆς ὁρίζουσα· καὶ λοιπόν,
διχόθεν περιγραφομένη, ἄνωθέν τε λέγω καὶ κάτωθεν,
ἀρχὴν καὶ τέλος ἔχουσα δείκνυται, τὸν τῆς ἀπειρίας οὐδόλως ἐπιδέξασθαι δυναμένη λόγον. Ὡσαύτως δὲ καὶ ἡ
ποσότης· οὐ μόνον ἡ τῶν ἐν γενέσει καὶ φθορᾷ, παντὶ
τρόπῳ ᾧ πέφυκε θεωρεῖσθαι, κατ'αὔξησιν κινεῖται καὶ
μείωσιν, ἀλλὰ καὶ ἡ πᾶσα καὶ πάντων τῷ κατ'ἄνεσιν
καὶ ἐπίτασιν λόγῳ κινουμένη καὶ ταῖς κατὰ μέρος διαφοραῖς κατὰ διαστολὴν εἰδοποιουμένη περιγράφεται,
τὸ ἐπ'ἄπειρον χεῖσθαι οὐκ ἔχουσα, καὶ συνάγεται πάλιν
ἀναποδίζουσα, τὸ κατ'αὐτὰς ἀλλ'οὐ τὸ συμφυὲς εἶδος
ἀπολύουσα. Ὁμοίως δὲ καὶ ἡ ποιότης· οὐ μόνον ἡ τῶν

essence and are added to it through the correct judgment of
intellect and reason (which are the capacities that constitute
them) – but[100] what is simply called the essence itself is moved
as well. Not only is the essence of what exists in the realm of
coming to be and destruction moved when it comes into being
and is destroyed, but it is also the case that the essence of all
beings has been moved and continues to be moved in terms of
the logic and modality of expansion and contraction. For it is   C
moved from the most general genus through descending levels
of generality to the species, through which and into which it
is naturally divided as it proceeds, until it arrives at the most
specific species, by which the expansion of an essence is limited, for its existence is thus enclosed in relation to what is below. It is gathered again from the most specific species, returns
through the more general, until it arrives at the most general
genus, by which the contraction of an essence is limited, for
its existence is defined in this way in relation to what is above.
And finally, being enclosed on both sides, I mean from above
and below, it is shown to have a source and final end and to
be absolutely unable to exhibit the very thing that defines
infinity. This is the case with quantity as well. The quantity   113
of what exists in the realm of coming to be and destruction
is not only moved in terms of increase and decrease in every
mode in which it is naturally observed; it is also the case that   D
the quantity of every being, in being moved with respect to
the logic of relaxation and tension, and in receiving its form, is
enclosed by the particular differences that result from expansion, for it cannot be poured out to infinity, and in returning
it is gathered together again, resolving the species that exists
as a differentiated thing but not the species in its nature as
such. A similar dynamic holds with respect to quality as well:
not only is the quality of what exists in the realm of coming to

---

100   59. Contemplating the contraction and expansion of substance, quality, and quantity, in accordance with which things without a source cannot
exist

ἐν γενέσει καὶ φθορᾷ κινεῖται κατ'ἀλλοίωσιν, ἀλλὰ καὶ
ἡ πᾶσα καὶ πάντων τῷ τρεπτῷ τε καὶ σκεδαστῷ τῆς
κατ'αὐτὴν διαφορᾶς κινουμένη, διαστολὴν καὶ συστο-
λὴν ἐπιδέχεται. Οὐδεὶς δὲ τὸ πεφυ|κὸς σκεδάννυσθαί   1180
τε καὶ συνάγεσθαι λόγῳ ἢ ἐνεργείᾳ εἴποι ἂν εὐφρονῶν
ἀκίνητον εἶναι παντάπασιν – εἰ δὲ μὴ ἀκίνητον, οὐδὲ
ἄναρχον· εἰ δὲ μὴ ἄναρχον, οὐδὲ ἀγένητον δηλονότι –,
ἀλλ'ὥσπερ οἶδεν ἠργμένον κινήσεως τὸ κινούμενον,
οὕτω καὶ τῆς πρὸς τὸ εἶναι γενέσεως ἦρχθαι τὸ γεγενημένον ἐπίσταται καὶ ἐκ τοῦ μόνου καὶ ἑνὸς ἀγενήτου τε
καὶ ἀκινήτου τὸ εἶναί τε καὶ τὸ κινεῖσθαι λαβόν· τὸ δὲ
κατὰ τὴν τοῦ εἶναι γένεσιν ἠργμένον οὐδαμῶς ἄναρχον
εἶναι δύναται.

* Ἵνα δὲ ἐάσω λέγειν ὅτι καὶ αὐτὸ τὸ εἶναι τῶν ὄντων
τὸ πῶς εἶναι ἔχον, ἀλλ'οὐχ'ἁπλῶς, ὅπερ ἐστὶ πρῶτον
εἶδος περιγραφῆς, ἰσχυρόν τε καὶ μέγα πρὸς ἀπόδειξιν
τοῦ ἦρχθαι κατ'οὐσίαν καὶ γένεσιν τὰ ὄντα, τίς ἀγνο-
εῖ ὅτι παντὸς τοῦ ὁπωσοῦν ὄντος, πλὴν τοῦ θείου καὶ
μόνου, τοῦ καὶ ὑπὲρ αὐτὸ τὸ εἶναι κυρίως ὑπάρχοντος,
προεπινοεῖται τὸ ποῦ, ᾧ πάντη τε καὶ πάντως ἐξ ἀνάγκης συνεπινοεῖται τὸ ποτέ· οὐ γὰρ τοῦ ποτὲ διωρισμέ-
νον κατὰ στέρησιν δυνατόν ἐστιν ἐπινοῆσαι τὸ ποῦ· τῶν
γὰρ ἅμα ταῦτά ἐστιν, ἐπειδὴ καὶ ὧν οὐκ ἄνευ τυγχά-
νουσιν. Εἰ δὲ τοῦ ποῦ τὸ ποτέ, ᾧ συνεπινοεῖσθαι πέφυκεν, οὐδαμῶς διώρισται κατὰ στέρησιν, πάντα δὲ ὑπὸ
τὸ ποῦ ὡς ἐν τόπῳ ὄντα δείκνυται – οὐ γὰρ ὑπὲρ τὸ
πᾶν αὐτὸ τὸ πᾶν τοῦ παντός (τοῦτο γὰρ πως καὶ ἄλογον
καὶ ἀδύνατον, αὐτὸ τὸ πᾶν ὑπὲρ τὸ ἑαυτοῦ πᾶν εἶναι θεσπίζειν), ἀλλ'ὑφ'ἑαυτοῦ ἐν ἑαυτῷ τὴν περιγραφὴν ἔχον
μετὰ τὴν πάντα περιγράφουσαν τοῦ παναιτίου ἄπειρον
δύναμιν, αὐτὸ τὸ πέρας ἑαυτοῦ τὸ ἐξώτερον· ὅπερ καὶ
τόπος ἐστὶ τοῦ παντός, καθὼς καὶ ὁρίζονταί τινες τὸν

be and destruction moved in terms of variation, but also every quality of everything indeed, in being moved by the alteration and scattering that come from the difference that pertains to it, admits of expansion and contraction. No one in his right   1180A mind would say that what is naturally scattered and gathered together is entirely unmoved in its essential idea or activity – if something is not unmoved, it is not without source; if it is not without source, then clearly it is not without becoming – but just as you know that what is moved has a source of the beginning of its movement, so also you understand, from the fact of its coming into existence, that what has come into being and has received both its existence and its motion from the single and only one who is without becoming and without motion had a source for its beginning. That which has begun to exist by coming into being cannot in any way exist without a source.

I[101] will leave to the side the fact that the existence of beings   1180B itself is conditioned in a certain way and does not exist simply, which is the first kind of limiting enclosure, a fact that makes a strong and formidable demonstration that existing things   114 have a beginning both to their essence and to their coming to be. Even so, who doesn't know that the concept "where," with which the concept "when" is likewise absolutely and in every respect necessarily conceived, is conceptually prior to any existing thing whatsoever, except the divine and unique one, which, properly speaking, exists beyond even existence itself? Indeed, it is not possible to conceptualize "where" in a definition that does not include the notion of "when," and all beings exist together with these two, since they do not occur without them.   C If "when" is never defined without the concept of "where," with which it is naturally conceptualized, then everything is shown

---

101   60. *Demonstration that everything whatsoever except God must be in a place and because of this is necessarily also in time, and that what is in a place must also have had a temporal beginning to its existence*

τόπον, λέγοντες· τόπος ἐστὶν ἡ ἔξω τοῦ παντὸς περιφέρεια ἢ ἡ ἔξω τοῦ παντὸς θέσις ἢ τὸ πέρας τοῦ περιέχοντος, ἐν ᾧ περιέχεται τὸ περιεχόμενον –, καὶ ὑπὸ τὸ ποτὲ
ὡς ἐν χρόνῳ πάντως ὄντα συναποδειχθήσεται, ἐπειδὴ
μὴ ἁπλῶς ἀλλὰ πῶς τὸ εἶναι ἔχουσι πάντα ὅσα μετὰ
θεὸν τὸ εἶναι ἔχει, καὶ διατοῦτο οὐκ ἄναρχα· πᾶν γὰρ
ὅπερ καθ᾽ὁτιοῦν τὸν τοῦ πῶς ἐπιδέχεται λόγον, κἂν εἰ
ἔστιν, ἀλλ᾽οὐκ ἦν. Ὅθεν τὸ θεῖον εἶναι λέγοντες οὐ τὸ
πῶς εἶναι λέγομεν, καὶ διατοῦτο καὶ τὸ ἔστι καὶ τὸ ἦν
ἁπλῶς καὶ ἀορίστως καὶ ἀπολελυμένως ἐπ᾽αὐτοῦ λέ-
γομεν· ἀνεπίδεκτον γὰρ παντὸς λόγου καὶ νοήματος τὸ
θεῖόν ἐστι, καθ᾽ὃ οὔτε κατηγοροῦντες αὐτοῦ τὸ εἶναι λέγομεν αὐτὸ εἶναι· ἐξ αὐτοῦ γὰρ τὸ εἶναι, ἀλλ᾽οὐκ αὐτὸ
τὸ εἶναι· ὑπὲρ γάρ ἐστι καὶ αὐτοῦ τοῦ εἶναι, τοῦ τε πῶς
καὶ ἁπλῶς λεγομένου τε καὶ νοουμένου. Εἰ δὲ πῶς, ἀλ-
λ᾽οὐχ᾽ἁπλῶς ἔχει τὰ ὄντα τὸ εἶναι, ὥσπερ ὑπὸ τὸ ποῦ
εἶναι διὰ τὴν θέσιν καὶ τὸ πέρας | τῶν ἐπ᾽αὐτοῖς κατὰ   1181
φύσιν λόγων, καὶ ὑπὸ τὸ ποτὲ πάντως εἶναι διὰ τὴν ἀρχὴν ἐπιδείξεται.

to be subject to the notion of "where" since everything is in a place. Indeed, the totality of the universe is not beyond the universe itself (for how irrational and impossible that would be, to declare that the universe itself is beyond its own totality) but rather possesses self-enclosure from itself after the all-enclosing infinite power of the cause of all, which is its outer limit. This is the place of the universe, as some would define place, by saying that the surface outside of the universe or the position outside of the universe or "the limit of what encompasses," in "which that which is encompassed is encompassed," "is place."[102] Moreover, everything all together will be shown to be subject to the concept "when," since everything is certainly in time, for all things have existence not simply but rather as conditioned in some way inasmuch as they have existence after God, and because of this they are not without a source; anything what- D
soever that admits the idea of a condition into its definition, even if it does exist now, has not always been. For this reason, when we say the Divine exists, we are not saying that it exists in a certain conditioned way, and because of this we attribute "is" and "was" to the Divine simply, indefinitely, and absolutely, for there is no word or thought that applies to the Divine, 115
and because of this we say It exists though we are not thereby attributing existence to It. Rather, existence derives from It, but It is not Itself existence. It is beyond even existence itself, whether when spoken and thought of in a conditioned way or simply. If beings have a conditioned manner of existence and do not exist simply, just as they possess existence as subject to the concept "where" because of their specific location and the limit of the essential ideas that pertain to them by nature, then 1181A
they must be subject to the concept of "when," because they have a beginning from a source.

---

102   NEM. EMES., *Nat. Hom.* 3, p. 41.22–42.1.

* Καὶ πάλιν· εἰ ἡ πάντων οὐσία, πολλῶν ὄντων τῶν πάντων, ἄπειρος εἶναι οὐ δύναται – πέρας γὰρ ἔχει αὐτῶν τῶν πολλῶν ὄντων τὴν ἐν πλήθει ποσότητα, περιγράφουσαν αὐτῆς τόν τε τοῦ εἶναι καὶ τοῦ πῶς εἶναι λόγον· οὐ γὰρ ἄφετος ἡ τῶν πάντων οὐσία –, οὐδὲ ἡ τοῦ καθ'ἕκαστον δῆλον ὑπόστασις ἔσται δίχα περιγραφῆς, ἀλλήλαις τῷ ἀριθμῷ καὶ τῇ οὐσίᾳ κατὰ λόγον περιγεγραμμέναι. Εἰ δὲ περιγραφῆς οὐδὲν τῶν ὄντων ἐλεύθερον, πάντα τὰ ὄντα δηλονότι ἀναλόγως ἑαυτοῖς καὶ τὸ ποτὲ εἶναι καὶ ποῦ εἶναι εἴληφε – τούτων γὰρ ἄνευ τὸ παράπαν οὐδὲν εἶναι δυνήσεται, οὐκ οὐσία οὐ ποσότης οὐ ποιότης οὐ σχέσις οὐ ποίησις οὐ πάθος οὐ κίνησις οὐχ'ἕξις οὐχ'ἕτερόν τι τῶν οἷς τὸ πᾶν περικλείουσιν οἱ περὶ ταῦτα δεινοί –, οὐδὲν οὖν τῶν ὄντων ἄναρχον, ᾧ τι ἕτερον προεπινοεῖσθαι, οὐδὲ ἀπερίγραφον, ᾧ τι ἕτερον συνεπινοεῖσθαι δύναται. Εἰ δὲ τῶν ὄντων οὐδὲν ἄναρχον ἢ ἀπερίγραφον, ὡς ἔδειξεν ἀκολούθως τῇ φύσει τῶν ὄντων ἑπόμενος ὁ λόγος, ἦν πάντως ποτὲ ὅτε τι τῶν ὄντων οὐκ ἦν. Εἰ δὲ οὐκ ἦν, πάντως γέγονεν, εἴπερ οὐκ ἦν· οὐ γὰρ ἄμφω ἐνδέχεται καὶ εἶναι καὶ γενέσθαι χωρὶς τροπῆς καὶ ἀλλοιώσεως. Εἰ γὰρ ἦν καὶ γέγονεν, ἐτράπη, εἰς ὅπερ οὐκ ἦν μεταχωρῆσαν κατὰ τὴν γένεσιν, ἢ ἠλλοιώθη, προσθήκην οὗ ἐστέρητο κάλλους ἐπιδεξάμενον· πᾶν δὲ τρεπόμενον ἢ ἀλλοιούμενον ἢ ἐλλιπὲς εἴδους, αὐτοτελὲς εἶναι οὐ δύναται. Τὸ δὲ μὴ ὂν αὐτοτελὲς ἑτέρου πάντως προσδεηθήσεται τοῦ παρέχοντος αὐτῷ τὴν τελειότητα· καὶ ἔστι τέλειον μὲν τὸ τοιοῦτον, ἀλλ'οὐκ αὐτοτελὲς διὰ τὸ μὴ φύσει, μεθέξει δέ, τὸ τέλειον ἔχειν. Τὸ δὲ ἑτέρου προσδεόμενον πρὸς τελείωσιν, καὶ πρὸς αὐτὸ τὸ εἶναι πολλῷ μᾶλλον προσδεηθήσεται. Εἰ γὰρ εἴδους κρείττων, ὥς φασιν, ἡ οὐσία καθέστηκε, ταύτην δὲ ἑαυτῷ παρασχεῖν ἢ ἁπλῶς ἔχειν δεδύνηται ἐκεῖνο τὸ ὄν, ὅπερ αὐτοὶ φάναι βούλονται, πῶς πρὸς τὸ ἔχειν ἁπλῶς ἢ παρασχεῖν ἑαυτῷ τὸ ἧττον, φημὶ δὴ τὸ εἶδος, οὐκ ἐπήρκεσεν; Εἰ δὲ πρὸς τὸ παρασχεῖν ἑαυτῷ τὸ ἧττον ἢ ἁπλῶς ἔχειν ἐκεῖνο τὸ ὄν, ὅπερ

Further,[103] if the whole of being cannot be infinite, even if there are many individual things – for it has as its limit the quantifiable amount of the many things themselves, which encloses the essential idea of the existence of the whole of being and the manner of its existence, for the being of all things is not free of all constraint – neither, clearly, will the actual existence of each thing be completely unenclosed, since B they are, by definition, enclosed by each other with respect to number and substance. If no being is free of enclosure, then it is clear that all beings have assumed temporal and spatial existence in the way that is ideally suited to them, for nothing at all could exist without these, neither essence, nor quantity, quality, relation, creativity, affectivity, motion, habit, or anything else with which experts in these matters delimit the universe.[104] Therefore if something has something else that can be conceived of before it, it is not without source, and neither is it unenclosed if something else can be conceptualized along with it. If nothing is without source and unenclosed, as the foregoing argument showed sequentially for the nature of beings, there must have been a "when" when a certain ex- 116 isting thing did not exist. And if a thing did not exist, then it must have come into being, if indeed it was not, for it C does not have the quality of either being or becoming without change and alteration. If something was and has become, it has changed by having gone over to what it was not through becoming, or it has been altered by receiving the addition of a good that it lacked, for anything that is changed or altered or has something left out of its form cannot be complete in and of itself. That which is not complete in and of itself will require, of necessity, something else to provide completeness to it; such a thing is then complete, but not complete in and

---

103   61. *Demonstration that it is impossible for the universe to be to be infinite, and because of this the universe is not without source if it is something that has existence according to a quantifiable amount*
104   Cf. Arist., *Cat.* 4.1b26–27.

εἴτε οὐσίαν εἴτε ὕλην καλεῖν βούλονται οἱ τὸ ἄναρχον
τοῖς μετὰ θεὸν καὶ ἐκ θεοῦ προσάπτειν τολμῶντες – οὐ
γὰρ περὶ τούτου διαφερόμεθα –, οὐκ ἐπήρκησε, πῶς τὸ
κρεῖττον, αὐτὸ τὸ εἶναί φημι, ἢ ἁπλῶς ἢ παρ’ἑαυτοῦ
ἔχειν δεδύνηται τὸ πρὸς τὸ ἔχειν τὸ ἧττον ἀδυνατῆσαν;
Εἰ δὲ παρ’ἑαυτῆς ἢ ἁπλῶς ἔχειν τὸ ἧττον οὐδαμῶς ἡ
ὕλη δεδύνηται, πολλῷ μᾶλλον | αὐτὸ τὸ εἶναι ἁπλῶς ἢ   1184
πῶς παρ’ἑαυτῆς ἔχειν οὐ δυνηθήσεται. Ἆρ’οὖν ἡ πρὸς τὸ
ἔχειν, ὡς δέδεικται, τὸ ἧττον, λέγω δὲ τὸ εἶδος, ἀτονή-
σασα, οὐδὲ τὸ κρεῖττον, αὐτὸ τὸ εἶναί φημι, κἂν ὁπωσοῦν ἔχειν δυνηθείη ποτέ. Εἰ δὲ τοῦτο, πάντως ἐκ θεοῦ
τὸ εἶναι τοῖς οὖσι καὶ τὸ εἶδος δεδώρηται, ἐπείπερ εἰσίν.
Εἰ δὲ ἐκ θεοῦ πᾶσα οὐσία καὶ ὕλη καὶ εἶδος ἅπαν ἐστίν,
οὐδεὶς ἂν μὴ πάντη σώφρονος λογισμοῦ ἐστερημένος
εἰπεῖν ἀνάσχοιτο ἄναρχον ἢ ἀγένητον τὴν ὕλην, θεὸν εἰδὼς τῶν ὄντων ποιητὴν καὶ δημιουργόν.

* Καὶ πάλιν· εἰ ἦν, ὥς τινές φασιν, ἡ ὕλη, οὐ γέγονε
δηλονότι· εἰ δὲ μὴ γέγονεν, οὐδὲ κινεῖται· εἰ δὲ μὴ κινεῖται, οὔτε τοῦ εἶναι ἤρξατο· εἰ δὲ τοῦ εἶναι μὴ ἤρξατο, πάντως ἄναρχον· εἰ δὲ ἄναρχον, καὶ ἄπειρον· εἰ δὲ
ἄπειρον, πάντως καὶ ἀκίνητον – ἀκίνητον γὰρ πάντως
τὸ ἄπειρον· οὐ γὰρ ἔχει ποῦ κινηθῆναι τὸ μὴ ὁριζόμενον –. Εἰ δὲ τοῦτο, δύο πάντως τὰ ἄπειρα καὶ ἄναρχα

of itself, because it has its completion not by nature but by participation. That which requires something else for its completion will require all the more something for its very existence. For if, as they say, being is superior to form, and if what exists has been able to provide its own being or to possess it simply, which is what they want to say, how was it not sufficient to possess simply or provide for itself the lesser reality of form? If that existing thing, which is called either   D "substance" or "matter" by those who dare to apply the quality of being without a source to what comes after God and is from Him – for we do not make a distinction concerning this – is not sufficient to provide the lesser reality for itself or to possess it simply, how is it, when it was unable to possess a lesser reality, able to possess either simply or from itself what is superior, existence itself? If matter is not at all able to possess a lesser reality, either from itself or simply, all the more will it be unable to possess existence itself, whether   1184A simply or in some conditioned manner, from itself. Therefore, |117 since it is too weak, as it has been shown, to possess the lesser reality of form, it would never in any way be able to possess what is superior, existence itself. If this is so, then existence and form must have been given to beings by God, if indeed they exist at all. If all substance, matter, and every form are from God, then no intelligent person who has not completely lost his mind would maintain that matter is without a source or did not come into being, for he would know that God is the creator and fashioner of what exists.

To[105] continue with this line of thought, if matter has always   B existed, as some say, then clearly it has not come into being; if it has not come into being, then it is not moved; if it is not moved, then it has no beginning of its existence; if it has no

---

105   62. *Demonstration that everything that is moved, or is always seen together with another distinction of substance, cannot be infinite, and that duality is not a source and is not without source, and that the Unity alone is properly source and without source*

καὶ ἀκίνητα, θεὸς καὶ ὕλη· ὅπερ εἶναι ἀμήχανον. Δυὰς
γὰρ οὔτε ἄπειρος οὔτε ἄναρχος οὔτε ἀκίνητος, οὔτε
μὴν ἀρχὴ καθόλου τινὸς εἶναι δυνήσεται, καθ᾽ἕνωσίν
τε καὶ διαίρεσιν περιγραφομένη· καθ᾽ἕνωσιν μέν, ὡς
ὕπαρξιν ἔχουσα τῶν μονάδων τὴν σύνθεσιν, ὑφ᾽ὧν ὡς
μερῶν περιέχεται καὶ εἰς ἃς ὡς μέρη τέμνεσθαι δύναται – οὐδὲν δὲ διαιρετὸν ἢ διαιρούμενον ἢ σύνθετον ἢ
συντιθέμενον κατὰ φύσιν ἢ θέσιν ἢ ἄλλον τινὰ ἐπινοη-
θῆναι δυνάμενον τρόπον, ἀλλ᾽οὐδὲ αὐτὴ ἡ ἁπλῶς λεγομένη διαίρεσις ἢ σύνθεσις, ἄπειρον εἶναι δυνήσεται, ὅτι
μὴ καὶ ἁπλοῦν καὶ μόνον, καὶ μὴ ἀριθμητὸν ἢ ἀριθμούμενον ἢ συναριθμούμενον, ἢ πάσης ἁπλῶς ἐλεύθερον
τῆς οἱασδήποτε σχέσεως (πάντα γὰρ ταῦτα ἐν σχέσει
θεωρεῖται, τὸ δὲ ἄπειρον ἄσχετον· οὐ γὰρ ἔχει τί κατὰ
σχέσιν συνημμένον παντάπασι) –, κατὰ διαίρεσιν δέ, ὡς
ἀριθμῷ κινουμένη, ἐξ οὗπερ ἤρξατό τε καὶ ὑφ᾽οὗ περιέχεται, ἐπείπερ οὐ φύσει τὸ εἶναι καὶ ἄσχετον ἔχει· *
ἀριθμῷ γὰρ πᾶσα δυάς, καὶ πᾶσα μονὰς εἰς μέρος αὐτῆς
συντελοῦσα, εἶναι καθέστηκε, καθ᾽ὃν ἀλλήλων αἱ κα-
τ᾽αὐτὴν μονάδες ἀφαιροῦνται τὸ ἀπερίγραφον. Οὐδεὶς
δὲ μεμοιραμένος κἂν ὁπωσοῦν τοῦ λογίζεσθαι εἴποι ἂν
ἄπειρον εἶναι ᾧ ἐξ ἀϊδίου συνθεωρεῖταί τι ἢ συνεπιθεωρεῖται κατ᾽οὐσίαν διάφορον, εἰδὼς διαπεσεῖσθαι πάντως αὐτῷ τὸν περὶ τοῦ ἀπείρου λόγον οὕτω φρονοῦν-

beginning of its existence, then it must be without a source; if it is without a source, it is also infinite; if it is infinite, then it must be unmoved, for that which is infinite must be unmoved because that which is unbounded has nowhere to which it could be moved. If this is so, there must be two infinite, sourceless, and unmoved realities, God and matter, which is impossible. For duality is neither infinite, nor without a source, nor unmoved, nor can it be the source of anything at all, since it is enclosed in terms of both unity and division. It   C
is enclosed in terms of unity since it has its existence as the synthesis of singular realities, by which, as parts, it is comprised and into which, as parts, it can be separated. Nothing divisible or divided or synthesizable or synthesized according to nature or placement or any other mode that could be conceived, nor what is called in an absolute sense "division" or   118
"synthesis" itself, could ever be infinite since such a thing is neither simple nor alone, nor can what is countable or counted or counted together with something else, or free of every habitual relation whatsoever in a general sense (for all of these things are thought in terms of habitual relation, and the infinite is unconditioned by relation, for it does not have anything connected to it in any way by relation). Duality is enclosed in terms of division in that it is caused by counting from which it takes its beginning and by which it is comprised,   D
since indeed it does not possess existence and unrelatedness by nature. For[106] every duality, and every unity that makes up a part of it, exists as a function of counting, and as such the singular realities that pertain to a duality prevent each other from being unenclosed. No one who can think at all would call something "infinite" if rthere is always something essentially different from it observed along with it or at the same time as it, for he would know that someone who thinks like that has

---

106   *63. That every duality is called "duality" with respect to counting, and that every unity that makes up a part of a duality is called "unity" with respect to counting, but is not called "unity" in the simple sense*

τι. Τὸ γὰρ ἄπειρον κατὰ πάντα καὶ λόγον καὶ τρόπον
ἐστὶν ἄπειρον, κατ᾽οὐσίαν κατὰ δύναμιν κατ᾽ἐνέργειαν
κατ᾽ἄμφω τὰ πέρατα, τὸ ἄνω τε λέγω καὶ τὸ κάτω,
τουτέστι κατὰ τὴν ἀρχὴν καὶ τὸ τέλος. Ἀχώρητον γὰρ
κατὰ τὴν οὐσίαν καὶ ἀπερινόητον κατὰ τὴν δύναμιν καὶ
κατὰ τὴν | ἐνέργειαν ἀπερίγραφον καὶ ἄναρχον ἄνωθεν   1185
καὶ ἀτελεύτητον κάτωθεν ἐστὶ τὸ ἄπειρον καί, ἁπλῶς
εἰπεῖν ἀληθέστερον, κατὰ πάντα ἀόριστον, ὡς οὐδενὸς
τὸ παράπαν καθ᾽ἕνα τῶν ἀπηριθμημένων τρόπων συνεπινοηθῆναι αὐτῷ δυναμένου. Καθ᾽ὃν γὰρ ἂν εἴποιμεν
λόγον ἢ τρόπον δύνασθαί τι ἕτερον αὐτῷ κατ᾽οὐσίαν
διάφορον παραβάλλεσθαι, τὸν ὅλον τῆς ὅλης ἀπειρίας
αὐτῷ συναφαιρούμεθα λόγον. Εἰ δὲ ἄπειρόν τι εἶναι
οὐ δύναται, ᾧ ἐξ ἀϊδίου συνυπάρχει ἕτερόν τι κατ᾽οὐ-
σίαν διάφορον, ἄπειρον εἶναι οὐδαμῶς ἐνδέχεται δυάδα. Αἱ γὰρ κατ᾽αὐτὴν μονάδες, ἀλλήλαις κατὰ παράθε-
σιν συνυπάρχουσαι, ἀλλήλας ὁρίζουσιν, οὐδ᾽ἑτέρας τὴν
ἑτέραν ἀορίστως ὁρᾶσθαι συγχωρούσης παρακειμένην,
ἀλλ᾽οὐχ᾽ὑπερβαίνουσαν ἐχούσης, καὶ τὸν τῆς ἀπειρίας
εἰκότως ἀλλήλων συναφαιροῦνται λόγον.

Εἰ δὲ ἄπειρον, ὡς δέδεικται, μὴ ἐνδέχεται εἶναι δυάδα, οὔτε ἄναρχον δηλονότι – ἀρχὴ γὰρ πάσης δυάδος
μονάς –· εἰ δὲ μὴ ἄναρχον, οὐδὲ ἀκίνητον – κινεῖται γὰρ
τῷ ἀριθμῷ ἐκ μονάδων καθ᾽ἕνωσιν, καὶ εἰς αὐτὰς κατὰ
διαίρεσιν τὸ εἶναι λαμβάνουσα –· εἰ δὲ μὴ ἀκίνητον,
οὐδὲ ἄλλου τινὸς ἀρχὴν εἶναι – τὸ γὰρ κινούμενον οὐκ
ἀρχή, ἀλλ᾽ἐξ ἀρχῆς δηλαδὴ τοῦ κινοῦντος –. Μονὰς δὲ
μόνη κυρίως ἀκίνητος, ὅτι μήτε ἀριθμός ἐστι μήτε ἀριθμητὸν ἢ ἀριθμούμενον – οὔτε γὰρ μέρος ἢ ὅλον ἢ σχέσις
ἐστὶν ἡ μονάς –, καὶ κυρίως ἄναρχος, ὅτι μὴ δ᾽ἕτερον
ἑαυτῆς ἔχει πρεσβύτερον, ἐξ οὗ κινουμένη δέχεται τὸ

no understanding of the essential idea of infinity. For the infinite is infinite with respect to every essential idea and every modality of being, in terms of essence, potentiality, activity, and both limits, above and below, that is, according to source and final end. For the infinite is uncontainable with respect essence, incomprehensible with respect to potentiality, unenclosed with respect to activity, without source from above, and without final end from below.[107] To put it simply and in fact more truly, it is undefinable in all aspects, since nothing at all can be conceived along with it with respect to any one of the modes here enumerated. For should we mention an essential idea or mode such that something other, which is different in essence, could be put alongside it, then we would remove the whole essential idea of the whole of infinity along with it. If it is not possible for an infinite reality to have something else that is different in essence coexisting along with it from eternity, then it is absolutely impermissible for duality to be thought of as infinite. For the singular realities that constitute it, by coexisting in juxtaposition with each other, set a bound to each other, and neither of them allows the other lying next to it to be seen as boundless, but rather each restrains the other so that neither is transcendent, and thus they also actually negate the essential idea of infinity from each other.

1185A

119

If, as it has been shown, duality cannot be infinite, then duality is clearly also not without a source, for unity is the source of every duality. If it is not without source, it is not unmoved, for it is moved numerically from the unities to form a unified reality, and its existence is separated back out into the unities when it is considered as a divided reality. If it is not unmoved, it is not the source of something else, for that which is moved is not a source, but is from a source, which is obviously that which produces movement. Unity alone is really without mo-

---

107   "from above and below," that is, without the defining limits of genus and species.

εἶναι μονάς, καὶ ἄπειρον κυρίως, ὅτι μηδὲν ἔχει συν-
υπάρχον ἢ συναριθμούμενον, καὶ ἀρχὴ κυρίως, ὅτι
παντὸς καὶ ἀριθμοῦ καὶ ἀριθμουμένου καὶ ἀριθμητοῦ
αἰτία τυγχάνει, ὡς πάσης σχέσεως καὶ παντὸς μέρους
καὶ ὅλου ἐξῃρημένη, καὶ κυρίως καὶ ἀληθῶς πρώτως
τε καὶ μόνως καὶ ἁπλῶς, ἀλλ᾽οὐ πῶς, πρώτη τε μονὰς
ὑπάρχουσα καὶ μόνη. Καὶ τοῦτο λέγοντες οὐκ αὐτὴν ὡς
ἔστι σημαίνομεν τὴν μακαρίαν θεότητα, ἀπείρως κατὰ
πάντα καὶ λόγον καὶ τρόπον καὶ νῷ καὶ λόγῳ παντὶ καὶ
ὀνόματι ἀπρόσιτον οὖσαν παντελῶς καὶ ἀπροσπέλα-
στον, ἀλλ᾽ἑαυτοῖς ὅρον τῆς εἰς αὐτὴν πίστεως παρέχο-
μεν βάσιμον καὶ ἡμῖν ἐφικτόν τε καὶ πρόσφορον. Οὐ
γὰρ ὡς παραστατικὸν πάντως τοῦτο, φημὶ δὲ τὸ τῆς
μονάδος ὄνομα, τῆς θείας καὶ μακαρίας οὐσίας ὁ θεῖος
διαγορεύει λόγος, ἀλλ᾽ὡς ἐνδεικτικὸν τῆς παντελοῦς
αὐτῆς ἁπλότητος, τῆς ἐπέκεινα πάσης ποσότητός τε
καὶ ποιότητος καὶ τῆς οἰασδήποτε σχέσεως, ἵνα γνῶμεν
ὅτι μὴ ὅλον τί ἐστιν ὡς ἐκ μερῶν τινων, μηδέτι μέρος
ἐστὶν ἐξ ὅλου τινός. Ὑπεράνω γὰρ πάσης διαιρέσεώς
τε καὶ συνθέσεως καὶ μέρους καὶ ὅλου ἡ θεότης – ὅτι
ἄποσον – καὶ πάσης τῆς κατὰ θέσιν ὑπάρξεως καὶ τῆς
πῶς εἶναι αὐτὴν ὁριζομένης ἐννοίας ἀπῳκισμένη – ὅτι
ἄποιον – καὶ τῆς πρὸς ἄλλο πᾶν πάσης συναφείας τε
καὶ οἰκειότητος ἐλευθέρα καὶ ἄφετος – ἄσχετον γάρ –,
τὸ πρὸ αὐτῆς ἢ μετ᾽αὐτῆς ἢ μετ᾽αὐτὴν οὐκ ἔχουσα – ὡς
πάντων ἐπέκεινα – καὶ μηδενὶ τῶν ὄντων | κατ᾽οὐδένα   1188
λόγον ἢ τρόπον συντεταγμένη.

Καὶ τοῦτο τυχὸν ἐννοήσας ὁ μέγας καὶ θεῖος Διονύ-
σιός φησι· Διὸ καὶ μονὰς ὑμνουμένη καὶ τριὰς ἡ ὑπὲρ πά-

tion, since it is neither a number, nor countable, nor counted, for Unity does not exist partially or as a whole, nor is it a relation. Unity alone is really without source, since there is nothing else that is older than it, from which Unity receives existence by being moved. Unity alone is really infinite, since it has nothing that exists along with it or is counted along with it. Unity alone is really a source, since it is the cause of every number, of everything that is counted, and of everything that is countable and is at a far remove from every relation and from every part and whole. Unity is really and truly, primar- C ily, uniquely, and simply – but without condition – primary and alone. And in saying this, we are not signifying the bless- ed Divinity Itself as It is, since It is infinitely unapproachable and absolutely unreachable for intellect and for all reason and naming with respect to any idea or mode. Rather, we provide for ourselves a definition from our faith in It that is accessible, 120 attainable, and useful for us. For divine discourse does not de- clare the name of "Unity" to be entirely representative of the divine and blessed essence, but rather as indicative of its com- plete simplicity, which goes beyond every quantity and quality and any sort of relation, so that we should know that it is nei- D ther a whole composed of parts, nor is it a part of a whole. Di- vinity is far beyond every division and synthesis and part and whole because It is unquantifiable, and It dwells far from every existence characterized by placement and from every concept that would define It as existing in a certain way, because It has no relative qualities. It is free from and unconstrained by any combination and appropriation in relation to anything else, be- cause It is without relation as such, and there is nothing before It or with It or after It since It is beyond all things, nor has It 1188A been arranged alongside any existing thing in accordance with any logical structure or particular mode.

And it is probably in thinking this that the great and divine Dionysius says, "Therefore while both Unity and Trinity are

ντα θεότης οὐκ ἔστιν οὔτε μονὰς οὔτε τριὰς ἢ πρὸς ἡμῶν
ἢ ἄλλου τινὸς διεγνωσμένη, ἀλλ'ἵνα καὶ τὸ ὑπερηνωμένον
αὐτῆς καὶ τὸ θεογόνον ἀληθῶς ὑμνήσωμεν, τῇ τριαδικῇ
καὶ ἑνιαίᾳ θεωνυμίᾳ τὴν ὑπερώνυμον ὠνομάσαμεν καὶ τοῖς
οὖσι τὴν ²ὑπερούσιον. Οὐδαμῶς οὖν τις δυάδα ἢ πλῆθος
ἄναρχον ἢ ἀρχὴν τὸ σύνολόν τινος εἶναι λέγειν δυνήσεται ζῆν εὐσεβῶς δι'ἀληθείας βεβουλημένος – εἷς γὰρ διὰ
πάσης τῆς κατὰ λόγον καὶ νοῦν θεωρητικῆς δυνάμεως
καὶ ἐπιστήμης αὐτῷ θεὸς ἀναφανήσεται, πάσης ἀπειρίας
ὑπάρχων ἐπέκεινα καὶ μηδενὶ καθόλου τῶν ὄντων καθοτιοῦν, πλὴν τοῦ διὰ πίστεως μόνον γινώσκεσθαι, καὶ
τοῦτο ἐκ τῶν αὐτοῦ ποιημάτων ὅτι ἐστίν, οὐχ'ὃ τί ποτέ
ἐστι, διεγνωσμένος, καὶ παντὸς αἰῶνος καὶ χρόνου καὶ
πάντων τῶν ἐν αἰῶνι καὶ χρόνῳ ποιητής τε καὶ δημι-
ουργός –, οὐδὲν τὸ παράπαν ἐξ ἀϊδίου καθ'ὃν οὖν τινα
τρόπον αὐτῷ συνεπινοῶν, εἰδὼς ὅτι μὴ δ'ἕτερον τῶν
ἅμα κατὰ τὴν ὕπαρξιν ἀλλήλοις ἐξ ἀϊδίου συνόντων εἶναι δύναται τοῦ ἑτέρου ποιητικόν – ἀσυλλόγιστον γὰρ
τοῦτο παντάπασι καὶ ἀνένδεκτον καὶ τοῖς νοῦν ἔχουσι
καταγέλαστον ἐπὶ τῶν ἐχόντων ἅμα τὸ εἶναι ποιεῖσθαι
ἄλλο ἄλλου ποιητικόν –, ἀλλ'ἐκ θεοῦ τοῦ ἀεὶ ὄντος τὰ
πάντα ἐκ τοῦ μὴ ὄντος γενέσθαι παντελῶς τε καὶ ὁλικῶς, ἀλλ'οὐ μερικῶς τε καὶ ἀτελῶς, ὡς ἐξ αἰτίας ἀπει-
ρογνώστου καὶ ἀπειροδυνάμου σοφῶς παρηγμένα,
δέξεται, καὶ ἐν αὐτῷ συνεστακέναι τὰ πάντα, ὡς ἐν παντο-
κρατορικῷ πυθμένι, φρουρούμενά τε καὶ διακρατούμενα,
καὶ εἰς αὐτὸν τὰ πάντα ἐπιστρέφεσθαι καθάπερ εἰς οἰκεῖον
ἕκαστα πέρας, ὥς που φησὶν ὁ μέγας Ἀρεοπαγίτης Δι

hymned, the Divinity beyond all things is neither Unity nor Trinity, nor is It known either by us or by anything else, but so that we might truly hymn both Its transcendent unity and Its divine fecundity, we name the Divinity that transcends naming by means of a three-fold and unified divine name and the Divinity beyond being by means of beings."[108] Therefore, there is no way that anyone wanting to live piously in the truth will be able to say either that a duality itself is fully without a source or is itself the all-sufficient source of something, for the one God, who exists beyond   121 all infinity and is not known definitively by any existing thing, except insofar as He is known by faith alone – and   B this is the knowledge that He is, which is derived from His creatures, not the knowledge of what He is essentially – will appear to him through every possibility of contemplation and understanding in reason and intellect as the creator and fashioner of all eternity and time, and of everything that exists in eternity and in time. He will not think that anything at all exists with God from everlasting in any way, for he would know that if two things have been together in existence from everlasting one cannot be the creator of the other, for it would be totally irrational, impermissible, and absurd for those with understanding to make one thing the creator of something else when they exist together. Rather, he will admit that everything has come to be from non-being complete and whole – with God who always is as its source – and has not come into being partially and with no purpose, since all things have been wisely led forth by an infinitely-knowing and infinitely-powerful cause: "and in Him all things have been established, since they are kept and held fast in an all-de-   C termining foundation, and unto" Him "all things return, as each to its own proper limit,"[109] as the great Dionysius the

---

108   Ps. Dion. Areo., *Div. Nom.* XIII.3, p. 229.6–10.
109   Ps. Dion. Areo., *Div. Nom.* IV.4., p. 148.13–15.

ονύσιος. * Καὶ προνοητὴν αὐτὸν εἶναι **πεισθήσεται** τῶν ὄντων, δι'ὧν ὅτι καὶ θεός ἐστιν **ἐδιδάχθη, δίκαιον εἶναι κρίνων καὶ εὔλογον μὴ ἄλλον εἶναι φύλακα καὶ ἐπιμελετὴν τῶν ὄντων ἢ μόνον τὸν τῶν ὄντων δημιουργόν. Αὐτὴ** γὰρ ἡ τῶν ὄντων διαμονὴ καὶ ἡ τάξις καὶ ἡ θέσις **καὶ ἡ κίνησις καὶ ἡ ἐν ἀλλήλοις τῶν ἄκρων διὰ τῶν μέσων συνοχή, μηδὲν κατὰ τὴν ἐναντιότητα λυμαινομένων ἀλλήλοις, ἥ τε τῶν μερῶν πρὸς τὰ ὅλα σύννευσις καὶ τῶν ὅλων πρὸς τὰ μέρη διόλου ἕνωσις καὶ αὐτῶν πρὸς ἄληλα τῶν μερῶν |** ἡ ἄμικτος διάκρισις   1189 **κατὰ τὴν ἰδιάζουσαν ἑκάστου διαφορὰν καὶ ἀσύγχυτος ἕνωσις κατὰ τὴν ἀπαράλλακτον ἐν ὅλοις ταυτότητα καὶ ἡ πάντων πρὸς πάντα, ἵνα μὴ τὰ καθ'ἕκαστον λέγω, σύγκρισίς τε καὶ διάκρισις καὶ ἡ πάντων καὶ ἑκάστου κατ'εἶδος διαδοχὴ ἀεὶ φυλαττομένη, μηδενὸς τὸ παράπαν τοῦ οἰκείου τῆς φύσεως λόγου παραφθειρομένου καὶ πρὸς ἄλλο συγχεομένου τε καὶ συγχέοντος, δείκνυσι σαφῶς τὰ πάντα τῇ προνοίᾳ συνέχεσθαι τοῦ πεποιηκότος θεοῦ·** οὐ γὰρ οἷόν τε ἐστιν ἀγαθὸν ὄντα τὸν θεὸν **μὴ καὶ** εὐεργετικὸν **πάντως** εἶναι, **μὴ δὲ** εὐεργετικὸν ὄντα **μὴ καὶ** προνοητικὸν **πάντως εἶναι, καὶ διατοῦτο τῶν ὄντων θεοπρεπῶς ἐπιμελούμενον σοφῶς αὐτοῖς, ὥσπερ τὸ εἶναι, καὶ τὴν κηδεμονίαν χαρίζεσθαι. Πρόνοια** γάρ ἐστι, **κατὰ τοὺς θεοφόρους πατέρας,** ἡ ἐκ θεοῦ εἰς τὰ

Areopagite says somewhere. Such[110] a person will be persuaded, moreover, that "He is the one who makes provision for
what exists, and through these things" he is "also" taught
"that God is," for he will judge it to be right and reasonable   D
that there is nothing else that is guardian and care-giver   122
for beings or that God is only the fashioner of beings. "For"
the fact that "the endurance of beings, their arrangement,
placement," motion, the co-inherence through intermediaries
of the extremes in them, which do not destroy each other
when they are brought into combination with each other, the
convergence of the parts with the wholes and the complete
union of wholes with the parts, the unmixed differentiation   1189A
of the parts themselves in relation to each other in accordance with the particularizing difference of each, the unconfused union that pertains to the unwavering identity in the
wholes, the mixture and differentiation of everything with
everything – to avoid speaking about every reality individually – and the succession of all things and of each individually according to its species, are all alike always guarded
and preserved, there being absolutely no inherent essential
idea of nature that is destroyed and is either commingled
or actively commingles with something else: all this clearly
shows that all things are held together by the providence of
God who has made them.

Indeed, it is not as though "God is good" but not also fully
"one who does good," nor "is He one who does good" and
not "also" fully "one who provides,"[111] and because of this He
wisely takes care of beings in a way that befits His Divinity
by granting to them His careful attention, just as He grants
them existence. For "God's care for beings," according to the
God-bearing fathers, "is providence. They also define it this   B

110   64. Contemplating, by way of demonstration, the fact that the providence of God is naturally over all things
111   NEM. EMES., Nat. Hom. 42, p. 122.22–24.

ὄντα γινομένη ἐπιμέλεια· ὁρίζονται δὲ αὐτὴν καὶ οὕτως·
πρόνοιά ἐστι βούλησις θεοῦ, δι'ἣν πάντα τὰ ὄντα τὴν πρόσφορον διεξαγωγὴν λαμβάνει. Εἰ δὲ θεοῦ βούλησις ἐστίν,
ἵνα αὐτοῖς τῶν διδασκάλων χρήσωμαι τοῖς λόγοις, πᾶσα
ἀνάγκη κατὰ τὸν ὀρθὸν λόγον γίνεσθαι τὰ γινόμενα, τὴν
κρείττω μὴ ἐπιδεχόμενα τάξιν. Αὐτὸν **οὖν** εἶναι προνοητὴν
**ἐκ παντὸς τρόπου εἰπεῖν ἐναχθήσεται ὁ τὴν ἀλήθειαν
ὁδηγὸν ἔχειν ἑλόμενος** ὃν καὶ ποιητὴν **ἔγνω** τῶν ὄντων·
οὐ γὰρ ἄλλου τινὸς τὸ προνοεῖν ἐστι τῶν ὄντων ἀληθῶς
ἢ τοῦ πεποιηκότος τὰ ὄντα θεοῦ, εἴπερ κἂν τοῖς ζῴοις,
ὅταν ταῖς κατὰ λόγον ἐφόδοις τοῖς οὖσιν ἐμβάλλωμεν
ἡμῶν τὸ νοερόν, εὑρίσκομεν ἔμφασιν οὐκ ἀγεννῶς τὰ
ὑπὲρ λόγον εἰκάζουσαν. Ἐκεῖνά τε γὰρ ὁρῶντες κατὰ
γένος τῶν ἐξ αὐτῶν φυσικῶς ἐπιμελούμενα, θαρροῦ-
ντες καὶ ἡμεῖς τὸν περὶ τοῦ προνοητὴν μονώτατον εἶναι τὸν θεὸν πάντων τῶν ὄντων μετ'εὐσεβοῦς παρρη-
σίας εὐσεβῶς ἑαυτοῖς λόγον διοριζόμεθα, καὶ οὐ τῶν
μέν, τῶν δὲ οὔ, καθάπερ τινὲς τῶν τὰ ἔξω φιλοσοφησάν-
των, ἀλλὰ πάντων ὁμοῦ κατὰ μίαν τῆς ἀγαθότητος
**καὶ ἀπαράλλακτον βούλησιν, τῶν τε καθόλου καὶ τῶν
καθ'ἕκαστον,** εἰδότες ὡς τῶν κατὰ μέρος πάντων **τῷ μὴ
προνοίας τυγχάνειν καὶ φυλακῆς τῆς πρεπούσης** διαφθειρομένων, καὶ τὰ καθόλου συνδιαφθαρήσεται – ἐκ γὰρ
τῶν κατὰ μέρος τὰ καθόλου συνίστασθαι **πέφυκε** –, **τὴν
περὶ τούτου λογικὴν ἀπόδειξιν διὰ τῆς εὐλόγου ἀντι-
στροφῆς πρὸς τὴν ἀλήθειαν ὀρθῶς ποδηγοῦσαν ἑαυτοῖς
προβαλλόμενοι. Εἰ γὰρ τὰ καθόλου ἐν τοῖς κατὰ μέρος
ὑφέστηκεν,** οὐδαμῶς τὸ παράπαν **τὸν τοῦ καθ'αὑτὰ εἶναί τε καὶ ὑφεστάναι λόγον ἐπιδεχόμενα, τῶν κατὰ
μέρος διαφθειρομένων, πάντῃ που δῆλόν ἐστιν ὡς οὐδὲ
τὰ καθόλου στήσεται· τὰ μέρη γὰρ ἐν ταῖς ὁλότησι καὶ
αἱ ὁλότητες ἐν τοῖς μέρεσι καί εἰσι καὶ ὑφεστήκασι.**

way: providence is the will of God, through which all beings receive a suitable way of life. If it is the will of God," to use the very words of the teachers, "then it is entirely necessary that what has come to be has come to be in accordance with right reason, that they are not expecting a better arrangement." Therefore, the one who has chosen to have truth as a guide will be persuaded to say that "He is the one who provides" in every sense, the one whom he knows "also to be   123 the creator of beings."[112] For there is truly no one who makes provision for beings other than God who has made them, if indeed, whenever we apply our thinking to beings with a reasonable approach, we see even in animals something that shows that reality is not simply base and irrational. For when we see those creatures that naturally care for their progeny, we are confident piously to determine for ourselves with pious bold-   C ness the idea that God is the unique provider of all beings, and not only of some but not others, as some of those who philosophize in a way foreign to us say, but of all together according to a single and unwavering good will, of all things as a whole and of each individually. We know "that if all things in their parts are destroyed" by not having their existence founded in providence and in a preservation appropriate to them," then the universals will also be destroyed along with them, for universals are" naturally "constituted of particulars."[113]

We can adduce for ourselves a rational demonstration of this, which will lead us safely to the truth through a well-reasoned argument that will turn the opposing view against itself. If universals exist actually in particulars, since they can't contain the essential idea either of their being or of their actual existence in themselves, then when the particulars are de-   124 stroyed, it is absolutely clear that the universals will not per-   D sist, for parts are and exist actually in wholes and wholes in

---

112   NEM. EMES., *Nat. Hom.* 42, p. 125.4–10.
113   NEM. EMES., *Nat. Hom.* 43, p. 130.13–14.

Καὶ οὐδεὶς ἀντερεῖ λόγος πλὴν ὅτι, ὑπὸ τῆς ἀληθείας
ὥσπερ δεσμούμενοι, ἄκοντες καὶ αὐτοὶ τῆς προνοίας
τὴν δύναμιν ἐξαγγέλλουσι καὶ διὰ πάντων διήκειν κα-
τασκευάζουσι, δι᾽ ὧν αὐτῆς κατεσπούδασαν. Λέγοντες
γὰρ ὑπὸ τῆς προνοίας ἄγεσθαι μόνα τὰ καθόλου, λελήθα-
σιν ἑαυτοὺς καὶ τῶν κατὰ **μέρος** εἶναι πρόνοιαν λέγοντες,
ἐξ ἀνάγκης πρὸς τὴν ἀλήθειαν, ἣν φεύγειν σπουδάζου-
σιν, ὑπαγόμενοι. Εἰ γὰρ χάριν | διαμονῆς τὰ καθόλου   1192
προνοίας ἀξιοῦσθαί φασι, ταύτης πολλῷ πρότερον ἀξι-
οῦσθαι τὰ κατὰ μέρος εἰσάγουσιν, ἐν οἷς ἡ τῶν καθόλου
ἐστὶ διαμονὴ καὶ ὑπόστασις· συνεισάγεται γὰρ ἀλλήλοις ταῦτα διὰ τὴν κατὰ φύσιν ἀδιάλυτον πρὸς ἄλληλα σχέσιν καί, θατέρου πρὸς διαμονὴν συντηρουμένου,
μὴ δὲ τὸ ἕτερον ταύτης εἶναι τῆς φυλακῆς ἀλλότριον,
καί, ἑνὸς πάλιν τῆς πρὸς διαμονὴν φυλακῆς διαπίπτον-
τος, μὴ δὲ τὸ ἄλλο ταύτης τυγχάνειν λέγειν ἀκόλου-
θον.

Ἄλλως τε δὲ κατὰ τρεῖς τρόπους τὸ μὴ πάντων τῶν
ὄντων προνοεῖν τὸν θεὸν λέγεται· ἢ γὰρ ἀγνοεῖν αὐτὸν
λέγουσι τῆς προνοίας τὴν μέθοδον, ἢ μὴ βούλεσθαι, ἢ μὴ
δύνασθαι. Ἀλλὰ μὴν κατὰ τὰς κοινὰς πάντων ἐννοίας
ἀγαθὸς ὢν καὶ ὑπεράγαθος ὁ θεὸς ἀεὶ πάντως τὰ καλὰ
βούλεται καὶ πᾶσι, καὶ σοφὸς ὑπάρχων καὶ ὑπέρσοφος,
μᾶλλον δὲ πάσης σοφίας πηγή, γινώσκει πάντως τὰ
συμφέροντα, καὶ δυνατὸς ὤν, μᾶλλον δὲ ἀπειροδύνα-
μος, ἐνεργεῖ πάντως θεοπρεπῶς ἐν πᾶσι τὰ ἐγνωσμένα
αὐτῷ καὶ βεβουλημένα καλὰ καὶ συμφέροντα, ὡς ἀγαθὸς καὶ σοφὸς καὶ δυνατὸς διικνούμενος διὰ πάντων
τῶν τε ὁρατῶν καὶ τῶν ἀοράτων καὶ τῶν καθόλου καὶ
τῶν μερικῶν καὶ τῶν μικρῶν καὶ τῶν μεγάλων καὶ πάντων τῶν κατὰ πᾶσαν τὴν οἱανοῦν οὐσίαν τὸ εἶναι ἐχόντων, μηδὲν ὑφιεὶς τῆς κατὰ τὴν ἀγαθότητα καὶ τὴν

parts. And the only argument contradicting this is made by those who, as if bound by the truth, themselves unwillingly proclaim the power of providence and establish its extension throughout all things, even though they attempt to deny a place for providence in all particular things. For, by saying that "universals" alone are directed by providence, "they are saying unbeknownst to themselves that providence also pertains to" particulars and thus are necessarily submitting to the truth, which they try fervently to flee. For if they   1192A
say that universals are worthy of providence thanks to their endurance, they already introduce well in advance that the particulars are worthy of providence, since it is in the particulars that the endurance and actual existence of universals are found. For these are brought in together because of their natural insoluble relation to each other and, when one is maintained in endurance, the other is not excluded from the preservation of the first one, and when one again falls away from its enduring preservation, we do not say that something different happens to the other.

In any case, there are "three" aspects to the assertion that God does not extend His providence to all beings. They say either that He "does not know" how to make providence work, "is unwilling, or is unable."[114] But according to concepts that are common to all, God, who is good and beyond good, surely also always wills what is good for all, and since He is wise and beyond wise , or rather is the font of all wis-   B
dom, surely He knows what is expedient, and since He is powerful, or rather, infinitely powerful, surely He divinely achieves in all things what is known by Him, the good   125
things willed by Him, and what is expedient. Because He is good, wise, and powerful He thereby reaches into all things visible and invisible, universals and particulars, the small and the great, all things that possess existence in any es-

114   NEM. EMES., *Nat. Hom.* 43, p. 130.7–10.

σοφίαν καὶ τὴν δύναμιν ἀπειρίας, καὶ πάντα κατὰ τὸν ἑκάστων τοῦ εἶναι λόγον πρός τε ἑαυτὰ καὶ ἄλληλα κατὰ τὴν ἀδιάλυτον πάντων σχετικὴν ἁρμονίαν τε καὶ διαμονὴν συντηρῶν.

Τί δὲ αὐτὴν καθ᾿ἑαυτὴν οὐ κατανοοῦμεν τὴν φύσιν περὶ τοῦ εἶναι τὴν ἐπὶ πάντα τοῦ θεοῦ πρόνοιαν σαφῶς οὖσαν διδάσκαλον; Τεκμήριον γὰρ οὐ σμικρὸν τοῦ φυσικῶς ἡμῖν ἐνεσπάρθαι τὴν τῆς προνοίας γνῶσιν ἡ φύσις αὐτὴ δίδωσιν, ὁπηνίκα ἂν ἡμᾶς ἀδιδάκτως ὥσπερ ὠθοῦσα πρὸς τὸν θεὸν διὰ τῶν εὐχῶν ἐν ταῖς ἐξαίφνης περιστάσεσιν ἐκεῖθεν ζητεῖν τὴν σωτηρίαν παρασκευάζῃ· ὑπ᾿ἀνάγκης γὰρ ἄφνω συλληφθέντες, ἀπροαιρέτως, πρίν τι καὶ σκέψασθαι, τὸν θεὸν ἐπιβοώμεθα, ὡς ἂν τῆς προνοίας αὐτῆς πρὸς ἑαυτὴν καὶ λογισμῶν χωρὶς ἑλκούσης ἡμᾶς καὶ τὸ τάχος τῆς ἐν ἡμῖν νοερᾶς νικώσης δυνάμεως καὶ πάντων ἰσχυροτέραν τὴν θείαν προδεικνυούσης βοήθειαν. Οὐκ ἂν δὲ ἡμᾶς ἦγεν ἀπροαιρέτως ἡ φύσις ἐπὶ τὸ μὴ φύσιν ἔχον γίνεσθαι; Πᾶν δὲ τὸ ὁτῳοῦν φυσικῶς ἑπόμενον, ὡς πᾶσιν εὔδηλον, ἰσχυρὰν ἔχει καὶ ἀκαταμάχητον κατὰ τὴν ἀπόδειξιν τῆς ἀληθείας τὴν δύναμιν. Εἰ δὲ ὅτι ἀκατάληπτος ἡμῖν τῆς τῶν κατὰ μέρος προνοίας ὁ λόγος, ὥσπερ οὖν καὶ ἔστι κατὰ τὸ Ὡς ἀνεξερεύνητα τὰ κρίματα αὐτοῦ καὶ ἀνεξιχνίαστοι αἱ ὁδοὶ αὐτοῦ, διὰτοῦτο φαῖεν μὴ δὲ πρόνοιαν εἶναι, οὐκ ὀρθῶς ἐροῦσι κατὰ τὸν ἐμὸν λόγον· εἰ γὰρ πολλὴ τίς ἐστιν ἡ διαφορὰ καὶ ἀκατάληπτος τῶν ἀνθρώπων ἑκάστου πρὸς ἕκαστον καὶ ἡ πρὸς ἑαυτὸν ἑκάστου ἐναλλαγὴ ἔν τε βίοις καὶ ἤθεσι καὶ γνώμαις καὶ προαιρέσεσι καὶ ἐπιθυμίαις ἐπιστήμαις τε καὶ | χρείαις καὶ ἐπιτηδεύμασι καὶ αὐτοῖς   1193 τοῖς κατὰ ψυχὴν λογισμοῖς, ἀπείροις οὖσι σχεδόν, καὶ πᾶσι τοῖς καθ᾿ἑκάστην ἡμέραν καὶ ὥραν ἐπισυμβαίνουσι συμμεταβαλλομένου – ἀγχίστροφον γὰρ τοῦτο τὸ ζῷον ὁ

sence whatsoever, compromising nothing of His infinity in goodness, wisdom, and power, and maintains all things in accordance with the essential idea of existence belonging to each thing, with respect to itself and in relation to each other thing, in the insoluble relational harmony and endurance that hold all things together.

Why do we not comprehend that nature in itself teaches the   C fact that the providence of God clearly pertains to all things? "For nature" itself gives "not an insignificant proof that the knowledge of providence has naturally been sown" in us, whenever it prepares "us without teaching," as if it were pushing us toward God, to seek salvation there with Him "through prayer in our immediate" circumstances. "For" when we have been seized unawares "by necessity, involuntarily, and before anything is considered, we call upon God," as if providence itself were drawing us towards itself, even without our rational awareness, and as if it were showing forth the swiftness of our intellectual power, which overrides everything else, and the divine help that is stronger than all things. "Nature would not lead us" involuntarily "to something that does not happen naturally. Everything whatsoever that proceeds naturally," as is perfectly clear to all, "possesses a strong" and   126 invincible power for "the demonstration" of truth.[115] I grant that "the essential idea of how providence guides particulars is ungraspable for us, and indeed it is, according to the verse, *how unsearchable are His judgments, and His ways past finding out* (Rom 11.33)," but "if" they were to say on account of this that "there is" no "providence," they will not, to my mind, be speaking rightly. "For" if there is an "immense" and ungraspable "difference" between one human being and another "and a variation in each in relation to himself in ways of life," ethics, mental inclinations, purposes, "desires," understanding, "tasks, pursuits," and the very reasonings of the soul,   1193A

---

115   NEM. EMES., *Nat. Hom.* 43, p. 132.10–21.

ἄνθρωπος, ὀξέως τοῖς καιροῖς καὶ ταῖς χρείαις συμμετα-
βαλλόμενον –, ἀνάγκη πᾶσα καὶ τὴν πρόνοιαν, **προγνωστι-
κῶς πάντα συνειληφυῖαν κατὰ περιγραφὴν τὰ καθ'ἕκαστα**, διάφορόν τε καὶ ποικίλην **φαίνεσθαι** καὶ πολυσχιδῆ
καί, τῇ τῶν πεπληθυσμένων ἀκαταληψίᾳ συνεκτεινομένην,
ἑκάστῳ προσφόρως καθ'ἕκαστον **καὶ πρᾶγμα καὶ νόημα
μέχρι καὶ τῶν ψιλῶν κινημάτων τῶν κατὰ ψυχὴν καὶ
σῶμα συνισταμένων** ἁρμόζεσθαι. **Εἰ οὖν** τῶν κατὰ μέρος
ἀκατάληπτός ἐστιν ἡ διαφορὰ καὶ τῆς ἁρμοζούσης αὐτοῖς
εἰκότως προνοίας ἄπειρος ὁ λόγος, **ἀλλ'οὐκ, ἐπειδὴ** ἄπει-
ρός **τε** καὶ ἄγνωστος ἡμῖν **τῆς τῶν κατὰ μέρος προνοίας
ὁ λόγος τυγχάνει**, τὴν **ἰδίαν** ἄγνοιαν ἀναίρεσιν ποιεῖσθαι
τῆς **πανσόφου** τῶν ὄντων κηδεμονίας **ὀφείλομεν**, πάντα
δὲ **ἁπλῶς καὶ** ἀνεξετάστως **θεοπρεπῶς τε καὶ συμφερόν-
τως** τὰ τῆς προνοίας **ἀνυμνεῖν** ἔργα **καὶ** ἀποδέχεσθαι **καὶ**
καλῶς γίνεσθαι **τὰ γινόμενα πιστεύειν, κἂν ἡμῖν ὁ λόγος
ἐστὶν ἀνέφικτος. Πάντα δὲ λέγων, τὰ τῆς προνοίας φημί,
οὐ γὰρ τὰ κακῶς ὑφ'ἡμῶν κατὰ** τὸν τοῦ ἐφ'ἡμῖν λόγον γι-
νόμενα· **ταῦτα γὰρ τοῦ κατὰ τὴν πρόνοιαν λόγου παντελῶς ἀλλότρια.**

Τὸν μὲν οὖν σημαινόμενον τρόπον περὶ τῆς τῶν
ἁγίων κατὰ τὸν λόγον καὶ τὴν θεωρίαν δυνάμεώς τε
καὶ χάριτος ὑπὸ τοῦ μεγάλου τούτου διδασκάλου, κατὰ
τὸ δυνατόν, στοχαστικῶς ἀλλ'οὐκ ἀποφαντικῶς – πολλῷ γὰρ ἀπολείπεται τῷ μέτρῳ τῆς κατ'αὐτὸν ἀληθείας

which are nearly infinite, "and each person changes together
with" everything that "happens through the course of each
day" and hour – "for this animal," man, "turns about suddenly, changing abruptly together with occasions and tasks
– then it is also entirely necessary that providence," which
has presciently comprehended all things by enclosing them
in their individuality, be manifest as "diverse, manifold, and
many faceted." It is necessary moreover that "providence,
in extending itself right along with the incomprehensibili-
ty of the things that have proliferated, accommodate itself
closely to each thing in its individuality," both "as action"
and as thought, extending even as far as the basic movements achieved in soul and body. Therefore, if "the difference between things in their parts" is ungraspable, "and the
essential idea of the providence that harmonizes them" in a
seemly way "is infinite," we are not, even if the essential idea
of how providence guides particulars happens to be "infinite
and unknowable for us, bound to regard this" specific "ig-   B
norance as somehow the destruction of" an all-wise "concern   127
for beings." Rather, we are bound to hymn and "accept all
of the works of providence" simply, "without prying," in a
way that befits the Divine and is coherent, and to believe
that all things that have come to be "have come to be beautifully," even if the essential idea of this is unattainable
for us. "When I say 'all things,'" I mean "what comes from
providence," for wicked things that happen within our own
power in accordance with "the logic of our own agency" are
not the result of providence,[116] for such things are entirely
foreign to the essential idea of providence.

I have made my way, then, through what Gregory has said as
if following after the tracks it has left, in order to interpret
what was meant by this great teacher concerning the power
and grace of the saints in their "reason and contemplation" as

---

116   Nem. Emes., *Nat. Hom.* 43, p. 133.2–22.

ὁ ἡμέτερος νοῦς – διὰ τῶν εἰρημένων ὑποδραμὼν τῷ
λόγῳ καὶ ὥσπερ ἰχνηλατήσας, τοιόνδε καθ'ὑπόνοιαν
μόνον φημι, * διὰ δὲ τοῦ ὑπὲρ τὴν ὑλικὴν δυάδα γενέσθαι διὰ τὴν ἐν τῇ τριάδι νοουμένην
ἑνότητα τὸ ὑπὲρ τὴν ὕλην γενέσθαι καὶ τὸ εἶδος, ἐξ
ὧν τὰ σώματα, τοὺς ἁγίους λέγειν αὐτόν ὑπονοῶ, ἢ
τὴν σάρκα καὶ τὴν ὕλην, ἅσπερ διασχόντας ἔφη θεῷ
συγγενέσθαι καὶ τῷ ἀκραιφνεστάτῳ κραθῆναι
φωτὶ καταξιωθῆναι, τουτέστι τὴν πρὸς τὴν σάρκα τῆς
ψυχῆς σχέσιν καὶ διὰ τῆς σαρκὸς πρὸς τὴν ὕλην, ἢ καθόλου εἰπεῖν, πάσης τῆς αἰσθητικῆς οὐσίας πρὸς τὴν αἰσθητὴν ἀποθεμένους φυσικὴν οἰκειότητα, τῆς δὲ θείας
μόνης γνησίως ἐπιλαβομένους ἐφέσεως διὰ τήν, ὡς
ἔφην, νοουμένην ἐν τῇ τριάδι ἑνότητα. Μέσην
γὰρ κειμένην θεοῦ καὶ ὕλης τὴν ψυχὴν ἐγνωκότες καὶ
τὰς πρὸς ἄμφω ἑνοποιοὺς δυνάμεις ἔχουσαν, τὸν νοῦν
λέγω πρὸς τὸν θεὸν καὶ πρὸς τὴν ὕλην τὴν αἴσθησιν,
τὴν μὲν αἴσθησιν μετὰ τῶν αἰσθητῶν παντελῶς αὐτῆς
ἀπετινάξαντο κατὰ τὴν ἐν διαθέσει σχετικὴν ἐνέργει-
αν, κατὰ δὲ τὸν νοῦν μονώτατον ἀρρήτως | αὐτὴν τῷ   1196
θεῷ προσῳκείωσαν, πρὸς ὃν ὅλον ἀγνώστως ἑνωθεῖσαν
ὅλην, ὡς ἀρχετύπου εἰκόνα, κατὰ νοῦν καὶ λόγον καὶ
πνεῦμα, ὡς ἐφικτόν, καθ'ὁμοίωσιν ἔχουσαν τὸ ἐμφερὲς
θεασάμενοι, τὴν ἐν τῇ τριάδι νοουμένην ἑνότητα
μυστικῶς ἐδιδάχθησαν.

far as this is possible, but I have done so speculatively and not
as though proving something, for my mind falls far short of
the measure of the truth in it, and I speak here by conjecture C
only. With[117] the phrase, "by transcending material duality
through the unity in the Trinity as it is known by the mind"
I think he means that the saints come to transcend "matter"
and form, which give rise to bodies, or flesh and matter, and
by "parting" them, he says, they have been deemed worthy
"to attain kinship with God and to be mixed with the purest
light." That is, by having put off the relation of the soul to D
the flesh and through the flesh to matter, or to speak gen- 128
erally, having put off the natural kinship of the essence of
all sensuality with sensual nature, they nobly attained desire
for the Divine alone "through," as he says, "the unity in the
Trinity as it is known by the mind." For having known that
the soul is set between God and material reality and has the
potential of being made one with both, I mean the intellect
with God and sense-perception with matter, they completely
suspended the normal disposition of sense-perception in its activity relative to sensual reality, and they ineffably brought 1196A
the soul in intellect, reason, and spirit, through the intellect
in its pure solitude, into communion with God, with whose
fullness the soul is fully united, though without the mediation
of knowledge, as an image with its archetype, as far as this is
attainable. In this they saw the soul's resemblance to God as
a likeness, and thus were mystically taught "the unity by the
Trinity as it is known by the mind."

---

117   65. *Contemplating the material duality that has been traversed by the
saints in a different way, and the question, What is "the unity in the Trinity
as it is known by the mind"?*

Τυχὸν δὲ καὶ τὸν θυμὸν καὶ τὴν ἐπιθυμίαν ὑλικὴν δυάδα προσηγόρευσεν ὁ διδάσκαλος διὰ τὸ προσύλους καὶ τοῦ παθητικοῦ τῆς ψυχῆς μέρους αὐτὰς εἶναι δυνάμεις καὶ πρὸς τὸν λόγον στασιαζούσας καὶ εἰς πολλὰ σκεδάσαι τὸν νοῦν δυναμένας, εἰ μή, ἐξ ἀρχῆς ἐπιστημόνως ἄγχων, ἑαυτῷ ὑποζεύξειεν. Ὧν εἴ τις κρατήσειε καὶ ἐφ'ἃ δεῖ πρεπόντως φέρεσθαι πείσειε, δουλικῶς ὑπεζευγμένας τῇ δυναστείᾳ τοῦ λόγου, ἢ καὶ παντελῶς αὐτὰς ἀπολιπὼν ἀπολίποι καὶ μόνης τῆς ἀρρεποῦς κατ'ἀγάπην γνωστικῆς διὰ λόγου καὶ θεωρίας ἔχεται θέλξεως καὶ πρὸς μίαν καὶ μόνην ἐκ τῶν πολλῶν καθαράν τε καὶ ἁπλῆν καὶ ἀδιαίρετον τῆς κατ'ἔφεσιν ἀρρενωτάτης δυνάμεως κίνησιν συνεστάλη, καθ'ἣν περὶ θεὸν ἀκαταλήκτως ἐν ταυτότητι τῆς κατ'ἔφεσιν ἀεικινησίας ἑαυτῷ φιλοσόφως ἐπήξατο τὴν μονιμότητα, μακάριος ὄντως ἐστί, τῆς ἀληθοῦς τε καὶ μακαρίας τυχών, οὐ μόνον ἑνώσεως τῆς πρὸς τὴν ἁγίαν τριάδα, ἀλλὰ καὶ ἑνότητος τῆς ἐν τῇ ἁγίᾳ τριάδι νοουμένης, ὡς ἁπλοῦς καὶ ἀδιαίρετος καὶ μονοειδὴς κατὰ τὴν δύναμιν πρὸς τὴν ἁπλῆν καὶ ἀδιαίρετον κατὰ τὴν οὐσίαν γεγενημένος καὶ κατὰ τὴν ἕξιν τῶν ἀρετῶν, τὴν ὡσαύτως ἔχουσαν ἀγαθότητα, κατὰ τὸ ἐφικτὸν ἐκμιμούμενος καὶ τὴν ἰδιότητα τῶν κατὰ φύσιν μεριστῶν δυνάμεων διὰ τὴν τοῦ ἑνωθέντος θεοῦ χάριν ἀποθέμενος. * Διαιρεῖται γάρ, ὥς φασι, τὸ παθητικὸν τῆς ψυχῆς εἴς τε τὸ ἐπιπειθὲς λόγῳ καὶ τὸ μὴ πειθόμενον λόγῳ· καὶ τὸ μὲν λόγῳ μὴ πειθόμενον διαιροῦσιν εἰς τὸ θρεπτικόν, ὃ καλοῦσι φυσι

Freedom from Passion

The teacher may also have been referring to aggression and appetite with his use of the phrase "material duality," because they are the materially oriented powers and derive from the passionate part of the soul. They are at odds with reason and can scatter the intellect into multiplicity, unless, by strangling them from the beginning with understanding, reason has subjugated them to itself. If someone masters them and compels them to be moved only as far as is necessary, such that they are subjugated like a servant by the rule of reason, or even if someone abandons them completely and is possessed of only the unwavering knowledge-filled enchantment of love "through reason and contemplation" and is drawn   B
from multiplicity to the single, unique, pure, simple and indivisible movement of the exceedingly virile power of desire,   129
with which one ceaselessly and philosophically attains stability with God for oneself in an invariable and continuous movement of desire, such a person is truly "blessed." He will have attained not only true and blessed union with the holy Trinity but also the "unity in the" holy "Trinity as it is known by the mind," for he will have gained the power to become simple, undivided, and uniform with the Trinity, which is simple and undivided in essence, and he will possess the virtues, as the Trinity likewise possesses goodness. In this way, such a person closely imitates the holy Trinity as far as this is possible and puts off, by the grace of the unified God, the characteristic property of the powers that are divisible by nature. For[118] the   C
passionate element of the soul "is divided," as they say, "into that part which is obedient to reason and that part which does not" obey "reason."[119] Moreover, they divide "the part that does not obey reason" into "the nutritive faculty," which

---

118   *66. Explanation of the passionate aspect of the soul and of its general divisions and subdivisions*
119   Nem. Emes., *Nat. hom.* 15, p. 72.19–20.

κόν, καὶ **εἰς τὸ σφυγμικόν, ὃ καλοῦσι ζωτικόν (ὧν οὐδέτε-
ρον λόγῳ πειθόμενον ἄγεται) – οὐκ ἐπιπειθὲς δὲ λόγῳ
καλεῖται, ἐπειδὴ μὴ πέφυκεν ἄγεσθαι λόγῳ·** τὸ γὰρ αὐ-
ξάνειν ἢ ὑγιαίνειν ἢ ζῆν οὐκ ἔστιν ἐν ἡμῖν –, τὸ δὲ ἐπιπειθὲς λόγῳ διαιρεῖται εἰς δύο, τό τε ἐπιθυμητικὸν καὶ τὸ
θυμικόν – **ἐπιπειθὲς δὲ λόγῳ καλοῦσιν αὐτό, διότι λόγῳ
πέφυκεν ἐν τοῖς σπουδαίοις ἄγεσθαί τε καὶ ὑποτάσσε-
σθαι –.** Πάλιν δὲ τὸ ἐπιθυμητικὸν διαιροῦσιν εἰς ἡδονὴν καὶ
λύπην· ἐπιτυγχάνουσα γὰρ ἡ ἐπιθυμία ἡδονὴν **ἐργάζεται,**
ἀποτυγχάνουσα δὲ λύπην. **Καὶ** πάλιν, καθ'ἕτερον τρόπον
φασὶ τὴν ἐπιθυμίαν διαιρουμένην τέσσαρα σὺν ἑαυτῇ τὰ
πάντα εἴδη ποιεῖν, **ἐπιθυμίαν ἡδονὴν φόβον καὶ λύπην.**
Καὶ ἐπειδὴ τῶν ὄντων τὰ μέν ἐστιν ἀγαθά, τὰ δὲ φαῦλα,
ταῦτα δὲ ἢ παρόντα ἢ μέλλοντά ἐστι, προσδοκώμενον μὲν
ἀγαθὸν ἐπιθυμίαν **ἐκάλεσαν,** παρὸν δὲ ἡδονήν, **καὶ** πάλιν,
προσδοκώμενον κακὸν φόβον, παρὸν δὲ λύπην, **ὡς εἶναί τε
καὶ θεωρεῖσθαι** | περὶ μὲν τὰ **καλά, εἴτε τὰ ὄντως ὄντα,**   1197
εἴτε τὰ νομιζόμενα, τὴν ἡδονὴν καὶ **τὴν** ἐπιθυμίαν, περὶ
δὲ τὰ φαῦλα **τὴν** λύπην καὶ **τὸν** φόβον. **Πάλιν** δὲ τὴν λύπην **διαιροῦσιν εἰς** τέσσαρα, **εἰς ἄχος εἰς ἄχθος εἰς φθόνον εἰς ἔλεον· καὶ τὸ μὲν ἄχος εἶναί φασι** λύπην, ἀφωνίαν
ἐμποιοῦσαν οἷς ἂν ἐγγένηται διὰ τὴν εἰς βάθος πάροδον
τοῦ λογιστικοῦ, τὸ δὲ ἄχθος λύπην βαροῦσάν τε **καὶ διοχλοῦσαν ἐπ'ἀβουλήτοις συμβάσεσι, τὸν** δὲ φθόνον λύπην ἐπ'ἀλλοτρίοις ἀγαθοῖς, **τὸ δὲ ἔλεος** λύπην ἐπ'ἀλλοτρίοις
κακοῖς. Κακὸν δὲ πᾶσαν λύπην **ἔφασαν** τῇ ἑαυτῆς φύσει

"they call 'natural,' and 'pulsation," which "they call 'living,'"[120] (neither of which is led on in its activity by obeying reason). It is referred to as "not obedient to reason" because it is not naturally led by reason, for growing, being in good health, and living are not in our power. "And the part that is obedient to reason is divided into two, the appetitive and the aggressive faculties."[121] They call this part "obedient to reason" because it is naturally led by and subject to reason in those who are diligent.

"They divide the appetitive aspect into pleasure and distress, for when appetite attains its object" it produces "pleasure, and when it fails to attain it," it produces "distress." And "again, in a different mode, they say that when appetite is divided it yields with itself all four forms": appetite, pleasure, fear, and distress. "Since, among existing things, there are good things and base things," and these are either "present" or impending, they call "an expected good 'appetite,' a present good 'pleasure,'" and "moreover," they call "an expected evil 'fear,' and a present evil 'distress.'" This is because "pleasure and appetite" exist and are observed as pertaining to things that are beautiful, whether they really be such or are simply considered to be so, "whereas distress and fear exist and are observed as pertaining to what is base."[122] To continue, they divide "distress into four: shock, grief, envy, and pity." They say "shock is distress that renders" those whom it befalls "silent" by driving the rational faculty down into the depths. "Grief is distress that weighs us down" and vexes us with unwanted circumstances. "Envy is distress in reaction to someone else's possession of good things, and pity is distress in reaction to someone else's experience of evil." They say "every form of distress is an evil thing in virtue of its own nature,

120 NEM. EMES., *Nat. hom.* 22, p. 82.20–22.
121 NEM. EMES., *Nat. hom.* 16, p. 73.11–12.
122 NEM. EMES., *Nat. hom.* 17, p. 75.9–19.

κἂν γὰρ ὁ σπουδαῖος **ἐπ'ἀλλοτρίοις** λυπῆται **κακοῖς, ὡς ἐλεήμων,** ἀλλ'οὐ προηγουμένως κατὰ πρόθεσιν, ἀλλ'**ἐφεπομένως** κατὰ περίστασιν, ὁ **δὲ** θεωρητικὸς **κἂν τούτοις** ἀπαθὴς **διαμένει,** συνάψας **ἑαυτὸν τῷ** θεῷ **καὶ** τῶν τῇδε **πάντων** ἀλλοτριώσας. Τὸν δὲ φόβον **πάλιν** διαιροῦσιν εἰς ἕξ, εἰς ὄκνον εἰς αἰδῶ εἰς αἰσχύνην εἰς κατάπληξιν εἰς ἔκπληξιν εἰς ἀγωνίαν· **καὶ τὸν μὲν** ὄκνον εἶναί **φασιν** φόβον μελλούσης ἐνεργείας, **τὴν** αἰδῶ **δὲ** φόβον ἐπὶ προσδοκίᾳ ψόγου, **τὴν δὲ** αἰσχύνην φόβον ἐπ'αἰσχρῷ πεπραγμένῳ, **τὴν** δὲ κατάπληξιν φόβον ἐκ μεγάλης φαντασίας, **τὴν δὲ ἔκπληξιν** φόβον ἐκ **μεγάλων ἀκουσμάτων τὴν αἴσθησιν ἀφαιρούμενον, τὴν** ἀγωνίαν δὲ φόβον διαπτώσεως, τουτέστιν ἀποτυχίας – φοβούμενοι γὰρ ἀποτυχεῖν ἀγωνιῶμεν –, **καλοῦσι δέ τινες αὐτὴν καὶ δειλίαν.**

Τὸν δὲ θυμὸν **πάλιν** εἶναι **λέγουσι** ζέσιν τοῦ περὶ καρδίαν αἵματος ἢ ὄρεξιν **ἀντιλυπήσεως, διαιροῦσι δὲ καὶ τοῦτον εἰς** τρία, **εἰς** ὀργήν, ἥν **τινες** ἐκάλεσαν χολὴν καὶ χόλον, **καὶ εἰς** μῆνιν **καὶ εἰς** κότον· **καὶ τὴν μὲν ὀργὴν εἶναί φασι θυμὸν πρὸς ἐνέργειαν** ἀρχὴν καὶ κίνησιν ἔχοντα **ἢ θυμὸν ἐνεργούμενον, τὴν δὲ χολὴν τὴν δι'ἄλλου ἄμυναν τοῦ λυπήσαντος, τὸν δὲ χόλον τὴν δι'ἑαυτοῦ τοῦ λυπηθέντος ἐπεξέλευσιν εἰς τὸν λυπήσαντα, τὴν δὲ μῆνιν θυμὸν εἰς** παλαίωσιν – εἴρηται **δὲ** παρὰ τὸ μένειν καὶ τῇ μνήμῃ **παρακατέχεσθαι –, τὸν δὲ κότον θυμὸν** ἐπιτηροῦντα καιρὸν εἰς τιμωρίαν – εἴρηται δὲ παρὰ τὸ κεῖσθαι οὗτος –.

for" even if "a diligent person is in distress" over someone else's experience of evil, as one who has pity, "not as being guided in accordance with a purpose, but rather" incidentally in reaction "to circumstances, the contemplative" remains "free from passion" even in these circumstances, for he will have connected" himself "to God," and "will have estranged himself from" all things "here below."[123] To continue on again, "they divide fear into six: hesitation, embarrassment, shame, terror, panic, and anguish." They say "hesitation is the fear of a future eventuality; embarrassment is fear because of an expectation of blame; shame is the fear that comes because of a shameful deed that has already been committed; terror is the fear that comes from some great apparition; panic is the fear" that comes from great rumors that deprive a person of his senses; and "anguish is the fear of falling, that is, of failure – for when we are afraid of failing we are in anguish" –,[124] and some also call this cowardice.

131

|B

With respect to "aggression" then, they say "it is the boiling of the blood around the heart or the desire" to inflict pain in retribution, and they divide this into three: wrath, which" some "call bile and gall," and "rage," and "rancor." They say wrath is aggression that "has a beginning and moves" towards actualization or that it is actualized aggression; bile is revenge gained through another person upon someone who has caused pain; gall is the vengeance one who was afflicted with pain himself visits upon the one who has caused pain. Rage is aggression "directed towards something past – it is called this because it remains" and is stored up "in the memory." And "rancor" is aggression "that watches out for an occasion for retribution – it is called this because it lies in wait."[125]

C

123   NEM. EMES., *Nat. hom.* 19, p. 80.13–20.
124   NEM. EMES., *Nat. hom.* 21, p. 81.15–21.
125   NEM. EMES., *Nat. hom.* 20, p. 81.2–10. These last two definitions contain etymological explanations in the Greek: μῆνις (rage), μένειν (remain), μνήμη (memory); κότος (rancor), κεῖσθαι (lying in wait).

Διαιροῦσι δὲ καὶ τούτων ἕκαστον εἰς ἄλλα πολλά, ἅπερ εἰ βουληθείη τις δι'ἀκριβοῦς ἐξετάσεως παραδοῦναι γραφῇ, πολὺν ἀθροίσει λόγον καὶ χρόνον δαπανήσει, ὡς μὴ δὲ ἀνεκτὸν εἶναι τοῖς ἐντυγχάνουσι διὰ τὸ πλῆθος.

Μέγα οὖν καὶ θαυμαστὸν ὄντως ἐστὶ καὶ πολλῆς δεόμενον προσοχῆς τε καὶ σπουδῆς καὶ πρὸ τούτων τῆς θείας ἐπικουρίας τὸ δυνηθῆναι πρῶτον μὲν τῆς ὑλικῆς δυάδος τῶν ἐμφύτων κρατῆσαι δυνάμεων, θυμοῦ λέγω καὶ ἐπιθυμίας, καὶ τοῦ κατ'αὐτὰς μερισμοῦ, καὶ μακάριος ὅστις ἄγειν ἑτοίμως ταύτας ὅποι τῷ λόγῳ δοκεῖ δεδύνηται, μέχρις ἂν τοῖς πρακτοῖς διὰ τῆς ἠθικῆς φιλοσοφίας τῶν προτέρων καθαίρηται μολυσμῶν, | 1200
* ἔπειτα δὲ καὶ ὑπὲρ αὐτὰς γενέσθαι καὶ παντελῶς ἀπώσασθαι, ὡς τὴν Ἄγαρ καὶ τὸν Ἰσμαὴλ ὁ Ἀβραὰμ ἐκεῖνος ὁ μέγας, τοῦ λογιστικοῦ ἤδη περὶ τὰ θεῖα κατὰ τὸν Ἰσαὰκ ἐκεῖνον γυμνασθῆναι δυναμένου θεάματα, ὑπὸ τῆς κατὰ τὴν γνῶσιν φερομένης θείας φωνῆς διδασκόμενος μὴ δύνασθαι τὸ κατὰ νοῦν θεῖον τῆς ἐλευθέρας κατὰ πνεῦμα γνώσεως γέννημα, τῷ δουλικῷ τῆς σαρκὸς ἐπισυνημμένον σπέρματι, τῆς μακαρίας τυχεῖν ἐπαγγελίας, ἥτις ἐστὶν ἡ κατ'ἐλπίδας προκειμένη τοῖς ἀγαπῶσι τὸν κύριον τῆς θεώσεως χάρις, ἣν ἤδη τυπικῶς ὑπῆρχε προειληφώς, τῷ περὶ μονάδος λόγῳ διὰ πίστεως μυστικῶς συναφθείς· καθ'ὃν ἑνοειδὴς γενόμενος, μᾶλλον δὲ ἐκ πολλῶν εἷς, μόνος πρὸς μόνον διόλου τὸν θεὸν μεγαλοπρεπῶς συνήχθη, μηδένα τὸ παράπαν τῆς οἱασοῦν περί τι ἄλλο τῶν σκεδαστῶν γνώσεως τύπον ἑαυτῷ συνεπιφερόμενος· ὅπερ οἶμαι δηλοῦν τὴν τοῦ δοθέντος εἰς προσθήκην τοῦ ὀνόματος ἄλφα γράμματος δύναμιν. Διὸ καὶ πατὴρ τῶν διὰ πίστεως προσαγομένων θεῷ κατὰ στέρησιν πάντων τῶν μετὰ θεόν ἐχρημάτισεν, ὡς τοὺς αὐτοὺς κατὰ πίστιν ἐν πνεύματι τύπους τῷ πατρὶ τῶν τέκνων ἐμφερῶς ἔχειν δυναμένων.

They also divide each of these into many other concepts, which, if someone wanted to transmit them in a thorough written account, it would take up so many words and consume so much time that it would be unbearable because of   132
its length for those who would try to read it.

Therefore, it is a great and truly wonderful thing requiring much attention and diligence, and divine aid above all, to be able, first of all, to achieve mastery over the innate powers of "material duality," that is, aggression, appetite, and all   D
their various aspects. Blessed indeed is the one who is able willingly to guide these in the direction that seems fitting to reason, until he should be cleansed of his former defilements by the practices of ethical philosophy, since[126] he will also be   1200A
able "to transcend" them and drive them away completely, as that great man Abraham did with Hagar and Ishmael.[127] His rational faculty will have already been ready to be stripped down for training in divine visions like that man Isaac,[128] for he was taught by the divine, knowledge-bearing voice, that the divine intellectual offspring of free spiritual knowledge cannot, when it has been joined to the servile seed of the flesh, attain the blessed promise, which is the hoped-for grace of deification appointed for those who love the Lord. It was Abraham who had already initiated this as its primary example when he received it, when he was joined mystically   B
to the essential idea of Unity through faith. Having acquired unity of form in accordance with this essential idea, or rath-   133
er, a unity out of multiplicity, he was magnificently led alone to God who is completely alone,[129] carrying with himself no knowledge of any other scattered reality whatsoever. This in-

---

126   67. Contemplating from Scripture how it is not necessary that the one with true knowledge join the word of wisdom to the law of nature, and what the addition of the letter "alpha" to the name of Abraham means

127   Cf. Gen. 16.1–16; 21.9–14.

128   Cf. Gen 24.63.

129   Cf. PLOT., Enneads V.i.6.11; VI.ix.11.51.

* Τοῦτο τυχὸν ἐν ἀρχῇ τῆς γνωστικῆς ἀγωγῆς καὶ
ὁ μέγας Μωϋσῆς ἐκεῖνος, διδασκόμενος ὑπὸ τῆς θείας
φωνῆς, ἐπαιδεύετο, ἡνίκα προσῆγεν ἰδεῖν τὸ ἐν τῇ
βάτῳ μυστικῶς φανταζόμενον φῶς, φασκούσης λῦσον
τὰ ὑποδήματα ἀπὸ τῶν ποδῶν σου· ὁ γὰρ τόπος ἐν ᾧ
ἔστηκας γῆ ἁγία ἐστί, τὸ δεῖν, ὡς οἶμαι, τῶν σωματικῶν ἁπάντων ἀπολελύσθαι κατὰ διάθεσιν τὴν ψυχήν,
μέλλουσαν τὴν διὰ θεωρίας πρὸς τὴν τῶν ὑπερκοσμίων
νόησιν γνωστικὴν ποιεῖσθαι πορείαν καὶ τελείαν τοῦ ἐν
σχέσει σαρκὸς προτέρου βίου ἀλλοτρίωσιν διὰ τῆς τῶν
ὑποδημάτων ἔχειν ἀποθέσεως.

* Τοῦτο πάλιν ἴσως ὁ αὐτὸς θειότατος Μωϋσῆς ἐν
ταῖς τῶν θυσιῶν διατάξεσι παρεδήλου, τῶν ἱερείων
ἀφαιρεῖν τὸ στέαρ καὶ τοὺς νεφροὺς καὶ τὸ στηθύνιον
καὶ τὸν λοβὸν τοῦ ἥπατος ἐπιτάσσων, τὸ δεῖν αὐτάς τε
τὰς γενικὰς τῶν ἐν ἡμῖν παθῶν δυνάμεις, τὸν θυμὸν
λέγω καὶ τὴν ἐπιθυμίαν, τὴν ὄντως ὑλικὴν δυάδα,
καὶ τὰς ἐνεργείας αὐτῶν ἀφαιρεῖν, καὶ τῷ θείῳ πυρὶ
τῆς κατὰ γνῶσιν μυστικῆς ἐκτῆξαι δυνάμεως, τῆς μὲν
ἐπιθυμίας διὰ τῶν νεφρῶν, τῆς δὲ ἐνεργείας αὐτῆς,
τουτέστι τῆς ἡδονῆς, διὰ τοῦ λίπους ἤτοι τοῦ στέατος
δηλουμένης καὶ τοῦ θυμοῦ | διὰ τοῦ στηθυνίου, τῆς δὲ   1201
κατ᾽αὐτὸν ἐνεργείας διὰ τοῦ λοβοῦ τοῦ ἥπατος, ἐν ᾧ ἡ
πικρὰ καὶ δριμυτάτη πέπηγε χολή, σημαινομένων.

dicates, I think, the significance of the letter "alpha," which was given as an addition to his name.[130] For this reason, the father of those who are led through faith to God by the denial of everything that is after God have acted in this way, so the children are able to possess the same traits by faith in spirit, similar to their father.

The[131] great Moses probably learned this in the beginning of   C his journey to knowledge, when he was taught by the divine voice as he went forth to see the light mystically appearing in the bush, when the voice said, *put off your shoes from your feet, for the place where you are standing is holy ground* (Ex 3.5). He learned, I think, that it is necessary to release the disposition of the soul from all bodily realities, for the soul is destined to make its way through contemplation towards the knowledge-filled thought of what transcends worldly reality and to acquire complete estrangement from the fleshly condition of its former life. He learned all this through the symbol of removing his sandals.

Perhaps[132] this same most divine Moses also hinted at this idea in the ordinances concerning sacrifices, when he ordered the removal of the tallow, the kidneys, the breast, and the lobe of the liver from the sacrificial animals.[133] He indicated in these ordinances that it is necessary to remove the generative powers of the passions in us, I mean aggression and appetite, the real "material duality," as well as their actualizations, and to melt them out with the divine fire of knowledge-filled mystical power. Appetite is signified here by the kidneys, and its actualization, pleasure, is indicated through the fat or tallow,

---

130   Cf. Gen. 17.5. Maximus here refers to the practice of negating a concept by affixing the Greek letter α as a prefix to the word.

131   *68. Contemplating Moses, specifically his sandals being removed*

132   *69. Contemplating the parts of sacrifices*

133   Cf. Ex. 29.13, 22, 26–27, etc.

* Τοῦτο πάλιν κἂν τῷ περὶ λέπρας τόπῳ σοφῶς αὐτὸν οἶμαι παρεμφαίνειν δι᾿αἰνιγμάτων συμβολικῶν τὴν ἀφὴν τῆς λέπρας εἰς τέσσαρα γένη μερίσαντα, εἰς λευκὸν καὶ χλωρὸν καὶ ξανθὸν καὶ ἀμαυρόν, δι᾿ὧν τό τε θυμικὸν καὶ τὸ ἐπιθυμητικὸν εἰς τὰ ὑπ᾿αὐτὰ εἴδη διῃρημένα δείκνυται, τῆς μὲν ἐπιθυμίας διὰ τοῦ λευκοῦ καὶ τοῦ χλωροῦ εἰς ἡδονὴν καὶ λύπην μερίζεσθαι δηλουμένης, τοῦ δὲ θυμοῦ διὰ τοῦ ξανθοῦ καὶ τοῦ ἀμαυροῦ εἰς ὀργὴν καὶ μῆνιν καὶ τὴν κεκρυμμένην κακουργίαν τῆς ὑποκρίσεως τεμνομένου· ταῦτα γὰρ πρῶτα γένη τῶν ὑπ᾿αὐτὰ παθῶν, ὥς φασι, καὶ πάντων ἀρχηγικώτερα τῶν τοῦ θυμοῦ καὶ τῆς ἐπιθυμίας γεννήματα, οἷς τὴν νοσηλευομένην ψυχὴν οὐχ᾿οἷόν τε, ἕως ὑπὸ τούτων κατέστικται, τοῖς τῆς θείας ἠξιωμένοις παρεμβολῆς ἐναρίθμιον εἶναι.

* Τοῦτο καὶ τὸν θαυμαστὸν οἶμαι Φινεὲς ἐκεῖνον τῷ καθ᾿ἑαυτὸν ζήλῳ παραινίττεσθαι. Τὴν γὰρ Μαδιανῖτιν τῷ Ἰσραηλίτῃ συγκαταιχμάσας μυστικῶς διὰ τοῦ δόρατος τὴν ὕλην τῷ εἴδει καὶ τῷ θυμῷ τὴν ἐπιθυμίαν καὶ τὴν ἀλλόφυλον ἡδονὴν τῷ ἐμπαθεῖ λογισμῷ διὰ τῆς τοῦ ἀρχιερέως λόγου δυνάμεως συναπωθεῖσθαι χρῆν παντάπασι τῆς ψυχῆς ἐνέφαινεν· εἴδους γὰρ πρὸς ὕλην τρόπον ἐπέχει ὅ τε θυμὸς πρὸς τὴν ἐπιθυμίαν, τῷ προσεγγισμῷ διδοὺς αὐτῇ κίνησιν, καθ᾿ἑαυτὴν οὖσαν ἀκίνητον, ὅ τε λογισμὸς πρὸς τὴν ἡδονήν, εἰδοποιεῖν αὐτὴν πεφυκώς, ἀνείδεον καὶ ἄμορφον κατὰ τὸν ἴδιον λόγον ὑπάρχουσαν. Δηλοῖ δὲ τοῦτο καὶ αὐτὴ τῶν ὀνομάτων ἡ δύναμις· Χασβὴ γὰρ ἡ Μαδιανῖτις ὀνομάζεται, ὅπερ ἐστὶ γαργαλισμός μου, καὶ Ζαμβρὶ ὁ Ἰσραηλίτης,

while aggression is signified by the breast and its actualiza-   1201A
tion by the lobe of the liver, where bitter and pungent bile is
stored.

I[134] think he also gives a wise indication of this same idea
through enigmatic symbols in the passage concerning leprosy,
where he distinguished the infection of leprosy into four types:
white, green, yellow, and dark.[135] Through these, the faculties
of aggression and appetite are shown to be divided into the
different species classified under them: we see appetite separated into pleasure and distress, and these are symbolized by
the white and green, and aggression divided into wrath, rage,
and the hidden evil work of hypocrisy, these being symbolized
by the yellow and the dark. These are the primary species   B
of the passions that are classified under them, as they say,
and are the original offspring of all that belongs to aggression
and appetite. Because of these, the sickened soul is not in any
condition to be counted among those who are worthy of divine
visitation while it is still covered with blemishes induced by
them,

I[136] think that marvelous man Phineas also suggests this by   135
his zeal.[137] For when he struck down the Midianite woman
along with the Israelite man he mystically indicated with his
spear that it is absolutely necessary for materiality along with
form, and appetite along with aggression, and foreign pleasure along with impassioned thought, to be expelled from the
soul through the power of high-priestly reason. For as it is   C
with form in relation to matter so aggression is predominant
in relation to appetite: it gives motion to it by its proximi-
ty though it remains motionless in itself. Thought, likewise,

---

134   70. *Briefly contemplating the different forms of leprosy in the law*
135   Cf. Lev 13–14.
136   71. *Contemplating Phineas and those who were destroyed by him*
137   Cf. Num 25.6–13.

ὅπερ ἐστὶν ᾆσμά μου, τουτέστι μετεωρισμός μου. Ἐπειδὰν οὖν τῆς θείας ἀπονεῦσαν μελέτης τε καὶ ἐνατενίσεως τὸ λογιστικὸν τῆς ψυχῆς καὶ μετεωρισθὲν τῷ ὑλικῷ
τῆς σαρκὸς γαργαλισμῷ συμπλακῇ κατὰ τὴν κάμινον
τῆς ἁμαρτίας, τοῦ ζηλωτοῦ πάντως δεῖται ἀρχιερέως
λόγου πρὸς ἀναίρεσιν μὲν τῶν οὕτω κακῶς ἀλλήλοις
συμπεπλεγμένων, ἀποστροφὴν δὲ τῆς φερομένης θείας
ἀγανακτήσεως.

   * Τοῦτο καὶ αὐτὸς ὁ κύριος, ὡς ἔμοιγε δοκεῖ, τυχὸν
παρεδήλου, τοῦτο μὲν ἐν οἷς φησι *μὴ δῶτε* | *τὸ ἅγιον*   1204
τοῖς κυσὶ μὴ δὲ βάλλετε τοὺς μαργαρίτας ὑμῶν ἔμπρο-
σθεν τῶν χοίρων, ἅγιον ἴσως καλῶν τὸ ἐν ἡμῖν νοερόν,
ὡς θείας ἀπεικόνισμα δόξης, ὅπερ μὴ κακῶς ἐᾶν ὑπὸ
τῶν θυμικῶν κινημάτων καθυλακτούμενον ἐκταράσ-
σεσθαι παρεγγύησε, μαργαρίτας δὲ τὰ θεῖα καὶ λαμπρὰ
τούτου νοήματα, οἷς τίμιον ἅπαν κοσμεῖσθαι πέφυκεν,
ἅπερ διαφυλάττειν ἀμόλυντα καὶ τῶν ἀκαθάρτων τῆς
ὑλικῆς ἐπιθυμίας παθῶν ἐλεύθερα δεῖν παρεκελεύσατο,
τοῦτο δὲ ἐν οἷς πρὸς τοὺς ἁγίους αὐτοῦ μαθητὰς ἀπο-
στελλομένους ἐπὶ τὸ κήρυγμα περὶ τοῦ πῶς εὐσταλεῖς
αὐτοὺς εἶναι καὶ ἀπερίττους διατυπῶν. Καὶ τοῦτο πρὸς
τοῖς ἄλλοις φησὶ *μὴ δὲ πήραν αἴρετε εἰς τὴν ὁδόν, μήτε*
ῥάβδον μήτε ὑποδήματα εἰς τοὺς πόδας ὑμῶν, ὡς δέον
τὸν τῆς ὑψηλῆς κατὰ τὴν γνῶσιν πορείας ἐπειλημμέ-
νον παντὸς μὲν ὑλικοῦ βάρους ἐλεύθερον εἶναι, πάσης
δὲ τῆς κατ' ἐπιθυμίαν καὶ θυμὸν ἐμπαθοῦς διαθέσεως
καθαρόν, ὡς δηλοῖ ἥ τε πήρα καὶ ἡ ῥάβδος, ἡ μὲν τὴν
ἐπιθυμίαν, ἡ δὲ τὸν θυμὸν ἐπισημαίνουσα, μάλιστα δὲ
τῆς καθ' ὑπόκρισιν γυμνὸν κακουργίας, τῆς οἷον, ὑπο-
δήματος δίκην, τοῦ βίου τὸ ἴχνος ἐπικαλυπτούσης καὶ

is predominant in relation to pleasure and naturally confers form upon it, while pleasure exists as formless and shapeless in its own logic. The very meaning of the names shows this as well, for the Midianite woman is named Chasbe, which means "my stimulation," and the Israelite is named Zambri, which is "my song," that is "my arousal." Therefore, whenever the rational faculty of the soul has turned its attention and gaze away from the Divine and has been aroused by the material stimulation of the flesh and is bound up thereby in the furnace of sin, it certainly needs the high-priestly reason of the zealot D
to destroy what had thus been wickedly wrapped around each 136
other to avert the approaching divine wrath.

It[138] seems to me that perhaps the Lord Himself has also addressed this same theme. For example, He says, *Do not give that which is holy to the dogs, neither cast your pearls before* 1204A
swine (Matt 7.6). He is probably calling *"holy"* that which is intellectual in us, since it is an image of the divine glory, which He insisted should not be thrown vilely into horrible confusion, being barked at by angry movements. The *pearls* are its divine and luminous thoughts. Every valuable thing is naturally adorned with them, and He exhorts us that it is necessary to keep them undefiled and free of the impure passions of material appetite. Another example is when he described to His holy disciples how they were to be lightly equipped and unencumbered when they were being sent out for preaching. With respect to this second example, among other things, He says, *Take neither purse for your journey, nor staff, nor shoes* for your feet (Matt 10.10; Lk 9.3, 10.4), since one who has undertaken the exalted pathway of knowledge B
must be free of every material weight and pure of every passionate disposition of appetite and aggression, as the *purse* and

---

138   72. *Contemplating the phrase, "Give not that which is holy unto the dogs" (Matt 7.6), and that it was necessary for the apostles to take "neither staff, nor purse, nor shoes" (Matt 10.10)*

τὸ ἐμπαθὲς τῆς ψυχῆς ἐπικρυπτούσης ἐπιεικείας πλά-
σματι· ἣν ὑποδησάμενοι ἀφρόνως οἱ Φαρισαῖοι μόρφω-
σιν εὐσεβείας ἀλλ'οὐκ εὐσέβειαν ἔχοντες, κἂν εἰ λαθεῖν
ἐνόμιζον, ὑπὸ τοῦ λόγου ἐλεγχθέντες ἐδείχθησαν.

* **Ταύτης** τῆς ὑλικῆς δυάδος, **τῆς κατὰ θυμὸν
λέγω καὶ ἐπιθυμίαν, πάλιν ὁ κύριος ἠλευθέρωσεν, ὡς
οἶμαι, τὸν σεληνιαζόμενον, μᾶλλον δὲ τοῦ πυρί, τῷ
θυμῷ, καὶ ὕδατι, τῇ ἐπιθυμίᾳ, αὐτὸν βουληθέντος ἀπο-
λέσαι πονηροῦ δαίμονος ἐπέσχε τε καὶ κατήργησε τὴν
μανιώδη λύσσαν. Σελήνης γὰρ οὐδὲν διενήνοχεν ἡ πρὸς
τὰ** γινόμενα καὶ ἀπογινόμενα **σχέσις τῶν ἡττημένων τοῖς
ὑλικοῖς ἀνθρώπων· ἧς ἐπιλαβόμενος ὁ τὰ πάθη δια-
γείρων δαίμων, ὥσπερ ὕδατι καὶ πυρί, τῇ ἐπιθυμίᾳ καὶ
τῷ θυμῷ, ἐμβάλλων τὸν νοῦν καὶ ἐναποπνίγων οὐ παύε-
ται, ἕως ὁ τοῦ θεοῦ λόγος παραγενόμενος τὸ μὲν ὑλικὸν
καὶ πονηρὸν ἀπελάσειε πνεῦμα, δι'οὗ ὁ παλαιός τε καὶ
χοϊκὸς χαρακτηρίζεται ἄνθρωπος, τὸν δὲ ἐνεργούμενον
τῆς πονηρᾶς ἐλευθερώσειε τυραννίδος, τὴν φυσικὴν
αὐτῷ σωφροσύνην ἀποδοὺς καὶ χαρισάμενος, δι'ἧς ὁ
νέος καὶ κατὰ θεὸν κτιζόμενος ἄνθρωπος διαδείκνυται.**

the *staff* show, where the *purse* signifies appetite, and the *staff* aggression. And such a person must especially be stripped of hypocritical malice, which obscures, as it were, the pathway   137
of a person's life like a *shoe* and hides the passionate state of the soul with an artificial equanimity. Because the Pharisees had mindlessly put this on as a *form of piety* (II Tim 3.5) – although they did not actually *possess* piety – and even if they thought they were escaping notice, they were shown to stand refuted by the Word.

C

It[139] was from this "material duality," I mean the duality of aggression and appetite, that, again, I think the Lord freed the epileptic,[140] that is to say, He freed him from the evil demon that wanted to destroy him with fire, which is aggression, and water, which is appetite, when He came against his raving madness and made it of no effect. For the habitual relation to "things that come to be and pass away," which characterizes people who have yielded to material things, is no different than the moon.[141] The demon attacks by means of this relation in order to stir up the passions, and does not stop casting the intellect into appetite and aggression, as though into water and fire, choking it with them, until the Word of God comes near and destroys the material and evil spirit, which characterizes the *old* and *earthly man* (I Cor 15.47; Eph 4.22), and sets free the one possessed by this evil tyranny by allowing and granting to him a naturally sound mind. The new man, D
who is created in accordance with God (Eph 4.24), is then shown to all in his soundness of mind.[142]

---

139   *73. Contemplating the epileptic*
140   Cf. Matt 17.14–21; Mk 9.14–29; Lk 9.37–42.
141   The word for "epileptic," ὁ σεληνιαζόμενος ("lunatick" in the King James Version), is related to the word for "moon," ἡ σελήνη.
142   Cf. Lk 9.42.

Οὕτω μὲν οὖν πάντες οἱ ἅγιοι, τοῦ θείου καὶ ἀπλα-
νοῦς λόγου γνησίως ἐπειλημμένοι, τὸν αἰῶνα τοῦτον
διέβησαν, οὐδενὶ τῶν ἐν αὐτῷ τερπνῶν τὸ τῆς ψυχῆς
ἴχνος ἐναπερείσαντες· πρὸς γὰρ τοὺς ἄκρους τῶν ἀνθρώποις ἐφικτῶν περὶ θεοῦ λόγους, τῆς ἀγαθότητός τέ
φημι καὶ τῆς ἀγάπης, τὸν νοῦν μάλα γε εἰκότως ἀνα-
πετάσαντες, οἷς κινηθέντα τὸν θεὸν τὸ εἶναί τε δοῦναι
τοῖς οὖσι καὶ τὸ εὖ εἶναι χαρίσασθαι ἐπαιδεύθησαν, εἴ-
περ κίνησιν ἐπὶ θεοῦ τοῦ μόνου ἀκινήτου | θέμις εἰπεῖν,   1205
ἀλλὰ μὴ μᾶλλον βούλησιν τὴν πάντα κινοῦσάν τε καὶ εἰς
τὸ εἶναι καὶ παράγουσαν καὶ συνέχουσαν, κινουμένην
δὲ οὐδαμῶς οὐδέποτε. Τούτοις καὶ αὐτοὶ σοφῶς ἑαυτοὺς ἀπετύπωσαν, τοῦ ἀφανοῦς καὶ ἀοράτου κάλλους
τῆς θείας μεγαλοπρεπείας εὐμιμήτως φέροντες φαι-
νομένην διὰ τῶν ἀρετῶν τὴν ἰδιότητα. Διατοῦτο ἀγα-
θοὶ καὶ φιλόθεοι καὶ φιλάνθρωποι εὔσπλαγχνοί τε καὶ
οἰκτίρμονες γεγόνασι καὶ μίαν πρὸς ἅπαν τὸ γένος διάθεσιν ἔχοντες ἀγάπης ἐδείχθησαν· ὑφ'ἧς τὸ πάντων
ἐξαίρετον εἶδος τῶν ἀρετῶν, τὴν ταπείνωσιν λέγω,
διὰ πάσης αὐτῶν τῆς ζωῆς βεβαίαν κατασχόντες, τὴν
φυλακτικὴν μὲν τῶν ἀγαθῶν, φθαρτικὴν δὲ τῶν ἐναν-
τίων, οὐδενὶ τὸ παράπαν ἁλώσιμοι τῶν διοχλούντων
γεγόνασι πειρασμῶν, τῶν τε ἑκουσίων καὶ τοῦ ἐφ'ἡμῖν
λόγου καὶ τῶν ἀκουσίων καὶ οὐκ ἐφ'ἡμῖν, τῷ τοῖς μὲν
δι'ἐγκρατείας ἀπομαραίνειν τὰς ἐπαναστάσεις, τῶν δὲ
δι'ὑπομονῆς τὰς προσβολὰς ἀποσείεσθαι. Διχόθεν γὰρ
βαλλόμενοι, ὑπό τε *δόξης καὶ ἀτιμίας*, διέμενον ἄσει-
στοι, πρὸς ἄμφω ἀκινήτως ἔχοντες, μήτε ὕβρεσι τιτρω-
σκόμενοι διὰ τὴν ἑκούσιον ὕφεσιν, μήτε δόξαν προσιέ-
μενοι δι'ὑπερβάλλουσαν πτωχείας οἰκείωσιν· ὅθεν οὐ
θυμὸς οὐ φθόνος οὐκ ἔρις οὐχ'ὑπόκρισις οὐ δόλος οὐκ
εἰρωνευτική τις καὶ ἐπίκλοπος τῷ φαινομένῳ πλάσμα-

Conclusion

Thus have all the saints completed their passage through this   138
age by genuinely attaining to divine and unwavering reason,
for they did not allow the soul to become distracted on its
way by any of this age's delights. They very fittingly indeed
laid bare their intellect to the highest essential ideas about
God that are attainable for human beings, I mean goodness
and love. They were taught by them that God is moved to
give existence and to grant existence in the good to beings, if
I may be permitted to speak of motion with respect to God,
who alone is unmoved, instead of will, which moves all things   1205A
and both leads them to and holds them together in existence
but is never itself moved in any way. They have wisely formed
themselves in accordance with these, bringing to manifestation the distinctive property of the non-appearing and invisible beauty of divine magnificence in an accurate imitation
through the virtues. Because of this they became good, friends
of God and man, compassionate and merciful and were shown
to have a single disposition towards all people out of love.
Having throughout their whole life kept firm through love the
preeminent form of all the virtues, I mean humility, which
preserves good things but destroys the opposite, they became
impervious to the attacks of every vexing temptation, both
freely chosen temptations that belong to the logic of our own
agency and those that are not feely chosen and do not depend
upon us, putting down rebellions with self-control with respect
to the former, and fending off the attacks of the latter through
endurance . For, when they were attacked from both sides,   B
by *glory and dishonor* (II Cor 6.8), they remained unshaken   139
and kept themselves unmoved in relation to either, neither
being wounded by acts of insolence through willing compla-
cency nor accepting glory by taking on an exaggerated state
of poverty. Thus neither aggression, nor malice, nor strife, nor

τι δι'ἀπάτης ὑποσύρουσα πρὸς ἄλλο στοργή, τὸ πάντων
παθῶν ὀλεθριώτατον, οὐκ ἐπιθυμία τῶν κατὰ τὸν βίον
δοκούντων εἶναι λαμπρῶν, οὔτε τι ἕτερον τῆς πονηρᾶς
τῶν παθῶν πληθύος, οὐκ ἀπειλαὶ παρ'ἐχθρῶν ἐπανατει-
νόμεναι, οὐδέ τις θανάτου τρόπος αὐτῶν ἐκυρίευσε.

Διὸ καὶ μακάριοι δικαίως παρὰ θεῷ καὶ ἀνθρώποις
ἐκρίθησαν, ὅτι τῆς φανησομένης ἀρρήτου καὶ περιφα-
νοῦς δόξης κατὰ τὴν χάριν τοῦ μεγαλοδώρου θεοῦ ἐμ-
φανεῖς εἰκόνας ἑαυτοὺς κατέστησαν, ἵνα χαίροντες ὡς
γνωρίμοις τοῖς λόγοις τῶν ἀρετῶν, μᾶλλον δὲ θεῷ,
ὑπὲρ οὗ καὶ καθ'ἑκάστην ἡμέραν ἀποθνήσκοντες διε-
καρτέρησαν, ἑνωθῶσιν, ἐν ᾧ πάντων οἱ λόγοι τῶν ἀγαθῶν, ὥσπερ πηγῇ ἀειβλύστῳ, προϋφεστήκασί τε κατὰ
μίαν ἁπλῆν καὶ ἑνιαίαν τῶν πάντων περιοχήν, καὶ πρὸς
ὃν ἕλκουσι πάντας τοὺς καλῶς καὶ κατὰ φύσιν ταῖς ἐπὶ
τούτῳ δοθείσαις χρωμένους δυνάμεσιν.

hypocrisy, nor treachery, nor any false and cunning devotion to anything else that deceitfully seduces us when something delusional appears – this delusion being the most destructive of all the passions – nor the appetite for what seem to be the splendid things of life, nor any other member of the evil throng of passions, nor threats brandished by their enemies, nor any form of death, had power over them.

Therefore, the saints were justly considered by God and men   C
to be "blessed," for they established themselves as radiant images of the ineffable and all-encompassing glory of the generous God, which will be made manifest by grace, so that they might rejoice when they are united with the essential ideas that make known the virtues, or rather with God Himself, for whose sake they have endured to the end, even as they had died each day.[143] It is in God that the essential ideas of all good things have the source of their constitution, as in an ever-living spring, in one simple, single, all-encompassing embrace, and it is towards God that the saints draw all things that have beautifully and naturally acquired the powers that have been given by Him.

143   Cf. I Cor 15.31.

Note on the translation of λόγος in *Ambiguum* 10

Joshua LOLLAR

(*Lawrence, Kansas*)

I am grateful for the opportunity to place my translation of Maximus the Confessor's *Ambiguum* 10 alongside the learned studies contained in this volume. The translation is based on Carl Laga's forthcoming critical edition of the *Ambigua to John*. My complete translation of the *Ambigua* appears as Volume 45 of *Corpus Christianorum in Translation*[1] and will be followed by a full commentary on the work. I explain my approach to translating the *Ambigua* in the introduction to the CCT volume, and I will not repeat that here. It will be useful, however, to give at least a brief explanation of my translation of Maximus's well-known term λόγος.

Translating Maximus's λόγος magnifies the general, familiar problems of translation – accuracy, precision, gaps in meaning, comprehensibility – not simply because λόγος is multifaceted in Greek (many words in Maximus's lexicon are), but because it is a word that is basically associated with the meaning of language itself. Trying to translate the word for "word" from one language to another combines the instability of translation with the bewilderment of what language is and does, of how it is bound up with thought and world. Some Maximus scholars choose to leave λόγος, when it refers to the λόγοι of beings, untranslated.[2] Indeed, "logos" is among the philosophical terms discussed in the fascinating, and fascinatingly subtitled, *Vocabulaire Européen des*

---

[1] LOLLAR, Maximus the Confessor – Ambigua to John, Volume I: Translation.

[2] See, e.g., F. MORESCHINI, *Ambigua: problemi metafisici e teologici su testi di Gregorio di Nazianzo, Dionigi Areopagita*; Milano, 2003; T. TOLLEFSEN, *The Christocentric Cosmology of St. Maximus the Confessor*, Oxford, 2008; CONSTAS, 2014,1.

Ambiguum *10 of Maximus the Confessor in Modern Study: Papers Collected on the Occasion of the Budapest Colloquium on Saint Maximus, 3–4 February 2021*, ed. By Alexis LÉONAS & Vladimir CVETKOVIC, with the collaboration of Daniel HEIDE, Turnhout, 2025 (IPM 97), pp. 195–199
© BREPOLS ☙ PUBLISHERS   10.1484/M.IPM-EB.5.141860

Philosophies: Dictionnaire des Intraduisibles, and leaving the untranslatable λόγος untranslated does have the advantage of avoiding the misrepresentations that inevitably enter through any vernacular rendering.

However, the danger of abstracting λόγος from the rest of Maximus's thinking by such a non-translation introduces a different, and perhaps worse, kind of misrepresentation. It tends to treat the λόγοι as discrete objects that created things have,[3] but this misses something fundamental to Maximus's conception. The λόγοι of the beings of creation, of which we are a part, speak to the λόγος (reason) in us, which is in the image of the Λόγος τοῦ Θεοῦ, the Word of God. The λόγος of a being is that being leading us to the knowledge of the reality it embodies, "the Word of God who is God Himself".[4] The λόγος of a being is Divine-human communion in the world through contemplation. It is an answer to the question that the being raises: "When a question arises it breaks open the being of the object, as it were. Hence the logos that explicates this opened-up being is an answer".[5]

To approach the richness of this meaning, I use the phrase "essential idea" to translate Maximus's λόγος, where "idea" connotes both the openness of creativity at the heart of beings and the foundation of explicated meaning.[6] The λόγος of a being is the word God speaks as creation; it is the idea, the meaningfulness God gives in creating.

A generation before Maximus, John of Scythopolis, the sixth century commentator on Dionysius the Areopagite, connected "ideas" (ἰδέαι) to the λόγοι of beings through Dionysius's use of the term παραδείγματα, which refer in Dionysius to "the λόγοι which preexist as a unity in God and which produce the essences of things".[7] Maximus

---

[3] See E. D. PERL, *Methexis: Creation, Incarnation, Deification in Saint Maximus the Confessor*, Yale, 1995, p. 152, for helpful comments.

[4] *Amb. Ioh.*, PG 91, 1084D.

[5] H.-G. GADAMER, *Truth and Method*, 2nd rev. trans. by W. GLEN-DOEPEL et al, New York, 1989, p. 362; *Wahrheit und Methode: Grundzüge einer philosophischen Hermeneutik*, Tübingen, 1975, p. 345.

[6] H.-U. VON BALTHASAR, *Kosmische Liturgie: Das Weltbild Maximus' des Bekenners*, Einsiedeln – Trier, ²1988, uses "Idea/Ideen" to translate λόγος/λόγοι.

[7] Dionysius the Areopagite, *Div. Nom.* V.8, 188.6–8; cf. *Pseudo-Dionysius: The Complete Works*, trans. by C. LUIBHÉID & P. ROREM, New York, 1987, p. 102.

quotes this passage in *Ambiguum* 7, though he refers there to Diony-sius's definition of the λόγοι as "pre-determinations and divine acts of will".[8] For John, the παραδείγματα, which Dionysius identifies with the λόγοι, are also called ἰδέαι, "ideas",[9] as we also see much earlier in Philo of Alexandria, for whom "the world of ideas" is to be found in "the divine λόγος". Philo is drawing the philosophical, Platonic language of ἰδέαι towards the λόγοι, which more readily align with his Biblical refer-ence point, where the Word of God is the creative and ordering principle of all things.[10] While it should be noted that Maximus does not follow John of Scythopolis's verbal identification of λόγοι with ἰδέαι in *Ami-guum* 7,[11] I am more interested here in the range of meaning that "idea" has in English, as suggested by the connection of ἰδέα and λόγος, than in the use (or non-use) of ἰδέα itself in Maximus's Greek. λόγος/idea as "predetermination" speaks to the purposeful conveyance of meaning, and λόγος/idea as "act of will" reflects Divine creativity.

The "idea" of a being for Maximus is that which can be understood and articulated about it, that which makes it intelligible and organizes its meaning. Or better: it *is* that being as intelligible and meaning-ful. Consider Ralph Waldo Emerson: "The key to every man is his thought... he has a helm which he obeys, which is the idea after which all his facts are classified".[12] Emerson makes this observation in his essay "Circles", which sees the world as an ever-expanding recapitula-tion, in form, of God:

> The eye is the first circle; the horizon which it forms is the second; and throughout nature this primary picture is repeated without end. It is the highest emblem in the cipher of the world. St. Augustine described the nature of God as a circle whose centre was everywhere and its circum-

---

[8] Dionysius the Areopagite, *Div. Nom.* V.8, p. 188.8–9; *Amb. Io.*, PG 91, 1085A.

[9] John of Scythopolis, *Prol. et Schol. in Dion. Areo. Lib. De Divinis Nomini-bus*, ed. by B. R. SUCHLA, Berlin-Boston, 1990, p. 339.1; cf. *ibid.*, p. 326.3–4.

[10] Philo of Alexandria, *De opificio mundi*, 20, noted in G. WATSON, *Phanta-sia in Classical Thought*, Galway, 1988, p. 83 n. 2.

[11] JOHNATAN D. WOOD argues that Maximus is precisely *not* equating λόγοι with ἰδέαι as John of Scythopolis does: J. D. WOOD, *The Whole Mystery of Christ: Creation as Incarnation in Maximus Confessor*, Notre Dame, 2022, pp. 68–72. Wood's metaphysical distinctions are not my concern here.

[12] R. W. EMERSON, *Essays and English Traits*, New York, 2001, p. 150.

ference nowhere. We are all our lifetimes reading the copious sense of this first of forms.[13]

I invoke this usage in my translation of λόγος as "essential idea". The One Λόγος is many λόγοι and the many are One; the One Essential Idea of God, Who is with God and is God, is many essential ideas, which appear with God and reveal God's presence and are One.[14] And again, the One Circle is many circles and the many are One.

Closely related to this is a set of terms that are derived from λόγος: ἀναλογία – ἀναλόγως – κατ' ἀναλογίαν. These terms are often rendered as "proportion/proportionally" or simply as "analogy/according to analogy". I think it is best for a translation of these terms to be transparent to the link between ἀναλογία – ἀναλόγως – κατ' ἀναλογίαν, which describe how the Divine is present in a being, and the λόγος, which marks how a being is known and articulated as created by God. As such, I use the adverbial phrase "in the way that is ideally suited to", where "ideally" echoes the "essential idea" of a being.

A use of ἀναλόγως in the *Prologue* to Maximus's *Quaestiones ad Thalassium* is helpful here:

> the divine word (ὁ θεῖος λόγος) is like water, for just as water operates in different species of plants and vegetation and in different kinds of living things – by which I mean in human beings who drink the Word Himself – the Word is manifested in them through the virtues, in proportion (ἀναλόγως) to their level of knowledge and ascetic practice, like burgeoning fruit produced according to the quality of virtue and knowledge in each, so that the Word becomes known to others through other qualities and characteristics.[15]

Water is itself present to all different kinds of plants, but its activity and manifestation – how its presence is "known to others" – depend on the nature of the individual plant. Its singular presence is ideally suited to, in that it constitutes, each one in its particularity. The Word's presence is likewise made known according to, and as, the qualities of each person.

These translation choices, and the translation as such, are obviously based upon my understanding of the *Ambigua*. My goal in translat-

---

[13] EMERSON, *Essays and English Traits*, p. 149.

[14] Cf. *Amb. Ioh.*, PG 91, 1077C.

[15] *Q.Thal*, Prol. 99–107; trans. modified from CONSTAS, 2018, p. 77.

ing has been to get as close as I can to Maximus's thought through the words he used – as they sound in ours –, so that his teaching may inform our own thinking and experience.

Section Headings in *Ambiguum* 10

I have followed Professor Laga's edition in placing the traditional subdivisions of *Ambiguum* 10 into footnotes. While the subdivisions in *Amb.* 10 are very old – they occur in Carolingian manuscripts of Eriugena's Latin translation of the Ambigua[16] – in many instances they have been placed in the midst of a developing thought, sometimes in the middle of a sentence, so I have thought it best to remove them from the body of the text. I have numbered the subdivisions within the footnotes to set them off from the other sources.

---

[16] IOH. SCOT., *versio Max.*, p. lxvi (dates of the two manuscripts in question discussed at p. xiv and p. xxx).

II.

Studies:
Saint Maximus and his
intellectual context

Lecture typologique du récit de la Transfiguration : le schéma ternaire "démiurge, nature et temps"

L'*Ambiguum* 10 de Maxime à la lumière du *Timée* de Platon[*]

Pascal MUELLER-JOURDAN

(*Angers*)

Introduction

La littérature théologique byzantine comporte d'importantes traces de problèmes philosophiques remontant à la plus haute Antiquité, probables résurgences d'un fond de culture savante devenu, dans l'Antiquité tardive, commun au christianisme et au paganisme. On ne décèle souvent qu'avec peine l'origine parfois technique des questions philosophiques initiales. Tel pourrait être le cas d'une affirmation de Maxime le Confesseur, moine spéculatif du septième siècle byzantin, introduisant une interprétation symbolique du récit évangélique de la Transfiguration.[1]

Nous sommes loin d'une lecture littérale du texte biblique et nous serions sans doute autorisés à parler de lecture typologique dans la mesure où les Moïse et Élie du texte évangélique, apparus au côté du Christ transfiguré, représentent en type la nature et le temps tandis que le Christ, en tant que Verbe incarné, y apparaît comme le Démiurge. La Transfiguration du Christ donnerait ainsi à voir l'icône de l'acte créateur qui transcende lieu et temps et qui en un sens se produit dans un

---

[*] Cette recherche résulte du remaniement d'un premier travail paru en ligne dans la revue *Plato Journal* en 2006.

[1] Il existe trois récits évangéliques de la Transfiguration : Mt. 17 : 1–8 ; Mc. 9 : 2–8 ; Lc. 9 : 28–36.

Ambiguum *10 of Maximus the Confessor in Modern Study: Papers Collected on the Occasion of the Budapest Colloquium on Saint Maximus, 3–4 February 2021*, ed. by Alexis LÉONAS & Vladimir CVETKOVIĆ, with the collaboration of Daniel HEIDE, Turnhout, 2025 (IPM 97), pp. 203–220

10.1484/M.IPM-EB.5.141861

© BREPOLS ❧ PUBLISHERS

kairos constant. La concomitance de la nature et du temps produits hors du temps dans un premier maintenant inétendu pose à l'origine de toute la création deux principes qui présideront de façon constante à tous les processus naturels qui s'y donneront à observer ainsi qu'à leur ordre. Il pouvait en ressortir en particulier l'idée d'un temps premier, inétendu, principe de toutes les formes que connaîtra ultérieurement le temps quand il deviendra la mesure ordonnante et ordonnée de tous les mouvements naturels de l'univers créé. Il pouvait alors apparaître comme un principe d'ordre et de régularité toujours concomitant à la nature qui est par essence mouvement. C'est ce que nous chercherons en particulier à clarifier au cours de notre examen d'une brève portion de l'*Ambiguum* 10 qui voit Maxime, sous le motif d'élucider le sens symbolique du récit de la Transfiguration, exposer quelques-uns de ses principes les plus saillants concernant la cosmologie et la démiurgie. Nous convoquerons en support, et pour nous autoriser à une comparaison que nous croyons éclairante, quelques éléments du riche commentaire *Sur le Timée* de Proclus de Lycie dont le modèle explicatif de l'acte créateur converge assez mystérieusement avec celui qui nous est proposé par Maxime. En effet, sur le point particulier de la concomitance de la nature et du temps chez Maxime, du ciel et du temps chez Proclus, les deux modèles paraissent tomber d'accord comme nous tenterons de le démontrer.

1. *Theôria* sur Moïse et Élie

La portion de texte que nous tentons d'examiner ici, notamment la première proposition qui pourrait en constituer l'axiome, porte dans le livre X des *Ambigua* le titre de *théôria* ou contemplation. La *théôria* indique que ce qui doit être vu doit être vu par une perception toute divine en mesure d'accéder au travers de ce qui se donne à voir à tout ce qui jusqu'alors était inapparent. Ainsi le lecteur de Maxime est-il invité à se laisser conduire par-delà le voile et la matérialité du texte vers ce qui est au-delà du texte. Le texte présente ainsi un caractère iconique et diaphane puisqu'il donne accès à un degré de la réalité qui le transcende. Par nature sensible, la lettre du texte donne accès à un niveau de réalité qu'on peut qualifier d'intelligible et de spirituel.

1.1 Le texte à commenter

> Tous ceux qui sont après Dieu qui sont nés de Dieu, c'est-à-dire la nature des êtres et le temps, apparaissent ensemble auprès de Dieu qui se manifeste réellement, autant qu'il est possible, comme cause et créateur.

De ces deux, [B] Moïse serait "type du temps", non seulement comme celui qui enseigne le temps et le nombre qui lui correspond (ce Moïse en effet fut le premier à nombrer le temps d'après la genèse du monde) ou comme celui qui introduisit un culte inscrit dans le temps mais aussi comme celui qui ne devait pas entrer corporellement dans le repos final avec ceux-là même qu'il avait charge d'instruire avant l'annonce de la divine Bonne Nouvelle.

Le temps n'est-il pas en effet aussi de cette sorte ? Ne devançant, ni ne se mouvant avec ceux qu'il avait naturellement charge d'escorter jusqu'à la vie divine de l'aiôn à venir. Il saisit en effet Jésus qui est le successeur de tout, et du temps et de l'aiôn même si par ailleurs les logoi du temps demeurent en Dieu comme le montre sous voile [μυστικῶς] l'entrée de la loi dans le désert, loi donnée par Moïse à ceux qui ont reçu la terre en possession.

Le temps en effet est aiôn quand le mouvement est arrêté et l'aiôn est temps quand, [C] porté par le mouvement, il est mesuré. De sorte que je dis, pour le saisir en une définition, que l'aiôn est temps privé de mouvement et que le temps est aiôn mesuré par le mouvement.

Quant à Élie, il serait "type de la nature", non seulement pour avoir gardé inaltérés les logoi de sa propre nature et être resté libre, pour ce qui les concerne et selon l'opinion, de pensées instables issues des passions, mais aussi pour avoir éduqué à juger, par exemple "ce qu'est la loi naturelle", ceux qui font un usage contre-nature de la nature. Car la nature même est telle qu'elle sanctionne autant ceux qui entreprennent de la corrompre que ceux qui s'exercent à vivre contre-nature. Elle les sanctionne par le fait qu'ils ne possèdent plus naturellement la pleine puissance de la nature même, étant déjà réduits dans leur intégrité naturelle et par là sanctionnés dans la mesure où, inconsciemment et de façon irréfléchie, [D] ils se donnent à eux-mêmes une carence d'être par inclinaison vers le non-être.[2]

1.2. *Premières étapes et observations*

Dans le prolongement de cette citation, on trouve deux comparaisons, l'une entre Moïse et le monde sensible dans la mesure où la naissance et la mort du prophète sont un fait avéré et nous sont connues, et l'autre entre Élie et le monde intelligible car il se trouve que l'histoire biblique ne dit rien de la naissance d'Élie, même si celle-ci a eu lieu, ni si sa der-

---

[2] Maxime le Confesseur, *Amb.Ioh.* 10, *PG* 91, 1164AD.

nière apparition, son élévation sur un char de feu,[3] fut suivie de mort et de corruption.

Bien que ce texte et sa thématique soient denses et parsemés d'importantes difficultés qui mériteraient un traitement approfondi, nous voudrions limiter le propos de cette notice à l'axiome qui l'introduit : *Tous ceux qui sont après Dieu, qui sont nés de Dieu, c'est-à-dire la nature des êtres et le temps, apparaissent ensemble* [συνεκφαίνεσθαι] *auprès de Dieu qui se manifeste réellement, autant qu'il est possible, comme cause et créateur.*

L'apparition de Moïse et d'Élie entourant le Christ transfiguré représenterait, selon le moine érudit, le "type" du temps pour Moïse et le "type" de la nature des êtres pour Élie révélés ensemble auprès du Verbe Démiurge.[4] Le schéma ternaire démiurge/nature des êtres/temps que nous nous proposons d'analyser dans son acclimatation byzantine n'est pas sans rappeler quelques lignes du *Timée* qui rapporte une configuration similaire, semble-t-il largement admise à l'époque de Platon et qui pourrait s'appuyer – comme le mentionne Timée au début de son exposé – sur la foi d'hommes de sens[5] : la concomitance du ciel (ou monde)[6] et du temps. On la trouve dans la reprise résumée de la section où Timée expose la naissance du temps : *Le temps est donc né en même temps que le ciel afin que, engendrés en même temps, ils soient dissous en même temps, si jamais ils doivent connaître la dissolution.*[7] Cette affirmation de Platon dit au moins deux choses qui feront l'objet d'importants commentaires dans l'Antiquité tardive.

La première porte sur la question de la génération du monde. Le propos de Platon laisse ouverte une telle possibilité soulevant une

---

[3] Cf. IV Reg. 2:11, dans, *Septuaginta*, vol. I, éd. par A. RAHLFS, Stuttgart, 1935.

[4] L'expression est de Maxime. Cf. *Amb.Ioh.* 10, *PG* 91, 1164D.

[5] Cf. le début du discours de Timée, dans, Platon, *Timée* 29e.

[6] Le flottement du vocabulaire utilisé jusque chez les commentateurs tardo-antique du *Timée* (cf. Proclus, *In Platonis Timaeum commentaria* II. 100.3–4, éd. par Gerd VAN RIEL (Oxford, 2022) proviendrait de Platon lui-même : *"Soit le ciel dans son ensemble ou le monde – s'il arrive qu'un autre nom lui convienne mieux, donnons-lui ce nom"*, Platon, *Timée* 28b.

[7] Platon, *Timée* 38b.

aporie qui produira même parmi les platoniciens des interprétations divergentes.[8]

La deuxième indication que nous fournit ce texte est le rapport de concomitance qui lie radicalement ciel et temps. Ces derniers en effet naissent ensemble et en même temps.

Il ne nous revient pas ici d'analyser dans le détail les raisons de cette disposition qui, dans le *Timée* lui-même, semble s'imposer et qui paraît assez claire à première lecture, mais plutôt de tenter d'observer ce qu'elle va devenir dans l'ébauche d'une théologie byzantine du monde créé dans un environnement de pensée influencé par la philosophie tardo-antique. L'objectif de nos remarques se limitera donc à identifier quelques éléments concernant l'assimilation chrétienne de ce point de cosmologie antique.

Rompu à la pratique de l'exégèse symbolique des textes des Saintes Écritures, Maxime le Confesseur trahit cependant une bonne familiarité avec les problèmes discutés dans les Écoles philosophiques de l'Antiquité tardive. La principale difficulté concernant son style provient du fait que Maxime n'est pas un compilateur à l'instar de Jean

---

[8] On pourra se reporter par exemple à la lecture critique que Proclus effectua de deux auteurs médio-platoniciens, Atticus et Plutarque de Chéronée, qui tendaient à comprendre littéralement et temporellement le mythe vraisemblable du *Timée* faisant ainsi naître le temps dans le temps. Voir, l'interprétation de Platon, *Timée* 30a2–6 par ces deux auteurs pour qui le monde n'est pas né avec le temps mais à un certain moment du temps, dans, Proclus, *In Platonis Timaeum commentaria* I.381.26–382.12, voir également I.276.27–277.3. Y font suite les arguments *contra* de Porphyre et de Jamblique. Philopon, en revanche, tout en admettant, comme Proclus, que le monde est né avec le temps (cf. Philopon, *De Opificio Mundi* 8.1–9.4), défendra de façon énergique l'idée d'une génération absolue du cosmos avec le temps, comme on peut en convenir de la réfutation qu'il fit des dix-huit arguments de Proclus en faveur de l'éternité du monde. Voir, Philopon, *Contra Proclum. De Aeternitate Mundi*, éd. par H. Rabe, Leipzig, 1899. Nous avons nous aussi discuté les convergences et divergences entre Proclus et Philopon sur cette question dans une récente contribution : P. Mueller-Jourdan, L'immutabilité et l'inengendrement de la matière première du monde en question. Les soubassements métaphysiques d'un cas d'École : Philopon versus Proclus, dans, *Platonism and Christianity in Late Ancient Cosmologies. God, Soul, Matter*, éd. par A. Palanciuc & J. Zachuber, Leyde, 2022, pp. 168–183.

Damascène, mais un penseur qui a profondément assimilé les sources dont il se sert à nouveau dans des contextes parfois fort différents de leur origine. Retrouver les théories philosophiques qu'ils convoquent dans son propre système devient par conséquent singulièrement difficile à entreprendre mais pas tout à fait impossible.

2. Les idées convoquées pour l'exégèse typologique du récit de la Transfiguration

L'interprétation symbolique de Maxime veut donc voir dans la présence de Moïse au côté du Christ le "type du temps". Maxime en donne deux raisons. La première s'appuie sur le fait que Moïse est, pour l'Antiquité, l'auteur du récit de la *Genèse*. Ce récit expose non seulement les conditions et les étapes de la naissance du monde mais dévoile également l'institution du temps. Moïse – premier à compter le temps relativement à la genèse du monde – enseigna, aux dires de Maxime, non seulement la notion de "temps" mais également le nombre qui lui correspond. La deuxième s'enracine dans le fait que Moïse fut l'instigateur d'un culte inscrit dans le temps. De cette explicitation symbolique d'un Moïse "type du temps", Maxime va tirer parti pour exposer une conception finalement assez traditionnelle du temps qu'il pouvait d'ailleurs avoir hérité du Pseudo-Aréopagite.[9]

Quant à la présence d'Élie le Prophète, elle serait symboliquement le "type" de la nature des êtres. Là aussi le moine byzantin en donne la raison. Élie, pour avoir gardé inviolé en lui les raisons de la nature, fut aussi celui qui eut pour charge d'éduquer ceux qui usèrent "contre-nature" de la nature, eux qui du fait de leur mauvaise inclination penchaient vers le non-être. Élie représente donc en type l'être de la nature dans son intégrité.

Il ne présente que peu d'intérêt de discuter ici la validité de la méthode et la pertinence de ce genre d'exégèse assez fréquent chez Maxime, mais les notions mobilisées et mises en parallèle sont révélatrices d'une certaine vision de la démiurgie qu'il nous peut être utile de déchiffrer.

Apparemment, lorsque Maxime allègue : *Tous ceux qui sont après Dieu, qui sont nés de Dieu, c'est-à-dire la nature des êtres et le temps, apparaissent ensemble auprès de Dieu qui se manifeste réellement, autant qu'il*

---

[9] Denys l'Aréopagite, *De divinis nominibus* X.3. [216.2–217.4] ; voir également, Platon, *Timée* 37d ; Plotin, *Ennéades* III.7 [45].

est possible, comme cause et créateur, – il ne dit que peu de choses du rapport qui pourrait exister entre la nature des êtres et le temps, sinon deux aspects fondamentaux. (1) Ils viennent *après* Dieu [τὰ μετὰ Θεὸν πάντα] et (2) ils apparaissent *ensemble* auprès de Dieu [παρὰ τῷ Θεῷ ὄντα συνεκφαίνεσθαι].

Commençons par trois précisions.

- Précision I. Par la mention "après Dieu" [μετὰ Θεὸν], Maxime entend bien distinguer sans équivoque Créateur et créatures.[10] À ce titre, il convoque volontiers dans ses écrits de maturité l'opposition "sans principe" [ἄναρχος] et "pas sans principe" [οὐκ ἄναρχα] pour désigner respectivement le divin seul, dont la puissance infinie, cause de tout et circonscrivant tout, étant "hors catégories", précède métaphysiquement le "tout" (cf. *Ambiguum* 10, 1180c) et tout ce qui vient après Dieu.

- Précision II. Dans le contexte de cet *Ambiguum*, "nature des êtres" embrasse, à la manière du vocable "ciel" dans le *Timée*,[11] tout ce qui a été, est et sera contenu dans le monde. Il n'est pas invraisemblable que Maxime nous offre par le choix du mot "nature" une version d'un platonisme mâtinée d'une forme d'aristotélisme qui lui est propre. Ce choix – pour peu qu'il ait été conscient – lui permettait notamment d'échapper au problème, très sérieux pour la conscience chrétienne, du statut du ciel. Celui-ci, pour les commentateurs platoniciens d'Aristote, ne pouvait avoir commencé et ne pouvait être soumis aux conditions de génération et de corruption du monde sublunaire.[12]

---

[10] Il l'avait fait dès les *Chapitres sur la charité* qui sont la première œuvre du moine byzantin. Cf. Maxime le Confesseur, *Car.* III.28 ; IV.6.

[11] Cf. Platon, *Timée* 28b, 30d, 31b qui connaîtra sur ce point une large postérité. Voir, Aristote, *Physique* IV [212b17–22] ; Philopon, *De Opificio Mundi* 12.6–17.

[12] Pour comprendre les éléments du problème, il faut renvoyer à l'article de Philippe Hoffmann qui rassemble les principales pièces de ce dossier que Maxime le Confesseur ne peut avoir ignorées. Voir donc, Ph. HOFFMANN, Sur quelques aspects de la polémique de Simplicius contre Jean Philopon : De l'invective à la réaffirmation de la transcendance du ciel, dans *Simplicius, sa vie, son œuvre, sa survie*. Actes du colloque international de Paris (28 sept.–1er oct.1985), éd. par I. HADOT, Berlin – New York, 1987, pp. 183–221.

– Précision III. Rien n'est dit du statut exact du "temps". On relève toutefois sa proximité de la nature des êtres avec laquelle il partage le privilège de représenter tous ceux qui venant après Dieu sont nés de Dieu.

Dans ce paragraphe, Maxime ne mentionne donc "nature" et "temps" qu'en rapport à "ce dont ils proviennent" [ἐκ Θεοῦ γεγονότα] sans préciser ce qu'il en est de leur rapport mutuel et particulièrement de leur "statut" à proximité du Démiurge. Toutefois, l'ensemble de l'*Ambiguum* 10, dans lequel s'inscrit pour Maxime la thèse de la concomitance du temps et de la nature, comporte d'autres éléments en mesure de satisfaire les besoins de notre propos.

3. Les présupposés de base du système du monde de Maxime le Confesseur

Dans l'*Ambiguum* 10, le savant byzantin dévoile un postulat fondamental, passé souvent inaperçu, de son système :

> Tous les êtres ont de toute évidence pris – à proportion de ce qu'ils sont eux-mêmes – l'être "quand" et l'être "où". Sans ceux-ci absolument rien ne pourra être, ni essence, ni quantité, ni qualité, ni relation, ni action, ni passion, ni mouvement, ni disposition, ni aucune autre parmi les catégories dans lesquelles les experts en ces matières enferment le tout.[13]

Par ailleurs, toujours selon le moine byzantin, *tous les êtres, quels qu'ils soient,*[14] *se meuvent.*[15] Il est notoire que pour Maxime le Confesseur, à

---

[13] Pour un examen approfondi de cette importante thèse recueillie et reformulée par Maxime, voir notre étude, P. MUELLER-JOURDAN, *Typologie spatio-temporelle de l'ecclesia byzantine. La Mystagogie de Maxime le Confesseur dans la culture philosophique de l'Antiquité tardive*, Leyde, 2005, pp. 42–71.

[14] Même idée mais plus développée dans l'*Amb.Ioh.* 7 [1072ab] : *"Les esprits se meuvent de manière spirituelle, les choses sensibles de façon sensible, ou bien en ligne droite, ou en cercle, ou en spirale"*. Sur les trois formes de mouvement, Aristote, *Physique* IV [261b.28] ; Simplicius, *In Aristotelis physicorum libros commentaria* 602.22–23 & 603.7–8 ; Simplicius, *In de Caelo* 132. 24–26. Voir l'enquête méticuleuse conduite par L. CHVATAL, "Mouvement circulaire, rectiligne et spiral. Une Contribution à la recherche des sources philosophiques de Maxime Le Confesseur", *Freiburger Zeitschrift für Philosophie und Theologie*, 54,1/2 (2007), pp. 189–206.

[15] Maxime le Confesseur, *Amb.Ioh.* 10, *PG* 91, 1177AB.

l'instar du Stagirite sur ce point, le mouvement est universel et intrinsèque à la nature de tout ce qui, d'une manière ou d'une autre, vient après le moteur immobile.[16] S'il est certainement un point qui, dans le soubassement philosophique de la cosmologie maximienne, unit nature et temps, c'est leur rapport respectif au mouvement. La nature est non seulement de l'être en mouvement mais principe de mouvement et de repos[17] et il est largement admis, depuis Aristote, que le temps est mesure du mouvement. On peut, par ailleurs, rappeler que le mouvement est la raison invoquée par Timée pour expliquer la naissance du temps (cf. Platon, *Timaeum* 37cd) sans qu'il faille dans l'absolu introduire un rapport chronologique autre que celui qu'impose la nature du discours entre l'apparition du mouvement et celui du temps.

La question de savoir si le temps est extrinsèque ou intrinsèque à la nature est dans le cas de Maxime assez délicate à trancher. Pour Maxime, l'être de la nature, soit l'être en mouvement, n'a de réalité que dans et par le temps toujours conjoint au lieu [τόπος] bien qu'il ne soit pas question de ce dernier dans le contexte de l'apparition de Moïse et d'Élie autour du Verbe Démiurge. On aura noté que sur la liste des catégories adoptées ici par Maxime figure le mouvement, lequel est par conséquent dépendant lui aussi des conditions espace – temps nécessaires à l'existence de l'être des étants.

Il est enfin clair qu'on ne saurait introduire de la chronologie dans le rapport de succession logique qui découle de ce que le temps, conjoint au lieu, est dans le cas qui nous intéresse ici, la condition du mouvement. Comme si le premier avait dû en quelque manière précéder "chronologiquement" le second. La priorité du temps, conjoint au

---

[16] Voir sur ce point le texte explicite du même *Ambiguum* : *"Aucun mouvement n'est sans commencement puisqu'il n'est pas sans cause, car le moteur est un principe, et la fin – qui appelle et attire – vers laquelle tout se meut est une cause. Si le moteur est principe de tout mouvement de tout mû, et fin, la cause vers laquelle est porté le mû (rien ne se meut sans cause), aucun des êtres n'est immobile si ce n'est le premier moteur (le premier moteur en effet est immobile car aussi sans commencement) ; aucun des êtres donc n'est sans commencement car aucun n'est immobile"*, *Amb.Ioh.* 10 [1176d–1177a]. Maxime fait converger dans le même *Ambiguum*, peut-être sans véritable intention, le Démiurge-artisan du *Timée* et le Moteur immobile de la *Métaphysique* d'Aristote.

[17] Cf., Aristote, *Métaphysique* Δ,4 [1014b16–20] ; *Physique* I [192b13–16, 20–23] ; *Physique* III [200b12–13] ; voir également chez Maxime : *Op.* 26, *PG* 91, 276A.

lieu, est métaphysique mais, intimement lié à l'être dont il est, avec le lieu, la condition d'existence, il lui est concomitant. Il y a donc simultanéité dans la naissance de la nature comme "être en mouvement" et du temps.

En bref, pour Maxime, il y a, nés de Dieu, après Dieu et apparaissant ensemble auprès de Dieu, de la nature, du mouvement et une mesure, le temps transcrit en rapports mathématiques, en rapports numériques.[18]

4. Coïncidence du ciel/monde et du temps dans le commentaire de Proclus sur le Timée

En fonction du schéma ternaire de notre texte initial, demiurge/nature/ temps, il est manifeste que nature et temps apparaissent et, comme nous le verrons ci-après, subsistent ensemble en conséquence du même et unique acte créateur. Leur statut paraît ne pas être initial seulement, mais transcendantal en ce sens qu'ils demeurent simultanément comme principe sans être affectés par le et les mouvements multiples consécutifs à ces principes premiers posés.

Une comparaison avec quelques points fondamentaux du commentaire de Proclus *Sur le Timée* de Platon contribue à éclairer les bases métaphysiques que le moine byzantin paraît embrasser.

Nous retiendrons ici quatre brèves sections où Proclus se donne pour tâche d'apporter quelques explications au rapport de simultanéité existant entre le temps et le ciel (ou monde). Nous pensons que nous sommes bien en présence d'un topique similaire à celui que propose Maxime bien que dans le présent cas ce dernier substitue au vocable ciel et/ou monde, le vocable "nature" à consonance plus aristotélicienne.

Texte 1 : Proclus, *In Platonis Timaeum commentaria* III. 49.29–50.7 (explication de Platon, *Timée* 38b).

> Les mots "pour que, étant nés ensemble, ils soient ensemble aussi dissous, si jamais ils doivent se dissoudre" montrent clairement que le Ciel est inengendré et impérissable. En effet, s'il est né, c'est dans le Temps qu'il est né. Mais s'il est né "avec le Temps", il n'est pas né dans le Temps :

---

[18] Cf. Maxime le Confesseur, *Amb.Ioh.* 10, *PG* 91, 1164B. Dans le cas qui nous intéresse, il pourrait s'agir simplement du "décompte" des jours de la création puisque c'est à partir de ce premier comptage du temps que Moïse est dit, selon l'exégèse qu'en fait Maxime, "type du temps". Ce décompte revêt dans tous les cas une forme paradigmatique.

car le Temps non plus n'est pas né dans le Temps, pour qu'il n'y ait pas du Temps avant le Temps. Si donc le Ciel est né "avec le Temps", il n'a pas eu de commencement : car tout ce qui naît doit être postérieur au Temps. Or le Ciel n'est d'aucune façon postérieur au Temps.[19]

Texte 2 : Proclus, *In Platonis Timaeum commentaria* III. 52.9–16 (Temps et Ciel se soutiennent mutuellement).

Chacun des deux n'est donc pas né pour soi seul ni non plus pour l'autre seul, mais en vue de l'œuvre démiurgique tout entière, pour qu'elle soit rendue le plus possible parfaite et semblable aux modèles – ou plutôt en vue de la bonté du Père de toutes choses, bonté par laquelle la Création aussi atteint son point suprême –. Et une fois devenu ce qu'il est pour l'autre, chacun des deux aide grandement aussi tous les êtres encosmiques à posséder permanence, ordre, bon état.[20]

Texte 3 : Proclus, *In Platonis Timaeum commentaria* III. 52.16–33 (Temps unique et total vs temps fragmenté)

Ici s'achève tout l'exposé philosophique de Platon sur le Temps unique, totale, capable de mesurer toutes choses, qui a été mis en branle et qui fait procession à partir du seul Démiurge et de la monade qui lui est propre. Pour le reste, dans la suite, Platon traitera du Temps tel qu'il se manifeste dans le Ciel et qu'il est comme pluralisé et comme fragmenté en fonction des divers circuits des astres [...] Et quand on voit que les planètes, parmi lesquelles ont été comptés et le soleil et la lune, sont dites avoir été créées pour que ce Temps secondaire se présente visible-

---

[19] Proclus, *In Platonis Timaeum commentaria* III. 49.29–50.7, trad. par A.-J. FESTUGIÈRE : "τὸ δ' ἵνα ἅμα γεννηθέντες ἅμα καὶ λυθῶσιν, ἐάν ποτε λύσις τις αὐτῶν γίγνηται, σαφῶς ἀγένητον καὶ ἄφθαρτον δείκνυσι τὸν οὐρανόν· εἰ γὰρ γέγονεν, ἐν χρόνῳ γέγονεν. εἰ δὲ μετὰ χρόνου γέγονεν, οὐκ ἐν χρόνῳ γέγονεν· οὐδὲ γὰρ ὁ χρόνος ἐν χρόνῳ γέγονεν, ἵνα μὴ πρὸ χρόνου χρόνος ᾖ. εἰ ἄρα μετὰ χρόνου γέγονεν, οὐ γέγονε· δεῖ γὰρ πᾶν τὸ γιγνόμενον μεταγενέστερον εἶναι χρόνου. ὁ δ' οὐρανὸς οὐδαμῶς ἐστι χρόνου μεταγενέστερος".

[20] Proclus, *In Platonis Timaeum commentaria* III. 52.9–16, trad. par A.-J. FESTUGIÈRE : "γέγονε μὲν οὖν ἑκάτερος οὐχ ἑαυτοῦ μόνου οὐδ' αὖ τοῦ ἑτέρου χάριν, ἀλλὰ τῆς συμπάσης δημιουργίας, ἵνα ὡς ὅτι τελειοτάτη καὶ ὁμοιοτάτη τοῖς παραδείγμασιν ἀποτελεσθῇ· μᾶλλον δὲ τῆς ἀγαθότητος εἵνεκα τῆς τοῦ πατρὸς τῶν ὅλων, δι' ἣν καὶ ἡ ποίησις ἔχει τὸ τέλειον. γενόμενος δὲ ἐστι θατέρῳ ὁ ἕτερος καὶ πᾶσι τοῖς ἐγκοσμίοις ἑκάτερος πρὸς διαμονὴν καὶ τάξιν καὶ εὐμοιρίαν μεγάλα συναίρεται".

ment sur la scène, devienne aisément reconnaissable à tous au moyen des astres qui en font voir clairement les mesures partielles et se montre ainsi plus divisé, combien grande ne doit-on pas penser qu'est la dignité qui a été attribuée au Temps tout premier et unique par le Philosophe, ou plutôt par le Démiurge universel lui-même ?[21]

Texte 4 : Proclus, *In Platonis Timaeum commentaria* II. 100.1–6 (co-subsistance du ciel et du temps en raison d'un même acte créateur)

"Qui doit être à un certain moment [ποτὲ ἐσόμενον <θεόν>]", d'autre part, ne désigne pas le commencement dans le temps, comme le pense Atticus, mais le fait que le Monde a son être coexistant au temps. En effet le temps est né avec le Ciel, et tout à la fois le Monde est dans le temps et le temps est dans le Monde : car ils ont été créés en connexion l'un avec l'autre et ils subsistent ensemble en conséquence d'un même acte créateur.[22]

Ce bref sondage dans le commentaire de Proclus *Sur le Timée* décrit assez clairement, nous semble-t-il, les présupposés en jeu dans l'axiome maximien discuté ici et contribue notamment à élucider le cadre philosophique et la tradition exégétique dans lesquels doit être replacé l'interprétation symbolique du récit de la Transfiguration et le rapport ciel

---

[21]   Proclus, *In Platonis Timaeum commentaria* III. 52.16–33, trad. par A.-J. Festugière : "Καὶ τοσαῦτα μὲν περὶ τοῦ ἑνὸς καὶ ὅλου καὶ μετρητικοῦ τῶν πάντων κἀκ μόνου τοῦ δημιουργοῦ κἀκ τῆς οἰκείας μονάδος κινηθέντος καὶ προϊόντος χρόνου τῷ Πλάτωνι πεφιλοσόφηται. λοιπὸν δὲ ἐν τοῖς ἑπομένοις περὶ τοῦ κατ' οὐρανὸν ἐκφαινομένου καὶ οἱονεὶ πληθυομένου καὶ οἱονεὶ συμμεριζομένου ταῖς ποικίλαις τῶν ἄστρων φοραῖς διαλήψεται, ὃς οὐκ ἂν ὑπέστη μὴ τῆς ταὐτοῦ καὶ τῆς θατέρου περιφορᾶς περὶ τὸν ἀφανῆ καὶ ἕνα κυκλουμένης χρόνον καὶ ἀπ' αὐτοῦ τὸ πρόσφορον ἑαυτῇ μέτρον ἑκατέρας ὑποτεμνομένης καὶ ἐκφηνάσης καὶ διὰ παντὸς φυλαττούσης. ὅπου δέ, ἵνα καὶ οὗτος ὁ δεύτερος χρόνος καὶ εἰς τὸ ἐμφανὲς προϊὼν καὶ πᾶσι γνώριμος διὰ τῶν τὰ μερικὰ αὐτοῦ μέτρα προχειριζόντων καὶ μᾶλλον μεριστὸς ὑποστῇ, τὰ πλανητὰ τῶν ἄστρων, ἐν οἷς καὶ ὁ ἥλιος καὶ <ἡ> σελήνη κατηρίθμηνται, γεγενῆσθαι λέγεται, πηλίκον δεῖ νομίζειν ἀξίωμα τῷ πρωτίστῳ καὶ ἑνὶ χρόνῳ παρὰ τοῦ φιλοσόφου, μᾶλλον δὲ παρ' αὐτοῦ τοῦ δημιουργοῦ τῶν ὅλων ἀποκεκληρῶσθαι;".

[22]   Proclus, *In Platonis Timaeum commentaria* II. 100.1–6, trad. par A.-J. Festugière : "τὸ δὲ αὖ ποτὲ ἐσόμενον οὐ τῆς κατὰ χρόνον ἐστὶν ἀρχῆς σημαντικόν, ὡς οἴεται Ἀττικός, ἀλλ' ὅτι τὴν οὐσίαν ἔχει τῷ χρόνῳ συνεζευγμένην· χρόνος γὰρ ἅμα οὐρανῷ γέγονε, καὶ ὅ τε κόσμος ἔγχρονος καὶ ὁ χρόνος ἐγκόσμιος· συμπαρήχθησαν γὰρ ἀλλήλοις καὶ συνυπέστησαν ἀπὸ τῆς μιᾶς δημιουργίας".

(cosmos)/temps pour Proclus ainsi que celui du rapport nature/temps chez Maxime.

5. Deux sens principaux du vocable "temps" chez Maxime

À l'instar des textes de Proclus retenus *supra* (Texte 4), le schéma ternaire démiurge/nature/temps est supratemporel et permanent dans le système du moine byzantin et exprime la continuité de l'action providentielle du divin dans l'univers assurant à tous les êtres une permanence, soit la raison de nature qui leur a été assignée, ainsi qu'un ordre ou rang et une position.[23] Le temps dont il est dès lors question et qui assure dans l'Univers l'ordre ou rang revêt un statut métaphysique évident, nécessaire et surtout positif, en ce sens qu'il tranche sur l'expérience intramondaine selon laquelle tout se dissout sous l'effet du temps.[24] Dans les *Centuries sur la théologie et l'économie de l'Incarnation du Fils de Dieu*, Maxime avait affirmé que tout ce qui est créé dans le temps [ἐν χρόνῳ] est créé selon le temps [κατὰ χρόνον].[25] Cela contraint à distinguer deux sens principaux du vocable "temps" chez le moine byzantin.

(1) On relève tout d'abord tout comme chez Proclus une sorte de "temps premier" qui possède un caractère générique. Il est produit comme condition *sine qua non* de l'être des étants mais n'est pas créé dans le temps ou selon le temps [κατὰ χρόνον].[26]

---

[23] Décrivant les effets de l'agir providentiel divin dans l'Univers, Maxime soutient : *"Les saints considérèrent d'une part, le bon ordre de la création, la proportion et le commerce que chacun y entretient avec le tout [...] et d'autre part, la permanence, l'ordre et la position des êtres qui y sont nés, leur évolution selon laquelle chacun selon sa forme particulière demeure sans confusion et libre de tout mélange"*, Amb.Ioh. 10, 1176bc. Ce texte introduit chez Maxime la description des mouvements intramondains réguliers comme le parcours des astres, le cycle de l'année, l'alternance des jours et des nuits. Voir également, *Amb.Ioh.* 10, *PG* 91, 1188D.

[24] Cf. Aristote, *Physique* IV [221a30–b.2].

[25] Cf. Maxime le Confesseur, *Th. Oec.* I.35, *PG* 90, 1096C. Cf. l'édition récente par K. HAJDÚ et A. WOLLBOLD, *Capita theologica et oeconomica – Zwei Centurien über die Gotteserkenntnis (Fontes Christiani 66)*, Freiburg, 2016.

[26] Son rapport à l'activité démiurgique ne peut être temporel puisqu'avant le temps il n'y a pas de temps. Il est donc créé à titre de cause primordiale comme mesure du mouvement interne à la nature des étants.

Affirmer le contraire n'aurait pas mis une telle thèse à l'abri de la critique solidement argumentée que Proclus adressait à l'encontre de la doctrine d'Atticus (*supra*, Texte 1, Texte 4). Ce paralogisme conduisait à l'impossible création du temps dans le temps ou création temporelle du temps. Doctrine erronée si l'on s'en tient à l'apparition simultanée du temps et du ciel qui subsistent ensemble en raison d'un même et unique acte créateur.[27]

La thèse d'un "temps premier et générique" découle donc assez naturellement de l'apparition simultanée de la nature et du temps "auprès de Dieu" manifesté autant qu'il est possible, avait affirmé Maxime, comme cause et créateur. En bref, on peut admettre dans ce système l'existence d'un temps transcendant, condition *sine qua non* de l'être et de toutes ses déterminations énumérées en "catégories", comme nous l'avons vu précédemment. Ce "temps tout premier", dont le caractère générique embrasse de façon unitaire toutes les formes du temps est aussi la première expression dans l'ordre de la création des *logoi* du temps qui demeurent en Dieu selon la formule de Maxime.[28]

(2) On relève ensuite un *temps relatif.* Il est, simultanément au mouvement dont est naturellement caractérisé tout être en devenir, objet de perception sensible. Il est relatif aux entités individuées et à leurs inévitables successions, marquées qu'elles sont par les lois de la génération, de la croissance et de la corruption. Ces dernières sont obligatoirement soumises à une certaine durée et donc produites dans le temps et selon le temps, soit produites en un certain temps pour disparaître en un certain autre.[29] Par comparaison au "temps premier", ce temps duratif

---

[27]   Cf. Proclus, *In Platonis Timaeum commentaria* II.100.1–6.

[28]   Cf. Maxime le Confesseur, *Amb.Ioh.* 10, PG 91, 1164B.

[29]   On perçoit nettement le problème que pourrait poser le statut du monde angélique qui ne tombe évidemment pas sous le coup des lois énoncées ici. Les anges ne sont pas "sans principe" [οὐκ ἄναρχα]. Ἄναρχος est pour le moine byzantin une prérogative du divin seul. Les anges ont pour Maxime un commencement mais ne connaîtront pas de fin. Ils participent toutefois, en raison de leur statut d'êtres créés qui ne fait aucun doute chez notre auteur, au temps intégral qui finalement, toujours chez le savant byzantin, est étroitement associé à l'*aiôn* (cf. Maxime le Confesseur, *Th. Oec.* I.5, PG 91, 1085A ; mais également : "Αἰὼν γάρ ἐστιν ὁ χρόνος, ὅταν στῇ τῆς κινήσεως, καὶ χρόνος ἐστιν ὁ αἰών, ὅταν μετρῆται κινήσει φερόμενος", *Amb.Ioh.* 10, PG 91, 1164c). Nous sommes conscients d'esquiver en partie ici le problème du rapport "temps-aiôn". Nous

en exprime les principales caractéristiques au niveau des entités individuées à savoir, l'ordre selon l'antérieur et le postérieur et la mesure de leurs mouvements et processus naturels qui peuvent connaître plusieurs variantes[30] mais qui n'ont qu'un seul ordre, le commencement, le milieu et la fin[31] soit, plus philosophiquement, de l'antérieur et du postérieur distingués par un certain "maintenant".

Comme on l'aura relevé, nous esquivons en partie le problème du statut d'un temps "autre" qui, si Maxime l'avait traité de façon directe, se classerait comme une variante du temps relatif. Nous voulons en effet faire mention du temps relatif au mouvement du ciel. Maxime l'avait, certes, observé[32] mais ne semble pas avoir tiré de sa régularité la raison de sa perpétuité et ceci parce que, pour le moine byzantin, "tout mû a commencé par du mouvement" [πᾶν κινούμενον πάντως καὶ ἤρξατο τῆς κινήσεως].[33] Il est difficile d'évaluer le degré de maîtrise que Maxime put avoir de ce délicat dossier mais sa position se rapproche sur ce point de celle que tint Jean Philopon, notamment de l'exégèse que le grammairien alexandrin fit de l'affirmation du *Timée* qui portait à la fois sur la concomitance du ciel et du temps et sur l'hypothèse de leur engendrement simultané.[34]

---

nous permettons de renvoyer aux observations que nous avons consignées dans l'une de nos précédentes études : P. MUELLER-JOURDAN, *Typologie spatio-temporelle de l'ecclesia byzantine. La Mystagogie de Maxime le Confesseur dans la culture philosophique de l'Antiquité tardive*, Leyde, 2005, pp. 171–172 ; 176–178. On consultera également avec profit : P. PLASS, "Transcendant Time in Maximus the Confessor", *The Thomist*, 44 (1980), pp. 259–277.

[30] Cf. Aristote, *Physique* III [200b32–201a20].

[31] Cf. Maxime le Confesseur, *Th. Oec.* I.5, PG 90, 1085A.

[32] Sur le mouvement des astres qui toujours se produit de la même manière sans jamais dévier en rien, sur l'égale durée de l'année, sur l'alternance des nuits et des jours, voir, Maxime le Confesseur, *Amb.Ioh.* 10, PG 91, 1176C.

[33] Cf. *Amb.Ioh.* 10, PG 91, 1176d–1177a.

[34] Cf. PLATON, *Timée* 38b. Voir également, Philopon, *De Opificio Mundi* 8.1–9.4 : *De même que les savants appellent point [σημεῖον] le commencement de la ligne, qui est un point inétendu et indivisible, et ne l'appellent pas ligne, de même ils considèrent que le commencement du temps n'est pas un temps mais cela même qu'ils dénomment maintenant "commencement du temps". Si en effet quelqu'un estimait que cette chose est un temps bref, il ne saisirait pas encore le commencement du temps considéré, mais une partie de ce temps, correspondant à un dixième ou à*

Remarques conclusives

Le temps et la nature, premiers et dotés de caractères génériques, qui sont le propre du monde conçu dans sa totalité originelle ne peuvent avoir dans le système maximien qu'un statut universel englobant d'innombrables réalisations particulières à savoir l'interpénétration de la nature et du temps dans la réalisation de cet être particulier, de cet autre et de cet autre encore, etc.[35]

Il est dès lors vraisemblable que le temps dont Moïse est le "type", c'est-à-dire l'expression visible et autorisée, est en priorité le temps "transcendant". Mais il peut également être, par la nature même du système maximien, type d'un "temps" relatif – objet de perception sensible – en tant que Moïse reproduit dans son histoire individuelle (naissance – croissance – mort) l'ordre chronologique de toute entité individuée et finalement de ce monde-ci qui se trouve dès lors conçu comme un vivant sensible.

Quant à la nature dont Élie est le type, elle ne peut être que la nature telle qu'elle fut originellement voulue par le Démiurge, à savoir dotée

---

quelque autre fraction. Ainsi donc le premier élément du temps considéré dans sa totalité, est le commencement de toute son existence, mais ce n'est pas encore le temps. Puisque le temps est la mesure du mouvement circulaire des corps célestes – les jours, les mois et les années sont des parties du temps et le temps n'est pas autre par rapport à eux ; mais quand ils parcourent un cycle par rapport à eux-mêmes, le temps s'accroît, lui, selon lequel nous comptons aussi l'existence de ces corps célestes – ainsi donc, avant que le ciel ne fût, il n'y avait rien de tout cela. Le temps n'existait donc pas avant que le ciel ne fût.

Donc, puisque Dieu fixa le temps en même temps que le ciel et que dans le premier fragment indivisible de temps, qui est le commencement du temps, Dieu fit le ciel et la terre, Basile dit que le commencement temporel de la création de ces choses est ce point ténu et indivisible. C'est de là que Platon reçut l'intuition qui le fit écrire cette magnifique phrase : "le temps fut avec le ciel pour que les choses créées en même temps se dissolvent en même temps, si jamais elles doivent se dissoudre". Cette première signification de "principe" dans lequel Dieu fit le ciel et la terre, me semble la plus importante et la plus vraie.

[35] Un bon exemple en est fourni dans les étapes de développement de l'embryon observées par Damascius et rapportées par Simplicius [διὰ τὸν χρόνον ἄλλο τι πρὸ ἄλλου δημιουργεῖται τῶν τοῦ ἐμβρύου μερῶν] Simplicius, *In Aristotelis physicorum libros octo commentaria* 626.13–14.

d'un certain nombre de déterminations et de processus internes qui en constituent la loi. Ces déterminations requièrent, comme nous l'avons signalé dans le postulat fondamental du système maximien, des conditions spatio-temporelles d'existence. Comme expression de l'agir providentiel du Démiurge, la nature est non seulement principe de mouvement et de repos mais surtout le garant d'une conformité et d'une permanence du rapport de tout être passé, présent et futur envers sa raison essentielle. Telle est sans conteste la doctrine de Maxime le Confesseur.[36]

Le temps, dont les *logoi*, soutient Maxime, demeurent en Dieu, est non seulement l'expression d'une intention et d'un agir démiurgiques à l'égard de l'être de la nature mais le garant d'un ordre qui s'impose à l'ensemble des êtres qui viennent après Dieu. La notion d'un temps, non seulement ordre ordonné mais ordre ordonnant, expression de la providence – soit de l'action continue du divin dans l'Univers – devait naturellement en découler. Sur ce point, Maxime pouvait s'autoriser d'une déjà longue tradition philosophique qu'on peut faire remonter au *Commentaire sur le Timée* de Jamblique, commentaire aujourd'hui perdu mais dont Simplicius a consigné plusieurs extraits dans le *Corollarium de tempore*.[37]

La notion d'un temps, cause de perfection et d'ordre, pouvait être tirée de l'intention démiurgique du *Timée* [37cd]. Cette compréhension de Platon qu'autorisait, ou même que nécessitait, l'univers fortement hiérarchisé du néoplatonisme en raison de l'extension de l'être "en mouvement"[38] devait trancher assez fortement sur l'opinion largement admise dans un cadre strictement aristotélicien pour lequel le temps était, certes, "mesure du mouvement" mais aussi cause de destruction et d'oubli. Maxime ne nous semble pas avoir pu ignorer tous les éléments de ce dossier.

---

[36] Cf. Maxime le Confesseur, *Amb.Ioh.* 10, *PG* 91, 1176BC.

[37] Voir en particulier, Simplicius, Corollarium de tempore 792.20–795.3, *In Aristotelis physicorum libros octo commentaria*.

[38] Cf. Simplicius, *In Aristotelis categorias commentarium* 364.11–15 : "τὰ δὲ γενητὰ καὶ μεριστὴν ἔχοντα τήν τε οὐσίαν αὐτὴν καὶ τὴν τοῦ εἶναι παράτασιν, ταῦτα τοῦ μὲν χρόνου ἐδεήθη μὴ συγχωροῦντος μήτε σκεδάννυσθαι μήτε συγχεῖσθαι τὴν τοῦ εἶναι παράτασιν, ἀλλ᾽ ὡς δυνατὸν ἐν τάξει κατὰ τὸ πρότερον καὶ ὕστερον συνάγοντος αὐτὴν καὶ συνεχίζοντος".

Dans le cas de la manifestation concomitante du temps et de la nature des êtres (passé, présent et futur), il en est non seulement la condition *sine qua non* d'existence mais aussi la limite salutaire, la mesure, présidant "de façon immobile" au mouvement de tout ce qui se meut vers la Transfiguration, à terme pour l'homme vers la déification autant qu'il est possible à une nature créée.[39]

[39] Le temps du monde comporte pour Maxime deux périodes majeures. Dans le système du moine byzantin, Dieu a divisé les siècles en deux grandes périodes. Une première partie des siècles appartient au temps de la descente de Dieu vers l'homme, l'autre au temps de l'élévation de l'homme vers Dieu. La première période est vouée à réaliser l'incorporation de Dieu dans l'humanité, la seconde vise à produire la déification de l'homme. Cf. *Q.Thal.* 22.4–16, in *CCSG* 7.

Aristotelian Categories in *Ambiguum* 10 (1177b–1181a)

Torstein Theodor TOLLEFSEN

(*University of Oslo*)

There are sections in the tenth *Ambiguum* where St. Maximus treats of certain concepts that the philosophical tradition calls *categories*. When I call these "Aristotelian" it is because most of them originally belong to the list of categories defined by Aristotle in his famous writing of the same name. Maximus' list contains the following items: οὐσία (substance or essence), quantity, quality, "where", "when", relation, making, passion, movement, and habit.[1] We shall compare this with Aristotle's list in the *Categories*. However, when one wants to treat sections of *Ambiguum* 10, one is confronted with a challenge. In general, whenever we read a section of a larger text, we try to interpret it with a view to find out how the author situated it within the whole and why he did so. This is not easy to figure out when it comes to *Ambiguum* 10. It is the longest text in the collection of the earlier *Ambigua*, consisting of many sections. The reader may find it difficult to detect the red string that binds them all together. The text seems to fall into separate paragraphs that we are tempted to study for their own interesting content without a view to the whole. Louth comments on this challenge in his translation.[2] He says: "It is what sometimes is called 'lateral thinking', i.e. his [Maximus'] mind does not move straight ahead in conformity to a linear, logical argument, rather it moves sideways, and gathers together a collection of considerations that are gradually made to converge".[3] Maximus' starting point is a quotation from St. Gregory Nazianzen's

---

[1] *Amb.Ioh.* 10, *PG* 91, 1181B.

[2] Cf. A. LOUTH, *Maximus the Confessor*, London-New York, 1996, pp. 68–70 and 94–96.

[3] LOUTH, *Maximus*, p. 94.

Ambiguum *10 of Maximus the Confessor in Modern Study: Papers Collected on the Occasion of the Budapest Colloquium on Saint Maximus, 3–4 February 2021*, ed. by Alexis LÉONAS & Vladimir CVETKOVIĆ, with the collaboration of Daniel HEIDE, Turnhout, 2025 (IPM 97), pp. 221–236
10.1484/M.IPM-EB.5.141862

Homily 21, in which the latter seems to say, in Louth's words, that "the mind can reach God through reason alone, without the necessity of any engagement in ascetic struggle".[4] These words, probably, had been exploited by some "Origenist" monks.[5] Louth says further that Maximus makes his opinion clear in the opening sentence, when he says that the only truly satisfactory philosophy is true judgement concerning reality and activity, supported by ascetic struggle.[6]

The terms "true judgement concerning reality" and "ascetic struggle" point to Maximus' teaching of the threefold spiritual development. What we may expect to find according to this approach, and what we actually do find, is meditations concerning practical or ascetic philosophy together with natural contemplation and mystical theology. The sections I try to shed some light on below deal with natural contemplation. I suggest that what we find in these sections is philosophical meditations on what we may expect to contemplate on this level.

1. Categories

Let us start with Maximus' summary of the categories:

> Εἰ δὲ περιγραφῆς οὐδὲν τῶν ὄντων ἐλεύθερον, πάντα τὰ ὄντα δηλονότι ἀναλόγως ἑαυτοῖς καὶ τὸ ποτὲ εἶναι καὶ τὸ "ποῦ εἶναι" εἴληφε. Τούτων γὰρ ἄνευ τὸ παράπαν οὐδὲν εἶναι δυνήσεται, οὐκ οὐσία, οὐ ποσότης, οὐ ποιότης, οὐ σχέσις, οὐ ποίησις, οὐ πάθος, οὐ κίνησις, οὐχ ἕξις, οὐχ ἕτερόν τι τῶν οἷς τὸ πᾶν περικλείουσιν οἱ περὶ ταῦτα δεινοί. Οὐδὲν οὖν τῶν ὄντων ἄναρχον, ᾧ τι ἕτερον προεπινοεῖσθαι, οὐδὲ ἀπερίγραφον ᾧ τι ἕτερον συνεπινοεῖσθαι δύναται.[7]

> If no being is free of enclosure (περιγραφῆς), then it is clear that all beings have assumed temporal (πότε εἶναι) and spatial existence (ποῦ εἶναι) in the way that is ideally suited to them, for nothing at all could exist without these, neither essence, nor quantity, quality, relation, creativity (ποίησις), affectivity (πάθος), motion, habit, or anything else with which experts in these matters delimit the

---

[4] LOUTH, *Maximus*, p. 94.

[5] LOUTH, *Maximus*, pp. 68–69, who states the probability that "Origenist" monks are the target with some caution.

[6] *Amb.Ioh.* 10, *PG* 91, 1108A.

[7] *Amb.Ioh.* 10, *PG* 91, 1181B; LAGA, *supra*, p. 150; CONSTAS 2014, 1, pp. 294–296.

universe (τὸ πᾶν περικλείουσιν). Therefore if something has some-thing else that can be conceived of before it, it is not without source (ἄναρχον), and neither is it unenclosed (ἀπερίγραφον) if something else can be conceptualized along with it.[8]

This paragraph, rich in content, needs several comments. Aristotle lists the following items in his *Categories*: οὐσία, quantity, quality, re-lation (πρός τι), "where?" (ποῦ), "when?" (ποτὲ), posture, having, do-ing (ποιεῖν), and being-affected (πάσχειν).[9] The traditional translation of οὐσία in Aristotelian contexts is "substance". If we look at different contexts in ancient and late ancient philosophy, the term is not easy to translate with one term only. In connection with Maximus, the transla-tions "being" or "essence" seem to fit most contexts best. I suppose the Maximian term ποίησις fits the sense of Aristotle's ποιεῖν. The same is probably the case with Aristotle's πάσχειν and Maximus' πάθος. We are now going to focus on the deviations from Aristotle's conceptions of the categories.

First, in Aristotle's *Categories*, he seems to deal mainly on classify-ing terms for subjects and predicates. According to Ackrill's influential interpretation, however, the *Categories* are primarily about things, not terms:[10] "Though the items in categories are not expressions but 'things", the identification and classification of these things could, of course, be achieved only by attention to what we say'. On the other hand, an early interpreter like Porphyry says the treatise is not about things *qua* things at all, "but instead is about the words that are used to signify things".[11] Porphyry's view seems reasonable enough to me, but it is quite clear that in his *Metaphysics*, Aristotle applies categories in an ontological way.[12] It is also clear from the quotation above that Maximus' use of categories is strictly ontological.

We shall next follow up the last claim a bit closer. According to Maximus, the categorical items *circumscribe* beings. They are attributes that *delimit* the universe. This is in contradistinction to the divinity,

---

[8] LOLLAR, *supra*, p. 127.

[9] *Cat.* 1b25-27.

[10] Aristotle's *Categories and De Interpretatione*, Translated with notes and Glossary by J. L. ACKRILL, Oxford, 1974, p. 78.

[11] Porphyrii, *Isagoge et In Aristotelis Categorias Commentarium*, ed. by A. BUSSE, Berlin, 1887, (*CAG* IV.I), p. 57.

[12] Cf. for instance *Metaphysics* Z, chapter 3.

which is strictly without beginning and beyond all cosmic being, as can be seen from the following quotation:

Ὑπεράνω γὰρ πάσης διαιρέσεώς τε καὶ συνθέσεως καὶ μέρους καὶ ὅλου ἡ θεότης, ὅτι ἄποσον, καὶ πάσης τῆς κατὰ θέσιν ὑπάρξεως καὶ τῆς πῶς εἶναι αὐτὴν ὁριζομένης ἐννοίας ἀπῳκισμένη, ὅτι ἄποιον, καὶ τῆς πρὸς ἄλλο πᾶν πάσης συναφείας τε καὶ οἰκειότητος ἐλευθέρα καὶ ἄφετος, ἄσχετον γὰρ τὸ πρὸ αὐτῆς ἢ μετ' αὐτῆς ἢ μετ' αὐτὴν οὐκ ἔχουσα, ὡς πάντων ἐπέκεινα, καὶ μηδενὶ τῶν ὄντων κατ' οὐδένα λόγον ἢ τρόπον συντεταγμένη.[13]

> Divinity is far beyond every division and synthesis and part and whole because It is unquantifiable, and It dwells far from every existence characterized by placement and from every concept that would define It as existing in a certain way, because It has no relative qualities. It is free from and uncontained by any combination and appropriation in relation to anything else, because It is without relation as such, and there is nothing before It or with It or after It since It is beyond all things, nor has It been arranged alongside any existing thing in accordance with any logical structure or particular mode.[14]

According to this saying, God transcends essence, quantity, place, quality, and relation. The categories are definitely applied ontologically; they delimit created beings and are transcended by God.

Thirdly, Aristotle does not reckon movement among the categories. Ammonius (in his commentary on Porphyry's *Isagoge*) says that movements and changes (αἱ κινήσεις καὶ αἱ μεταβολαί) occur in four categories, namely in essence (οὐσία), quantity, quality, and in the category of "where".[15] Movement or change are not, obviously, reckoned as category in their own right. Change in essence is generation and corruption, quantitative change is increase and diminution, qualitative change is alteration, and change of place is locomotion. For Maximus,

---

[13] *Amb.Ioh.* 10, *PG* 91, 1185D–1188A; LAGA, *supra*, pp. 158–160; CONSTAS 2014, I, p. 306.

[14] LOLLAR, *supra*, pp. 136–137.

[15] Ammonius, *In Porphyrii Isagogen*, ed. by A. BUSSE, Berlin, 1891 (*CAG* iv. iii), p. 113. Cf. Aristotle, *Physics* 5, especially 225a34 – b9 and 226a23–226b1 (Aristotle, *Physics*, ed. by W. D. ROSS, Oxford 1936). Aristotle does not divide change as strictly as this everywhere.

change is a basic feature delimiting the cosmos, and he, as we shall see below, acknowledges these four kinds of movement or change.

In the following paragraphs I discuss Maximus' application of the categories of essence, quantity, quality, "where", "when", and movement.

2. Essence (οὐσία) (1177b–c).

Maximus describes essence as subject to *movement*. He distinguishes between two sets of movement. These are (i) generation and corruption (γένεσις, φθορά) and (ii) expansion and contraction (διαστολή, συστολή). The last set is inclusive of all essences, while the first covers sensible beings only. This means that the movements of expansion and contraction includes sensible as well as intelligible beings, in short all created essences. The description of the dynamics of the last set (expansion and contraction) shows that Maximus considers all created essences as somehow related to one another. This should direct our attention to another text in the earlier *Ambigua*, namely *Ambiguum* 41. Maximus supplies two sketches to show how all created beings are interrelated. First, he sketches his famous five divisions of beings:[16] uncreated nature is divided from the totality of created nature, created nature is divided into the intelligible and the sensible (νοητὰ καὶ αἰσθητά), the sensible is divided into heaven and earth, earth is divided into paradise and the inhabited earth, and lastly the human being is divided into man and woman. Maximus then describes the human being as a microcosm, containing features of all the former divisions in itself, designed to unite these divisions and achieve union between all of creation and God. This task, Maximus shows, is fulfilled in the Incarnation of the Son of God.[17] The unity of creation is not preserved in the angelic being of intelligible creatures, but in the microcosmic nature of the human being. The human being is designed for the fulfilment of the divine purpose of achieving unity between all creatures and God. The relatedness of all beings to one another is further stressed in the recapitulation of everything in the Incarnate Logos. But there is more. In the second part of *Ambiguum* 41, Maximus stresses the interrelatedness between creatures from another

---

[16] *Amb.Ioh.* 41, *PG* 91, 1340D–1308A.
[17] *Amb.Ioh.* 41, *PG* 91, 1308C–1309D.

angle, using the logical terminology of genus, species, and difference.[18]
He shows, in short, how particulars are gathered into a whole in their
species, how species are unified in genera, and how all genera, considered in a hierarchical system, are unified in divine Wisdom, even the
Lord Jesus Christ himself. Created beings are not completely separated
entities without bonds that bind them together, rather they are ontologically related or connected, which is exactly what Maximus lets us see
in the passage we are investigating in *Ambiguum* 10.

According to *Ambiguum* 10, all created essences, intelligible as well
as sensible, are subject to the movements of διαστολή and συστολή.
These terms are known from ancient medicine. According to Liddell
and Scott, for instance in Galen they denote certain movements of
the heart, namely its expansion and contraction. Διαστολή, from the
verb διαστέλλω, means *drawing apart*, while συστολή, from συστέλλω,
means *drawing together*. The usage in St. Maximus, however, is not
medical, but metaphysical. The terms fit conceptually into late ancient
metaphysics, especially of the Platonic schools, with their idea of the
procession and conversion (πρόοδος and ἐπιστροφή) of beings in relation to the demiurgic source.

However, the expansion and contraction scheme described by
Maximus is not exactly the same as the procession and conversion scheme of Neoplatonism. First, this is an instance of Maximus'
"reformed" Platonism, or of his transformation of Platonist metaphysical structures into his own Christian metaphysics. In this regard, we
need to be aware of both likenesses and differences between pagan
Platonism and Maximus' thought. Secondly, while procession in
Maximus means *creation out of nothing*, conversion means that created
beings suffer eschatological *transformation*. Expansion and contraction, on the other hand, seems to specify a certain cosmic *arrangement*
that is an aspect of this procession-conversion scheme. Expansion and
contraction are definitely not one of the four kinds of movement or
change from the Aristotelian tradition. It is difficult to see how they
qualify as movements at all.

We shall first sketch the features of Maximus' procession and conversion scheme. There is an interesting presentation of this in *Ambiguum*
7. In a Christian thinker like Maximus, this scheme is worked out from
Christian as well as Neoplatonist principles. On the one hand, St. Paul

---

[18] *Amb.Ioh.* 41, *PG* 91, 1312B–1313B.

uses prepositional terms to describe the dependence of the world on God. In Romans (11:36) he says that "from Him and through Him and to Him are all things" (ὅτι ἐξ αὐτοῦ καὶ δι' αὐτοῦ καὶ εἰς αὐτὸν τὰ πάντα). Maximus refers explicitly to this when he describes procession and conversion in *Ambiguum* 7. However, his own scheme is more developed. He adopts and adapts the Neoplatonist triad of remaining-proceeding-converting in his description of the divine Economy. One Neoplatonic statement that illustrates this triad is Proclus' famous saying in the *Elements of Theology* (proposition 35): "Every effect remains in its cause, proceeds from it, and reverts upon it" (Πᾶν τὸ αἰτιατὸν καὶ μένει ἐν τῇ αὑτοῦ αἰτίᾳ καὶ πρόεισιν ἀπ' αὐτῆς καὶ ἐπιστρέφει πρὸς αὐτήν). The effect remains in the cause in a unitary and perfect essential condition. The procession accounts for the distinction between cause and effect, and the conversion is the desire for well-being that constitutes the effect as participating in the ideal paradigm in the cause. What Maximus describes in *Ambiguum* 7 is similar to what Proclus puts forward in his *Elements of Theology*. First, there is an original *remaining*. Maximus says a creature is a "portion of God" in the sense that its *logos*, meaning the principle of its essence, exists eternally in God.[19] He also puts it another way and says the *logoi* of all beings are "steadfastly fixed" (βεβαίως...πεπήγασι) in God as the principles of making of creatures.[20] The procession is called τὴν ἀγαθοπρεπῆ εἰς τὰ ὄντα τοῦ ἑνὸς ποιητικήν τε καὶ συνεκτικὴν πρόοδον, "the creative and together-keeping procession of the One to beings, which is befitting goodness".[21] He calls the conversion τὴν εἰς τὸν ἕνα τῶν πολλῶν ἐπιστρεπτικήν τε καὶ χειραγωγικὴν ἀναφοράν τε καὶ πρόνοιαν, "the converting and hand-leading ascent and providence of the many to the One". Maximus also stresses that the conversion is the way of well-being. The major difference between Maximus and Proclus is that in the former the scheme of remaining-proceeding-converting is centred in the particular Christian idea of the "mystery of Christ" motivated by God's eternal love for His creatures, combined with his doctrine of a temporal creation out of nothing.

In Maximus, procession is the act of creation, while conversion is the gathering of beings in the gracious eschatological fulfilment. On the

---

[19] *Amb.Ioh.* 7, *PG* 91, 1080B–C and 1080A.

[20] *Amb.Ioh.* 7, *PG* 91, 1081A.

[21] *Amb.Ioh.* 7, *PG* 91, 1081C.

other hand, the scheme of expansion-contraction specifies an aspect of this arrangement. It denotes a particular ontological and metaphysical structuring of the totality of created beings within the tension of unity and plurality. Procession is described as a "together-keeping procession" and conversion as a "hand-led ascent". It seems to me that expansion and contraction respectively are elaborations of these qualifications. Expansion elaborates the notion of "together-keeping" and contraction describes a feature that facilitates the "hand-leading". While procession and conversion set the limitations of the cosmos as its beginning and end, the expansion and contraction highlight the metaphysical structure of the created essence within these limits.

In the text we are interpreting from *Ambiguum* 10, Maximus describes expansion as a movement of essence, a movement from the most generic genus, through the more generic genera to the species, culminating in the most specific species. What is this "movement"? How can essence move or be moved? Maximus thinks obviously not of generation and corruption or of any other kind of movement from the Aristotelian tradition that we have listed above. On the other hand, essence is arranged in the system of genera and species, and for Maximus genera and species are, even if universals, created beings.[22] Expansion could therefore be interpreted as God's bringing forth this arrangement of genera and species in the act of creation. Expansion is, simply speaking, distribution namely a system in which something (essence) is distributed. I therefore suggest we take his notion of movement of essence simply to mean that God provides for the created order and that expansion and contraction is God's way of *ordering* the system of created essence.

But why describe this system as expansion *and* contraction? Let go that expansion may mean the establishment of a cosmic system of genera and species, but how does contraction enter the picture? We must not miss that Maximus in fact describes both expansion and contraction as dynamic structures. The system is not static like an everlasting and static Porphyrian tree. The system shows how essence (in the singular) is created and distributed in such a way that all entities are interconnected from top to bottom and this facilitates the conversion as a contractive movement that brings all being together into a

---

[22] Cf. *Amb.Ioh.* 7, *PG* 91, 1080B.

community united in God. The scheme is therefore another elabora-tion of the structures we found in *Ambiguum* 41.

The system of expansion and contraction is delimited above and below. There is a limit above since the all-inclusive genus of essence col-lects all kinds together at the border line between created being and the uncreated and transcendent reality of God. The most specific species (τῶν εἰδικωτάτων εἰδῶν) are below the limit. This term denotes, as in Porphyry, the lowest species, beyond which there are no other subordi-nate species.[23] Beyond this border line there is only non-being. One may wonder why Maximus does not include the particulars in the scheme. Particulars are definitely basic realities in the Maximian system. I sup-pose the answer is that Maximus sketches the distribution of *essence* and there are no essences below the last species. This does of course not exclude the particulars. All particulars are *the same* in the sense that they all have the same essence. Human beings, for instance, may differ in many ways but they all have one and the same essence. *Qua* human beings they do not differ. In *Ambiguum* 41, Maximus includes the par-ticulars in one of his divisions of creatures but not as if they represented a lowest division of essence.[24] He rather stresses their specific identity.

This stress on the sameness of the human species is important in Maximus' spiritual theology.[25] If one consults *Ambiguum* 7 and 41, one gets the impression that the totality of created being, all kinds, species, and particulars, is destined to convert to a glorified condition of intimate communion with God. The metaphysical "divisions" we have commented on above, expressed in part in the terminology of Aristotelian-Porphyrian logic, are, according to Maximus' view, insti-tuted in the cosmos in order to facilitate this kind of universal salvation. If we look at the philosophical sections of *Ambiguum* 10 in light of this, we understand why natural contemplation is a step on the way to expe-rience union with God.

---

[23] Cf. Porphyrii, *Isagoge et in Aristotelis categorias commentarium*, ed. by A. BUSSE, Berlin, 1887 (*CAG* IV.I), p. 4.

[24] *Amb.Ioh.* 41, *PG* 91, 1312D.

[25] See for instance *Car.* 1.13, *PG* 90, 964B–C, and cf. *Q.Thal.* introductio, in *CCSG* 7, p. 33.

3. Quantity and quality (1177c–1180a).

Maximus says that the being of beings (τὸ εἶναι τῶν ὄντων) has being in a certain manner (τὸ πῶς εἶναι ἔχων) and not simply (οὐκ ἁπλῶς).[26] It seems reasonable to understand this as referring to the delimitation beings suffer when they are quantitatively and qualitatively determined and receive their "where" and "when". Maximus' comments on quantity and quality are rather dense and obscure. His sketches are so scanty that the interpreter has a hard job unravelling the sense. Both categories are treated with a view to *movement*. The most obvious quantitative movement is of sensible things subject to generation and corruption, namely increase and decrease (αὔξησις and μείωσις) in bulk. In addition to this, beings, probably including intelligible as well as sensible entities, suffer the quantitative movement of ἐπίτασις and ἄνεσις. Louth translates ἐπίτασις as tightening and ἄνεσις as loosening, while Constas translates ἐπίτασις as augmentation and ἄνεσις as diminution.[27] What Maximus has in mind is far from obvious. It may be of help if we can discover how earlier philosophers used these terms. Barnes comments on them in his commentary on Porphyry's *Introduction*.[28] He points out that ἐπίτασις is literally "the stretching or extension of a cord or string", while ἄνεσις "is its relaxing". Barnes says both have a common musical application. His preferred translations are augmentation (ἐπίτασις) and diminution (ἄνεσις), which fit several contexts. Porphyry's point is that while differences, genera, species, and properties do not suffer augmentation and diminution or "the more and the less", accidents do.[29] Something may be more or less white, more or less good or bad, in general entities have more or less of any accidental characteristic. Will this interpretation fit into what Maximus says?

I think we may gain more background material for interpreting Maximus if we turn to Ammonius' commentary on Porphyry's *Introduction*. There we find a discussion of something Aristotle says in his *Categories*, namely that substances or essences do not admit of the more and the less.[30] Ammonius says: "Since even if one agreed that the

---

[26] *Amb.Ioh.* 10, *PG* 91, 1180B.

[27] LOUTH, *Maximus*, p. 138; CONSTAS, 2014, I, p. 288.

[28] Porphyry, *Introduction*, trans by J. BARNES, Oxford, 2008, pp. 172–176.

[29] See Barnes' discussion of the problems involved.

[30] Ammonius, *In Porphyrii Isagogen*, ed. by A. BUSSE, Berlin, 1891 *(CAG* IV.III), pp. 96–98. Cf. Aristotle, *Categories*, 3b24–4a9.

more and the less is in them, it will not be in the horizontal ones, but in the vertical ones". Ammonius continues by explaining that essence is more so in animal than in human being, and more in human being than in Socrates. Horizontal entities, like Socrates and Plato, however, are not more or less of an essence compared with one another. In the series essence-animal-human being-Socrates, there is a "more" the higher up in the hierarchy, and a "less" for each step downwards. Ammonius then comments on the terms ἐπίτασις and ἄνεσις: "These names have been taken metaphorically from strings, for in that domain a tightened string produces an intense sound, and a loosened one a lesser sound. Thus, the philosophers call augmentation (ἐπίτασις) an intense apprehension of a thing, and diminution (ἄνεσις) a lesser one". When a string is tightened or augmented, it is stretched and gives an intense sound. Analogically, higher entities are more of an essence than the lower ones. There is, to use other terms, a stretching, augmentation, or intensification of essence higher up in the hierarchy. Lower down, there is a loosening or diminution of essence.

It does not seem to me that this background information on the meaning of the terms helps much in the interpretation of Maximus. It is important to note that there is no Neoplatonic hierarchy of universal essences existing "between" God and the particulars. How, then, are we to solve the problem? The text seems to indicate that for Maximus, augmentation and diminution has to do with the *differences* introduced in the scale of being. In several instances, he uses the term "difference" technically in accordance with the Aristotelian-Porphyrian tradition of logic. A difference is in that case an essential characteristic. There is a movement of *expansion* with the introduction of a number of partial differences (ταῖς κατὰ μέρος διαφοραῖς). These partial differences are form-making (εἰδοποιουμένη). Then there occurs an opposite movement when things are brought together and return, without loss of the natural form (εἶδος). This should be the movement of *contraction*. On this background we may guess that in this short note on quantity, Maximus sketches the *numerical* aspect of expansion. Expansion is like stretching the boundaries of the set to include a great number of differentiated entities, each with its proper form, but this stretching does not go on infinitely. The opposite movement of contraction or loosening does not mean that entities lose their form. It means that differences are relaxed and that entities are brought together or collected into some kind of unity-in-plurality.

If we sum up, the picture shows that given the expansion of essence, this movement is numerically limited: there is a definite number of entities, of genera, species, and particulars. The number is stretched to a certain limit. From this limit, there occurs a contraction which does not mean the loss of differences, but that some kind of unity is achieved. This unity could probably be the eschatological unification in love of all created beings. I do not claim that this is the only possible interpretation. However, it gives some sense to the obscure passage.

Maximus' comments concerning quality are likewise sketchy. Once again he points to beings subject to generation and corruption that suffer the change of *alteration* (ἀλλοίωσις). Alteration is the term usually applied to characterize shift of qualities in the Aristotelian tradition: an apple may for instance suffer the change of colour from green to red. Then Maximus once again widens the perspective to include qualities in intelligible as well as sensible creatures. It further seems that qualities are gained and again lost in the expansive and contractive movement. There is nothing in the text itself that makes it possible to amplify Maximus' short statements into a kind of theory.

4. On "when" and "where" (1180b–1181c).

The sketchy presentation of the categories quantity and quality is frustrating for the interpreter. However, the main point in both presentations is clearly to stress the limited reality of created beings, both with regard to number and qualitative characteristics. We are much better off when we come to Maximus' interesting treatment of "when" and "where". Aristotle lists "when" and "where" as separate categories.[31] He does not, however, treat them as equivalent with *place* and *time* (τόπος and χρόνος), the latter being kinds of *quantity*.[32] Simplicius says in his commentary on the *Categories* that "when" and "where" "do not denote time and place, but a relation to (σχέσιν πρός) time and place".[33] So, if it is predicated of me that I was writing in the *late afternoon*, this denotes not time but a relation to a time-scheme. Aristotle defines time in the *Physics* as "the number of movement with respect to before and after".[34]

---

[31] Cf. *Cat.* 1b25–27.

[32] Cf. *Cat.* 4b20–25.

[33] Simplicius, *In Aristotelis Categorias commentarium*, ed. C. KALBFLEISCH, Berlin, 1907 (*CAG* VIII), p. 342.

[34] *Physics* 4.11: 219b1–2.

Time may be distinguished into past, the present moment, or "now" (τὸ νῦν), and future. Aristotle further discusses the "now" and says it may have two senses:[35] "In one way, it is potentially a division of time; in another, it is the limit and the unity of both [parts of time]". He then comments on the term "when" and says it means a time related to the "now" in the first sense. In the *Categories* Aristotle uses examples like "yesterday" and "last year".[36] Examples of "where" are "in the Lyceum", "in the market-place".[37] It is not altogether clear that Maximus actually takes over this view and distinguishes between "when" and "where", on the one hand, and time and place, on the other. However, the text in *Ambiguum* 10 is compatible with such a distinction. When he speaks of "where" as being "in place" (ἐν τόπῳ) and "when" as being "in time" (ἐν χρόνῳ) this definitely points in such a direction.[38]

Maximus claims that "when" and "where" cannot be thought of separately from each other. Rather they exist simultaneously (ἅμα).[39] This seems to give good sense: if something exists at some time, it clearly exists somewhere as well. The opposite seems obvious as well: being somewhere implies being "there" at some moment or "when". Simplicius, in his comments on "when" and "where", says that some categories are arranged together because of their inclination to one another, like action and being-affected, "when" and "where", "since they make a common and equal contribution towards the whole [process of] generation".[40] One of the main objectives for Maximus is to show how created beings are delimited and finite. Creatures possess being in a certain way and not simply like God. He says that no being is "without beginning" (ἄναρχον) temporally if something can be thought of before it (προεπινοεῖσθαι) or "uncircumscribed" (ἀπερίγραφον) spatially if something can be thought of together with it (συνεπινοεῖσθαι).[41] Every created entity is, therefore, temporally and spatially finite. But what about the totality of creatures?

Maximus has a short but interesting note on the place (τόπος) of "the all" (that is *the universe*) (τὸ πᾶν). He says:

---

[35] *Physics* 4.13: 222a17–19.

[36] *Cat.* 2a2.

[37] *Cat.* 2a1–2.

[38] *Amb.Ioh.* 10, *PG* 91, 1180C–D.

[39] *Amb.Ioh.* 10, *PG* 91, 1180B–C.

[40] Simplicius, *In Aristotelis Categorias commentarium* (*CAG* VIII), p. 342.

[41] *Amb.Ioh.* 10, *PG* 91, 1181B.

Οὐ γὰρ ὑπὲρ τὸ πᾶν αὐτὸ τὸ πᾶν τοῦ παντός (τοῦτο γὰρ πως καὶ ἄλογον καὶ ἀδύνατον αὐτὸ τὸ πᾶν ὑπὲρ τὸ ἑαυτοῦ εἶναι πᾶν θεσπίζειν), ἀλλ᾽ ὑφ᾽ ἑαυτοῦ ἐν ἑαυτῷ τὴν περιγραφήν ἔχον, μετὰ τὴν πάντα περιγράφουσαν τοῦ παναιτίου ἄπειρον δύναμιν, αὐτὸ τὸ πέρας ἑαυτοῦ τὸ ἐξώτερον. Ὅπερ καὶ τόπος ἐστὶ τοῦ παντός, καθὼς καὶ ὁρίζονται τινὲς τὸν τόπον λέγοντες, Τόπος ἐστὶν ἡ ἔξω τοῦ παντός περιφέρεια, ἢ ἡ ἔξω τοῦ παντός θέσις, ἢ τὸ πέρας τοῦ περιέχοντος ἐν ᾧ περιέχεται τὸ περιεχόμενον.[42]

> Indeed, the totality of the universe is not beyond the universe itself (for how irrational and impossible that would be, to declare that the universe itself is beyond its own totality) but rather possesses self-enclosure from itself after the all-enclosing infinite power of the cause of all, which is its outer (ἐξώτερον) limit. This is the place of the universe, as some would define place, by saying that the surface outside of the universe or the position outside (ἔξω) of the universe or "the limit of what encompasses," in "which that which is encompassed is encompassed," is place.[43]

Maximus' last phrase (τόπος ἐστὶν τὸ πέρας τοῦ περιέχοντος ἐν ᾧ περιέχεται τὸ περιεχόμενον) comes rather close to how Nemesius defines place in his *De natura hominis*:[44] "[...] place is the limit of that which contains, by which it contains what is contained (τόπος γάρ ἐστι πέρας τοῦ περιέχοντος καθ" ὅ περιέχει τὸ περιεχόμενον)'. Since we know that Maximus read Nemesius, we may take it for granted that the latter influenced Maximus' formulation. The background is, however, richer. The problem Maximus faces is a traditional one. Aristotle's definitions of place created puzzles that led many later commentators to discuss the concept.[45] He defines place as "the first unchangeable limit of that which surrounds".[46] Aristotle further says:

---

[42] *Amb.Ioh.* 10, PG 91, 1180C; LAGA, *supra*, pp. 146–148; CONSTAS 2014, I, p. 292.

[43] LOLLAR, *supra*, p. 125.

[44] Nemesius of Emesa, *De natura hominis*, PG 40, 600b.

[45] See for this the summaries in R. SORABJI, *The Philosophy of the Commentators*, Vol. 2, London, 2004, chapter 13.

[46] *Physics* 4.4: 212a20–21.

Τὸ γὰρ πού, αὐτό τε ἐστὶ τι, καὶ ἔτι ἄλλο τι δεῖ εἶναι παρὰ τοῦτο ἐν ᾧ ὁ περιέχει. Παρὰ δὲ τὸ πᾶν καὶ ὅλον οὐδὲν ἐστιν ἔξω τοῦ παντός, καὶ διὸ τοῦτο ἐν τῷ οὐρανῷ πάντα.[47]

> What is somewhere is both itself something, and, in addition,
> there must be something else besides that, in which the thing is,
> and which surrounds. But there is nothing besides the all and the
> whole, nothing which is outside (ἔξω) the all; and this is why every-
> thing is in the world (ἐν τῷ οὐρανῷ πάντα).[48]

The consequence is that there cannot be anything that surrounds the
uttermost sphere of the universe, and that it cannot therefore itself be
in a place. Aristotle illustrates his point by saying that the earth is in the
water, the water is in the air, the air is in the ether, the ether is in the
world (e.g. heaven), and the world is not in anything.[49] This, however, is
rather a puzzle. We may generally note that the all or universe comprises all sensible or bodily beings. Taken as what it is, namely as *all* there
is, there is no sensible or bodily being beyond it. Maximus obviously
thinks the universe has a place, and this place of the universe is an *outside* limit that circumscribes the totality of the cosmic system within it.
However, this outside limit is for him not a puzzling additional body,
nor a likewise puzzling nothingness, but the circumscription, the "outside", is "the infinite power of the cause of all that circumscribes all".
This notion recalls St. Paul's words from Acts 17:28: "for in Him we live
and move and have our being [...]". The power of God is the place of
the universe. Whether this solves the philosophical problems may be an
open question but Maximus obviously thinks it does.

Maximus sums up his treatment with claiming that the application
of categories demonstrates the limitations of the created world. Beings
are delimited essentially, quantitatively, and with respect to "when"
and "where".[50] In his short comment on the latter two he claims that
without "when" and "where" nothing could exist, neither essence, nor
quantity, quality, relation, action, affection, movement, habit, nor any
other possible category that delimit the universe (τὸ πᾶν περικλείουσιν).

[47] *Physics* 4.5: 212b14–17.

[48] Aristotle, *Physics*, trans. by H. G. APOSTLE (Bloomington and London
1980; first pub. 1969).

[49] *Physics* 4.5: 212b20–22.

[50] *Amb.Ioh.* 10, *PG* 91, 1181A–B.

It is obvious that no sensible essence can exist without temporal and spatial determinations, and none of the other categories could exist without being determinations of some essence.

Final remarks

The list of categories was the starting-point of the above interpretation and discussion. The way he treats them demonstrates Maximus' knowledge of at least parts of the philosophical tradition. What remains rather puzzling is how Maximus' highly theoretical exposition fits into his concept of spiritual development. I said at the end of my introduction above that what we find in these sections is philosophical meditations on what we may expect to contemplate on a certain level. I deliberately used the term "meditations" on what we may contemplate since I suppose Maximus would not claim that his expositions are equivalent with natural contemplation. He probably wants to shed some light on what kind of topics the contemplative would dwell on. But how could such highly theoretical subjects fit into a spiritual quest? Spiritual development has three stages, the practical or ascetical, natural contemplation, and mystical theology. There is a paragraph in *Ambiguum* 10 where Maximus elaborates on "the five modes of contemplation". These are concerned with essence, movement, difference, mixture, and position.[51] The points made by Maximus are intricate, so we shall not investigate all details, but just sketch what they might suggest. These modes lead to the vision and acknowledgement of God as the cause of the cosmos or as the cause of *essence*. They further lead to a vision of a cosmos in which one sees beings providentially ordered in their *movement* and as fitted together in the divine preservation of *differences*. One contemplates the distribution of beings according to natural potentialities, in their *mixtures* and *positions*. One also contemplates how human inclinations, when virtuously adjusted, are transformed into a "divinely-fitting" cosmos, a well-ordered state of the human person that is to be seen as a microcosm in harmony with the structure of the macrocosm. This is the purpose of natural contemplation. It brings the human being to study and understand the universe from the point of view of divine providence. It brings the human being into a virtuous and contemplative movement that contributes to the unification of all of God's creature.

---

[51] *Amb.Io.* 10, *PG* 91: 1133A–1136B.

Maximus the Confessor on Symbols of Manifestation of God the Word in the World

Lyubomira Stefanova

(*Sofia*)

Patristic scholars have always considered the teachings of St. Maximus the Confessor in relation to the *Corpus Areopagiticum*, which the saint interprets in his works. A central theme of the *Corpus* involves the ontological commitment of God to created being, expressed through the model of the procession of the Divine energies to created reality, and the reversion of creatures back to the Creator. According to Torstein Tollefsen, St. Maximus makes a connection between the idea of reversion in the procession model on the one hand, and the expansion of universal to individual, on the other.[1] The pattern μονή – πρόοδος – ἐπιστροφή[2] is considered by Maximus in the context of the expansive manifestation of God, while the opposite is seen as contraction, i.e., the reversion of beings to God (διαστολή-συστολή). Drawing upon the geometric representation of the two models, Vladimir Cvetković focuses on St. Maximus' understanding of the ontological relationship between the universal and the individual. This relationship can be seen as a pulsation of the One God, the outpouring of His gracious energy towards man.

In this study, I present St. Maximus' view of the manifestation of God the Word in creation, outlining how each form carries its own individual *logos*, while also being an expression of God in its particular mode, or *tropos*, of being. In the course of this study, I will focus on

---

[1] T. Tollefsen, *Christocentric Cosmology of St. Maximus the Confessor*, Oxford, 2008, pp. 64–68.

[2] The term ἐπιστροφή, used by the neo-Platonists was replaced by Maximos with ἐπιστρεπτικὴ καὶ χειραγωγικὴ ἀναφορά τε καὶ πρόνοια See: V. Cvetkovic, "Maximus the Confessors Geometrical Analogies Applied to the Relationship between Christ and Creation", in *Orthodox Theology and the Sciences*, ed. by G. D. Dragas, P. Pavlov & S. Tanev, Sofia, 2016, pp. 277–291.

Ambiguum *10 of Maximus the Confessor in Modern Study: Papers Collected on the Occasion of the Budapest Colloquium on Saint Maximus, 3–4 February 2021*, ed. by Alexis Léonas & Vladimir Cvetković, with the collaboration of Daniel Heide, Turnhout, 2025 (IPM 97), pp. 237–253
© BREPOLS ❧ PUBLISHERS   10.1484/M.IPM-EB.5.141863

the term *contemplation* in Maximus the Confessor, in order to trace the way in which human minds are joined to God the Word. The symbolic manifestations of the Divine Logos, bearing both sensory and irrational knowledge, are the basis of human's association with God. My thesis is that, in the teaching of St. Maximus, partaking in the sacrament of Communion, takes place incrementally and spontaneously. It takes place not only in time, but also outside of it. Thus, in each person the process of essential union with the Word has both an incremental and a radial paradigm. This pertains to what the Saint calls natural contemplation and may be considered in two ways: sensory-rational and metaphysical. This corresponds to the claim, made by Cvetković, that the manifestation of the Logos is tied directly to human individual nature in such a way that the ultimate point of identity of the *logos* of individuals is at the center of the circle representing the Logos of God.[3] Indeed, the dynamic relationship between God the Word and the created world will be examined, both ontologically and anthropologically.

The primary focus of our analysis will center on St. Maximus' treatment of the concept of contemplation within both philosophical and biblical contexts, specifically within the *Ambigua to John* 10 and 67 texts. These texts exemplify a specific numerical theology, as they elucidate how creation expands from God as the Monad and subsequently returns to Him through a structured arithmetic progression, beginning with the monad and progressing through the triad, pentad, heptad, and duodecad before ultimately converging back to the monad. Nevertheless, it's important to clarify that we do not intend to equate God directly with the monad. In *Ambiguum* 10.41, St. Maximus asserts that while God can be appropriately referred to as the "monad", this term does not fully encompass His transcendent nature. St. Maximus' intention is not to establish an equivalence between the Monad and the divine essence, but rather to emphasize that the term "monad" signifies absolute simplicity, devoid of any attributes such as quantity, quality, or relational characteristics. This implies that when we refer to God as the monad, we are asserting that God lacks any divisible parts within Himself. It's essential to note that this does not suggest that the Trinity constitutes parts of the divine monad. Since God as the monad exists beyond the realm of relation, He also exists beyond the possibility of

---

[3] CVETKOVIC, "Maximus the Confessor's Geometrical Analogies", p. 287.

division. St. Maximus draws support for this concept from Dionysius, as evidenced by his quotation:

> Therefore while both Singularity and Trinity are hymned, the Divinity beyond all things is neither Singularity nor Trinity nor is It known either by us or by anything else, but in order that we might truly hymn both Its transcendent unity and Its divine fecundity, we name the Divinity that transcends naming by means of a three-fold and unified divine name and the Divinity beyond being by means of being.[4]

In the theocentric model exposed in *Ambiguum* 10.3, St. Maximus simultaneously posits the triad: *being – well-being – eternal being* as progressive stages of divine knowledge for human being, as well as a radiation of the entire creation. According to St. Maximus, this is because God created all things by fitting them into these three states of creation. The human being, who is endowed with essence and existence, projects these two realities into these three states of being. Within this triad of stages, the state of well-being aligns with the existence of humanity, whereas the first and the last stages relate to the essence of humanity. St. Maximus contends that the first and last stages are entirely the result of God's intention, while the middle stage is contingent upon human mentality and motion. Nonetheless, the intermediate stage holds significant influence over the ultimate stage, for if an individual fails to achieve goodness and reach a state of well-being, the final term, which is eternal being, would not manifest as eternal well-being. In St. Maximus' view, the first and last terms are regarded as the extremes, while the middle term functions as a mean or a term that upholds the truth of these extremes. Given that the middle term is contingent on human mentality and motions, achieving well-being necessitates the alignment of humanity's focus towards God. This also implies that, at the level of the soul, humans should not engage in their natural activities in a way that goes against their natural disposition. The logos of an individual being is realized, and it achieves its proper mode (*tropos*)

---

[4] *Amb.Ioh.* 10.31d (*PG* 1168AB, here, pp. 128–129). Maximus relies here on Dionysius the Areopagite, *Div. Nom.*, XIII.3. The passages quoted from *Ambiguum* 10 refer to the translation from the Greek text by Joshua Lollar, according to the critical edition by C. Laga in this volume (referencing by the *PG* page numbers). In all other passages from *Ambigua* of St. Maximus the Confessor, the translations of N. Constas are used.

of existence, only when it is oriented toward the origin of its existence. Otherwise, if it is directed towards itself or anything other than God, a human being cannot ensure its own existence because it is not the creator of its own being. According to Maximus, in alignment with the teachings of the saints, the human intellect should have its focus solely fixed on God, engaging in contemplation of His virtues, and surrendering itself, without relying on human understanding, "to the ineffable glory of His blessedness".[5]

Precisely because *well-being* is the symbolic manifestation of the relationship between the transcendent God and His creatures, the Word is perceptible as food for a human being, both mentally and materially. As such, *well-being* is itself an expression of the ontological relationship between man and God, the object of contemplation of the Divine Logos which, according to St. Maximus is the highest attribute of God the Word manifested in creation. When he talks about contemplation, Maximus does not regard it simply as a means of spiritual growth on the path to knowledge of God, but as a vital act of nutrition that ensures man's existence in both the spiritual and physical sense.

In *Ambiguum* 10.19, St. Maximus expands the concept of triad in being to encompass a pentad. Creation, according to St. Maximus, is the object of contemplation in five main aspects – as being, motion, difference, mixture and position. Through these modes of contemplation, God reveals Himself to us, insofar as we gather from created entities the implicit traces of the Lord. The contemplative activity of the mind is directed towards the comprehension of being, movement, and difference, reducing them to the aspects of mixture and position. Through being, we look for the cause of beings and learn from them that such a cause exists, without trying to know what that cause is in its own essence. Motion, on the other hand, manifests the providence of beings, and through it we contemplate the immutable essential identity of beings in their particular forms. Difference means judgment, of the natural potential of things, commensurate with the substrate of their being (according to the principle of each), by which we have learned that the wise distributor is God. These three basic modes of contemplation are resolved in its aspects of mixture and position, which underlie the perception of God's goodness and love.

---

[5] *Amb.Ioh* 10, 1116D, here, p. 44.

St. Maximus proceeds from his earlier explanation in *Ambiguum* 10.3, illustrating that when the intellect is directed toward God, it doesn't solely acquire pious knowledge. Rather, through its orientation towards God, the human intellect encounters Him and, by means of virtue, transforms into the very essence it contemplates. The initial triad among the five principles – being, motion, and judgment – corresponds to the triad of being, well-being, and eternal being. In St. Maximus' theological perspective, being, or essence, holds the role of an teacher of theology, because it imparts the understanding that being is inherently linked to a cause. Nevertheless, through the contemplation of being, one cannot deduce the cause of being, as being itself does not reveal its underlying cause. Motion aligns with the concept of well-being, as well-being is essentially the outcome of the movement of creation toward its creator. According to St. Maximus, this motion mirrors divine providence for all beings. Through the contemplation of how a diverse array of distinct elements is harmoniously held and safeguarded within an unbreakable structure, one gains insight into God, who, in His ineffable unity, both binds all things together and maintains their distinctiveness from one another. Ultimately, the eternal beings are associated with the concept of judgment, which becomes apparent through the differences or distinctions in the inherent potentiality of the essence within each being. In His wisdom as a distributor and judge, God has bestowed upon every being an enduring consistency in its natural essence, or, to be more specific, the "what", "how", and "how much" of each being's existence has been ordained by Him.

The remaining two categories, namely mixture and position, provide the path towards achieving well-being and also serve as means to elevate well-being into eternal well-being. The motion discussed in relation to well-being is not simply any form of movement but rather a specific motion directed towards God as the eternal source of goodness. When the intellect is oriented towards God, it doesn't merely gather knowledge; rather, by mixing with the object of its knowledge, it assimilates divine virtues. Hence, St. Maximus regards this mixture as a representation of the intellect's inclination. Position or placement ensures the ongoing mixture of the intellect with divine virtues and its steadfastness in goodness.[6]

---

[6] *Amb.Ioh* 10, pp. 51–55.

The very existence of humanity is conceivable when the spiritual vision focuses on the goodwill and love of God, implicitly embedded in the state of well-being.[7] The divine Logos first penetrates and constitutes the higher realms in the human soul, which means that He feeds the mind first on the level of the *logos*. But since the cognitive faculties of man are inextricably linked with the sensible, it may be believed that at the same time the satiation of his material body takes place. The moment of satiation can therefore be seen as an expansion of the Word, which simultaneously penetrates both the mind and the sensory body of man. This act is connected with a special time – the time spoken of in the biblical text of Creation: "In the beginning God created the heavens and the earth"(Gen.1:1). In the theology of St. Basil the Great, this "beginning" stands outside the time unfolding within the sensible creation, but also outside the timelessness of the intelligible creation.[8] It is the principle of time that serves as a bridge between the transcendent God and the created world. It is in this special principle of time that the first creative manifestation of the Creator appears, namely light. Light thus becomes the bearer of all the fundamental elements in creation, from which the various forms of animate and inanimate natures are built. Speaking of this kind of satiation in a purely material sense, St. Maximus shows that it takes place precisely outside the time of creation. Or, if one may say so, satiation is the insertion of extraordinary time into the time of being. The link between the temporal and the timeless, or the spiritual and the material realms, is established by virtue of the pre-existing logos of creation. This logos predates the actual act of creation and takes on its definitive form through divine energies, ultimately leading to the realization of well-being.

In *Ambigua* 10.3 and 10.19, St. Maximus explores the broad dimension of divine care and providence, along with human contemplation of these concepts on a universal scale. However, in *Ambiguum* 10.42, he broadens the perspective of divine providence to encompass each individual created being. This concept is not an original one, as St. Maximus draws inspiration from St. Nemesius of Emessa. St. Nemesius contends that if all individual elements are annihilated, the universals will

[7] *Amb.Ioh* 10, p. 167.

[8] See: I. CHRISTOV, "Theological and Scientific Approaches to the Contemplation of Nature", in *Theology and the Sciences*, ed. by G. D. DRAGAS, P. PAVLOV & S. TANEV, Sofia, 2016.

likewise cease to exist because universals are inherently composed of particulars.[9] Nevertheless, St. Maximus advances this line of reasoning through his theology of logos. In essence, this implies that God, guided by a singular and steadfast benevolent will, extends His care not just to all things collectively but also to each individual thing. Each individual creature came into existence within the divine mind through the agency of its unique logos of being.[10] According to St. Maximus, when God granted existence to all things, He also bestowed upon them the grace of well-being.[11] Through this grace of well-being, individual beings have the capacity to respond to divine providence and orient their trajectory back toward their Creator.

In *Ambiguum* 10, Maximus primarily delves into abstract concepts, such as being, motion, distinction, virtue, everlastingness. When the intellect contemplates these concepts, it gains insight into the divine and becomes one with it. St. Maximus employs a geometrically inspired logic, progressing from the unity of the monad to the complexity of the triad and pentad, and then retracing this expansion to return to the monadic unity.

As it is mentioned above in the theology of St. Maximus, symbols are not understood as abstract allegories, but as real objects and manifestations of God, filling all of existence. Allegory is placed in opposition to the intuitive and supra-rational (mystical) perception given by grace. Due to the limitations (i.e. poverty) of our mind, knowledge of the Divine is only communicable through parables and the symbolic narratives of the Gospels.[12] Even so, one can never fully penetrate the mysteries of God's providence, including the inexplicable act of the Incarnation, which are only partially comprehensible to the human mind through the contemplation of creation. As such, St. Maximus' apophatic theology of the Logos transcends discursive knowledge. It is not through hymnody and discourse that the Word illumines our understanding, but through contemplation of the λόγοι in creation.[13] Insofar as the Word actually descends to the sensible and intelligible

---

[9] Nemesius of Emesa, *De natura hominis 43 ed. by M.* MORANI, Berlin 1987, *p. 130,15–18,* Cf. *Amb.Ioh* 10, *PG* 91, 1192BC), pp. 143–145.

[10] *Amb.Ioh.* 10, p. 145.

[11] *Amb.Ioh.* 10, p. 169.

[12] *Th. Oec.*II.60.7–8, *PG* 90, 1149D.

[13] *Th.Oec.* II.60.10–12, *PG* 90, 1151A.

nature, God reveals Himself to humans enabling us to perceive or think of Him through the multiplicity (τῇ ποικηλίᾳ) of His forms in nature.[14] This is why Maximus advises us not to grasp the Word by intellectual activity, but through perceiving His manifestations in the visible world through faith and the contemplation of creation.

Unlike *Ambiguum* 10, where St. Maximus employs philosophical concepts to elucidate the contemplation of creation, in *Ambiguum* 67, he leans on sensory imagery. This text focuses on the miracles of Christ and the interpretation of the Gospel narrative regarding the feeding of the great multitude of people with five loaves and two fishes. Taking the symbolic manifestations of the Word to be real, manifold, natural manifestations, St. Maximus shows that contemplation as a path of spiritual ascent takes place in every human mind through the joining of its *logos* with the divine Logos. The whole of creation, being the main object of contemplation, appears to human being as a means of gradual approach to God, and at the same time as an expression of a common and spontaneous attraction of the entire creation towards the single Principle.

I will briefly present the basic patristic conception of the manifestations of God and their participation in Him, which St. Maximus interprets and develops further. According to him, penetrating into the essence of creation with the help of the senses and the mind, we feel satiety and delight, approaching the works of God. Contemplating the visible creation, according to the saint, one "scientifically receives the contemplation of divine realities with greater concision" (κατ' ἐπιτομὴν τὴν τῶν θείων ἐπιστημόνως δέχεσθαι θεωρίαν).[15] In the *Divine Names*, Dionysius outlines the main points of the procession of God as the Source of existence of all things. According to Dionysius, this process includes two main stages: first, the emanation of the creative ideas of beings in God's pre-eternal Providence; second, the realization of these ideas in creation, where they exist as the individual λόγοι of beings. Therefore, contemplating the things of the sensory world, as well as feeling them, we join with their common *logos*, which is in the bosom of the Creator. The term εἰδοποιΐα[16] in the teaching of the Areopagite

---

[14] *Th.Oec.* II.60.11, *PG* 90, 1151A.

[15] *Amb. Ioh.* 67.2. 4–5 in CONSTAS, 2014, 2, pp. 286–287.

[16] εἰδοποιΐα – shaping of beings. According to Dionysius: "Εἰ δὲ καὶ ὑπὲρ πάντα τὰ ὄντα ἐστίν, ὥσπερ οὖν ἐστι, τἀγαθόν, καὶ τὸ ἀνείδεον εἰδοποιεῖ. Καὶ ἐν

has a broad ontological meaning while simultaneously expressing three stages of the overall development of man, both physically and spiritually. These are: the act of baptism, which is the giving of form to the formless; the act of God's incarnation, in which God assumes human form; and the state of contemplation of the Divine manifested in the sensible paradigms of immanent being.[17] These three stages can be referred to three human states that have both an anthropological and a metaphysical dimension: hunger, food intake and satiety. The latter is conceivable as a closure of the circular model of Divine Providence; namely, the process of reversion, or return to God. It is seen in the light

---

αὐτῷ μόνῳ καὶ τὸ ἀνούσιον οὐσίας ὑπερβολὴ καὶ τὸ ἄξωον ὑπερέχουσα ζωὴ καὶ τὸ ἄνουν ὑπεραίρουσα σοφία καὶ ὅσα ἐν τἀγαθῷ τῆς τῶν ἀνειδέων ἐστὶν ὑπεροχικῆς εἰδοποιίας", in Dionysius Areopagite, *De Divinis Nominibus*, DN IV.3 (697A), according to: *Corpus Dionysiacum I*, Pseudo-Dionysius Areopagita, *De Divinis Nominibus*. ed. by B.-R. SUCHLA, Berlin-New York, 1990, p. 146. Commenting on this part of the treatise "On the Divine Names", which speaks of the formation of the *eidos* in the bosom of God's Wisdom, even before their existence, Paul Rorem writes: "The name 'Wisdom' reaches out to everything which has to do with understanding, reason and sense perception, and surpasses them all" (816B, 97) [...] Thus we consider the name Being. Not that God is a being, or even that God "is" in the sense that a creature is. "Rather, He is the essence of being for the things that have being. Not only things that are but also the essence of what they are come from him who precedes the ages" (817D, 98). Now the attribute of being or existence is primal for all subsequent numbers and just as a circle's center point in the starting point for each radius (821A, 99–100). From this primal manner of individual beings, the ranks of angels and all souls and creatures (821CD, 100–101) and all facets of being such as time and eternity(825C, 103 and chapter 10). This section is both an ontology and a lyrical hymn of praise to the one beyond all being, "the eternity of being, the source and the measure of being.../who precedes essence, being, and eternity, .../the creative source, middle and end of all things"(824A, 101). Nevertheless, the attributes of finite beings can be applied to the infinite Preexistent One, if divinely understood: "That is, through the knowledge we have, which is geared to our faculties, we may be uplifted as far as possible to the Cause of everything" (825A, 102). See in P. ROREM, *Pseudo-Dionysius. A Commentary on the Texts and an Introduction to Their Influence*, New York-Oxford, 1993, pp. 153–155.

[17] CHRISTOV, "Theological and Scientific Approaches to the Contemplation of Nature", pp. 74–75.

of natural contemplation, where the mind, penetrating into the essence of individual created things, is spontaneously nourished by recognizing their involvement – firstly with itself and, secondly, with the Divine Logos, as their common Creator.

What is satiety of the mind? In his interpretation of the texts of Scriptures (Is.61:2, Luk.4:19), St. Maximus explains the procession of God's activity (*energeia*) into the world. The created world is bound in a circular manner to the "favorable year of the Lord",[18] that is, the time range of creation from its very beginning, to its end, in which God gives life and meaning to the existence of both animate and inanimate beings. This means that creation can be seen not only as evolving in time, but also in the projection of its temporal origin, which directly binds it to the moment it arises out of nothing. Where it arises, however, is in the bosom of the Primeval God, of the Logos, in Whom everything that exists has already been established as the original economy. In recognizing the *logos* of existent things, the mind suddenly discovers the meaning of its own existence. This moment of recognition of the Logos in every single object of creation is beyond time. It is the time of the Spirit, a time in the timeless creation of the world. Therefore, the mind joins everything that can be contemplated by experiencing satiety, in the sense of identifying itself as part of the Whole.

In this context, the Gospel stories of Christ's miracle of feeding the great multitude with five loaves and two fishes may be considered.[19] St. Maximus states:

> Jesus Himself, the pure perfection, knew how to feed five thousand men in the desert with five loaves; and again He knew how to feed four thousand with seven – and, in the former, after they were satisfied, there were twelve baskets left over, whereas in the latter there were seven baskets. None of these details, as it seems to me, is without a reason or unworthy of the Spirit. (trans. N. Constas)[20]

St. Maximus' approach reflects a long patristic tradition of symbolic interpretation of the number of the loaves, which goes back to Origen and possibly even precedes him. Already Origen associated the five loaves with the sensible words of the Scripture (since their number matches that of the five senses) and the two fishes with the inner and the outer

---

[18] *Amb.Ioh.* 46.4, Constans, 2014, 2, pp. 204–205.

[19] See: Mt. 14:13–21, 15:32–38; Mc. 6:34–44, 8:1–9; Lc. 9:10–17; Io 6:1–13.

[20] *Amb.Ioh* 67, CONSTAS, 2014, 2, p. 287.

meanings of the Scripture.[21] Cyril of Alexandria, commenting on the same numbers in John 6:9–13, equates the number of the loaves with the five books of Moses, seen as the prototype of coarser food in comparison with the two fishes, understood to signify evangelical and apostolic teachings (*Commentary on John* 3.4).[22] In addition, speculation on the numbers five, seven and twelve was prominent in Neo-Platonic discourse. In *Timaeus* Plato speaks of the five cosmoses (55D),[23] whereas in the Sophist he elaborates on five supreme principles (beginning with Being, *Sph.* 254D–255E).[24] In *Theaetetus* (195E–196A) the wrong opinion is exemplified by the addition of five and seven (= 11 or 12),[25] which numbers were later understood to be charged with a deeper meaning. Symbolic understanding of these numbers is amply discussed in *Theologoumena arithmeticae*[26] attributed to Iamblichus,[27] while the genuinely Iamblichian *On the General Science of Mathematics* lays out the speculative grounds of the procedure.[28] Keeping in mind this extensive hermeneutical and speculative background, let us return to St. Maximus.

[21] Origen, *Commentary on Matthew* 11.2, cf. Origène, *Commentaire sur l'Évangile selon Matthieu, tome I (Livres X et XI)*, ed. by R. GIROD, Paris, 1970 (SC 162), pp. 268–275.

[22] Cyril of Alexandria, *Commentaria in S. Joannis Evangelium*, PG 73, 456D–457B.

[23] Plato, *Timaeus* 55D, in "Platonis Opera", "Clitopho", "Respublica", "Timaeus", "Critias". Vol. IV, ed. by J. BURNET, Oxford, 1902.

[24] Plutarch, *On the E at Delphi* 391B, in Plutarch, Moralia, Vol. 5, trans. by F. COLE BABBITT, Cambridge, Mas. 1936.

[25] Plato, *Theaetetus* 147E–148A, in Platonis Opera, vol I, ed. by E. A. DUKE, W. F. HICKEN, W. S. M. NICOLL, D. B. ROBINSON, and J. C. G. STRACHAN, Oxford, 1995.

[26] On five, see Iamblichus, *Theologumena arithmeticae* 24.16–32, on seven see *id.*, 41.10–53.

[27] Iamblichus, *Theologumena arithmeticae*, ed. by V. DE FALCO, Leipzig, 1922; English translation in Pseudo-Iamblichus, *The Theology of Arithmetic*, ed. by R. WATERFIELD, Grand Rapids, 1988. See also K. STAEHLE, *Die Zahlenmystik bei Philon von Alexandreia*, Leipzig – Berlin, 1931.

[28] Iamblichus, *De communi mathematica scientia*, ed. N. FESTA, Leipzig, 1891 (²1975); English translation in IAMBLICHUS, *On the General Science of Mathematics*, trans. by J. DILLON & J. O. URMSON, London, 2020 (Ancient Commentators on Aristotle).

Delving into the meaning of the Gospel narrative, St. Maximus explains the satiation of hunger accomplished by Christ as invoking the contemplative abilities of the mind – both in His disciples and in the gathered crowd. It is these contemplative faculties that are at the heart of alleviating hunger. St. Maximus draws attention to two interrelated processes, taking place as two opposite movements – that of multiplication, expressed as radial growth, and of synthesis, expressed as the union of multiplicity. The dynamic expression of these two movements figuratively constitutes the paradigm of the Divine pulsation of the Word.

As multiplication (increase), Maximus considers the number seven represented in the Gospel text by the five loaves and the two fishes. The number of those whose hunger was satiated (5000 people) is a multiple of 5, therefore this number is considered as a synthesis. As the completion of these two processes, the paradigms of the numbers seven and five are resolved in the number twelve, which in the Gospel text is represented as "twelve full baskets of leftovers".[29] These twelve baskets are also a symbol of the twelve apostles, although the allegorical symbolism is not primary in the interpretation of St. Maximus. Attention is specifically directed to the leftovers which, expressed numerically, reveal the limitless potential of the contemplative faculty of the mind and its saturation through the fullness of the Word. According to St. Maximus, those places of Scripture are interpreted which illustrate how the Word, through the contemplative power of the mind, makes strong the leftover of the loaves.

Further, St. Maximus says that the five loaves indicate (παραδηλοῦσι) the words which are prepared for natural contemplation: "Thus, the five barley loaves are an allusion to the principles of natural contemplation that are readily accessible to us".[30] The 5000 satiated people (Mat. 14:21) exist within the limits of nature, although they are subject to the passions and the primitive thinking pertaining to the soul; however, their imagination appears as recognition of the Word, which is the true Bread.[31] The distribution of the loaves is regarded as a penetration of

[29] See: Mt. 14: 13–21.
[30] *Amb.Ioh* 67.2 "Οἱ κρίθινοι τοιγαροῦν πέντε ἄρτοι τοὺς προχείρους τῆς φυσικῆς θεωρίας παραδηλοῦσι λόγους" [Io 6:9, 13], Constans, 2014, 2, p. 286.
[31] Cf. *Io.* 6:9, 13 – where Jesus is said to have chosen from among His disciples the 12 apostles.

the Word into the minds of many people, including the twelve apostles.[32] The participation of the latter in the community makes them both receivers and distributors of the Word, insofar as they preserve the leftovers of the Word, related not to sensual desires, but to spiritual involvement with the Word. At the same time, the apostles satiated their hunger like ordinary people.[33]

The number twelve, says Maximus, appears both as time and as nature of the Word, fulfilled according to the compound sum of seven and five.[34] Seven is actually a symmetrical number consisting of two threes and a one (3+1+3). That is, within it lies the totality and completeness of the Divine Trinity, expressed once as a Unity and twice as a Trinity. The increase in number is actually a manifestation of the One as Trinity and the Trinity as One. This is precisely the principle on which the multiplication of the leftovers is based. By this division is expressed the idea that every unit in the community of the multiple ternary has the ability to divide into three. Here Figure1 represents the rising characteristic of the number seven vertically:

Fig. 1

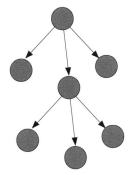

3:1

[32] Cf. Mt. 14: 21, 15:38.

[33] *Amb.Ioh* 67.2–3, CONSTAS, 2014, 2, pp. 286–287: "Οἱ δὲ τούτοις τρεφόμενοι πεντακισχίλιοι ἄνδρες [Mt. 14:21] τοὺς περὶ φύσιν μὲν κινουμένους, οὔπω δὲ πάντῃ τῆς περὶ τὸ παθητικὸν καὶ ἄλογον τῆς ψυχῆς μέρος ἐκκαθαρθέντας σχετικῆς διαθέσεως ἐμφαίνουσι ...ὅπερ δηλοῖ σαφῶς μὴ τῶν καθ' ἡδονὴν παντελῶς ἐπιθυμιῶν καὶ τῆς ἀτελοῦς τῶν λογισμῶν νηπιότητος αὐτοὺς ἠλλοτριῶσθαι".

[34] *Amb.Ioh* 67.2–3, CONSTAS, 2014, 2, pp. 288–289. "Ἐμφαίνει δὲ ὁ δωδέκατος ἀριθμος, ἢ τοὺς κατὰ χρόνον καὶ φύσιν λόγους, ὡς ἐκ πέντε καὶ ἑπτὰ κατὰ σύνθεσιν συμπληρούμενος".

Each triad consists of three equivalent monads, the middle one being raised in the sense of Maximus' explanation: "For time is sevenfold, moving as it does in a cyclical manner, and possesses a natural affinity for motion, maintaining the extremes at an equal distance from the mean".[35]

Dividing into three, each equivalent monad in turn is in position both as part of the triad and as a "high" monad from which the same division is derived (Fig. 1). The fact that St. Maximus calls one of the monads "high" determines the verticality of division. That is why we can conceive of this model as representing a growing, or expanding and contracting, universe. He also illustrates the expansive idea of the emanation of the divine Good-Being, of the uncreated divine energies, where time, presented as increasing towards itself, gives us the reason to perceive the movement itself as both an expansion and a contraction (inward to the self). On the other hand, this paradigm is also associated with what St. Maximus says about time; namely, it can be associated with the number seven. It is time that changes cyclically (moving away from itself) while at the same time moving increasingly towards itself. This division also expresses the idea that each single in the community of the trinitarian multiple has the ability to divide into three.

The second number indicates the process of synthesis or transformation of matter. Five is also a symmetrical number in which there are two by two and one: 2+1+2. In the text it is presented as an expression of the sensible things and their relation to God. The idea here is that everything in the sensible world strives for union with its Creator. St. Maximus states: "On the other hand nature is fivefold, because it is natural for it to be arranged under the number five" (Πενταδικὴ δὲ ἡ φύσις, ὑπὸ τὸν ἀριθμὸν τὸν πέντε πεφυκυῖα τάττεσθαι).[36]

Fig. 2

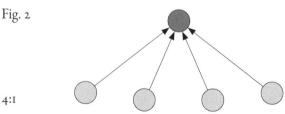

4:1

---

[35] *Amb.Ioh* 67.3., CONSTAS, 2014, 2, p. 288 "Ἑβδοματικὸς γὰρ ὁ χρόνος, ὡς κυκλικῶς κινούμενος, καὶ τὴν πρὸς τὸ κινεῖσθαι προσφυῶς ἔχων ἐπιτηδειότητα, τὴν τῶν ἄκρων ἀπὸ τοῦ μέσου κατὰ τὸν ἀριθμὸν τοῦτον ἴσην ἀπόστασιν".

[36] *Amb.Ioh* 67.3., CONSTAS, 2014, 2, p. 288.

Human nature has five senses, therefore the senses are also subject to fivefold division. However, matter itself is divided into four elements – fire, earth, water and air (Fig. 2). St. Maximus says that nature simply manifests the essence either through the *eidos* or through *eidos-formed* matter: "That is to say, the *eidos* of matter was formed before the nature" (Τὸ γὰρ εἶδος τῇ ὕλῃ προστεθὲν φύσιν ἀπεργάζεται).[37] The remarkable thing here is that the verb used ἀπ-εργάζομαι, can also be translated as "depicting". The meaning of this is connected with the superabundant formation of the forms in Divine Providence, where the primeval paradigms (energies of the Divine intellect) become causes of the origin of all creation. This idea, as shown at the beginning of this study, was developed through the reception of the Areopagite texts and remains fundamental to the Christian philosophical tradition.[38]

Through the story of the miraculous feeding of the five thousand with five loaves, St. Maximus manages to explain the essence of contemplation. Christ feeds the multitude of people precisely on the basis of multiplication and synthesis – as the Lord, multiplying and uniting Himself. This satiation, however, is done through the Word and in the fullness of the Word, through the contemplative faculties of the mind. Like hunger, the contemplative attitude is a condition inherent to the human mind.

Conclusion

Numerical relations in St. Maximus are considered in the context of the Gospel narrative to explain the relationship between the present being and the transcendent dimensions of time. Thus, the symmetry of the odd numbers reveals in a figurative way the interaction between eternal being and the present, while uniting them in well-being. Through the internal connections in the number seven is expressed the trinitarian mode of existence of God. It can be understood as a self-sufficient Monad, but at the same time it can also be perceived as a triple Unit, manifesting each of the three monads as the center of the other two,

---

[37] *Amb.Ioh.* 67, p. 288.

[38] I. CHRISTOV, "The Two-Level Emanation of the Divine and the Plurality in Mystical Vision", in *Nomina divina. Colloquium Dionysiacum Pragense (Prag, den 30.-31. Oktober 2009)*, ed. by L. KARFIKOVA, M. HAVRDA & L. CHVATAL, Fribourg, 2011, pp. 42–49.

because the three are at equal distances from each other, but at the same time each one is "raised" equidistant from the other two. If we assume that the monad is time, then there is a visual representation of a kind of dynamic synthesis of the divine trinity, as time growing towards itself (Fig. 1). Thus, in the pattern of the number seven we observe both an expansion of the monad into a triad and a contraction of the triad into a monad.

Simultaneous division and union is also observed in the second odd number of the Gospel text. The number five is that kinetic aspect of the Divine manifestation which expresses the materialization of His energies in the world in the form of the five elements which compose it (Fig. 2). Here, the presence of the idea of *logos* formation in God's pre-eternal providence also predetermines the natural attraction of every being towards the Creator as the initial and ultimate goal of its existence. The use of the verb ἀπεργάζομαι in the statement that "the *eidos* is created before the nature of the thing" (Τὸ γὰρ εἶδος τῇ ἤλῃ προστεθὲν φύσιν ἀπεργάσεις) also signifies the place of natural contemplation as part of the creative potential of the mind. It should also be borne in mind that the verb ἀπεργάζομαι, in addition to "creating", is also translated as "depicting". Penetrating through mental contemplation into the images, we increasingly comprehend and merge more deeply with the essence of every single form of Creation. In the contemplative process, the mind is constantly making additions and divisions of the *logos* of created things. Thus, one makes sense of, and at the same time is nourished by, the sense of this Divine pulsation, which is essentially an increase and contraction-aspiration to union with God, containing all the manifold forms of existence.

Contemplation is not some deliberate action exercised at a specially appointed moment. It is an enlightenment of the mind brought about by its purification and striving for union with the Word, in Whom all forms of existence are formed. In fact, the same logos-synthesis takes place in the mind, which is also outside the time of the creation itself, when the will of the Divine Providence for the existence of every form is realized. When the numbers seven and five are combined (Fig. 3), we get the number twelve as an expression of the fullness of Divine contemplation, through which the mind is satiated with the light of the Word.

Fig. 3

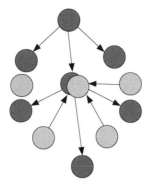

3:1 X 4:1

Figure 3 represents the satiety model. It is a combination between Figure 1 and Figure 2 and it explains the superimposition of the number five on the number seven – according to St. Maximus' explanations that refer to the relationship between God and the created world. Such an overlay is applied to every monad in the triadic model. Due to the fact that these abilities are laid down as fundamental in the formation of the individual *logos* of each person, spiritual union with the Creator is possible and takes place not only as an evolutionary spiritual process, but also spontaneously, involuntarily, by God's providence, and outside time, always through the contemplative attitudes of man, which are provoked by the manifestations of God in the world.

St. Maximus the Confessor and the Hermeticism

Possible Inspiration?

Aleksandar Djakovac

(*Belgrade*)

Saint Maximus the Confessor is among the most educated Byzantine authors, which is why it is possible to detect very diverse influences in his writings. In impact analysis, it is not always easy to determine what constitutes direct impact, what is indirect, and what are generalities that do not necessarily indicate a close relation. I believe that in some cases it is possible to point to immediate influences, even when direct citation or clear reference is lacking. Detecting such possible connections is significant because it allows us to better understand Maximus' conceptions, even though the context in which he uses certain ideas is very different from their original use.

1. The possibility of influence of hermetic ideas on St. Maximus the Confessor

First of all, it is necessary to determine whether there is even a possibility that the ideas we find in *Corpus Hermeticum* (= *CH*)[1] inspired St. Maximus. The possible connection between Maximus the Confessor and the *CH*[2] has not been – as far as I know – examined in detail to this day. This is also true of other sources belonging to the "Platonic Underworld" as John Dillon calls it.[3] However, these connections did not go complete-

---

[1] *La révélation d'Hermès Trismégiste*, 4 vols, ed. by A. D. Nock, A. J. Festugière, Paris, 1944–1954. English translation: W. Scott, *Hermetica: The Ancient Greek and Latin Writings which Contain Religious Or Philosophic Teachings Ascribed to Hermes Trismegistus*, 4 vols, Oxford, 1924.

[2] Including, of course, other hermetic sources.

[3] J. M. Dillon, *The Middle Platonists, 80 B.C. to A.D. 220*, New York, 1996, p. 384.

Ambiguum *10 of Maximus the Confessor in Modern Study: Papers Collected on the Occasion of the Budapest Colloquium on Saint Maximus, 3–4 February 2021*, ed. by Alexis Léonas & Vladimir Cvetković, with the collaboration of Daniel Heide, Turnhout, 2025 (IPM 97), pp. 255–275

© BREPOLS 쯸 PUBLISHERS   10.1484/M.IPM-EB.5.141864

ly unnoticed. At the beginning of his scholarly article, Wayne Meeks points to the connection between the *Nag Hammadi documents* and St. Maximus' teaching on the five divisions of nature, though he does not deal with this issue in detail.[4]

The complex history of *Corpus Hermeticum* has been explored in detail. As is known, the exact dating and place of origin cannot be determined, which makes it difficult to analyze their influence on certain authors. However, we can say with certainty that the texts were not created after the third century AD. There are indications that some of them are much older, although not in the form in which they came down to us.[5] The collection of texts preserved for us under this name represents "the end result of a process of conscious or unconscious selection on the part of Christian editors, in Byzantium or perhaps elsewhere".[6]

If we ask the question why Saint Maximus, in the first place, would use a non-Christian source like *CH*, we can find the answer in the tradition already present in the Church before him. That tradition goes back in the West to Lactantius and Augustine, and in the East to St. Cyril of Alexandria.[7] The *Corpus Hermeticum* was not unknown to Christian

---

[4] *Q.Thal.* 48. Cf. W. MEEKS, "The Image of the Androgyne: Some Uses of a Symbol in Earliest Christianity", *History of Religions* 13/3 (1974), pp. 165–208.

[5] *CH* represents the most complete part of the Hermetic tradition, which consists of the following three groups of texts: (1) the *CH* itself written in Greek, (2) tractate *Asclepius* in Latin, and (3) some 30 extracts from the *Anthologium Graecum* of Stobaeus. SCOTT *Hermetica*, I, *Introduction*, pp. 41–43; L. T. JOHNSON, *Among the Gentiles: Greco-Roman Religion and Christianity*, London, 2009, pp. 84–85. See more about the source identification methodology in P. HADOT & M. TARDIEU, *Recherches sur la formation de l'Apocalypse de Zostrien et les sources de Marius Victorinus: questions et hypotheses*, Bures-sur-Yvette, 1996.

[6] P. KINGSLEY, "Poimandres: The Etymology of the Name and the Origins of the Hermetica", *Journal of the Warburg and Courtauld Institutes*, 56 (1993), pp. 1–24: 22.

[7] It is important to mention that the influence of Hermeticism goes back even earlier, all the way to Philo of Alexandria, whose influence on the development of Christian theology is generally recognized. A large number of scholars have pointed out the connection between Philo of Alexandria and Hermeticism. For a bibliography on this topic, see A. D. DeCONICK, *Voices of the Mystics*, New York, 2004, p. 55 n. 86. Attempts to determine the influence

authors, and many fragments of the *CH* have been preserved in their works.[8] Some Christian authors – such as Eusebius, Lactantius, Justin and Tertullian – point to Hermes Trismegistus as a pre-Christian author in whom confirmation of some elements of Christian doctrine can be found.[9] Marcellus of Ancyra considered Hermes one of the sources of heresy.[10] Didymos quotes the *Corpus* in several places,[11] while St. Gregory the Theologian does not mention it by name, although he knows about it.[12]

Cyril of Alexandria (in *Against Julian*) also mentions Hermes Trismegistus, and thinks that he used some books of the Bible, which is why his language sometimes approaches to the language of Christian theology.[13] A lot of fragments from *CH* have been preserved in Cyril,

---

of Hermeticism on the New Testament writings have not proved to be viable, since there are no direct and clear evidences. Apparently, where we can talk about influences, they move in the opposite direction (W. C. GRESE, *Corpus Hermeticum Thirteen and Early Christian Literature*, Leiden, 1979, pp. 44–47). For testimonies about the mention of *CH* by later authors, mostly Christian, see: E. LAW, *Das Corpus Hermeticum – Wirkungsgeschichte: Transzendenz, Immanenz, Ethik*, Stuttgart-Bad Cannstatt, 2018 (Clavis Pansophiae 7,3.1), pp. 563–600.

[8] Translations of the fragments as well as their context are available in an excellent collection edited by David Litwa: D. LITWA. *Hermetica II: The Excerpts of Stobaeus, Papyrus Fragments, and Ancient Testimonies in an English Translation with Notes and Introduction*, Cambridge, 2018..

[9] Manichaeans also considered Hermes Trismegistus to be one of Mani's predecessors (A. MAGRIS, "Free Will According to the Gnostics", in *Fate, Providence and Free Will. Philosophy and Religion in Dialogue in the Early Imperial Age*, ed. by R. BOUWER & E. VIMERCATI, Leiden, 2020, pp. 174–195: 178).

[10] *On the Holy Church* 7–16, in A. LOGAN, "Marcellus of Ancyra (Pseudo-Anthimus), 'On the Holy Church': Text Translation, and Commentary", *Journal of Theological Studies* 51/1 (2000), pp. 81–112: 95–96; LITWA, *Hermetica II*, pp. 224–226.

[11] LITWA, *Hermetica II*, pp. 232–234.

[12] *Or.* 28.4, SC 250, 106–108; F. W. NORRIS. "Of Thorns and Roses: The Logic of Belief in Gregory Nazianzen", *Church History* 53/4, 1984, pp. 455–464: 456; LITWA, *Hermetica II*, pp. 230–231.

[13] LITWA, *Hermetica II*, pp. 205–214. It is interesting that in Origen we find only indirect but significant parallels with the teaching present in *CH*. It is certain that Origen was familiar with the Hermetic tradition, since his arguments

which is by no means without significance. It is known that St. Cyril was the supreme theological authority in Maximus' time.[14] Among the Christian authors who mention the Hermetic writings, there was a belief that they represented a pre-Christian testimony to the truths of the Christian faith. So the Suda lexicon mentions that Hermes speaks of the Holy Trinity. While Suda's reliance on Cyril is certain, this remark indicates a positive reception of the Hermetic writings by his Christian readers. An exact list of mentions and preserved fragments of *CH* in the works of the Fathers of the Church is provided by Mead.[15]

The ways of transmitting the ideas of *CH* to Maximus can also be followed through the Neoplatonic philosophers and *Corpus Dionysiacum* (= *CD*). The possibility of hermetic influence on Plotinus depends on the dating of texts from *CH*, which is uncertain. It is clear that certain ideas that we find in *CH* have their counterparts in the Enneads.[16] Although we cannot say this with confidence in the case of Plotinus, it is certain that the later Neoplatonists, especially Iamblichus, knew and highly valued the Hermetic tradition. According to Iamblichus: "those documents, after all, which circulate under the name of Hermes contain Hermetic doctrines, even if they often employ the terminology of philosophers; for they were translated from the Egyptian tongue by men not unversed in philosophy".[17]

Corpus Dionysiacum is certainly among the most significant links between Maximus and Neoplatonism. The question arises whether we can find evidence of the influence of *CH* in *CD*. Neoplatonist ideas could have reached Saint Maximus through the *CD*, in which we can see certain analogies with *CH*. The most noticeable parallelism

about the power of names and language as a gift of God have a counterpart in the arguments from *CH* (N. JANOWITZ, "Theories of Divine Names in Origen and Pseudo-Dionysius", *History of Religions* 30/4 (1991), pp. 359–372: 362.

[14] Maximus knew Cyril's writings well and quotes them verbatim (see for example: *Ep.* 12, *PG* 91, 472A–485A).

[15] G. R. S. MEAD, *Thrice-Greatest Hermes; Studies in Hellenistic Theosophy and Gnosis*, vol. III, London, 1906, pp. 133–175.

[16] As Dillon has shown, Numenius, who greatly influenced Plotinus, combined Platonic, Neo-Pythagorean, Gnostic, Jewish, Zoroastrian *and Hermetic* teachings (DILLON, *The Middle Platonists*, pp. 378).

[17] Iamblichus, *De mysteriis*, 8, 4; T. M. O'NEILL, *Ideography and Chinese Language Theory: A History*, Berlin, 2016, pp. 85–86.

between *CD* and *CH* is visible in the apophatic approach to the mystery of God. Although Neoplatonism is the more likely model for *CD*, the apophatic ideas we find in *CH* represent an integral part of the historical development of the doctrine of an unknown God.[18] However, in this case it is possible to indicate only an indirect conceptual connection between *CD* and *CH*.[19]

The assumption that Maximus knew and used *CH* becomes more likely if Pépin's assumption that Gregory of Nazianzus also used *CH* is correct.[20] Pépin believes that the "theologian" Gregory refers to in *Or.* 28,[21] is not Plato, as is commonly believed, but Hermes Trismegistus. If this assumption is correct, it further strengthens the possibility of a relationship between Maximus and *CH*.

The exact route of transmission of Hermetic ideas to Maximus is difficult to determine with any degree of precision; moreover, the question is perhaps not of essential importance. As a widely educated man, it is quite possible that Maximus was familiar with *CH* (or some of its writings) either directly or through anthologies, such as that of Stobaeus.[22]

2. The *locus communis* problem

At the first glance, similarities between certain ideas of Maximus the Confessor and the *Corpus Hermeticum* are evident. For example, Maximus, quoting the Areopagite, says that the soul is "the image and appearance of the invisible light" (εἰκόνα καὶ φανέρωσιν τοῦ ἀφανοῦς φωτός), an accurate mirror, very transparent, without flaw, undefiled,

---

[18] See: *CH* VI.4, XIII, 6; D. CARABINE. *The Unknown God: Negative Theology in the Platonic Tradition: Plato to Eriugena*, Louvain, 1995, pp. 67–68.

[19] See more details about the connection between *CD* and *CH* in G. KOCIJANČIČ, "The Identity of Dionysius the Areopagite: A Philosophical Approach", in *Dionysius the Areopagite between Orthodoxy and Heresy*, ed. by F. IVANOVIC, Newcastle, 2011, pp. 3–13.

[20] J. PÉPIN, "Grégoire de Nazianze, lecteur de la littérature hermétique", *Vigiliae Christianae* 36/3 (1982), pp. 251–260.

[21] *Or.* 28, 4: SC 250, 106–108.

[22] R. A. ARTHUR, *Pseudo-Dionysius as Polemicist: The Development and Purpose of the Angelic Hierarchy in Sixth Century Syria*, Hampshire – Burlington, 2008, pp. 33.

unstained, receiving in itself, if we are allowed to say this, the splendor of the divine model and purely illuminating in himself, as far as possible, the goodness of the silence of the inner recesses (τὴν ἀγαθότητα τῆς ἐν ἀδύτοις σιγῆς).[23]

A similar description may be found in *Poimandres*, where the mind is reflected in the water of nature so much so that it falls in love with its own reflection.[24] However, the representation of the world or of the soul as an image is not unique to Hermeticism or Maximus (who refers to the *CD*). Such an idea – if it is only an external performance – could easily have been mediated through Neoplatonism. Suffice it to refer to Plotinus.[25]

We will point to another possible parallel between the Maximus and the Hermetic tradition. In several places in the *CH* we find an emphasis on silence as the most suitable way of respecting theineffable. Thus in *CH* 1, 31 we read "You whom we address in silence, the unspeakable, the unsayable, accept pure speech offerings from a heart and soul that reach up to you".[26] It is known that St. Maximus repeatedly calls for "honorable silence" when it comes to the most sublime secrets of theology. It is possible that this idea came to him through Pseudo-Dionysius.[27] However, we also find the idea that silence is the most adequate expression of respect for God in earlier authors, such as Clement of Alexandria.[28] There is an important difference between the

---

[23] *Myst.* 23, CCSG 69, pp. 55, 881–882 = *PG* 91, 701C 11–12. (English translation: *Maximus the Confessor, Selected Writtings*, trans. by G. C. BERTHOD, New York, 1983, pp. 181–225: 206.

[24] *CH* I, 14.

[25] *Enn.* II.3.18,17.

[26] See: *CH* 1, 30: "My silence became pregnant with good", *CH* X, 4: "In the moment when you have nothing to say about it, you will see it, for the knowledge of it is divine silence and suppression of all the senses", the divine knowledge "is a secret kept in silence" (*CH* XIII, 16). See also: *CH* XIII, 2, *CH* XIII, 8, *Asclepius* 32.

[27] ARTHUR. *Pseudo-Dionysius as Polemicist*, pp. 32; CARABINE. *The Unknown God*, p. 70.

[28] Clement mentions silence in an ethical and theological context. The latter is particularly interesting to us, because it connects silence with what is ἐπέκεινα αἴτιον. (*Stromateis* 1.77.1); See R. MORTLEY, "The Theme of Silence in Clement of Alexandria", *The Journal of Theological Studies* 24/1 (1973), pp. 197–202: 199–200; H. F. HÄGG, *Clement of Alexandria and the Beginnings of Christian*

understanding of silence in *CH* and Maximus. In *CH*, silence is associated with the ineffability of the divinity,[29] while Maximus also resorts to silence concerning things that can be said, but which are better kept silent lest they be misunderstood. Although we cannot know what it was that Maximus did not want to tell us, the very fact that he believed that there were things in theology that were better left unsaid[30] suggests their possible connection with sources that were not acceptable in his time, such as Gnosticism or the Hermetic tradition.

If we accept Festugière's conclusion that the *CH* is dominated by the ideas "of popular Greek philosophical thought in a very eclectic form", the question arises as to how we might establish a definitive connection with Saint Maximus, who also used philosophy in this way. Careful analysis is crucial. In any case, this type of coincidence between Maximus and *CH* is important, and in some cases, *it is* possible to prove the connection between St. Maximus and *CH*.

We have to mention one more clue about the connection between Maximus and *CH*; namely, the famous term θέλησις, which is key to Maximus' Diothelite Christology. This term is used only about twenty times in all the surviving writings in Greek from the time of Homer to Clement of Alexandria. Half of the places where this term is used are in

---

Apophaticism, Oxford, 2006, pp. 175–177. M. Edwards, "Christian Apophaticism before Dionysius", in *The Oxford Handbook of Dionysius the Areopagite*, ed. by M. Edwards, D. Pallis, G. Steiris, Oxford, 2022, pp. 64–76: 69. The connection between Clement's (*Stromateis* 5.11.71) and Plotinus' (*Enn.* 4.8.7) use of περινοεῖν and the Hermetic λόγος περινοητικός (*CH Fr.* 17.6) has not gone unnoticed, although we will not deal with it in detail here (see R. E. Witt, "The Hellenism of Clement of Alexandria", *The Classical Quarterly* 25/3–4 (1931), pp. 195–204: 198).

[29] Authors of hermetic texts avoid term οὐσία θεοῦ. For a detailed analysis, see E. Hamvas, "Some Points to the Explanation of the Concept of οὐσία θεοῦ in the Hermetic Literature", *Acta Classica Universitatis Scientiarum Debreceniensis* 45 (2009), 29–43: 31.

[30] Maximus points to "more secret and higher interpretation" in several places. (*Q.Thal.* 21, CCSG 7, 153, col. 108–114. = *PG* 90, 316 D3–8. Cf. *Q.Thal.* Prol. CCSG 7, 37, col. 350–353 = *PG* 90, 260 A7–10: ...διὰ τῆς σιωπῆς τιμωμένου; *Cf.* B. E. Daley, "Apokatastasis and 'Honorable Silence' in the Eschatology of Maximus the Confessor", in *Maximus Confessor. Actes du Symposium sur Maxime le Confesseur, Fribourg 2–5 Septembre 1980*, ed. by F. Heinzer, C. von Schönborn, Fribourg, 1982, pp. 309–339: 316.

the Septuagint, and in *CH* it is found in three places (IV, 1a, 1b; V, 2).[31] Although it is possible and even probable that Maximus was inspired by the Septuagint for the use of this term, the fact that this rare term is used as many as three times in *CH* indicates a possible connection.

Although certain parallels can be drawn between the ideas we find in *CH* and those we find in Maximus, it is rarely possible to determine with certainty whether Maximus took them directly from the *CH*, or indirectly through other authors. Of course, this creates difficulty in establishing actual parallels. Therefore, it is necessary to find some idea that is specific to *CH* and Maximus, which rarely or never appears in other authors. In order to establish the existence of a parallel with *CH* in this case we need to understand the teaching of Maximus on this matter. Then it is necessary to show that such or a similar teaching can be found in *CH*, and finally to determine whether such teaching exists in authors who are possible mediators between Maximus and *CH*. I think it is worth paying attention to an example that I believe represents just such a case. It seems to me that we can establish such parallels when it comes to Maximus' teaching that the fall occurred simultaneously with creation.

3. Eating time

We will now try to outline Maximus' teaching on this matter. As is known, Maximus considered himself a man of the Church, and he constantly emphasizes that his teaching is in perfect agreement with the Holy Scriptures and the Holy Tradition. In *Ambiguum* 10 we find a description that at first glance agrees with the biblical account.

Ἀμέλει τούτῳ μὴ ἐπερείσας τῷ θείῳ φωτὶ τὸν τῆς ψυχῆς ὀφθαλμὸν ὁ προπάτωρ Ἀδὰμ τυφλοῦ δίκην εἰκότως ἐν σκότει τῆς ἀγνωσίας ἄμφω τὼ χεῖρε τὸν τῆς ὕλης φορυτὸν ἑκουσίως ἀφάσσων, μόνῃ αἰσθήσει ἑαυτὸν ὅλον ἐπικλίνας ἐκδέδωκε, δι'ἧς τοῦ πικροτάτου θηρὸς τὸν φθαρτικόν ἰὸν εἰσδεξάμενος οὐδ'αὐτῆς, ὡς ἠβουλήθη, ἀπέλαυσε τῆς αἰσθήσεως, δίχα θεοῦ, καὶ πρὸ θεοῦ, καὶ οὐ κατὰ θεόν, ὡς οὐκ ἔδει, ὅπερ ἀμήχανον ἦν, τὰ τοῦ θεοῦ ἔχειν ἐπιτηδεύσας. τὴν γὰρ σύμβουλον παραδεξαμένην τὸν ὄφιν θεοῦ πλέον παραδεξάμενος αἴσθησιν καὶ τοῦ ἀπηγορευμένου ξύλου,

[31] J. D. MADDEN. "The Authenticity of Early Definitions of Will (thelesis)", in *Maximus Confessor. Actes du Symposium sur Maxime le Confesseur*, ed. by F. HEINZER & C. von SCHÖNBORN, Fribourg, 1982, pp. 61–79: 64.

ᾧ καὶ θάνατον συνεῖναι προεδιδάχθην τὸν καρπὸν ὀρέγουσαν, βρώσεως ἀπαρχὴν ποιησάμενος πρόσφορον τῷ καρπῷ τὴν ζωὴν μετηλλάξατο, ζῶντα τὸν θάνατον ἑαυτῷ κατὰ πάντα τὸν χρόνον τοῦ παρόντος καιροῦ δημιουργήσας.[32]

> For instance, because our forefather Adam did not direct the eye of his soul toward this divine light as he groped about willingly in the darkness of ignorance for the rubbish of material reality with both hands like a blind man, he gave himself exclusively to sense-perception by having inclined himself entirely to it. In having received the noxious poison of the viciously spiteful beast through sense-perception, he did not enjoy his sensuality itself, as he wished, since he tried to possess the things of God without God, instead of God, and not in accordance with God, as though He were unnecessary, though this was actually impossible. For having accepted sense-perception which is symbolized by the snake and reaches out for the fruit of the forbidden tree, and which he had been taught was death's companion, over God, he exchanged his original life for food by producing what befits the fruit: he fashioned a living death for himself, and it has spread itself across the whole duration of the present time.

However, a closer reading reveals certain differences. Note that at the beginning of this section, St. Maximus speaks of the ancestor Adam before the fall and points out that he "did not direct the eye of his soul toward this divine light (μὴ ἐπερείσας τῷ Θεῷ φωτὶ τὸν τῆς ψυχῆς ὀφθαλμόν)". We also notice that at that time the serpent had not yet appeared and that Adam had not yet tasted the tree of knowledge. The initial problem is in the human will, and that is the place (τόπος) where the drama of the fall takes place. The problem arises in man's relation to matter: "as he groped about willingly in the darkness of ignorance for the rubbish of material reality with both hands like a blind man". Constas translates ὕλης φορυτόν as "confusion of matter" while Lollar suggests a more accurate solution – "rubbish of material". St. Maximus – as Sherwood has long shown – was not an Origenist and did not consider matter to be evil in itself. What makes matter "rubbish" is man's wrong attitude towards it.

---

[32] *Amb.Ioh.* 10.28, *PG* 91, 1156AD, cf. Joshua Lollar's translation in this volume (following the *PG* column numbering); cf. CONSTAS, 2014, I, p. 247.

In the continuation of the same *Ambiguum*, we notice that man not only tasted the forbidden tree, but that it was the first thing he did. Maximus further explains how the process of feeding is itself the introduction of death into life.

> βρώσεως ἀπαρχὴν ποιησάμενος πρόσφορον τῷ καρπῷ τὴν ζωὴν μετηλλάξατο, ζῶντα τὸν θάνατον ἑαυτῷ κατὰ πάντα τὸν χρόνον τοῦ παρόντος καιροῦ δημιουργήσας.

> he exchanged his original life for food by producing what befits the fruit: he fashioned a living death for himself, and it has spread itself across the whole duration of the present time.

In the Greek text we see the term ἀπαρχή which means "the beginning of a sacrifice, the primal offering". The very act of eating is a turning away from God. Maximus consciously passes over God's words in the book of Genesis (2,16): "You may freely eat of every tree of the garden". According to Maximus, eating as such is a problem. In his words:

> Εἰ γὰρ φθορὰ γενέσεως ὑπάρχει ὁ θάνατος, ἀεὶ δὲ τὸ δι'ἐπιρροῆς τροφῶν γινόμενον φυσικῶς φθείρεται σῶμα τῇ ῥοῇ διαπνεόμενον, ἀεὶ ἄρα δι'ὧν εἶναι τὴν ζωὴν ἐπίστευσεν ἀκμάζοντα ἑαυτῷ τε καὶ ἡμῖν τὸν θάνατον ὁ Ἀδάμ συνετήρησεν.[33]

> For if death exists as the destruction of coming into being, and the body that comes to be through the influx of nourishment is always naturally destroyed by flowing back out in its dissipation, then Adam secured a perpetually flourishing death for himself and for us through the nourishment which he believed to carry life.[34]

---

[33] Joshua Lollar' translation in this volume (= *PG* 91, 1156AD).

[34] Identical linking of eating with death is also found in *Ep.* 7: *PG* 91, 437C 12–440A 3. Εἰ γὰρ φθορὰ τῶν οὕτω συνισταμένων ὑπάρχει ὁ θάνατος σωμάτων, ἀεὶ δὲ τὸ δι' ἐπιρροῆς τροφῶν συνιστάμενον φθείρεται σῶμα, τῇ ῥοῇ διαπνεόμενον, διὰ τὴν τῶν ἐν αὐτῷ χυμῶν, ἐξ ὧν καὶ συνέστηκε, φυσικὴν ἀντιπάθειαν· (Because the perishability of bodies structured in this way represents physical death, and the body that is structured by taking food always decays due to the mutual natural opposition of the juices that flow through it and that make it up). In the sequel, Maximus criticizes those who believe that people will eat food even after the resurrection. By comparing these two sections we can conclude that Maximus' omission of a part of the biblical account is not accidental or incidental.

Continuation of the text shows that this interpretation is correct. Maximus explains that "all living things are naturally sustained by the type of food that is appropriate to them. But the food of that blessed life was the bread that came down from heaven and gave life to the world". For linking growth and corruption we can also find a parallel in *CH* X.15b. Hermes points to a small child who "has not yet grown to its full bulk". His body "is not yet fouled by the bodily passions". The context is different[35] since for Hermes it is the entry of a pre-existing soul into the body that makes it evil, while for Maximus the source of evil is the misdirection of the will. Both Hermes and Maximus see the growth of the body as something negative, which, despite the difference, can hardly be explained as a simple coincidence.

According to Maximus, the first man's movement was supposed to be directed to the Logos, which is his real food, and not towards the food that enables the growth of the body, which is actually death. Thus, we notice a certain difference in emphasis between the biblical account and Maximus' interpretation. We will see that this seemingly small difference in emphasis has great theological significance. An accurate understanding of this section of *Ambiguum* 10 is possible through comparison with some other places where Maximus deals with the same topic.[36]

4. Simultaneity

In his *Response to Thalassios* 61.2, Maximus presents his analysis of the dialectic of pleasure and pain. According to him, pleasure as such is not the cause of the fall, but it is his unnatural orientation towards sensual things instead of God.

> Ὁ τὴν φύσιν τῶν ἀνθρώπων δημιουργήσας Θεὸς οὐ συνέκτισεν αὐτῇ κατὰ τὴν αἴσθησιν οὔτε ἡδονὴν οὔτε ὀδύνην, ἀλλὰ δύναμίν τινα κατὰ νοῦν αὐτῇ πρὸς ἡδονήν, καθ᾽ ἣν ἀρρήτως ἀπολαύειν αὐτοῦ δυνήσεται, ἐνετεκτήνατο. Ταύτην δὲ τὴν δύναμιν – λέγω δὲ τὴν κατὰ φύσιν τοῦ νοῦ πρὸς τὸν Θεὸν ἔφεσιν – ἅμα τῷ γενέσθαι τῇ αἰσθήσει δοὺς ὁ πρῶτος ἄνθρωπος πρὸς τὰ

---

[35] This is primarily about the mythological context that is most clearly expressed in *Poimandres*, the first writing in *CH*. On the mythological content that provides a framework for all other writings, see JOHNSON, *Among the Gentiles*, pp. 88–92.

[36] Cf. *Q.Thal.* 61.2, *CCSG* 22, p. 85: 8–16.

266 ALEKSANDAR DJAKOVAC

αἰσθητὰ κατ' αὐτὴν τὴν πρώτην κίνησιν διὰ μέσης τῆς αἰσθήσεως ἔσχε παρὰ φύσιν ἐνεργουμένην τὴν ἡδονήν·.

> God, who fashioned human nature, did not create sensible pleasure or pain together with it, but instead devised for this nature a certain capacity for intelligible pleasure, where by human beings would be able to enjoy God ineffably. The first human being, however, at the same moment that he was brought into being, surrendered this capacity – I mean the intellect's natural desire for God – to physical sensation, and in his initial impulse toward sensory objects, mediated through his senses, he came to know pleasure activated contrary to nature.[37]

We will not deal with Maximus' understanding of pleasure and pain. Instead, we will refer to the interesting statement that man committed sin "at the same moment that he was brought into being (ἄμα τῷ γενέσθαι)". It is immediately clear that if the fall occurred simultaneously with creation, the entire biblical account can only be understood metaphorically. Of course, there remains the possibility of a different interpretation of this expression, in the sense that the fall occurred immediately after creation, although not simultaneously. But it seems that Maximus uses the term ἄμα in other places precisely to denote simultaneity. Thus in his *Response to Thalassios* 65.25 we read:

> Ἅμα γάρ τις τὴν τῶν ἀρετῶν λογικῶς μετέλθοι φιλοσοφίαν, ἅμα καὶ τὴν τῶν γραφῶν πρὸς τὸ πνεῦμα φυσικῶς μετήνεγκεν ἐκδοχήν, ἐν καινότητι πνεύματος πρακτικῶς διὰ τῶν ὑψηλῶν θεωρημάτων τῷ θεῷ λατρεύων, καὶ οὐ παλαιότητι γράμματος.[38]

> For at the very same time that a person advances in a reasonable manner to the philosophy of virtues, he will in that same moment have naturally transferred the interpretation of Scripture to the Spirit, worshiping God in practice through his sublime contemplations in the newness of the Spirit, and not in the oldness of the letter.

If there could be any doubt that the term ἄμα here really exclusively denotes simultaneity, the passage from *Response* 40 does not allow for a different interpretation.

[37] *Q.Thal.* 61, 2. English translation: CONSTAS, 2018.
[38] *Q.Thal.* 65.25: *CCSG* 22, 289: 593–596.

Ὁ τὴν φύσιν τῶν ἀνθρώπων δημιουργήσας Θεός, ἅμα βουλήσει τὸ εἶναι
αὐτῇ δέδωκεν, συνήρμοσεν αὐτῇ καὶ δύναμιν τῶν καθηκόντων ποιητικήν.[39]

> God, who created human nature, simultaneously gave it being and
> the power of intention, and thus joined to this nature the creative
> power to realize what is proper to it.

It is clear that it is not possible to imagine any distance between the
creation and the giving of being. Moreover, the thought that Maximus
expresses here is quite consistent with the statement from *Q.Thal.* 61, 2.
During creation, God simultaneously gifted being "and the power of
intention". God's desire was for man to use that power correctly. However, we could ask ourselves, does the fact that God *first* gave man "the
power of intention" and that man *then* committed a sin leave room for a
certain time gap between these two events? The answer to this question
seems to be found in Maximus' understanding of time.

Τὰ δὲ περὶ φύσιν ἐστὶ τὰ προεπινοούμενά τε καὶ συνεπινοούμενα· τὸ μέν,
ὅτι ποῦ καὶ πότε πάντως ἡ τῶν ὄντων ὑπέστη γένεσις· τὸ δέ, ὅτι ἅμα τῇ
πρώτῃ γενέσει τῶν ὄντων, συνεπεθεωρήθη καὶ ἡ καθόλου τῶν ὄντων θέσις
καὶ κίνησις, ἅπερ ἐστὶ χρόνος καὶ τόπος, ἐν οἷς κατὰ τὴν ἔξωθεν θέσιν, καὶ
τὴν πρὸς ἀρχὴν κίνησιν ἡ φύσις ἐστίν, ἀλλ᾽ οὐ καθ᾽ ὑπόστασιν.[40]

> What pertains to nature are those conditions that are conceived of
> as being both anterior and posterior to that nature. This is both
> because all created beings came into existence relative to a "where"
> and a "when", and because simultaneously with their coming into
> existence we may observe together with them their universal posi-
> tion and motion, which very things are place and time, by means
> of which nature exists relative to an outward position and in terms
> of its motion toward its principle of origin, but not according to its
> subsistence.

According to Maximus, position (θέσις) and motion (κίνησις) correspond to place (τόπος) and time (χρόνος). Since time is equated with motion, there can be no time before the first motion. According to Maximus, that first movement represented the wrong direction of man's will
towards sensual things instead of towards God. Since there can be no
time before motion, the first motion had to occur simultaneously (ἅμα)

---

[39] *Q.Thal.* 40.2: CCSG 7, 267, 4–6.
[40] *Q.Thal.* 55, sh.6: CCSG 7, 517, 50–54.

with creation. Moreover, Maximus argues that creation is inconceivable without motion, since motion is equated with life. In this sense, before the first movement of the created man, there can be no question of his real existence either. This is precisely why Maximus emphasizes the simultaneity of creation and fall. The first movement of created nature is identified with its creation and its fall. The first movement, because it is unnatural, is actually identical with original sin. Christ's purpose was to reveal the beauty toward which human nature failed to move when it was first created, "and to trample down the wickedness to which it, being deceived, unnaturally moved at the very moment it was created (ἅμα τῷ γενέσθαι), and which emptied it of all its power".[41]

The initial movement, which was ultimately proven to be unnatural, occurred simultaneously with creation. This first movement was intended to be the end (τέλος) at the same time. Here, one might question how movement can be equated with an end or goal since τέλος, strictly speaking, signifies the cessation of movement? The answer lies in the fact that, according to Saint Maximus, the initial movement of the created nature should have immediately transitioned into the cessation of all movement. In this sense, the initial movement, which should have been the final state, can be perceived as a goal. If the initial movement had been in harmony with nature, it would have transformed into stillness. In other words, deification would have occurred simultaneously with creation. However, due to the incorrect and unnatural direction of the will, the separation of the movement into successive sequences took place, resulting in the detachment of the beginning from what followed. This is precisely why what followed is defined as the Fall.

> Ἀφ' οὗ γάρ, ἔφασκεν, ἅμα τῷ εἶναι διὰ τῆς παρακοῆς τὴν οἰκείαν ἀρχὴν ὀπίσω ποιήσας ὁ ἄνθρωπος ζητεῖν οὐκ ἠδύνατο τὸ κατόπιν αὐτοῦ γεγενημένον, καὶ ἐπειδὴ φυσικῶς ἡ ἀρχὴ περιγράφει τῶν ὑπ' αὐτῆς γεγενημένων τὴν κίνησιν, εἰκότως προσηγορεύθη καὶ τέλος, εἰς ὅπερ, ὡς αἰτίαν τῆς τῶν κινουμένων κινήσεως, δέχεται πέρας ὁ δρόμος.[42]

> He further said that because man, at the very moment of his coming into being, put his own beginning behind him through disobedience, he was unable to seek what lay behind him; and since

---

[41] *Amb.Ioh.* 42.7, *PG* 91, 1321AB = CONSTAS, 2014, 2, p. 134: 7, 4–14.
[42] *Q.Thal.* 59.12, *CCSG* 22: 61, 263–268.

the beginning delimits the motion of beings that owe their existence to it, the beginning is rightly called the end as well, in which,
inasmuch as it is also the cause of motion, the course of beings in
motion has its terminus.

The thesis about the fall happening ἅμα τῷ γενέσθαι is completely in
line with Maximus' teaching on deification. His description of the state
of the deified creation as στάσις ἀεικίνητος (based on the teaching of
St. Gregory of Nyssa on ἐπέκτασις), implies a movement towards the
goal or end (τέλος). Only man's κίνησις towards God, who is his τέλος,
represents movement in accordance with his inner logos: "For from
God come both our general power of motion (for He is our beginning),
and the particular way that we move toward Him (for He is our end =
τέλος)".[43] That is why there were only two possibilities: the first movement could only be a fall or deification – nothing else. Since movement
is inherent in created nature, there was no movement before creation.

> But the beginning of every natural motion is the origin (genesis) of the
> things that are moved, and the beginning of the origin of whatever has
> been originated is God, for He is the author of origination. (*Amb.* 15: *PG*
> 91, 1217CD = Constas I, 369)

We can conclude that St. Maximus uses the term ἅμα τῷ γενέσθαι in a
very specific way. We will now analyze the use of this expression by certain authors who use it in a sense that bear similarities with Maximus'
usage.

5. Similarities and differences

The use of the expression ἅμα τῷ γενέσθαι before St. Maximus is not
common. We have been able to find only a few examples where this
phrase is used in a sense somewhat similar to Maximus' usage. Sextus
Empiricus uses this expression in connection with animals: "Hence,
also, the Epicureans suppose themselves to have proved that pleasure
is naturally choiceworthy; for the animals, they say, as soon as they are
born (ἅμα τῷ γενέσθαι), when still unperverted, seek after pleasure and
avoid pains".[44] The similarity of the use of the phrase ἅμα τῷ γενέσθαι

---

[43] *Amb.Ioh.* 7, *PG* 91, 1073C = Constas, 2014, 1, p. 87.
[44] Sextus Empiricus, *Outlines of Pyrrhonism* 3.194. LCL 273, p. 458.

with *Q.Thal.* 61, 2 is reflected in the context of the relationship between pleasure and pain. But the similarity seems to end there.

Proclus uses this term when explaining the nature of demonic powers. According to him, demons are capable of making real what they want, simultaneously with desire:

> ἔτι δὲ αὖ κατὰ τοὺς θεολόγους εἶναί τινας καὶ κρείττους ἡμῶν δυνάμεις χρωμένας δραστηρίοις φαντασίαις καὶ ἅμα τῷ γενέσθαι ποιητικαῖς, ὧν ἂν ἐθέλωσι, καὶ τὰς φωταγωγίας ἀπεργάζεσθαι καὶ δεικνύναι θείας τινὰς μορφὰς ταῖς ἑαυτῶν κινήσεσι, τοιαύτας ἔξω δεικνύσας τοῖς θεᾶσθαι δυναμένοις ὄψεις.

> And, again, according to the theologians there are also certain powers, superior to us, which make use of images which are efficacious and able to bring about whatever they wish the moment they appear. [These powers] practice the art of drawing down [supernatural] illuminations and display certain divine forms by means of their own movements, exhibiting outward appearances of this kind to those who are able to see them.[45]

This simultaneity of desire and its realization recalls Maximus' use of the expression ἅμα τῷ γενέσθαι. The actual identity of the meaning could be established only if we assume that Maximus understood the first man as incorporeal, which is in contrast to his opposition to the Origenist teaching about the preexistence of souls.[46]

In *De opificio mundi*, Philo of Alexandria also presents a parallel perspective. While interpreting Moses' account of creation over six days, Philo highlights that the Creator did not require time to bring forth everything that exists, stating that "God surely did everything at the same time (ἅμα γὰρ πάντα δρᾶν εἰκὸς θεόν)".[47] The reason for the gradual process of creation, according to Philo, is the necessity of order for things that come into existence. Philo further emphasizes

---

[45] Proclus, *Procli Diadochi in Platonis Timaeum commentaria*, 3 vols, ed. by E. DIEHL, Leipzig (repr.), 1965, vol. 1, 395D, col. 31. English translation:, *Proclus: Commentary on Plato's Timaeus*, trans. by D. T. RUNIA & M. SHARE vol. II, Cambridge, 2008, p. 270.

[46] A. DJAKOVAC, "Soul According to St. Maximus the Confessor: Entity or Person?", *SP* CXXI, 2021, pp. 67–82.

[47] Philo of Alexandria, *De opificio mundi*, 13: Leopold Cohn, *Philonis Alexandrini, Opera Qvae Svpersvnt*, vol. I, Berlin, 1887 pp. 3, 12–24.

that those who believe creation occurred within time are mistaken, as time presupposes the movement of heavenly bodies that were not yet in existence. Thus, time was created in conjunction with the world – "simultaneously with it, or after it (ἢ σὺν αὐτῷ γέγονεν ἢ μετ' αὐτόν)".[48] Although both Philo and Maximus discuss simultaneity in the context of creation, a direct parallel between them cannot be established conclusively, although some potential influence may be present. Philo's focus in the first instance is apologetic, suggesting that God did not create everything simultaneously to bring order to the created world. In the second instance, Philo argues that time emerges simultaneously with the created world or, as he notes, after creation.

Among Christian authors, we find this expression in Saint Athanasius the Great and Didymus the Blind. Athanasius, disputing with the Arians, as proof that the Son is not a creature who was subsequently deified, cites the testimonies of the Scriptures about people who were deified without any special merits. As an example, he mentions Adam, whom he says was placed in paradise simultaneously with creation: καὶ γὰρ Ἀδὰμ προλαμβάνων τὴν χάριν καὶ ἅμα τῷ γενέσθαι τεθεὶς ἐν τῷ παραδείσῳ.[49] It is interesting that the context of the use of this expression is the same as that of St. Maximus, but it is used in a completely opposite sense.

In another place, Athanasius explains that the Father did not hand over the world to the Son simultaneously with creation, since everything was created in the Son as Logos:

> Εἰ δὲ, ἅμα τῷ γενέσθαι τὴν κτίσιν, παρεδόθη αὐτῷ πᾶσα· χρεία οὐκ ἦν παραδόσεως· πάντα γὰρ δι' αὐτοῦ ἐγένετο, καὶ περιττὸν τὸ παραδίδοσθαι τῷ Κυρίῳ ταῦτα, ὧν αὐτός ἐστι δημιουργός.[50]

> > But if simultaneously with the origin of the Creation it was all "delivered" to Him, such delivery were superfluous, for "all things were made by Him" (Jn. 1:3), and it would be unnecessary for those things of which the Lord Himself was the artificer to be delivered over to Him.

[48] *De opificio mundi*, 26: Cohn, pp. 6, 13–21.

[49] Athanasius, *De decretis Nicaenae synodi*, in Athanasius Werke, II/1, ed. by H. G. OPITZ, Berlin, 1935–1941, p. 6. 6.1–2.

[50] Athanasius, *In illud: Omnia mihi tradita sunt*, in *Athanasius Werke, I/1: Die dogmatischen Schriften, Lfg. 5: Epistulae dogmaticae minores*, ed. by K. SAVVIDIS, Berlin – Boston, 2016, p. 768, . 10–13.

Athanasius' logic and sense of the use of the expression ἅμα τῷ γενέσθαι are quite clear. However, this quote can help us because it shows that when the term ἅμα τῷ γενέσθαι is used in the cosmological sense it always has the meaning of absolute, and not relative, simultaneity.

With Didymus, we meet the expression in a somewhat different context. In *Fr.* 26[51] he claims that God is not the creator of evil, and that no evil originates from Him. He then interprets the words of Scripture that the devil "when he lies, he speaks his native language" and points out that "this does not mean that he is evil by nature (εἰ δὲ τοῦτο, οὐκ ἔστιν κατ' οὐσίαν κακός·)" because he did not become a liar *simultaneously with creation* (οὐ γὰρ ἅμα τῷ γενέσθαι) and by foundation (καὶ εἰς ὑπόστασιν), but the lie was spoken later. So, at least when it comes to the devil, Didymus' point of view seems to be the opposite of Maximus'. If sin occurred ἅμα τῷ γενέσθαι, according to Didymus, it would mean that creation is like that by nature, and that God is to blame for the existence of evil.

6. Corpus Hermeticum

We find some interesting parallels in the *Corpus Hermeticum*. I will point out two places: *CH* IX, 8–9 and *Fr.* IV, 8 preserved in Stobaeus. In *CH* IX, 8–9 we find an explanation of the relationship of God the Father and the Cosmos. The Cosmos is called the Son of God, and he takes care of the arrangement of everything that exists.

> πάντων οὖν τῶν ζῴων ἡ αἴσθησις καὶ νόησις ἔξωθεν ἐπεισέρχεται, εἰσπνέουσα ὑπὸ τοῦ περιέχοντος, ὁ δὲ κόσμος, ἅπαξ λαβὼν ἅμα τῷ γενέσθαι, ὑπὸ τοῦ θεοῦ λαβὼν ἔχει.[52]

> Now the sense and thought of all living creatures enter into them from without, being breathed into them from the atmosphere; but the Cosmos received sense and thought simultaneously with creation, and has got them from God.

The difference between the Cosmos and living beings is that they receive sense and thought subsequently and indirectly, while the Cosmos receives them simultaneously with creation (ἅμα τῷ γενέσθαι) and directly from God. Here, the concept of ἅμα τῷ γενέσθαι is related to sense

---

[51] Didymus, *Fragmenta in Psalmos, Fr.* 26, *PTS* 15, p. 132, . 9–12.

[52] English translation, partially altered: Scot, *Hermetica*, 1, p. 185.

and thought. Although it is the Cosmos and not man who receives them directly from God, the transition from the cosmological to the anthropological aspect does not seem unusual for Maximus.

The basis for this shift can be found in the hermetic writings themselves. Thus in *Fr.* IV,[53] Hermes tells Tat that a body cannot hold together without a soul, but that a body without a soul can still have forces working within it. When the soul leaves the body, the body disintegrates, but the disintegration process itself is possible because some forces are still at work in the body. Forces are also found in those bodies that do not have a soul and enable them to do everything that such bodies do. Hermes further explains that every force is incorporeal but that it works in the body and with the help of the body. Forces are incorporeal and immortal, but they cannot work apart from bodies, so it follows that bodies must always come into being, since forces are dependent on bodies. Forces act both in the soul and in the body. While the soul is not always in the body, forces cannot exist without the body. Hermes goes on to say that:

παρέπονται δὲ τῇ ψυχῇ οὐκ ἀθρόως παραγιγνόμεναι, ἀλλά τινὲς μὲν αὐτῶν ἅμα τῷ γενέσθαι τὸν ἄνθρωπον ἐνεργοῦσιν ὁμοῦ τῇ ψυχῇ περὶ τὰ ἄλογα οὖσαι, αἱ δὲ καθαρώτεραι ἐνέργειαι κατὰ μεταβολὴν τῆς ἡλικίας τῷ λογικῷ μέρει τῆς ψυχῆς συνεργοῦσαι.

> The forces which accompany the soul do not all arrive at the same time. Some of them arrive at the moment of the man's birth, entering into his body together with the soul, and acting on the irrational parts of the soul; but the purer forces arrive when he reaches the age of adolescence, and co-operate with the rational part of the soul.[54]

---

[53] *Fr.* IV, 8 vol. III, p. 23. We can see a certain similarity between the Hermetic teachings about the forces and the soul with the teachings of Numenius of Apamea (see: *Fr* 4b, *Numénius, Fragments*, ed. by E. DES PLACES *(Collection Guillaume Budé)*, Paris, 1973, pp. 46–48). If we bear in mind the importance of Numenius for the development of Neoplatonism on the one hand, and the similarity of his teaching with *CH* on the other, it is clear that this significantly increases the possibility of CH's influence on Maximus (G. BOYS-STONES. *Platonist Philosophy 80 BC to AD 250, An Introduction and Collection of Sources in Translation*, Cambridge, 2018, p. 296).

[54] English translation in SCOT, *Hermetica*, I, p. 399.

From here we can see a certain similarity with Maximus' teaching about the fall that occurs ἅμα τῷ γενέσθαι. Maximus is not talking about the gradual progress of man. In Maximus, unlike in Irenaeus of Lyons, there is no question of any kind of justification of man because of the Fall. According to Maximus, man did not commit sin because he was not yet mature enough. Connecting the Fall with irrationality is the moment where these two concepts meet. Maximus understands the state of the first man as a potentiality.[55] All the forces are present in him (to use the language of hermetics), but it is the irrational force that was first activated and led to the fall.

The similarities we have pointed out here are by no means absolute. However, the use of the term ἅμα τῷ γενέσθαι in *CH* is closest to the one we find in Maximus, if we compare it with the use of this term in the other authors we have analyzed. The idea that certain forces act in man simultaneously with creation and that these forces are irrational, really brings us close to the teaching of Maximus.

Conclusion

Based on the presented analysis, we can conclude that it is possible to establish certain parallels between *CH* and Maximus the Confessor. The term ἅμα τῷ γενέσθαι is very specific and relatively rare in authors who precede Saint Maximus. Moreover, when we come across this expression it is used either in a different context, or with a meaning opposite to the one we find in Maximus. Only in *CH* do we find this phrase in a similar context and with a similar meaning as in Saint Maximus. Of course, the possibility remains that Maximus came up with this idea completely independently of *CH*. In support of this solution is the fact that the thesis about the fall happening simultaneously with creation fits very well into Maximus' theological system, and is especially compatible with his understanding of time as movement and the future eschatological state as rest. Even so, it is likely that Maximus was familiar with the Hermetic tradition, with which he must have come into contact at least through St. Cyril of Alexandria. The most likely assumption is that certain ideas from *CH* served Maximus as inspiration for developing his own theo-

---

[55] J. LOLLAR, *Christ and the Contemplation of Nature in Maximus the Confessor's Ambigua to John*, Turnhout, 2013 (Monothéismes et Philosophie, 18), p. 252.

logical theories. This is supported by his tendency to make certain elements of his teachings secret. A possible reason for this secrecy could be precisely the sources he used, which were not in accordance with the orthodoxy of his time and which would undoubtedly arouse the suspicion of his contemporaries.[56] If the thesis that Maximus knew and used *CH* is correct, the possibility of further research in this field (which includes other unorthodox sources) will perhaps provide better insights into the development and meaning of his thought.

[56] As we know, such suspicion was certainly shown during the trial of Saint Maximus, when he was accused, among other things, of being a follower of Origen, whom he immediately anathematized. These accusations show us that Maximus' possible fear of openly referring to unorthodox teachings, if there was one, was by no means unfounded.

III.

St. Maximus the Christian Philosopher

Maximus Confessor's Threefold Doctrine of Creation *Ex Nihilo*

Daniel HEIDE

(*Montréal*)

Introduction

I have argued elsewhere for the continuity between the metaphysics of monism of Plotinus and Proclus and the metaphysics of mono-theism of Dionysius and Maximus.[1] For these thinkers – pagan and Christian alike – the world issues from God or the One as the sole *archē* of existence, the irreducible simplicity constitutive of being. Plotinus express-es this in terms of the derivation of all things *from* the One (ἐξ ἑνός);[2] Maximus articulates this in the terminology of creation *from* God (ἐκ Θεοῦ).[3] Though importantly and crucially modified by its Christian context, I maintain that Maximus' understanding of the Trihypostatic Monad as the necessary Ground[4] of being is in onto-logical continui-

---

[1] D. HEIDE, *The World as Sacrament: The Eucharistic Ontology of Maximus Confessor*. Doctoral Dissertation, McGill University, 2022.

[2] *Enn.* VI.7.15, 20. (*LCL*).

[3] See *Myst.* § 2, 225 [*CCSG* 16]; § 1, 190 [*CCSG* 13]; § 5, 335 [*CCSG* 22]; *Amb. Ioh.* 41, PG 91, 1312B, 10; *Amb.Ioh.7*, 1080A; *Amb.Ioh.* 15, PG 91, 1217D *passim*.

[4] I employ "Ground" as a way of translating and combining the ideas of πηγή, "fount" "source" "origin", with ἀρχή, "origin" "first principle". Maximus' use of πηγή follows that of Plotinus and Dionysius. See *Amb.* 10, PG 91, 1205D where Maximus refers to God as an "ever-flowing spring" (πηγῇ ἀειβλύστῳ). The term ἀρχή is ubiquitous in the writings of Maximus. While a somewhat free rendering of these terms, I like the versatility of Ground, which enables me to speak of the God/world relation in terms of "Ground" and "grounded", or of God in apophatic terms as the "Groundless Ground".

Ambiguum *10 of Maximus the Confessor in Modern Study: Papers Collected on the Occasion of the Budapest Colloquium on Saint Maximus, 3–4 February 2021*, ed. by Alexis LÉONAS & Vladimir CVETKOVIĆ, with the collaboration of Daniel HEIDE, Turnhout, 2025 (IPM 97), pp. 279–299
© BREPOLS ❧ PUBLISHERS   10.1484/M.IPM-EB.5.141865

ty with that of the pagan Neoplatonists: all things *are* only insofar as they are *one*; that is, insofar as they partake of the unity bestowed upon them from their Cause.[5] I argue that creation ἐκ Θεοῦ, in conjunction with the various metaphors of emanation employed by both pagans and Christians, points unequivocally to Maximus' sacramental ontology, to the theophanic character of the cosmos as derived from, and thus grounded in, God.

This leads to a least two possible objections: the first pertains to the philosophical problem of otherness. If the world is derived from God how is it crucially other than God? I argue here that it is precisely Maximus' adoption of the Christian doctrine of creation *ex nihilo* that accounts for this otherness. Indeed, Maximus states not merely that the world is created from God (ἐκ Θεοῦ), but equally that it is created from nothing (ἐκ τοῦ μὴ ὄντος).[6] It is this nothingness of the world that definitively distinguishes it from God, and that establishes it as genuinely other. The second objection is terminological. If, as I contend, the preposition ἐκ indicates the derivation of beings *from* God (ἐκ Θεοῦ), what are we to make of the same preposition in relation to creation *from* nothing (ἐκ τοῦ μὴ ὄντος)? Must it not mean something analogous in relation to *ex nihilo*? In what sense are beings created *from* (ἐκ) nothing? I propose three possible solutions to this problem: the first, is that creation from nothing is simply a way of saying creation *not from something*.[7] That is to say, creation *ex nihilo* as rejection of ontological dualism. The second possibility is to interpret the *nihil* (μὴ ὄν) in a more relative sense as potential being; creation *ex nihilo* as the creaturely motion *from* (ἐκ) potential existence in God to actual existence as other. Thirdly, creation *ex nihilo* may be taken in a temporal sense as the rejection of an eternal cosmos.

---

[5] See Proclus, *Elements of Theology*, Prop. 1.

[6] See *Amb.Ioh.* 10.41, *PG* 91, 1188C.

[7] See comments by G. MAY, *Creatio ex Nihilo: The Doctrine of "Creation out of Nothing" in Early Christian Thought*, Edinburgh, 1994, p. 7 n. 27. In fact, two classic Biblical source texts for creation *ex nihilo* express it in precisely this way. 2 Maccabees 7:28 literally states that God made things "not from beings (οὐκ ἐξ ὄντων ἐποίησεν)", while Hebrews 11:3 says that "the things which are seen were not made of things which are visible (τὸ μὴ ἐκ φαινομένων τὸ βλεπόμενον γεγονέναι)".

In what follows, I argue that Maximus' doctrine of creation *ex nihilo* can be read on these three distinct yet interrelated levels: 1) creation *ex nihilo* as rejection of ontological dualism (creation *not* from beings); 2) creation *ex nihilo* as movement from potentiality to actuality (creation from *not yet* being); 3) creation *ex nihilo* as temporal creation (creation *not from eternity*). Taken together, these three senses of *ex nihilo* help us to understand how beings can be derived *from* (ἐκ) nothing without reifying the nothing as a quasi-something. More importantly, all three levels work together to unequivocally affirm the otherness of the world from God, yet without undermining the crucial continuity between them. Creation *ex deo* and creation *ex nihilo* are not opposed, but seen to be two complementary poles of a single sacramental reality.[8] The world is created not merely from God, but *from God from nothing* (ἐκ Θεοῦ... ἐκ τοῦ μὴ ὄντος).[9]

1. Creation *ex nihilo* as rejection of ontological dualism

The first level on which to approach Maximus' doctrine of creation *ex nihilo* involves the Christian rejection of the doctrine of creation from preexistent matter such as one finds, for example, in Plato's *Timaeus*. The rejection of preexistent matter means, in essence, the uncompromising rejection of ontological dualism in favour of the view that God alone is the supreme *archē* of existence. From this point of view, creation *ex nihilo* in fact coincides with creation *ex deo* – the two are not opposed to each other as some might presume, but rather complementary ways of talking about the same thing; namely, the derivation of all things from God as the solitary Ground of being.[10] As such, creation *ex nihilo* as rejection of ontological dualism does not, in itself, repre-

---

[8] For an alternative account of *creatio ex nihilo* (and *ex deo*) in Maximus see, R. KNEŽEVIĆ, "Maximus' *Opuscula* and the Concept of the Hypostatic Union A Critical Interrogation of the Ontology of Absolute Non-Being", in *Studies in Maximus the Confessor's Opuscula Theologica et Polemica*, ed. by V. CVETKOVIĆ & A. LEONAS Turnout, 2022, pp. 162–200.

[9] *Amb.*Ioh.10.41, *PG* 91, 1188C. Constas obscures the reference to ἐκ Θεοῦ in his English translation. See CONSTAS, 2014, I, p. 309.

[10] It is not without reason that Eriugena, that great Latin commentator upon the Greeks, explicitly – albeit not unproblematically – equates them in *Periphyseon* III.

sent a radical break with the Platonic tradition – for the Neoplatonists themselves modified Plato's position in a way that brings them quite close to that of the Christians. Just as for the Christians matter itself is created, so for Plotinus and Proclus matter is derived from the One as the term of the emanative process. The crucial difference emerges with the Christian rejection of an eternal creation as illustrated in our case by Maximus' second and third levels of *ex nihilo*.

Needless to say, the Christian doctrine of creation *ex nihilo* has a long history, one which we can only touch upon in the most cursory manner.[11] Traditionally, evidence for this doctrine is found in Scriptural passages such as 2 Maccabees 7:28 in which the mother of the seven martyrs encourages her youngest son "to look at heaven and earth and see everything in them, and know that God made them out of nothing (ὅτι οὐκ ἐξ ὄντων ἐποίησεν αὐτὰ ὁ θεός)". In Romans 4:17 we read that God "calls those things which do not exist as existing (καλοῦντος τὰ μὴ ὄντα ὡς ὄντα)", while Hebrews 11:3 states that "the things which are seen were not made of things which are visible (τὸ μὴ ἐκ φαινομένων τὸ βλεπόμενον γεγονέναι)". Finally, the *Shepherd of Hermas* states that God created "that which exists out of that which does not exist (ἐκ τοῦ μὴ ὄντος τὰ ὄντα)".[12] As Gerhard May points out, however, none of these passages *in themselves* unequivocally bear witness to the Christian doctrine of creation *ex nihilo* understood as the rejection of the doctrine of creation from preexistent matter.[13] Such an understanding only emerges in the second–third centuries after a lengthy process of theological reflection as witnessed first in the writings of Tatian († *c.* AD 185), and then more definitively in Theophilus of Antioch († *c.* AD 183–185), and Irenaeus of Lyons († *c.* AD 202).[14] Only from Athanasius († *c.* AD 373) onwards does the formal Christian doctrine of creation *ex nihilo* becomes an accepted premise in patristic theology.[15] Prior to these thinkers, the language of *ex nihilo* – as one

[11] For a thorough treatment of this topic, see G. MAY, *Creatio ex nihilo: The Doctrine of "Creation Out of Nothing" in Early Christian Thought*, Edinburgh, 1994.

[12] *Shepherd of Hermas* 1 (I.1) 6.

[13] See MAY, *Creatio Ex Nihilo*, p. 27.

[14] See MAY, *Creatio Ex Nihilo*, pp. 148–178.

[15] See A. LOUTH, *The Origins of the Christian Mystical Tradition: From Plato to Denys*, Oxford, 2007, p. 76.

finds it in Philo or Clement, for example – remains ambiguous and arguably still refers to the ancient model of world formation from pre-existent matter, the relative nonbeing[16] of formless *hyle*.[17]

Athanasius offers a clear statement of the meaning of creation *ex nihilo* as rejection of preexistent matter. Athanasius singles out Plato "that giant among the Greeks" as chief among those who taught that God created the world from preexistent and uncreated matter. Just as a carpenter is dependent upon his building materials without which he cannot manufacture anything, so God, according to the Platonic view, "is not able to make anything unless matter preexisted". For Athanasius, such a demiurgic view of creation is unacceptable insofar as it imputes weakness and limitation to God, "for if he is not himself the cause of matter, but simply makes things from pre-existent matter, then he is weak, not being able without matter to fashion any of the things that exist".[18] Such a god may well be called "craftsman" after the analogy of human artisans who also depend upon external materials, but he cannot rightly be called "Creator" or "Maker". For Athana-

---

[16] The distinction that is made among some commentators and philosophers between "relative" nonbeing as μὴ ὄν and "absolute" nonbeing as οὐκ ὄν does not appear to have a historical basis. In many cases the two expressions are used interchangeably by ancient philosophers and theologians without difference in meaning (this is evident even in the quotations from 2 Maccabees, the Epistles, and the *Shepherd*). See MAY, *Creatio Ex Nihilo*, p. 17, n. 73. A. Louth observes that the Divine Liturgy of St. John Chrysostom uses both expressions without any difference in meaning. See A. LOUTH, "Theology of Creation in Orthodoxy", *International Journal of Theology*, 8.3 (2017), p. 56.

[17] See MAY, *Creatio Ex Nihilo.*, pp. 6–26. MAY points to Philo's *De Opificio Mundi* 8 where Philo invokes the Stoic doctrine of an active and passive principle: "the former is the perfect Nous – God – the latter is no doubt the formless matter" (10). This would seem to find confirmation later at *De Opif.* 22 where Philo appears to speak of God as bestowing order upon an original substance destitute of form, order and distinction, very much as Plato does in the *Timaeus*. There is also the interesting case of the Hellenistic Jewish Wisdom of Solomon 11:22 which states that God "created the world out of unformed matter (κτίσασα τὸν κόσμον ἐξ ἀμόρφου ὕλης)". For Clement, see MAY's comments p. 178.

[18] Athanasius, *On the Incarnation*, ed. by John BEHR, Yonkers, N.Y., 2014, p. 2.

sius, these terms are reserved for the omnipotent God of Genesis who brought the universe into being "from nothing and having absolutely no existence".[19] In support of his understanding of creation *ex nihilo* as rejection of the demiurgic model of world formation from preexistent matter, Athanasius invokes the above mentioned passages from the *Shepherd of Hermas* and Hebrews 11:3. As noted above, however, the formal *doctrine* of creation *ex nihilo* does not originate with these passages; rather, it derives from a lengthy process of theological reflection which gradually comes to recognize the unacceptable dualism of the demiurgic model of world formation. While Athanasius frames his discussion in terms of divine omnipotence, the ontological implications of creation *ex nihilo* are apparent: God alone is the supreme *archē* of existence, such that matter cannot stand as a rival principle or even an auxiliary cause – for God Himself is the cause of matter.

The ontological implications in Athanasius are more explicitly worked out by Maximus, who fully accepts the by now well-established Christian doctrine of creation *ex nihilo* while providing it with a more robust philosophical foundation. In *Amb.* 10, Maximus argues against the eternity of matter on the grounds that whatever is subject to motion, or genesis, or some kind of limitation cannot be coeternal with God who alone is unmoved, ungenerated, and infinite. Basing himself on the philosophical identification of matter as dyad,[20] Maximus argues that matter-as-dyad cannot be infinite or uncircumscribed because the *dyad* is quite literally composed of *two monads*. Matter by definition is *dyadic*, that is, composite and hence susceptible to division. As such, matter is not infinite but finite – it is both circumscribed by a prior principle of unity, the Monad, to which it owes whatever derivative unity it possesses, as well as limited by the individual monads which make up the dyad and which stand in finitizing relation to one another. In other words, a multiplicity of finitudes does not make a simple infinity.[21]

---

[19] *On the Incarnation*, p. 3.

[20] On matter as dyad, see John RIST, "The Indefinite Dyad and Intelligible Matter in Plotinus", *The Classical Quarterly* 12 (1962), pp. 99–107.

[21] See *Amb.Ioh.*10, 40, *PG* 91, 1184B–D; also *Amb.Ioh.*10, 41, *PG* 91, 1184D–1185B. The logic of Proclus' *Elements of Theology*, Props.1–6 on the priority of the One over the many seems to be lurking in the background here, though Maximus articulates it somewhat differently.

If, then, matter is not infinite but finite, argues Maximus, then neither can it be ungenerated or without beginning (ἄναρχον), "for the
beginning (ἀρχή) of every dyad is the monad".[22] Moreover, if matter-
as-dyad is generated or possesses a beginning, or principle (ἀρχή), of
its existence, then it is not without motion (ἀκίνητον) for the dyad is
constituted by the numerical motion of multiplication and division,
expanding from the One into multiplicity and resolving back from
multiplicity into unity.[23] Finally, if the dyad is not unmoved then,
Maximus concludes, "neither is it the beginning (ἀρχή) of something
else. For that which is moved (κινούμενον) is not a beginning, but *from
a beginning* (ἐξ ἀρχῆς), that is, from whatever set it in motion (τοῦ
κινοῦντος)".[24] This Unmoved Mover, as Maximus indicates, is the (Trihypostatic) Monad which alone is unmoved, ungenerated, and infinite.
Given that matter-as-dyad cannot serve as a self-subsistent, coeternal
principle alongside God-as-Monad, Maximus concludes that "there is
only one God (Εἷς Θεὸς), who is beyond all infinity", and who alone
is the creator and fashioner of all things. As such, he asserts, "it must
be accepted that all things have been created *from the eternally existing God from nothing* (ἐκ Θεοῦ τοῦ ἀεὶ ὄντος τὰ πάντα ἐκ τοῦ μὴ ὄντος
γενέσθαι)".[25]

Maximus' abstract argument, composed of a mesmerizing mixture
of Aristotelian metaphysics, Neopythagorean numerology, and Neoplatonic emanationism, requires some unpacking. To begin with, we
encounter the Proclean notion of the One as irreducible simplicity
constitutive of being. All things *are*, only insofar as they are one.[26] Yet
matter is not one – at least not in terms of its intrinsic nature, which is
dyadic. As unity-in-multiplicity, matter is contingent upon the One as
the principle of its existence "for the beginning (ἀρχή) of every dyad
is the monad". Insofar as matter is itself dependent upon something
prior, it cannot serve as an ontological principle alongside God. As
Maximus puts it, matter is "not a beginning, but *from* a beginning (ἐξ

[22] *Amb.Ioh.*10, 41, *PG* 91, 1185B.

[23] *Amb.Ioh.*10, 41, *PG* 91, 1185B–C.

[24] *Amb.Ioh.*10, 41, *PG* 91, 1185B–C, emphasis added.

[25] *Amb.Ioh.*10, 41, *PG* 91, 1188A, 1188C, emphasis added. I have significantly modified Constas' translation which entirely obscures the dual reference to
creation from God from nothing. See CONSTAS, 2014, 1, pp. 307–309.

[26] See Proclus, *Elements*, Prop. 1.

ἀρχῆς)". In other words, matter is itself derived *from* God as the sole *archē* of existence.[27] This in turn implicates matter in motion – for the very act of becoming involves a movement from nonexistence into being. Invoking Aristotle, Maximus insists that whatever is in motion cannot itself be the ultimate source of motion for this would lead to an infinite regress. Instead, only God as Trihypostatic Monad, as infinite and uncircumscribable, as perfect actuality (and so unmoved), can act as the Unmoved Mover of matter, and with it of the whole of creation. Hence Maximus arrives at his final conclusion: "it must be accepted that all things have been created *from the eternally existing God from nothing* (ἐκ Θεοῦ τοῦ ἀεὶ ὄντος τὰ πάντα ἐκ τοῦ μὴ ὄντος γενέσθαι)".

All of this is Maximus' considerably more complex way of reiterating Athanasius' position concerning the rejection of preexistent matter as a principle alongside God. What Athanasius expresses in theological terms, Maximus renders in the philosophical language of ontology. The first key point here is how the rejection of matter culminates in the doctrine of creation *ex nihilo*. Creation *ex nihilo* here simply means that beings are brought from nonexistence into being *without recourse to any additional principle apart from God*.[28] The Latin Anselm († AD 1109) in fact arrives at precisely the same solution. For him, creation *ex nihilo* "indicates the *manner* of the world's creation: affirming that it was made, *but not out of anything*".[29] The preposition ἐκ, then, may be affirmed as possessing the same meaning in the case of both *ex deo* (ἐκ Θεοῦ) and *ex nihilo* (ἐκ τοῦ μὴ ὄντος). In both cases, ἐκ has the meaning of "derived from". In the first case it affirms the derivation of beings from God, while in the second it *denies* their derivation

---

[27] See *Amb.Ioh.*10, 39, *PG* 91, 1184B: "And if every substance (οὐσία), and all matter (ὕλη), and all forms (εἶδος) are from God (ἐκ Θεοῦ), then no one, unless he had been deprived of his ability to think rationally, would say that matter is without beginning and uncreated, since God has created and given form to everything".

[28] See, S. BULGAKOV, *Sophia, the Wisdom of God: An Outline of Sophiology*, Hudson, N.Y., 1993, p. 61. The controversy surrounding Bulgakov's sophiology, it seems to me, obscures what an astute reader of Maximus he is. It is not surprising, therefore, that Bulgakov's understanding of creation comes close, in some respects, to that of Maximus.

[29] Ian MCFARLAND, *From Nothing: A Theology of Creation*, Louisville, 2014, p. 87.

from anything other than God. Hence, Maximus is able to assert that the world is created from God from nothing. This uncompromising rejection of ontological dualism means that God alone is the Ground of being. At this level, creation *ex nihilo* essentially means the rejection of ontological dualism; that is, creation *not* from beings.

This, then, brings us to our second key point – creation *ex nihilo* coincides here with creation *ex deo*. These two expressions are not opposed to each other but, as Maximus so vividly demonstrates, complementary perspectives upon a single reality – the world is created *from God from nothing*. Whereas creation from God gives positive expression to the metaphysics of monotheism whereby God alone is the Ground of being, creation from nothing expresses this negatively in terms of the rejection of preexistent matter. The first asserts the fundamental Unity at the heart of reality, the second represents the denial of duality. *Both* proclaim the radical *givenness* of the creature as wholly contingent upon God as its Ground. As such, it is equally possible to affirm the eucharistic character of creation as gift in terms of both *ex deo* and *ex nihilo*.[30]

If creation *ex nihilo* as rejection of ontological dualism coincides with creation *ex deo*, in what sense may it be said to serve as a means of distinguishing the world from God? The answer, of course, rests with the radical contingency of the world created from God from nothing. The distinction between Ground and grounded is in itself sufficient for Maximus to affirm "the infinite distance and difference (διάφορος) between the uncreated and the created".[31] Yet this ought not to be exaggerated, as Thunberg does, to imply "a basic gulf (χάσμα) between uncreated and created natures, which only the creative will can overbridge".[32] Nor should one unreservedly follow Florovsky's

---

[30]   For an insightful and balanced discussion concerning seemingly opposed views of creation among several prominent Orthodox theologians, see LOUTH, "Theology of Creation in Orthodoxy".

[31]   *Amb.Ioh.*7, PG 91, 1077A.

[32]   See L. THUNBERG, *Microcosm and Mediator: The Theological Anthropology of Maximus the Confessor*, Chicago, 1995, p. 53. See comments by V. KARAYIANNIS, *Maxime le Confesseur: essence et énergies de Dieu*, Paris, 1993, p. 28. Tollefsen would seem to follow Thunberg in this regard. See T. TOLLEFSEN, *The Christocentric Cosmology of St. Maximus the Confessor*, Oxford, 2008, p. 62.

interpretation of this "infinite distance" in terms of an ontological otherness so extreme that he can only describe it as a "*living duality of God and creation*".[33] With all respect to this great Orthodox theologian, Florovsky's views in this regard would seem to owe more to Duns Scotus(† AD 1308)[34] than to Maximus or any other Greek Father. For Maximus, Creation *ex nihilo* does not imply a radical rift between God, and the world created from God, such that they have absolutely nothing in common. Such an extreme view (however "orthodox" it may instinctively seem to us moderns) can only culminate in a desacralizing dualism.[35] Rather, as Maximus' conjunction of *ex deo* and *ex nihilo* illustrates, the world is both infinitely other than God insofar as it is wholly contingent upon God (creation *ex nihilo*), as well as intimately related to God from whom alone it derives its being (creation *ex deo*).

2. Creation *ex nihilo* as movement from potentiality to actuality

If, as I suggested above, the fundamental distinction between Ground and grounded is already sufficient to affirm the infinite distance and difference between God, and the world derived from God *from nothing*, this basic understanding of creation *ex nihilo* as rejection of ontological dualism nonetheless represents merely the first level of Maximus' doctrine. In a sense, this initial level is not so different from that of the pagan Neoplatonists who, though they do not employ the language of *ex nihilo*, equally reject ontological dualism while affirming the derivation

---

[33] G. FLOROVSKY, *Creation and Redemption*, Nordland, 1976, p. 47. Italics in original.

[34] Indeed it comes as little surprise that Florovsky explicitly praises the voluntarism of the "Subtle Doctor" a few pages later; See FLOROVSKY, *Creation*, p. 52. For an insightful analysis of the "sophiological subtext" of Florovsky's position see Paul GAVRILYUK, *Georges Florovsky and the Russian Religious Renaissance*, Oxford, 2014, pp. 132–158. Aristotle Papanikolaou points to a similar nominalist tendency in John Zizioulas; see "Creation as Communion", in *Toward an Ecology of Transfiguration: Orthodox Christian Perspectives on Environment, Nature, and Creation*, ed. by J. CHRYSSAVGIS & B. FOLTZ, New York, 2013, p. 119.

[35] For a helpful overview of the Orthodox debate concerning the God/world relation, see P. LADOUCEUR, *Modern Orthodox Theology*, New York, 2019, pp. 193–229.

of matter from God, or the One.[36] Where Maximus diverges crucially from the pagan philosophers is in his understanding of creation *ex nihilo* as, firstly, involving a movement from the world's potential existence in God to its actual existence as other; and, secondly, as creation in time. I shall deal with the first here, while concluding with the second in the following section.

In addition to creation *ex nihilo* as creation *not* from beings, then, Maximus' doctrine of creation *ex nihilo* (ἐκ τοῦ μὴ ὄντος) may be understood in terms of creation from not *yet* being; that is, as the world's movement *from* (ἐκ) its potential existence in God to its actual existence as other. This approach involves interpreting the nonbeing of *ex nihilo* in a more relative sense. Rather than understanding it purely in terms of negation, as creation "*not* from beings", it is possible to regard the *nihil* more positively as creation "from *potential* beings (ἐκ μὴ ὄντων)".[37] Aristotle, for example, equates the non-existent with potential existence when he observes that it is possible for non-existent things to be conceivable and desirable. This is because "although these things do not exist actually (οὐκ ὄντα ἐνεργείᾳ), they will exist actually; for some non-existent things (μὴ ὄντα) exist potentially (δυνάμει); yet they do not exist (οὐκ ἔστι), because they do not exist in complete reality (οὐκ ἐντελεχείᾳ ἐστίν)".[38] According to Aristotle, then, it is possible to understand nonbeing as "not *yet* being", as potentially being.

It might be tempting, in this regard, to take Maximus' use of the negation μή rather than ὀυκ as indicative of this relative nonbeing. Bulgakov, for example, distinguishes between the "relative" nonbeing of μὴ ὄν and the "absolute" nonbeing of οὐκ ὄν. The former corresponds merely to "nonmanifestation and nondefinition", the fecundity of potential existence, while the latter refers to the "full negation of being", the sterility of absolute nothingness.[39] Tempting though it may

---

[36] To insist that creation *ex nihilo* is somehow a radical break from the "Hellenistic" worldview, as Zizioulas does, is really quite misleading. Certainly, this is true for the "Hellenic" world inhabited by Plato; yet it is scarcely true for the "Hellenistic" world of Plotinus, Proclus, and countless other non-Christian philosophers. See LOUTH, "Theology of Creation in Orthodoxy", p. 55.

[37] See *Amb.Ioh.*28, *PG*. 91, 1272C. This use of the plural is rare in Maximus.

[38] *Metaphysics*, IX.3. 1047b.

[39] S. BULGAKOV, *Unfading Light: Contemplations and Speculations*, Grand Rapids, 2013, pp. 188–189.

be, this distinction would seem to have little bearing on Maximus' position. As several commentators have pointed out, both expressions are often used interchangeably by philosophers and theologians of antiquity without any discernible difference in meaning.[40] 2 Maccabees for example, uses οὐκ, while the *Shephard of Hermas* employs μή. The Divine Liturgy of St. John Chrysostom uses both particles of negation indifferently.[41] None of these sources are of an especially philosophical nature. Bulgakov's distinction between μὴ ὄν and οὐκ ὄν, while philosophically interesting in its own right, would seem ultimately to owe more to the genius of Schelling than to actual historical usage.[42] Maximus, for his part, exhibits a singular preference for μὴ ὄν which, I am arguing, he employs in a variety of distinct yet interrelated ways.

If the intriguing distinction between μὴ ὄν and οὐκ ὄν cannot help us here, it nonetheless remains possible to interpret the *nihil* of creation *ex nihilo* in the Aristotelian sense of potential existence, of creation from not *yet* being. Evidence for this is found in Maximus' discussion concerning the preexistence of the *logoi* of beings in God. From all eternity, Maximus insists, God "contained within Himself the preexisting *logoi* of created beings. When, in His goodwill, He formed out of nothing (ἐκ τοῦ μὴ ὄντος) the substance of the visible and invisible worlds, He did so on the basis of these *logoi*".[43] Maximus goes on to explain how a particular *logos* precedes and guides the creation of every particular being, whether in heaven or on earth, "at the appropriate time (τὸν δέοντα χρόνον)". Everything which receives its being from God (ἐκ Θεοῦ)[44] does so according to its own *logos* eternally preexisting in God and precisely for this reason is called a "portion of God".[45] Though the *logoi* of beings are eternal insofar as they represent the timeless intentionalities of God,[46] Maximus reiterates that beings created *according*

---

[40] See, MAY, *Creatio Ex Nihilo*, p. 17, n. 73.

[41] See LOUTH, "Theology of Creation in Orthodoxy", p. 56.

[42] See BULGAKOV, *Unfading Light.*, p. 469, n. 9.

[43] *Amb.Ioh.*7, *PG* 91, 1080A.

[44] See *Amb.Ioh.*7, *PG* 91, 1080B.

[45] "μοῖρα" καὶ ἔστι καὶ λέγεται "Θεοῦ", *Amb.Ioh.*7, 1080C. The quotation marks found in the Greek text indicate that Maximus is quoting and commenting upon the words of Gregory the Theologian.

[46] That is, the "predeterminations" (προορισμοί) and "divine wills" (θεῖα θελήματα). *Amb.Ioh.*7, *PG* 91, 1085A–B.

to (κατά) the *logoi* do not exist simultaneously with them. Here we approach the critical passage:

> Instead, in the wisdom of the Creator, individual things were created at the appropriate time (τῷ ἐπιτηδείῳ καιρῷ), in a manner consistent with their *logoi*, and thus they received in themselves actual existence as beings (τὸ εἶναι τῇ ἐνεργείᾳ). For God is eternally an active creator (ὁ μὲν ἀεὶ κατ᾽ ἐνέργειάν ἐστι Δημιουργός), but creatures exist first in potential (δυνάμει) and only later in actuality (ἐνεργείᾳ) [...][47]

Within this discussion of the *logoi* (painfully condensed for our purposes), we encounter a number of essential ideas: Maximus once again states both that beings are created from nothing *and* that they are created from God, while introducing the notion of creation in time. Maximus further associates his doctrine of creation with his doctrine of the *logoi*: all beings are created from God from nothing *in time* and *according to* the *logoi* eternally preexisting in God. All of this culminates in the idea that, while God is an eternally active Creator, beings exist first in potentiality and only later in actuality. Given Maximus' juxtaposition of these ideas, it would seem that the potential existence of beings, their "relative" nonbeing, is somehow equivalent (though not identical) to their respective *logoi*. As the "content" of the Logos, beings possess a kind of potential existence in God, while acquiring actual existence in their own right at the foreordained time. Creation *ex nihilo*, then, could be understood here as a movement *from* (ἐκ) the timeless not *yet* being of potentiality to the state of actual existence in time.

In what sense are the *logoi* simultaneously tied to the eternal activity of God and the potentiality of beings? They are the former insofar as they represent the unwavering will and eternal foreknowledge of God concerning every finite temporal creation. Following Dionysius, Maximus calls the *logoi* "predeterminations" (προορισμοί) and "divine wills" (θεῖα θελήματα); that is, the timeless intentionalities of God according to which beings are known and constituted. As Maximus puts it, "God knows beings as His own wills".[48] God's eternal creative activity thus consists in a kind of timeless self-contemplation which is simultaneously noetic and volitional, such that God wills from all eternity that

---

[47] *Amb.Ioh.7*, PG 91, 1081B; translation: CONSTAS, 2014, I, p. 101.
[48] *Amb.Ioh.7*, PG 91, 1085B-C.

which he intends to create in time.[49] Indeed, an essential part of God's timeless thought-willing is precisely the divinely determined time allocated to each individual being in accordance with the divine wisdom.[50]

If the *logoi* represent the eternal actuality of God, in what sense are they also the potentiality of beings? To begin with, we need to be careful to distinguish the *logoi*, the principles *according to* which beings are created, from the beings themselves. The former are God (for the many *logoi* are the One Logos) while the latter are creatures. Moreover, the *logoi* are not some sort of fully formed *kosmos noetos*, such that sensible beings become the pale instantiations of intelligible veracities. The many *logoi* simply *are* the One Logos in their transcendent aspect, only becoming manifold as the immanent principles of creation. Nor is this to say that beings possess some kind of murky, amorphous existence in God apart from the *logoi* prior to their actualization in time. Their potentiality, rather, is owing purely to the fact that God foreknows and forewills them in a transcendently unified manner. In other words, their existence is purely virtual: they have no existence in themselves whatsoever, but exist solely as concepts (or rather as a single unified Concept) within the divine Mind.[51] Their potential existence, in other words, is equivalent to nonbeing in the Aristotelian sense of not *yet* being – for creatures are eternally conceived and willed by God, and

---

[49] See *Amb.Ioh*.7, *PG* 91, 1080A.

[50] As to why God chose to create at a particular point in time, Maximus remains silent: "Seek the reason why God created, for this is knowledge. But do not seek how or why he only created recently, for this question does not fall under your mind..." *Car.* 4.5. *Maximus Confessor Selected Writings*, ed. and trans. by G. C. BERTHOLD, New York, 1985, p. 76.

[51] Maximus further illustrates this with the Biblical example of Levi. Just as Levi existed potentially (ἐν δυνάμει) in the loins of Abraham prior to his actual birth (κατ' ἐνέργειαν), says Maximus, so beings exist as formal possibilities in God prior to their actual creation. This masculine example is illuminating. It is not the case that beings possess a quasi-material existence in the womb of God, so to speak; rather, their potential existence is purely formal and hence indistinguishable from God. Just as Levi is, as it were, part of the very DNA of Abraham and only acquires separate, fleshly existence after his birth, so creatures are initially nothing other than the formal content of the Logos, acquiring a distinct, embodied existence only at the moment of creation. See *Amb.Ioh*.41, *PG* 91, 1328D. Also Hebr. 7:10.

as such possess a kind of potential existence. What is eternally actual in God – the *logoi* as timeless intentionalities – is potential in relation to created beings. Hence, creation *ex nihilo* (ἐκ τοῦ μὴ ὄντος) could be understood as the creaturely motion *from* (ἐκ) the timeless not *yet* being of potential existence to the state of actual existence in time.

If the first understanding of creation *ex nihilo* as rejection of onto-logical dualism established a fundamental distinction between Ground and grounded, this second conception of creation *ex nihilo* as move-ment from potentiality to actuality, as creation from not *yet* being, establishes the incommensurable otherness of Creator and creation:

> For God is eternally an active creator (ἀεὶ κατ' ἐνέργειάν), but creatures exist first in potential (δυνάμει), and only later in actuality (ἐνεργείᾳ), since it is not possible for the infinite (τὸ ἄπειρον) and the finite (τὰ πεπερασμένα) to exist simultaneously on the same level of being. Indeed no argument will ever be able to demonstrate the simultaneous (ἅμα) in-terdependence of being (οὐσία) and what transcends being (ὑπερούσιον), or of the measureless (τὸ ἄμετρον) and what is subject to measurement (τὸ ἐν μέτρῳ), or that the absolute (τὸ ἄσχετον) can be ranked with the relative (τὸ ἐν σχέσει), or that something of which no specific category can positively be predicated can be placed in the same class as what is constituted by all the categories. For in their substance and formation all created things are positively defined by their own logoi, and by the lo-goi that exist around them and which constitute their defining limits.[52]

The movement from potential being in God to actual existence as other means that the world is subject to all the categories of derivative exis-tence. As the transcendent Ground of being, the "Groundless Ground" as it were, God is not subject to any kind of categorization – for He is the very criterion of all possible categories, the measure of all things, the ultimate limit of all delimitation. As Logos, He is the Wisdom which governs the cosmos, beyond which no further ordering principle may be sought. All beings are defined and constituted by their *logoi* – that is, by God's eternal predeterminations concerning their being, time, place, relation, quantity, etc.[53] – and thus come to exist as distinct, particular *beings*. For to *be*, is to be determined, defined, delimited as a particu-

---

[52] *Amb.Ioh.7, PG* 91, 1081B; translation: Constas, 2014, I, p. 52.
[53] See Aristotle, *Categories* II, 1b 25.

lar *something* (τι).[54] Yet God, as the very Ground of being, is infinitely
beyond being – for if God were a being (even a so-called "Supreme Being"), then He, too, would require some prior determining principle,
and so on *ad infinitum*. Hence, God is the Unmoved Mover, the eternally actual Ground *in whom* all things abide as potentialities and *from
whom* they emerge from nonexistence into being as finite actualities.

3. Creation *ex nihilo* as temporal creation

This, then, brings us to Maximus' third level of creation *ex nihilo* as
temporal creation. If the first level of creation *ex nihilo* meant creation
not from beings, while the second level meant creation from not *yet* being, the third and final level, I conclude, means creation *not from eternity* or, as Maximus, puts it, "when once beings were not". The notion
of creation *ex nihilo* as creation in time follows closely upon the idea
of creation as involving a creaturely motion from potential existence in
God to actual existence as other. For Neoplatonists such as Proclus, the
eternal actuality of God had as its counterpart an eternally actualized
cosmos, such that the latter could have no discernible beginning in time.
Maximus rejects this line of thinking. For him, the eternal actuality of
God in terms of the preexistent *logoi* does not result in a corresponding-
ly eternal creation. Instead, God eternally wills the creation of the world
"at the appropriate moment in time (τῷ ἐπιτηδείῳ καιρῷ)".[55] Creatures
first exist as potentialities in God only receiving actual existence as other
at the preordained time. It is precisely Maximus' insistence upon the
world's beginning in time that irrevocably separates him from the pre-
vailing pagan Neoplatonic position concerning the eternity of the cosmos. All things are created from God from nothing *in time*. In other
words, creation *not* from eternity.

One of Maximus' central arguments for creation in time rests upon
the idea of motion. God alone as the Prime Mover (πρώτως κινοῦν)
is absolutely unmoved (ἀκίνητον), while every being is in perpetual
motion (κινούμενον). And if beings are in motion, Maximus argues,
then it follows that they have a beginning in time "for whatever is in

[54] See Aristotle, *Metaphysics* VII, 1037a 25–27; 1038b 5.
[55] *Amb.Ioh.7, PG* 91, 1081B.

motion began to move [at a particular point in time (ἤρξατο)]".[56] More-over, if beings are in motion then they are neither without a beginning (ἄναρχος) nor without a cause (ἀναίτιος), for the *archē* is that which sets them in motion while the same as *aitia* draws them towards completion. God alone as the Ground of being, as the ultimate *archē* and *telos* of existence, is unmoved. It follows, Maximus concludes, that "no beings are without a beginning (ἄναρχος), since none of them is unmoved (ἀκίνητον)".[57] Now, strictly speaking, the idea of time is merely implicit in this argument (the verb ἤρξατο being amenable to a purely ontological interpretation). An Aristotelian or a Neoplatonist would have no difficulty interpreting Maximus' line of reasoning in ontological terms. The simple fact *that* beings are in motion (something Maximus assumes rather than demonstrates) in itself indicates nothing more than that there must be a principle of motion which both sets beings in motion (efficient cause), and draws them to completion (final cause). In order to avoid an infinite regress, there must be an ultimate Source of motion, an Unmoved Mover which sets all things in motion without itself being subject to motion.

That Maximus (with a certain delightful irony!) draws upon this Aristotelian argumentation to demonstrate that the world has not merely an ontological origin, but a temporal beginning becomes evident from the broader contours of Maximus' thought.[58] To begin with, as we noted in the previous section, Maximus associates the creaturely movement from potential existence in God to actual existence as other with time. All things, he says, "were created at the appropriate moment in time (τῷ ἐπιτηδείῳ καιρῷ), in a manner consistent with their *logoi*, and thus they received in themselves actual existence as beings (τὸ εἶναι τῇ ἐνεργείᾳ)".[59] This passage suggests that Maximus under-

---

[56] *Amb.Ioh.*10, *PG* 91, 1177A. The square brackets are my own. The bracketed section indicates Constas' paraphrase of the ambiguous Greek verb ἤρξατο which is more literally rendered simply as "beginning". Like the noun ἀρχή from which it is derived, ἤρξατο can refer both to a temporal and/or to an ontological beginning. The broader context, however, justifies Constas' rendering of it in temporal terms.

[57] *Amb.Ioh.*10, *PG* 91, 1177A–B.

[58] Maximus explicitly rejects the pagan notion of an eternal creation at *Car.* 4.6.

[59] *Amb.Ioh.*7, *PG* 91, 1081B.

stands motion in Aristotelian terms as a movement from potentiality to actuality.[60] Insofar as beings have their primordial origin in God, the "beginning" (ἤρξατο, ἀρχή) of beings is simultaneously ontological *and* temporal – for all beings are derived from God from nothing at the divinely preordained time. Unlike Aristotle, God for Maximus is not merely the final cause of an eternal cosmos, but also the efficient cause of a temporal creation.[61] God alone is eternally actual; beings exist first in potentiality and only later in actuality. To be created is to be subject to time, for time is inseparable from motion.[62] As to why God only created recently, Maximus maintains an apophatic silence: "Seek the reason why God created, for this is knowledge. But do not seek how or why he only created recently, for this question does not fall under your mind..."[63]

Maximus further subverts Aristotle by arguing for the temporal origin of the world in terms of the Aristotelian Categories. Who, he insists,

> Does not know that every kind of being whatsoever, with the sole exception of the Divine (which strictly speaking is beyond being), presupposes the concept of a "where", (ποῦ) which in absolutely every instance necessarily requires the related concept of a "when" (πότε)? For it is not possible for a "where" to be thought of separately from a "when" (for they belong to those things that are simultaneous (ἅμα), and do not exist apart from their mutual conditioning).[64]

We noted above that to be moved from potential existence in God to actual existence as other is to be subject to all the categories of existence, for "all created things are positively defined by their own *logoi*, and by the *logoi* that exist around them and which constitute their defining limits".[65] To *be* is to be *finite* – for which reason God as Ground is beyond being and beyond categorization. Here, Maximus essentially

---

[60] See also *Amb.Ioh.*7, *PG* 91, 1069B–C, 1072B–C.

[61] See Constas, 2014, 1, p. 489 n. 61. The nature of this modification would seem to involve the transposition of Aristotelian physics upon the plane of metaphysics. Just as every finite object (be it art or nature) has an efficient cause, so the entire world has God, the Demiurgos, as its efficient cause.

[62] See Aristotle, *Physics* IV, 217b30–224a15.

[63] *Car.*, 4.5.

[64] *Amb.Ioh.*10, *PG* 91, 1180B–C; translation: Constas, 2014, 1, p. 293.

[65] *Amb.Ioh.*7, *PG* 91, 1081B.

argues that to be subject to one of the categories of created being is to be subject to them all. To be in place is simultaneously (ἅμα) to be in time, for it is impossible to conceive of one in the absence of the other.[66] For Maximus, this is true not only of individual beings but of the entire cosmos. To be in place means to be circumscribed. Insofar as the entire world is circumscribed by God, the latter may be said to be its "place" (τόπος).[67] This, Maximus argues, demonstrates "that beings are subject to the category of 'when' (πότε), *as completely existing in time* (ἐν χρόνῳ), since no being after God (μετὰ Θεόν) exists simply (ἁπλῶς), but in a certain way (πῶς), and for this reason beings are not without a beginning (ἄναρχα)".[68] Here Maximus unambiguously identifies the *archē* with time. All beings in virtue of being created exist in God as their place and, hence, in time. By ingeniously transposing Aristotle's physics upon the plane of metaphysics, Maximus affirms the temporal origin of the world, arriving at a position diametrically opposed to that of the great Stagirite.

Finally, Maximus links the temporal origin of the world with the doctrine of creation *ex nihilo*. Continuing to argue from the Categories, Maximus states:

> Therefore no being is without a beginning (ἄναρχον) if its existence presupposes even a single qualitative distinction; neither is it without limits if its existence is conditioned by relation to something else. If, then, no being is without beginning (ἄναρχον) or limitation (as the argument has demonstrated, consistent with the nature of beings), *then there certainly was when each being was not* (ἦν πάντως <u>ποτὲ</u> ὅτε τι τῶν ὄντων οὐκ ἦν), from which it follows that, if it did not always exist (οὐκ ἦν), it was brought into being (γέγονεν), because there certainly *was when it was not* (εἴπερ οὐκ ἦν).[69]

To be without a beginning – in both the ontological and temporal sense – is impossible for finite creatures, whose delimited character points to their dependence upon a constitutive principle. And for Maximus, to

---

[66] See Aristotle, *Categories*, 6. 5–10.

[67] *Amb.Ioh.* 10, *PG* 91, 1180C–D.

[68] *Amb.Ioh.*10, *PG* 91, 1180D. Emphasis added.

[69] *Amb.Ioh.*10, *PG* 91, 1181C. I have modified the translation to bring out the terseness of Maximus' expression. As Constas notes, "This phrase would seem to pun on the Arian slogan that 'there was a time when He (i.e. the Son of God) was not'". See CONSTAS, 2014, I, P. 490 n.70.

be constituted means to be subject to all the categories of finite existence *including time*.[70] Here, Maximus expresses this temporal dimension in terms of the prior nonexistence of beings. If something has a beginning (as every creature must) then there was a "time" when it did not exist, and if there once was when it was not (οὐκ ἦν), then it must have been created (γέγονεν). To be a creature, then, means to have been brought from nonexistence into being in time; that is, creation *not from eternity* or, as Maximus puts it, when once it was not (οὐκ ἦν). The *nihil* of creation *ex nihilo*, then, may be understood in a temporal sense as the prior nonexistence of beings.[71] Insofar as there is, strictly speaking, no "time" prior to creation, creation in time essentially means creation as negation of eternity. In addition to creation *ex nihilo* as rejection of ontological dualism (creation *not* from beings) and as the creaturely motion from potentiality to actuality (creation from not *yet* being), we also have creation *ex nihilo* as temporal creation – creation *not from eternity*.[72]

Conclusion

Along with the preceding two understandings of creation *ex nihilo*, the equation of *ex nihilo* with temporal creation is crucial if we are to avoid

---

[70]   Maximus would regard the pagan notion of an eternal creation as a failure to properly distinguish between the Creator who transcends the categories, and creatures constituted by *all* of them. God alone is eternally unmoved; creatures are moved from nonexistence into being when once they were not (οὐκ ἦν).

[71]   Maximus expresses a parallel idea in his discussion of the eternal and temporal works of God: "the works of God beginning their existence temporally (χρονικῶς)", he states, "are all participating beings...since they have non-being (μὴ ὄν) prior to their existence. For there was a 'when' (πότε) when participating beings were not (οὐκ ἦν)" *Th.Oec.*, 1.48. Though the language here is Platonic rather than Aristotelian, the point is the same: all beings are contingent upon a prior constitutive principle – whether it be the unparticipated Godhead or the Unmoved Mover. It is worth noting that Maximus uses the negative particles μή and οὐκ interchangeably without any significant difference in meaning.

[72]   The first and the third levels parallel each other, though one is ontological and the other temporal. The emphasis of each, however, is unique. The aim of the first is the negation of pre-existent matter and thus tends to affirm the sameness of God and world, while the aim of the latter is the negation of an eternal creation and thus emphasises the otherness of God and world.

subtly reifying the *nihil* of creation as a quasi-something from which beings are created. The irony of such a reification – however unconscious or unintended – among radical proponents of creation *ex nihilo* is that it culminates in the very dualism that this Christian doctrine was designed to overcome. If the idea of creation *ex deo* carries with it the danger of pantheistic confusion, it is equally true that an exclusive emphasis upon creation *ex nihilo* tends towards the opposite extreme of a kind of gnostic dualism – one which threatens to undermine the very ground of the God/world relation. For if the world is not grounded in God, then it inevitably comes to be regarded as a separate, self-subsistent entity devoid of sacred significance. Maximus, to his eternal credit, charts a middle course: the world is created *both* from God *and* from nothing – or rather, from God alone who, from His own infinite resources brought it from nonexistence into being at the eternally predetermined time.

Maximus the Confessor on the Infinity of God:
Ambiguum 10, Sections 40–41

A Critical Reading

Miklós Vassányi

(*Budapest*)

Infinity (ἀπειρία) as a divine attribute or cosmogonical principle had run a famed and fabulous course over time from Pythagoras,[1] Anaximander,[2] Plato,[3] and Aristotle,[4] to Plotinus,[5] Proclus,[6] the Cappadocian Fathers,[7] and Dionysius the Areopagite,[8] to name only a few of the more eminent thinkers who commented upon it before Saint Maximus. In the course of that development, infinity had been alternatively viewed as a flaw, a lack of determination, or as a perfection, a token of unlimited power and creativity, before it was definitively enshrined in the ideal nature of the Christian God. For Maximus – as with a long line of authors after him including, among many others, Aquinas,[9] Scotus,[10] Suárez,[11] and Spinoza[12] – infinity is a core divine attribute exclusively characterizing God: *Only* God is unbounded. However, for Maximus, God is also exclusively monadic and unit-like, resembling the Platonic idea of the One in the First Hypothesis of the *Parmenides* (137 C4–142 A8), especially by reason of His partlessness and immobility. So at the end of the day, God, conceived by the Confessor as both infinite and monadic, will somehow resemble Plato's One, which, as a result of its partlessness, is also infinite: Ἄπειρον ἄρα τὸ ἕν (137 D8–9). Hence while

---

[1] As is known, Limit and Unlimited, πέρας καὶ ἄπειρον, are at the head of the ten Pythagorean principle pairs listed in Aristotle's *Metaphysics* I.5, 986a23–26. In the preceding passage, Aristotle suggests that πέρας καὶ ἄπειρον may have been conceived as cosmogonical principles by the Pythagoreans (cf. also Iamblichus, *De communi mathematica scientia* 3, where ἄπειρον is asserted to be the Pythagorean principle of mathematical substance: ὅτι μὲν οὖν τὸ πεπερασμένον καὶ ἄπειρον ἀρχαί εἰσι πάντων τῶν μαθημάτων καὶ πάσης μαθηματικῆς οὐσίας, παντὶ δῆλον, ὡς δοκεῖ τοῖς Πυθαγορείοις; see also his *In Nicomachi arithmeticam introductionem*, passim).

Ambiguum *10 of* Maximus the Confessor in Modern Study: Papers Collected on the Occasion of the Budapest Colloquium on Saint Maximus, *3–4 February 2021*, ed. by Alexis Léonas & Vladimir Cvetković, with the collaboration of Daniel Heide, Turnhout, 2025 (IPM 97), pp. 301–315
© BREPOLS ❦ PUBLISHERS   10.1484/M.IPM-EB.5.141866

[2] According to the well-known fragment B1 of Anaximander ἀρχὴν... εἴρηκε τῶν ὄντων τὸ ἄπειρον... ἐξ ὧν δὲ ἡ γένεσίς ἐστι τοῖς οὖσι, καὶ τὴν φθορὰν εἰς ταῦτα γίνεσθαι κατὰ τὸ χρεών· διδόναι γὰρ αὐτὰ δίκην καὶ τίσιν ἀλλήλοις τῆς ἀδικίας κατὰ τὴν τοῦ χρόνου τάξιν. For the ardent scholarly debate around the interpretation of the underdetermined ἄπειρον, see E. ASMIS, "What is Anaximander's Apeiron?", *Journal of the History of Philosophy*, 19/3 (1981), pp. 279–297; or the earlier, comprehensive analysis by H. B. GOTTSCHALK, "Anaximander's 'Apeiron'" *Phronesis* 10/1 (1965), pp. 37–53.

[3] For the late Plato, boundlessness is an attribute of the One according to the First Hypothesis of the *Parmenides* (137 D 8–9) while in the Second Hypothesis, infinity is chiefly understood as the boundless productivity of the One as it gives birth to an ἄπειρον πλῆθος (143 A 1) and by the time the Third Hypothesis takes the stage in the text, boundlessness even emerges as a quality shared by the multitude coming forth from the One (158 D 3–7). The *Philebus* apparently doubles down on these premises as it posits πέρας καὶ ἄπειρον as ontological and cosmological principles, accompanying the One and the Many: οἱ μὲν παλαιοί, κρείττονες ἡμῶν καὶ ἐγγυτέρω θεῶν οἰκοῦντες, ταύτην φήμην παρέδοσαν, ὡς ἐξ ἑνὸς μὲν καὶ πολλῶν ὄντων τῶν ἀεὶ λεγομένων εἶναι, πέρας δὲ καὶ ἀπειρίαν ἐν αὐτοῖς σύμφυτον ἐχόντων (16 C7–10 and 23 C9–30 B7).

[4] In the Aristotelian characteristics of God (*Metaphysics* XII, 7 = 1073a3–13), partlessness or indivisibility and infinite power are represented as belonging logically together in the resuming end-of-chapter argument, where the inexhaustibility of divine power is derived from God's endlessness over time: δέδεικται δὲ καὶ ὅτι μέγεθος οὐδὲν ἔχειν ἐνδέχεται ταύτην τὴν οὐσίαν ἀλλ' ἀμερὴς καὶ ἀδιαίρετός ἐστιν (κινεῖ γὰρ τὸν ἄπειρον χρόνον, οὐδὲν δ' ἔχει δύναμιν ἄπειρον πεπερασμένον...). On the other hand, in natural philosophy, Aristotle sees ἄπειρον as an imperfection, an opposite of "entire" and "perfect" (ἡ δὲ φύσις φεύγει τὸ ἄπειρον· τὸ μὲν γὰρ ἄπειρον ἀτελές, ἡ δὲ φύσις ἀεὶ ζητεῖ τέλος, *On the Generation of Animals* I, 1 = 715b14–16; see further the decisive passage in *Physics* III, 4–6 = 202 B30–207 A32).

[5] In the *Enneads*, ἀπειρία, often paired up with ἀόριστον, comes on stage in the theory of matter, designating a by excellence un-divine quality, indefiniteness, like in *Treatise 51* (= 1, 8, 6): Πέρατι δὴ καὶ μέτρῳ καὶ ὅσα ἔνεστιν ἐν τῇ θείᾳ φύσει, ἀπειρία καὶ ἀμετρία καὶ τὰ ἄλλα, ὅσα ἔχει ἡ κακὴ φύσις, ἐναντία... The early *Treatise 12* (= 2, 4), arguing in the same vein, still adds that the indeterminacy of matter has come from the One: καὶ εἴη ἂν γεννηθὲν ἐκ τῆς τοῦ ἑνὸς ἀπειρίας ἢ δυνάμεως ἢ τοῦ ἀεί, οὐκ οὔσης ἐν ἐκείνῳ ἀπειρίας ἀλλὰ ποιοῦντος.

⁶ Book III, Chapter 8 of the *Platonic Theology* specifies that πέρας καὶ ἄπειρον are the creative ontological hegemonic principles immediately following the One and preceding all the other principal henads (Being, Life, Mind, Soul).

⁷ In a familiar passage of *The Life of Moses*, Gregory of Nyssa derives divine infinity from the illimitability of God's ethical excellence: Τὸ πρώτως καὶ κυρίως ἀγαθόν, οὗ ἡ φύσις ἀγαθότης ἐστίν, αὐτὸ τὸ Θεῖον, ὃ τί ποτε τῇ φύσει νοεῖται, τοῦτο καὶ ἔστι καὶ ὀνομάζεται. Ἐπεὶ οὖν οὐδεὶς ἀρετῆς ὅρος πλὴν κακίας ἐδείχθη, ἀπαράδεκτον δὲ τοῦ ἐναντίου τὸ Θεῖον, ἀόριστος ἄρα καὶ ἀπεράτωτος ἡ θεία φύσις καταλαμβάνεται... (*PG* 44, 301 A8–14 = *GNO* 7/1, p. 4; cf. also *PG* 44, 404 B6–13 = *GNO* 7/1, p. 115: τὸ θεῖον κατὰ τὴν ἑαυτοῦ φύσιν ἀόριστον, οὐδενὶ περιειργόμενον πέρατι). Gregory Nazianzen, in turn, just brings in the infinity of God as an axiomatic argument against the materiality of God, whereby divine boundlessness is taken for granted as something self-evident: Τί γάρ ποτε ὑπολήψῃ τὸ θεῖον, εἴπερ ὅλαις ταῖς λογικαῖς πιστεύεις ἐφόδοις; ἢ πρὸς τί σε ὁ λόγος ἀνάξει βασανιζόμενος [...]; πότερον σῶμα; καὶ πῶς τὸ ἄπειρον, καὶ ἀόριστον, καὶ ἀσχημάτιστον, καὶ ἀναφές, καὶ ἀόρατον; (*Second Theological Sermon = Sermon 28, PG* 36, 33 B9–14 = *SC* 250, pp. 112–114).

⁸ For Dionysius, "infinite" does not, strikingly, line up among the divine names – while it still is the very essence of God, understood principally as illimitable productivity (cf. *On the Divine Names* XIII, 3). Mark that God is a simple and indivisible monad for Dionysius too: ἐν πάσῃ σχεδὸν τῇ θεολογικῇ πραγματείᾳ τὴν θεαρχίαν ὁρῶμεν ἱερῶς ὑμνουμένην ὡς μονάδα μὲν καὶ ἑνάδα διὰ τὴν ἁπλότητα καὶ ἑνότητα τῆς ὑπερφυοῦς ἀμερείας, ibid. I, 4).

⁹ *Summa theologiae*, p. 1, q. 7, a. 1: "Utrum Deus sit infinitus", where divine infinity is interpreted as a consequence of God's immateriality; and *Summa contra Gentiles* 1, 43: "Quod Deus est infinitus", where divine infinity is construed as boundless perfection.

¹⁰ *Tractatus de primo principio*, Chapter 4, Conclusion 9, where the infinity of God is understood as His unlimited mental capacity – which entails the infinity of the divine substance itself.

¹¹ *Disputationes metaphysicae* (1597) 28: "De prima divisione entis in infinitum simpliciter et finitum et aliis divisionibus quae huic aequivalent", Section 1. – In the Suárezian theological antithetics, portraying the relationship between Creator and creation, the opposition "infinite vs finite" is the fundamental one that grounds all the rest.

¹² *Ethica* 1, the well-known definition 6 and thesis 11, which point to infinity as the very essence of God; see also the *Korte verhandeling van God, de mensch en deszelvs welstand* 1, 1.

in *Ambiguum* 10, Sections 39–40, Maximus implicitly defies Platonism by rejecting the pre-existence of matter, a latent Platonizing tendency is still discernible in the deep structure of his idea of God. This is the point I would like to argue for here – but first we need to look into the textual constitution of our source.

1. Articulating the text: A philological preamble

Section 41,[13] as Andrew Louth points out, is separate from the previous section in Eriugena's Latin version,[14] produced between 862 and 864, while according to Jacques-Paul Migne's recension in *PG* 91 (1863), this bit is still part and parcel of Section 40 (*PG* 91, 1184 B–D). As Migne only revised Franciscus Oehler's 1857 edition,[15] the result is that in the single thirteenth-century manuscript (Gudianus Graecus 39) Oehler transcribed for his edition, Section 41 did not stand apart and consequently had no separate title either. This standoff between Eriugena's and Oehler's respective divisions of the text was recently resolved by Nicholas Constas's edition, which relies not on one but on six primary codices, four of which mark a text division here, whilst one (the twelfth-century Vaticanus Graecus 504) does not.[16] Hence it appears that in the majority of the manuscripts, the two sections had stood aloof but there was a minority that merged them. In terms of content, the two bits are never-

---

[13] *PG* 91, 1184 D1–1188 C4 (pp. 152–162 in the present volume). Apart from the critical text by Carl Laga and English translation of Joshua Lollar in this volume cf. the bilingual edition of *Ambiguum* 10 in CONSTAS, 2014, I, pp. 150–343. Section 41 is found on pp. 302–309. Another English translation, with explanatory notes, of the full text of *Ambiguum* 10 can be found in A. LOUTH, *Maximus*, pp. 94–154.

[14] "The text in Migne marks no division here. This is taken from Eriugena's version" (LOUTH, *Maximus the Confessor*, p. 210, n. 106). See Eriugena's Latin version in *Maximi Confessoris Ambigua ad Johannem iuxta Johannis Scotti Eriugenae latinam interpretationem*, ed. by É. JEAUNEAU, Turnhout, 1988 (*CCSG*, 18). Section 41 is on pp. 97–99.

[15] *S. P. N. Maximi Confessoris de variis difficilibus locis SS. PP. Dionysii et Gregorii ad Thomam V. S*. Librum ex codice manuscripto Gudiano descripsit et in Latinum sermonem interpretatus, post J. Scoti et Th. Gale tentamina, nunc primum integrum edidit Franciscus OEHLER, Halle, C. E. M. Pfeffer, 1857.

[16] CONSTAS, 2014, I, pp. 302, 457–461 and 468.

theless tightly knit together and the cohesion of the two passages is also underpinned by the presence of a γάρ in the opening sentence of Section 41. This cohesion is further corroborated by the partial overlap of the two titles,[17] both of which contrast the monad with the dyad, in an effort to make philosophical sense of Gregory of Nazianzus's phrase τὴν ὑλικὴν δυάδα, cited in the lemma standing at the head of *Ambiguum* 10.

Again developing a hint by Andrew Louth, we may say that Sections 35 through 42 (*PG* 91, 1176 B–1193 C) of *Ambiguum* 10 constitute a metaphysical treatise-within-a-treatise.[18] Although Maximus originally wanted to clarify the opening sentence of the second chapter of Gregory of Nazianzus's *Sermon* 21[19] (in terms of which blessed is the one who has been able to enjoy the company of God, the unique topmost object of desire beyond which there is nothing, τὸ τῶν ὀρεκτῶν ἔσχατον),[20] here the Confessor is constructing a metaphysical backdrop to an ascetical moral theology of his own. More specifically, however, in Sections 40–41, he is interested in clarifying the concept of the dyad mentioned by the Theologian. In these Sections, he is presumably offering an initial, metaphysical approach to the concept of the "material dyad" while a subsequent, moral philosophical approach will be proposed by him in Section 43 (*PG* 91, 1193 C–1196 C), whose title "Θεωρία διάφορος τῆς... ὑλικῆς δυάδος" reinforces this interpretation. The interjacent Section 42, a long development on divine providence seems to be a necessary complement to the argument of Section 41, which describes God as ultimately a relationless being – for Christian theology cannot put up with a God that does not relate in some positive manner to His own creation, the world.

---

[17]   The title to Section 40 ends with ὅτι ἡ δυὰς οὔτε ἀρχή ἐστιν οὔτε ἄναρχος, καὶ ὅτι ἡ μονὰς μονὴ κυρίως ἀρχὴ καὶ ἄναρχος while that of Section 41 reads ὅτι πᾶσα δυὰς ἀριθμῷ λέγεται δυὰς καὶ πᾶσα μονὰς εἰς μέρος συντελοῦσα δυάδος ἀριθμῶν λέγεται μονάς, ἀλλ᾽ οὐχ ἁπλῶς μονάς (CONSTAS, ed., *On the Difficulties*, pp. 298 and 302).

[18]   LOUTH, *Maximus*, p. 96: "Then after <sections 32–33...,> there follows a long series of discussions of metaphysical topics concerned with God's relationship to the cosmos, in particular, his providence (Sections 34–42)".

[19]   *Sermon 21* is "a panegyric of St. Athanasius, the Patriarch of Alexandria and defender of Nicene orthodoxy" (LOUTH, *Maximus*, p. 94).

[20]   *PG* 36, 1084B 8–9. Cf. *Grégoire de Nazianze, Discours 20-23*, ed. by Justin Mossay (*SC* 270), Paris, 1980, p. 112.

2. A philosophical outline of Maximus' train of thought

Maximus' entire metaphysical train of thought departs from the spring-board of the ascetic struggle expended on account of "the fleshly". For in order to understand what the ascetic wrestles with, one must eluci-date what essential attributes the natural material world has. This theo-retical quest is the driving force that leads Maximus to the point where he can specify the real difference between God and the material world, by virtue of the concept pair infinity *versus* finitude. So what is ultimate-ly at stake here is the infinity of God as the one grand divine prerogative.

As I suggested above one is inclined to do justice to Oehler and put Section 41 (*PG* 91, 1184 D–1188 D) into the broader context of espe-cially Sections 26 (1153 A–D) and 35–40 (1176 B–1184 D). As soon as it is put into that frame of reference, it becomes clear that as a first step towards his goal, Maximus is actually performing a formal full induc-tion to prove the *differentia realis* of God throughout Sections 26 and 36–38 (1176 D–1181 A). As a second step, then, he attacks the thesis of the pre-existence of matter with a *reductio ad absurdum* in Sections 39–40 (1181 A–1184 D), thereby implicitly designating Platonists and Peripatetics as his adversaries (or at least, so it seems to me). Last, Sec-tion 41 (1184 D–1188 D), as a dialectical climax, is a fully abstract and philosophical demonstration of the exclusive character of divine infin-ity understood according to the strong interpretation. Unlike at the beginning of *Ambiguum* 10, there are no longer any Scriptural ref-erences here, although a citation from the last part of Dionysius the Areopagite's authoritative *On the Divine Names* is used as a kind of cor-nerstone to seal off the argumentative part, as well as to introduce the recapitulation and conclusion.

The full induction I have specified as the Confessor's first dialectic move is a systematic inspection of whether the Aristotelian categories may be applied to God in any meaningful sense, or whether He tran-scends them.[21] Maximus passes in systematic review the categories of substance (οὐσία), relation (σχέσις), motion (κίνησις), or change (τροπή, ἀλλοίωσις), quantity (ποσότης), quality (ποιότης), place (ποῦ), time (χρόνος).[22] He even gives a list of them in Section 40: οὐσία, ποσότης,

---

[21] It just might be the case that Eriugena in Book 1 of the *Periphyseon* mod-elled his parallel but book-length quest on this precedent, which he also trans-lated and therefore knew well.

[22] Mark that position (κεῖσθαι), action (πράττειν), passion (παθεῖν), and pos-session (ἕξις) are missing if this is to be a seamless enumeration of the Aristote-

ποιότης, σχέσις, ποίησις, πάθος, κίνησις, ἕξις.[23] The basis upon which he refutes their applicability to God is generally that motion there is implicated in the Aristotelian categories, while God by contrast is regarded as motionless (changeless) and hence also without a beginning.

The fact that changelessness or impassibility is also the main defining feature of the Platonic idea as it is laid out in the *Symposium* (211 B1–2) or the *Timaeus* (28 A2) foreshadows the general Platonizing tendency of Section 41 (*PG* 91, 1184 D–1188 D). As a core attribute of the Platonic idea involves a full negation of the constant fluctuation of the natural universe, so Maximus' infinite will be revealed as the opposite, or negation, of the attributes characterizing the present visible world.

3. The in-depth argument for the exclusive character of divine infinity in Section 40

In more detail, then, still in Section 39 (*PG* 91, 1181 A–1184 B), the pre-existence of matter is refuted by an ingenious reasoning, hinged on the contention that matter cannot have acquired *existence* by itself (a big challenge) if it could not acquire *form* by itself (a smaller challenge) – which it was evidently unable to do.[24] Hence it must have been created and could not have existed forever.

But Maximus takes another, harder line in Section 40 (*PG* 91, 1184 B–D) to refute the eternity of matter. Here – by virtue of a reduction to absurdity – he departs from the evidently false supposition that matter is eternal. This, he argues, equals the beginninglessness (ἄναρχον) of matter, which in turn equals the *temporal* infinity (ἄπειρον) of matter. This infinity, then, would for him entail immobility; and if that is to be a property of matter (as it most certainly is not) then we apparently have two equally infinite, immobile, and beginningless things: Θεὸς καὶ ὕλη, God and matter. This is the absurdity (ὅπερ εἶναι ἀμήχανον) Maximus intended to expose and, from this point on, it is as if he were crossing over into a sort of Pythagorean arithmology. For such a dyad, consisting of God and matter, will be seen as a higher ἀρχή precisely

lian categories, while "motion" is an add-on perhaps as a substitute for action and passion together.

[23] This list is, again, incomplete, with position, place, and time wanting, if the list means to be "Aristotelian".

[24] *PG* 91, 1181C 13–1184A 10 (pp. 150–152 in the present volume); Constas, 2014, I, pp. 296–298.

on account of its being infinite, immobile, and beginningless. However, a dyad can never be truly infinite (δυὰς γὰρ οὔτε ἄπειρος) insofar as it breaks down into its constituents, the two monads, which as it were "move" it in the sense that the dyad comes to be from them (κατὰ διαίρεσιν δὲ ὡς ἀριθμῷ κινουμένη). So we are faced with a *contradictio in adiecto* which undermines the principle of contradiction. Hence, the idea of an infinite dyad must be abandoned.

This argument relies on the logically necessary interdependence between infinity and indivisibility, that is, between being endless and being monadic: whatever is infinite cannot be split into parts. In a classic manner, Maximus further breaks down the monadic character into simplicity and unicity (ἁπλοῦν καὶ μόνον). At the end of the day, for him, infinity presupposes simplicity and unicity – because "infinity is relationless" (τὸ δὲ ἄπειρον ἄσχετον) while divisibility and multiplicity imply relation. The logical connection between infinity and monadic character is, significantly, vested with an openly ontological meaning as soon as Maximus adds, in the last line of Section 40 (*PG* 91, 1184 B–D), that whatever is not infinite and monadic does not exist *a se* and is not unrelated: οὐ φύσει τὸ εἶναι καὶ ἄσχετον ἔχει. So the complex idea of ἀρχή, for the Confessor, combines in itself the aspects of infinity, monadicity, unrelatedness, and aseity. Monadicity, unrelatedness, and aseity may perhaps be brought under the common denominator of irreducibility, whilst infinity could be conceptualized as unrestrictability. Adding unicity to the list, I think, we come full circle and grasp the structure of Maximus' idea of God as an essence featuring unicity, irreducibility, and unrestrictability – which is a totally philosophical argument, not relying on either prior religious belief or Scripture.

An initial problem lying with this argumentation is the hidden and precarious conceptual transition it makes from temporal infinity (an *ex supposito* admitted point) to spatial infinity to divine infinity – that is, ἄπειρον, ἄναρχον, ἀκίνητον together – in the first part of the argument, at the beginning of Section 40.[25] This conceals an equivocal use of the term ἄπειρον; which is to say, to my mind at least, that the argument fails.

---

[25] ...εἰ δὲ ἄναρχον, καὶ ἄπειρον, εἰ δὲ ἄπειρον, πάντως καὶ ἀκίνητον (ἀκίνητον γὰρ πάντως τὸ ἄπειρον, οὐ γὰρ ἔχει ποῦ κινηθῆναι τὸ μὴ ὁριζόμενον)... (*PG* 91, 1184 B9–12; p. 152 in the present volume; CONSTAS, 2014, I, pp. 298–300).

A second, perhaps more serious dialectic difficulty is that as a premise, we have presupposed that matter is something beginningless, ἄναρχον. So to argue that a dyad is not an ἀρχή (and that therefore matter as a second candidate to infinity cannot be eternal) suffers from the vicious circle that once we have presupposed that matter is in no need of an ἀρχή (because it is ἄναρχος), there is no further necessity at all for a dyad to be the ἀρχή of anything, let alone matter. Hence it seems that the Maximian argument from the non-principial character of the dyad may be neglected insofar as it seems to beg the question.

Turning the query around, we may reasonably ask, finally, whether Maximus does not philosophically overshoot the mark when he attributes even spatial immobility to infinity in general – ἀκίνητον γὰρ πάντως τὸ ἄπειρον, οὐ γὰρ ἔχει ποῦ κινηθῆναι τὸ μὴ ὁριζόμενον. Placing no restrictions on the use of "the infinite" in this statement could implicate God too, were it not for the fact that Maximus has already ruled out that God may have any relation to the Aristotelian categories, including "place".

Despite all these logical difficulties, it is clear that the main pursuit of Section 40 (*PG* 91, 1184 B–D) is to drive home the point that an ἀρχή by excellence is irreducible, unrestrictable and unique at the same time (μονὰς μόνη κυρίως ἀρχὴ καὶ ἄναρχος); and that it hence coalesces within itself the contradictory features of lacking a boundary and yet being monadic in character. The final upshot of Section 40, then, resembles the outcome of the Second hypothesis of Plato's *Parmenides* (ἓν εἰ ἔστιν, "if the One exists", 142 B3–155 E3): that the One – that is, the monad – is the ἀρχή of the Many.

4. Divine infinity understood as all-round unrestrictability in Section 41

Proceeding to the truly theological Section 41 (*PG* 91, 1184 D–1188 D), we find Maximus elaborating on the concept of divine infinity, in the wake of his preceding argument against a possible duality of boundless ἀρχαί. Number, he says here, is the principle – that is, the efficient cause – of every dyad, as well as of every monad, if it is to be a constituent of a dyad. It is number – or plurality or multiplicity – at large that causes the monads composing an infinite dyad to no longer be illimitable or infinite, insofar as they will mutually circumscribe and hence restrict each other.[26] "Number" is hence understood here as being a *spiritus movens*, an agent that calls forth duality from singularity. But if the operation of number and the emergence of duality is a problem (as Maximus is now seeking a dialectically unproblematic first principle of all) then, apparently, he wants to reach back, by a regressive analysis, to a cosmogonic stage when number has not yet existed, has produced neither duality nor multiplicity. It is as though he were intent on reverting from the metaphysical situation explicated in the Second Hypothesis (involving the birth of "number" from the One, 144 A3–7) of the *Parmenides* to the absolute, relationless origin of the First Hypothesis.

This argument is slightly different from the one in Section 40, which was oriented toward the problematic concept of a dyad conceived as an infinite ἀρχή. There, Maximus considered the problematic from, as it were, a top-down perspective, looking at it from the upper position of the dyad. Here in Section 41, by contrast, he takes the opposite, bottom-up route as he examines the lower stratum where the two constitutive monads are positioned, and points us to a conceptual difficulty lying with infinity at this level. This new argument for the unicity of the absolute ἀρχή may be labeled as a proof from the *exclusivity of infinity*:

> Now no one with any intelligence would call "infinite" something that from eternity is seen to have or be marked by some essential difference, for if he thought about it he would recognize that this falls completely outside the definition of the infinite. For the infinite is infinite in every way and in all respects: according to substance, power, and activity, and in relation to the upper and lower limits of things, that is, the beginning and the end. For the infinite is incomprehensible in respect of its substance, inconceivable in respect of its power, and unlimited in respect of its activity, having no beginning on the upper end of the scale, and no end on the lower, and, to put it simply and more accurately, it is in every way unbounded, since absolutely none of the limiting factors that we have mentioned can be thought of in conjunction with it. For if we were to say, in any way whatsoever, that anything essentially different could be placed alongside it, we would in the same breath negate the principle of its infinity. And if the definition of infinity excludes the presence of

---

[26] Ἀριθμῷ γὰρ πᾶσα δυὰς καὶ πᾶσα μονὰς εἰς μέρος αὐτῆς συντελοῦσα εἶναι καθέστηκε, καθ' ὃν ἀλλήλων αἱ κατ' αὐτὴν μονάδες ἀφαριοῦνται τὸ ἀπερίγραφον. (*PG* 91, 1184 D1–4; p. 154 in the present volume; CONSTAS, 2014, I, p. 302).

something else essentially different existing together with it from eternity, then the dyad cannot be infinite.[27]

"Infinity" as such emerges here as something that does not bear up with a duplicate (unless an equally infinite counterpart is its own attribute). A truly infinite thing, suggests Maximus, is boundless in all essential and modal or accidental respects (κατὰ πάντα καὶ λόγον καὶ τρόπον): It is not to be encompassed in terms of essence; beyond the reach of intuition in terms of power; not to be circumscribed in terms of sphere of operation; removed from under the scope of efficient or final causality. Just as it exceeds the capacity of a finite mind to understand, so it ontologically excludes any parallel infinity, as it is conceived to be something expansive which has an ineluctable tendency of overstepping boundaries. Hence of eminently infinite things there can be only one, so an infinite dyad is, again, a *contradictio in terminis*.

For this argument to be convincing, infinity must be construed, from square one, as all-round unrestrictability or unlimited irreducibility or exclusive fundamentality. However, in this strong interpretation of infinity, it is still unclear how infinite *material* substance would restrict an infinite *spiritual* being which is also monadic. On the other hand, it remains philosophically unclarified how and why such a dynamically illimitable God would put up with anything finite (for instance, the world). Third, the final outcome that there can only be one all-round infinite thing invites a second argument that the one

[27] Οὐδεὶς δὲ μεμοιραμένος καὶ ὁπωσοῦν τοῦ λογίζεσθαι εἴποι ἂν "ἄπειρον" εἶναι, ᾧ ἐξ ἀϊδίου συνθεωρεῖταί τι ἢ συνεπιθεωρεῖται κατ' οὐσίαν διάφορον, εἰδὼς διαπεσεῖσθαι πάντως αὐτῷ τὸν περὶ τὸ ἄπειρον λόγον οὕτω φρονοῦντι. Τὸ γὰρ ἄπειρον κατὰ πάντα καὶ λόγον καὶ τρόπον ἐστὶν ἄπειρον, κατ' οὐσίαν, κατὰ δύναμιν, κατ' ἐνέργειαν, κατ' ἄμφω τὰ πέρατα, τὸ ἄνω τε λέγω καὶ τὸ κάτω, τουτέστι κατὰ τὴν ἀρχὴν καὶ τὸ τέλος. Ἀχώρητον γὰρ κατὰ τὴν οὐσίαν, καὶ ἀπερινόητον κατὰ τὴν δύναμιν, καὶ κατὰ τὴν ἐνέργειαν ἀπερίγραφον, καὶ ἄναρχον ἄνωθεν, καὶ ἀτελεύτητον κάτωθέν ἐστι τὸ ἄπειρον, καὶ ἁπλῶς εἰπεῖν ἀληθέστερον, καὶ πάντα ἀόριστον, ὡς οὐδενὸς τὸ παράπαν καθ' ἕνα τῶν ἀπηριθμένων τρόπων συνεπινοηθῆναι αὐτῷ δυναμένου. Καθ' ὃν γὰρ ἂν εἴποιμεν λόγον ἢ τρόπον δύνασθαί τι ἕτερον αὐτῷ κατ' οὐσίαν διάφορον παραβάλλεσθαι, τὸν ὅλον τῆς ὅλης ἀπειρίας αὐτῷ συναφαιρούμεθα λόγον. Εἰ δὲ ἄπειρόν τι εἶναι οὐ δύναται, ᾧ ἐξ ἀϊδίου συνυπάρχει ἕτερόν τι κατ' οὐσίαν διάφορον, ἄπειρον εἶναι οὐδαμῶς ἐνδέχεται δυάδα. (*PG* 91, 1184 D5–1185 A11 = CONSTAS, 2014 , 1, p. 302; English translation by Constas, *ibid*., p. 303; pp. 154–156 in the present volume).

remaining infinite thing we have pinpointed is God; that it is matter that has been eliminated from the controversial duality. But on this particular point, I think, Maximus may rely on what he has previously postulated for the eminently infinite thing – that it is also monadic in character, whereby matter is disqualified for good and all.

The rest of Section 41[28] is primarily dedicated by the Confessor to an often hymnic praise of the monad as an unconditioned, relationless (πάσης σχέσεως... ἐξηρημένη), beginningless principle (ἄναρχον and ἀρχή), the first efficient cause (αἰτία... πρώτη), which precedes number. As the monadic God antecedes and at the same time supersedes everything, He is also out of reach for intuition, discursive reasoning and naming alike. God is over and beyond (ἐπέκεινα and ὑπεράνω, even πάντων ἐπέκεινα), hypercategorical and unknowable, essentially by virtue of His relationlessness (ἄσχετον) – the spearhead of Maximus' account of the divine attributes in this latter part of Section 41.

5. Parallel passages in some other works of Maximus

For Maximus, then, infinity understood as illimitability complemented with indivisibility is at least ἐνδεικτικόν, if not παραστατικόν, of God: These attributes point to the one Creator. This coupling has one or two interesting parallels elsewhere in the Confessor's oeuvre, which are worth a brief mention here. One such passage is found in Chapter 1 of the second century of the *200 Chapters on Theology and Incarnation* (also known as the *200 Gnostic Chapters* or *Capita gnostica*; Hans Urs von Balthasar, a major expert, calls them the *200 Gnostische Centurien*).[29] In this terse statement, Maximus links up divine unicity with beginninglessness, simplicity, supraessentiality, partlessness, and indivisibility, by virtue of the implicit oneness of these properties: Εἷς Θεός, ὅτι μία θεότης· μονὰς ἄναρχος καὶ ἁπλῆ καὶ ὑπερούσιος· καὶ ἀμερὴς καὶ ἀδιαίρετος.[30] Although ἄπειρον itself is conspicuously missing from this particular list, all listed attributes come forward in an interconnected logical formation, as in the theology of *Ambiguum* 10.

[28]   That is, the text parts from p. 304 in CONSTAS, 2014, I = *PG* 91, 1185 B2–1188 A1.
[29]   H. U. von BALTHASAR, *Kosmische Liturgie. Das Weltbild Maximus' des Bekenners*, Einsiedeln – Trier, 1988, pp. 482–643.
[30]   *PG* 90, 1124 D12–1125 A2.

Again, a similar analytical transition from the concept of the super-eminent One to its relationlessness, and thence to its infinity and beginninglessness, all propped up by the unicity deriving from the One's simplicity, is found in Chapter 3 of the dubious *Moscow Gnostic Century* (*CPG Suppl.*, 7707, 11).[31] In logical terms, indivisibility and infinity are seen here as interdependent core attributes of God, very much like in *Ambiguum* 10.[32]

Lastly, the short *Ambiguum* 1,[33] on Gregory of Nazianzus' *Sermon* 29 (the 1st Sermon on the Son) and *Sermon* 22 (the 2nd Sermon on Peace), also places the divine monad in opposition to the dyad but in a trinitarian theological, rather than philosophical, analysis. Here, ἄπειρον, technically synonymous with πλῆθος, carries a strongly negative connotation as a non-divine quality. On the other hand, immobility, incorporeality, beginninglessness, supraessentiality, and supra-infinity (ὑπεράπειρος), figuring here as divine attributes, are all motifs well known from *Ambiguum* 10. All this is to say that indivisibility (or irreductibility), infinity (or unrestrictability), and unicity, inextricably interconnected in a logical structure, are apparently the constant metaphysical formula for Maximus – one that is capable of representing a God who is Himself beyond comprehension.

---

[31] Τὸ πάντῃ καὶ κυρίως ἓν οὐκ ἔχει διαφοράν· τὸ δὲ μὴ ἔχον διαφοράν, καὶ πάσης ἐκτός ἐστι σχέσεως· τὸ δὲ σχέσιν οὐκ ἔχον, καὶ ἄπειρον πάντως καὶ ἄναρχον· οὐκοῦν μόνον τὸ θεῖον ἄναρχον καὶ ἄπειρον καὶ ἄσχετον καὶ ἀδιάφορον, ὅτι καὶ μονώτατον φύσει κυρίως ἕν, ὡς ἁπλοῦν. (S. L. Epifanovič, *Materialy k izučeniyu žizni i tvoreniy prep. Maksima Ispovednika*, Kiev, 1917, pp. 33–56: "Glavy gnostičeskiya", p. 34). See also P. Sherwood, *An Annotated Date-List of the Works of Maximus the Confessor*, Rome, 1952 (Studia Anselmiana, fasc. 30), p. 24

[32] *The Oxford Handbook of Maximus the Confessor* is reticent on the authorship of the *100 capita gnostica*, see M. Jankowiak & Phil Booth, "A New Date-List of the Works of Maximus the Confessor" in *OHMC*, pp. 19–83. See also von Balthasar's opinion of this collection, which he styles as the "Moskauer Centurien", in his *Kosmische Liturgie*, chapter "Reduktion des Dualismus auf die Einheit", section "Dyas und Monas", pp. 631–638, more specifically p. 635.

[33] *PG* 91, 1033 D1–1036 A14 = Constas, 2014, 1, pp. 6–10.

Conclusion: Maximus' philosophical sources and objectives

It may be clear by now that, while Maximus' elaboration on the concept of infinity is partially directed against Platonism and Aristotelianism (insofar as it contests the eternity of matter), yet Section 41 (*PG* 91, 1184 D–1188 D) is a thoroughly Platonic elaboration on God as the infinite One.[34] True, Maximus has a precursor right before his eyes: Gregory himself, precisely before the commented lemma of *Sermon* 21, had already relied at length on Plato's analogy of the Sun in order to illustrate the relationship between God and the spiritual realm[35] – even though he targeted Plato's theory of ideas as a doctrine to be avoided in § 10 of *Sermon* 27 (the 1st sermon on theology). But whilst the doctrine of the supraessentiality and efficient causality of the first principle is certainly omnipresent in Maximus' *Ambiguum* 10, I think it is reasonable to believe that his philosophical inspiration, especially on account of his repeated arguments concerning number, may reach even further – to the First and Second Hypotheses of the *Parmenides*.

Again, that God is eternal (*Physica* VIII, 6 = 258 B16 259 A5), immobile (VIII, 5 = 256B20–258B9), indivisible (VIII, 10 = 266 A10–267 B26), etc., is also well-known Aristotelian theological doctrine (see further *Metaphysics* XII, 7 = 1073 A3–13). This is rehashed by Proclus in the final conclusions of Book II of his *Elements of Physics* (perhaps known to Maximus), where Proclus adds "infinite power", ἄπειρον δύναμιν to the list of divine attributes.[36] Still further, as Maximus actually describes God as being "beyond all" (ὡς πάντων ἐπέκεινα)[37] one should not overlook Plotinus' *Treatise 10* (*Ennead* 5, 1, 6) where the One is asserted to be ἐπέκεινα πάντων. Last, but not least, Part 13 of *On the Divine Names* by Dionysius the Areopagite is likewise an important source for the

---

[34] On Maximus' relation to Platonism in general, see Marius PORTARU's study titled "Classical Philosophical Influences: Aristotle and Platonism", in *OHMC*, pp. 127–148.

[35] *Sermon 21*, § 1 = *PG* 35, 1084 A10 – B6.

[36] τὸ δὴ Α < = τὸ κινοῦν τὴν πρώτην κίνησιν> εἰ ἔστι πρῶτον κινοῦν, ἀκίνητον ἔσται· τῶν γὰρ κινούντων πάντων ἡγεῖται τὸ ἀκίνητον. καὶ ἐπεὶ ἀίδιον κίνησιν κινεῖ, δύναμιν ἔχει τοῦ κινεῖν ἄπειρον· αἱ γὰρ πεπερασμέναι δυνάμεις καὶ τὰς ἐνεργείας ἔχουσι πεπερασμένας· ἀπὸ γὰρ τῆς δυνάμεως ἡ ἐνέργεια, ὥστ', εἰ αὐτὴ ἄπειρος, καὶ ἡ δύναμις. (*Institutio physica*, Book II, demonstration of thesis 21).

[37] *PG* 91, 1185 D9 = CONSTAS, 2014, I, p. 306.

Confessor, with its strong accent on divine infinity understood mainly as irrepressible productivity. In Section 42 (*PG* 91, 1188 D–1193 C) of *Ambiguum* 10, Dionysius' direct influence is also perceptible on how Maximus characterizes divine providence, and on specific divine attributes, some of which may be direct borrowings from *On the Divine Names* (e.g., ὑπερδύναμος, ὑπεράγαθος, ὑπέρσοφος).

It is perhaps not illegitimate to say that for Sections 40–41 (*PG* 91, 1184 B–1188 D) of *Ambiguum* 10 this distinguished philosophical heritage comes with baggage – for like the Neoplatonists, Maximus must strike a balance between the supereminent and the beneficent aspects of the first principle. Hence, the philosophically problematic upshot of the sections we have discussed, and *Ambiguum* 10 in general, is that Maximus is not ready to give up either aspect of God: neither the unrelated (ἄσχετος), nor the related (providential) aspect. This is because the philosophical theology of *Ambiguum* 10 is complemented by, or better, preceded by the articulate Christology of *Ambiguum* 5, with the doctrine of Incarnation and περιχώρησις, as well as by the mysticism and eschatology of *Ambiguum* 7. Which is to say that the miracle of God does not terminate at His ontological difference but only as it were "kicks off" there – because what is really unconceivable about God, and to be received only by faith, is that He is willing to transcend His own transcendence and condescend into immanence.

Wisdom in Maximus the Confessor's
Ambiguum 10.19[*]

Vladimir Cvetković

(*Belgrade – Bogotá*)

Ivan Nišavić

(*Belgrade*)

The topic of wisdom in St. Maximus the Confessor remains under-researched, despite the fact that it pervades all aspects of Maximus' voluminous work and, as Marcus Plested notes, constitutes a "master theme" of Maximus' theological vision.[1] This paper represents a modest contribution to the elucidation of wisdom in Maximus, with a special focus on the role of wisdom in his *Ambiguum* 10.19. Before embarking upon an analysis of wisdom in *Ambiguum* 10.19, it is important to mention three influential interpretations of wisdom in contemporary Maximian studies. Next, we intend to investigate, within the context of wisdom, the origin, meaning and purpose of Maximus' five modes of contemplation in *Ambiguum* 10.19; namely, movement, difference, mixture and position. Finally, we will analyze in parallel two pyramidal architectonical arrangements in which wisdom occupies a prominent place – one from *Ambiguum* 10.19, and another from *Mystagogia* 1–5, particularly *Mystagogia* 5.

---

[*] This research was realized with the support of the Science Fund of the Republic of Serbia, #GRANT No 1554, *Assessing Neoplatonism in the 14th and 15th century Balkans – ANEB* and the support of the Ministry of Science, Technological Development and Innovation of the Republic of Serbia, according to the Agreement on the realisation and financing of scientific research 451-03-66/2024-03/ 200025.

[1] M. PLESTED, "Wisdom in St. Maximus the Confessor", *SP* 42 (2006), pp. 205–209: 205.

Ambiguum *10 of Maximus the Confessor in Modern Study: Papers Collected on the Occasion of the Budapest Colloquium on Saint Maximus, 3–4 February 2021*, ed. by Alexis LÉONAS & Vladimir CVETKOVIĆ, with the collaboration of Daniel HEIDE, Turnhout, 2025 (IPM 97), pp. 317–339

10.1484/M.IPM-EB.5.141867

We would like to begin analyzing is Marcus Plested's view on wisdom, first developed in his article "Wisdom in St. Maximus the Confessor", and subsequently elaborated in his recent monograph *Wisdom in Christian Tradition*. Plested stresses several important aspects of this multifaceted and multivalent notion in Maximus. He acknowledges Maximus' distinction first between divine wisdom and human wisdom,[2] and then between the contemplative and practical wisdom that constitutes human wisdom.[3] He refers to the prologue to the *Ambigua to Thomas*, where Maximus distinguishes between wisdom, and "the beauty of wisdom" as knowledge in practice. Furthermore, on the basis of several passages from *Ambiguum* 10, Plested substantiates his claim that true philosophy as the love of wisdom is erroneous if it is not simultaneously practical and intellectual.[4] Commenting on the passages from *Ad Thalassium* 63,[5] Plested claims that wisdom is the unifying action of the *energeia* of the Holy Trinity, and is not only associated with the Son.[6] His claim is correct in affirming that St. Maximus holds that the divine energies belong equally to all three divine persons. Moreover, the example that Plested quotes from *Ad Thalassium* 63 proves that the Holy Spirit completes and perfects the divine activity, which springs from the Father, and passes through the Son.

The second interpretation of wisdom in St. Maximus consists of Paul Blowers' bold identification of Wisdom with the activity of Christ the Logos, in his monograph *Maximus the Confessor: Jesus Christ and the Transfiguration of the* World. Blowers acknowledges Maximus' understanding of divine wisdom and the true *philosophia* as a perennial quest for divine wisdom, constituted by monastic training and the reorientation of desire and will to the image of Christ.[7] Blowers is more keen developing the theme of divine wisdom. According to Blow-

---

[2] M. PLESTED, *Wisdom in Christian Tradition: The Patristic Roots of Modern Russian Sophiology*, Oxford, 2022, pp. 175–177.

[3] PLESTED, *Wisdom in Christian Tradition*, p. 178.

[4] PLESTED, "Wisdom in St. Maximus the Confessor", 206; PLESTED, *Wisdom in Christian Tradition*, p. 178.

[5] Maximus the Confessor, *Q.Thal*. 63 in *CCSG* 22, p. 219.

[6] PLESTED, "Wisdom in St. Maximus the Confessor", p. 208; PLESTED, *Wisdom in Christian Tradition*, p. 180.

[7] P. BLOWERS, *Maximus the Confessor: Jesus Christ and the Transfiguration of the World*, Oxford, 2016, p. 68.

ers, the Logos of God is embodied in creation as an imitation of divine Wisdom, and in salvation as a stabilizer of chaos, which is used as the raw material for an ever new creation.[8] Blowers rightly identifies wisdom with the activity of the Logos and Wisdom of God embodied in the structured order of creation as the one Logos and the many *logoi*, and realized in salvation as Christ's uniting the logos of nature with its proper mode, or tropos, of existence.

The third and final account of wisdom in Maximus is one proposed by Andrew Louth, who defines created wisdom (to recall Sergius Bulgakov's famous distinction between uncreated and created, or divine and creaturely wisdom)[9] as a virtue that sums up all other virtues.[10] Louth differentiates between two wisdoms: the Son and Logos as the uncreated Wisdom of God, and wisdom as that, by which human beings apprehend God. The first wisdom is omnipresent through Christ as the Wisdom of God, while the second wisdom, usually coupled in Maximus' language with knowledge (γνῶσις) and power (δύναμις), constitutes the entrance of human beings into the mystery of the Wisdom of God. In his article, "Sophia, the Wisdom of God, in St. Maximos the Confessor", Louth commences his investigation of wisdom by analyzing Maximus' *Centuries on Love*, followed by his *Responses to Thalassios* and *Ambiguum* 71, while concluding with Maximus' *Mystagogia* 1–5.[11] He elaborates the role of wisdom in epistemology and the virtues, and places wisdom in the context of liturgy. In contrast to Plested, for whom Maximus' sophiology is a "master theme",[12] Louth claims that there is nothing very obvious in St. Maximus' view of wisdom.[13]

---

[8]   BLOWERS, *Maximus the Confessor*, p. 109.

[9]   S. BULGAKOV, "The Wisdom of God", in *A Bulgakov's Antology*, ed. by J. PAIN & N. ZERNOV, London, 1976, pp. 144–156: 154–156.

[10]   A. LOUTH, "Readings and Misreadings of *Maximus the Confessor* by Paul Blowers", *Symposium*, at: https://syndicate.network/symposia/theology/maximus-the-confessor/.

[11]   A. LOUTH, "Sophia, the Wisdom of God, in St. Maximos the Confessor", in *Sophia: The Wisdom of God – Die Weisheit Gottes*, ed. by T. HAINTHALER *et al.*, Innsbruck – Vienna, 2017, pp. 349–358'.

[12]   PLESTED, "Wisdom in St. Maximus the Confessor", p. 205.

[13]   LOUTH, "Sophia, the Wisdom of God, in St. Maximos the Confessor", p. 250.

Let us begin our investigation of Maximus' sophiology with the relationship between the virtues and wisdom which, according to Louth, represents the cornerstone of Maximus' architecture of wisdom. In the *Second Letter to Thomas*, Maximus explains the link between wisdom and the virtues:

> Ὑπόστασιν μὲν σοφίας τὴν ἀρετὴν, οὐσίαν δὲ φασὶν ἀρετῆς εἶναι τὴν σοφίαν. Διὸ τῆς μὲν σοφίας ἀπλανὴς ἔκφανσίς ἐστιν, ὁ τρόπος τῆς τῶν θεωρητικῶν ἀγωγῆς, τῆς ἀρετῆς δὲ στερέμνιος βάσις ὁ λόγος τῆς τῶν πρακτικῶν θεορίας καθέστηκεν.[14]

> > They say that virtue is the real instantiation of wisdom, and that wisdom is the essence of virtue. Thus, the manner of life of those who practice contemplation is an unwavering demonstration of wisdom, and the principle of contemplation of those engaged in the practical life is the firmly established foundation of virtue.[15]

By considering only the first sentence, one may conclude that wisdom is manifested only by the virtues in their essence. This may inspire one to perceive virtue not only as necessary, but also as the most exclusive step toward wisdom. However, already in the second sentence Maximus challenges this view by claiming that the logos of contemplation (λόγος τῆς θεωρίας) is the solid basis for virtue. Thus, the development of the virtues necessitates contemplation, just as the virtuous life is a prerequisite for contemplation. Nevertheless, wisdom is demonstrated both in the beauty of wisdom as the practice of the virtues, and in the greatness of creation as the fruits of contemplation, though it is not exhausted by these activities. For Maximus, these two equally cherished activities "are the source of the pure mixture of the worthy ones with God in union".[16] Wisdom is revealed to a much greater extent in the union with God, than in contemplation and in practice of the virtues. Thus, the spiritual advancement toward the union with God is not a two-stage process, but rather consists of three stages.

---

[14]   *Ep.Sec.Th.*, prol., 5–8 in *CCSG* 48, p. 37.
[15]   Maximus the Confessor, *Ambigua to Thomas and Second Letter to Thomas*, trans. by J. LOLLAR, Turnhout 2010, p. 77.
[16]   *Ep.Sec.Th.*, prol. 12–13 (*CCGS* 48, 37); Maximus the Confessor, *Ambigua to Thomas*, 77.

Maximus describes these three stages of salvation as stages of virtue, knowledge, and theology.[17] The first requires courage and chastity in the practice of the virtues; the second requires righteousness, or the right discernment in natural contemplation; while the third requires the full perfection of wisdom. Maximus places these three stages in the context of his exegesis of the Transfiguration by identifying the first stage with Elijah, the second stage with Moses, and the third stage with Christ.[18]

The architecture of wisdom in the aforementioned works is quite simple. Both virtue and contemplation are instantiations of wisdom, and wisdom is their essence. Both virtue and contemplation are founded in wisdom, while virtue is established in contemplation. Thus, the virtuous life becomes the prerequisite for the contemplative life, while both are necessary for the acquisition of wisdom, which is the third stage.

In *Ambiguum* 10.19, which is our present focus, the architecture of wisdom is more complex.[19] Here, Maximus presents the theme of natural contemplation within the context of the five modes: being, movement, difference, mixture and position (οὐσία, κίνησιν, διαφορά, κράσιν, θέσιν).[20] The first three categories provide the knowledge of God as the fashioner, provider and judge, while the other two educate us in virtue and in assimilation to God. For Maximus, being is the teacher of theology (θεολογία), because it reveals the knowledge of God as creator. The movement of creation indicates the divine providence (πρόνοια) over the universe, while the divine judgement (κρίσις) instructs us in the difference in creation. The role of providence is to preserve the unvarying sameness of each of the things in universe and

---

[17] *Th.oec.* II, 16 in *PG* 90, 1132C. The English translation in Maximus the Confessor, *Selected Writings*, ed. and trans. by G. C. BERTHOLD, London. 1985 (Classics of Western Spirituality), p. 151.

[18] *Th.oec.* II, 16. See also *Amb.Ioh.* 10, 31; *PG* 91, 1168AD in CONSTAS, 2014, 1, pp. 268–273.

[19] In the analysis of the Ambiguum 10.19, We mostly rely on: V. CVETKOVIC, "Wisdom in Maximus the Confessor Reconsidered", in *Proceedings of the Conference "St. Emperor Constantine and Christianity"*, vol. 2, ed. by. D. BOJOVIĆ, Niš, 2013, pp. 197–215.

[20] *Amb.Ioh.* 10,19 (*PG* 91, 1133AB; CONSTAS, 2014, 1, pp. 202–205, *supra*, p. 72).

to preserve the universe in accordance with the *logoi* of which it consists. For Maximus, the role of providence is to hold the whole creation and every single being within the unity of God, and to preserve this unity amongst themselves. As judgment is indicative of difference the role of judgment is to preserve the wise distribution of beings, "which assures that all beings, consistent with the principles according to which they were created, possess an inviolable and unchanging equilibrium in their natural identity".[21] For Maximus mixture is the synthesis of the mind and the virtues which constitutes the intelligible cosmos, while position is the inclination and fixedness of the mind in the good.[22]

According to Maximus, the unification of position with motion, and mixture with difference led saints, through their contemplation of being, motion and difference, to understand that the cause "exists, it is wise and it is living" (εἶναι καὶ σοφόν εἶναι καὶ ζῶν).[23] By identifying God the Father with existence or being, the Son with divine wisdom, and the Holy Spirit with life, Maximus introduces wisdom into the entire scheme. Thus, it appears that the inner structure of creation reflects the inner structure of the Holy Trinity.

By considering the whole creation first from the perspective of position and then from the perspective difference, Maximus further reduces the five modes of contemplation. If the creation is beheld from the view of position, the five modes of contemplation are reduced to three domains of contemplation that correspond to earth, heaven, and what is between them (ἐξ οὐρανοῦ καί γῆς καί τῶν ἐν μέσῳ).[24]

Maximus identifies the contemplation of heaven, earth and what is between them with the domains of ethical, natural and theological philosophy, but it is unclear which philosophy corresponds to which contemplation. Thus, for Michael Harrington, natural philosophy deals with the earth; ethical philosophy deals with the people who live on the earth and theological philosophy deals with the sky or heaven.[25]

---

[21] *Amb.Ioh.* 10,19 (*PG* 91, 1133D; CONSTAS, 2014, I, pp. 206–207, *supra*, p. 76).

[22] *Amb.Ioh.* 10,19 (*PG* 91 1136B; CONSTAS, 2014, I, pp. 206–209, *supra*, p. 76).

[23] *Amb.Ioh.* 10,19 (*PG* 91, 1136B; CONSTAS, 2014, I, pp. 208–209, *supra*, p. 78).

[24] *Amb.Ioh.* 10,19 (*PG* 91, 1136C; CONSTAS, 2014, I, pp. 208–209, *supra*, p. 78).

[25] M. HARRINGTON, "Creation and Natural Contemplation in Maximus the Confessor's *Ambiguum* 10:19", in *Divine Creation in Ancient, Medieval, and Early Modern* Thought, ed. by W. OTTEN, W. HANNAM, & M. TRESCHOW, Leiden, 191–212: 206.

We are inclined to disagree here with Harrington and rather to connect earth with ethical philosophy, which for Maximus pertains to ascetic practices,[26] and to connect what is between earth and heaven with natural philosophy. In *Ad Thalassium* 5, Maximus identifies the "earth" with purification of the heart by ascetic practice, i.e. ethical philosophy; the "grass", which grows from the earth towards heaven, with natural contemplation, or natural philosophy; and the "bread" with the initiation into the mystery of theology, or theological philosophy.[27] Therefore, the contemplation of earth is to be found within the domain of ethical philosophy, the contemplation of beings living between earth and heaven is in the domain of natural philosophy, and finally the contemplation of heaven is in the domain of theological philosophy. These three modes of philosophy resemble the above-mentioned three stages that lead to salvation: of the virtues, of natural knowledge and of theology.

By considering the creation from the perspective of difference Maximus reduces these three modes of contemplations, dealing with earth, heaven and what is in between, to two modes of contemplation; namely, to what is contained and what is containing. Heaven is the containing principle containing what is beneath it, i.e. both earth and what is between earth and heaven. Thus, the three modes of contemplation, that is ethical, natural and theological philosophy are reduced to two modes, namely philosophy (φιλοσοφία) and wisdom (σοφία).[28] While wisdom "both receives all the pious ways attributed to it and as befits the divine and encloses within itself the mystical and natural essential ideas pertaining to realities", and philosophy "as constitutive of moral practice and mentality, of practical life and contemplation, and of virtue and knowledge, also refers to wisdom as its cause".[29]

Wisdom is revealed here in the ontological structure of the *logoi* of creation that are united in one logos of being of substance, which in its final instance leads to the divine Logos. Therefore, Maximus claims that many *logoi* are one Logos of God due to His converting and hand-lead-

---

[26] *Amb.Ioh.* 10,44 (*PG* 91, 1200A; CONSTAS, 2014, I, pp. 328–329, *supra*, p. 180).

[27] *Q.Thal.* 5, in *CCSG* 7, pp. 67, 40–45. See also CONSTAS, 2018, p. 107.

[28] *Amb.Ioh.* 10,19 (*PG* 91, 1136C; CONSTAS, 2014, I, pp. 208–211, *supra*, p. 78).

[29] *Amb.Ioh.* 10,19 (*PG* 91, 1136CD; CONSTAS, 2014, I, pp. 210–211, *supra*, p. 78; Lollar, *supra*, p. 79).

ing transference and providence (ἐπιστρεπτικὴ καὶ χειραγωγικὴ ἀναφορά τε καὶ πρόνοια).[30] Wisdom, or the state of wisdom, reveals the perfect unity of creation without confusing their parts, and at the same time it preserves the distinctions between beings, without separating or dividing them one from another.[31] By his insistence on the term "undivided" (ἀδιαίρετος), Maximus preserves the unity of the *logoi* among them, and with the one Logos, while by the insistence on the term "unconfused" (ἀσύγχυτος), he establishes all the beings as unique.

There is value in Harrington's remark that the difference between wisdom and philosophy is actually the difference between the state of wisdom and the love of wisdom.[32] The state of wisdom is order revealed in the structure of creation, while the love of wisdom represents the inclination of individual rational beings to act in accordance with their proper *logoi*, thus fulfilling the purpose of their existence; namely, of aligning themselves with the divine design. Unlike wisdom, which is transparent in its fullness, the love of wisdom, or philosophy, is wisdom in *via*. The true philosophy always tends towards the attainment of divine wisdom. According to Maximus' description, the transformation of the love of wisdom into the state of wisdom is effected through uniting the practical with the contemplative faculties in each rational being. Thus, by uniting the practical aspects of philosophy such as character (ἦθος), activity (πρᾶξις) and virtue (ἀρετή), with the contemplative aspects of philosophy such as inclination (γνώμη), contemplation (θεωρία) and knowledge (γνῶσις), the lover of wisdom appropriates the state of wisdom.[33] The epistemological process of transforming philosophy into wisdom is simultaneously the ontological process of preserving the mode of existence consistent with the natural logos.[34]

Therefore, Andrew Louth argues that the ascetic struggle which recovers the dispassion enabling us to practice natural contemplation, prevents the mode (τρόπος) from running counter to its fundamental logos.[35] While the creation of the universal essences designed accord-

---

[30] *Amb.Ioh.* 7 (*PG* 91, 1081C; CONSTAS, 2014, I, pp. 100–101).

[31] *Amb.Ioh.* 7 (*PG* 91, 1077C; CONSTAS, 2014, I, pp. 94–95).

[32] HARRINGTON, "Creation and Natural Contemplation", p. 208.

[33] *Amb.Ioh.* 10,19 (*PG* 91, 1136D; CONSTAS, 2014, I, pp. 210–211, *supra*, p. 78).

[34] *Amb.Th.* 5 (*CCSG* 48, 3, 99–104).

[35] A. LOUTH, *Maximus*, pp. 57–58.

ing to universal *logoi* bears the stamp of divine wisdom, the providence over the individual rational beings attains the state of wisdom when the personal inclination of these beings is reconciled with their particular *logoi*.

Finally, by considering the whole creation from the perspective of mixture, the mind is led through a single, harmonious cosmos to the Creator Logos, who reduces the two modes of contemplation into one mode. Thus, passing by simple movement through the many *logoi* of being, the *logoi* of providence and judgment, as well as the *logoi* of the virtues, the mind arrives at the cause of all these *logoi*, the One Logos of God.

Being the source of all *logoi*, the Logos of God is equally the source of all five modes of contemplation, as well as their final perfection:

> Θεὸν κυρίως εἶναι λοιπὸν ἐκ τῆς πρὸς τὰ ὄντα ἀκριβοῦς ἐνατενίσεως, καὶ οὐσίαν τῶν ὄντων καὶ κίνησιν καὶ τῶν διαφερόντων εὐκρίνειαν, καὶ συνοχὴν ἀδιάλυτον τῶν κεκραμμένων, καὶ ἵδρυσιν ἀμετάθετον τῶν τεθειμένων, καὶ πάσης ἁπλῶς τῆς ὁπωσοῦν νοουμένης οὐσίας, καὶ κινήσεως καὶ διαφορᾶς, κράσεώς τε καὶ θέσεως αἴτιον.[36]

>> God alone truly is and is the essence and motion of beings, the clear distinction of different things, the insoluble continuity of things that have been mixed together, and inmovable foundation of what has been established and that, in his simplicity, He is the cause of every essence, motion, distinction, mixture and placement (=position) that can be thought in any way whatsoever.

The origin of Maximus' five modes of contemplation still puzzles Maximian scholars. Despite admitting that their origin is hard to detect, Louth proposes that the "five greatest kinds", that is being, rest, motion, sameness and difference, from Plato's *Sophist* (254D–255C) might be a point of departure for this research.[37] Although the five modes of contemplation might be far beyond the Platonic and Neoplatonic heritage evident in Maximus,[38] we would nevertheless propose Porphyry's five logical predicates from his *Isagoge*, as a starting point for research

---

[36] *Amb.Ioh.* 10,19 (*PG* 91, 1137A, CONSTAS, 2014, 1, pp. 210–211, *supra*, p. 80; Lollar, *supra*, p. 81).

[37] LOUTH, *Maximus the Confessor*, p. 205, n. 46.

[38] S. E. GERSH, *Κίνησις ἀκίνητος: A Study of Spiritual Motion in the Philosophy of Proclus*, Leiden, 1973, pp. 19–20.

into the origins of Maximus' five modes. Maximus was among the few Christian theologians, such as Boethius and Philoponus, who wrote commentaries on Porphyry's *Isagoge* and Aristotle's *Categories*,[39] as his work *On the Isagoge of Porphyry and Categories of Aristotle* (*Additamentum* 34) confirms.[40]

While Porphyry employs the five logical predicates in defining specific things, Maximus transforms them into the five modes of philosophical contemplation, whereby one obtains knowledge of both the creation and the Creator. The five logical predicates in Porphyry, namely genus, species, difference, property, and accident (γένος, εἶδος, διαφορά, ἴδιον, συμβεβηκός) correspond to the five modes on natural contemplation; that is, being, movement, difference, mixture, and position in Maximus. Both Porphyry and Maximus consider being or substance as the highest genus. As species in Porphyry refers to certain divisions within one genus, for Maximus this process of division is described as the expanding movement of substance.[41] As such, he identifies species with the movement of expansion (διαστολή) within substance. Porphyry employs the category of difference to distinguish between the different species in one genus, while for Maximus difference serves to indicate the results of different movements within one substance.

Despite the fact that the predicates "property" and "accident" in Porphyry are terminologically different from Maximus' modes of mixture and position, they may point to the same thing. For Porphyry, property points to the innate substance, or essence, of each individual nature, such as rationality *qua* the distinctive characteristic of the human nature when compared with other sensible natures. Although the similarity between "property" in Porphyry and "mixture" in Maximus may not be recognized at the first glance, they point to the innate property of each nature or, according to Maximus, its *logos*. The knowledge of nature from the point of mixture or composition is not a passive process, or recognition of certain natural properties by mind or reason, but rather a transformation of the knower who, by mixing virtues with

---

[39] M. JANKOWIAK & P. BOOTH, "A New Date-List of the Works of Maximus the Confessor", in *OHMC*, pp. 19–83.

[40] B. ROOSEN, *Epifanovitch Revisited*, vol. 3. (PhD thesis), Leuven, 2001.

[41] *Amb.Ioh.* 10,37 (*PG* 91, 1177BC; CONSTAS, 2014, I, pp. 288–289, *supra*, p. 144).

mind, obtains the knowledge of the logos of each particular nature.[42] Mixture refers actually to the mixture between theological, natural and ethical philosophy, which provides a knower with the potential to discern in sensible nature the divine intention, or logos, of each thing, and this logos represents the innermost property of this thing. Accident in Porphyry points to those characteristics of a thing that are not fixed, but variable, like the skin colour of human beings, while position in Maximus corresponds to accident in Porphyry.

According to Maximus, "position is teacher of character".[43] However, as in the case of mixture, position is chosen by an inclination of the mind which, on the basis of reason, can understand and accept any kind of change, granted it is fixed in the good. The mentioned change pertains to variety that exists within certain species or nature. If the species within one genus are distinguished on the basis of difference in properties, the individuals within one species are distinguished on the basis of difference in accidents. Thus, the human being is distinguished from the other animals by being "rational animal, mortal, receptive of intellect and science, walking upright and having flat nails".[44] These characteristics are necessary to human species. However, one can distinguish Peter from Paul on the basis of Peter's curly white hair and beard, which are different from Paul's baldness and long dark beard. The whiteness or darkness of hair or beard, or curliness or baldness are accidental characteristics of human beings, but they appear as necessary in order to differentiate human individuals. Maximus again elevates the whole issue to the level of the *logoi*. Mixture helps the knower to distinguish between the *logoi* of different species, and to understand their innate nature in accordance with the divine intention for this particular nature, or species. Position, however, equips the knower with discernment what the individual logos of each rational created being

---

[42] HARRINGTON, "Creation and Natural Contemplation", p. 203.

[43] LOUTH, *Maximus*, p. 114.

[44] Maximus the Confessor, *Add.* 34. The English translation of *On the Isagoge of Porphyry and on the Categories of Aristotle* by Torstein T. Tollefsen is available in T. T. TOLLEFSEN, "St. Maximus the Confessor and Alexandrian Logic – some Observations", in *Philosophos – Philotheos – Philoponos: Studies and Essays as Charisteria in Honor of Professor Bogoljub Šijaković on the Occasion of His 65th Birthday*, ed. by M. KNEŽEVIĆ, Belgrade – Podgorica, 2021, pp. 296–304: 302.

is; that is, to understand what the divine intention was in creating this particular person and, by fixing his or her mind in goodness, to attain the logos of well-being.

The further similarity between Porphyry's five predicates and Maximus' five modes of contemplation is that Porphyry proposes the unification of (as well as the differentiation between) species and property and of difference and accident, while Maximus proposes the unification of position and motion, and of mixture and difference. According to Porphyry, "species are present equally in what participates in them",[45] that is, species are equally present in the properties that participate in them. Similarly, "common to difference and accidents is the fact that they are said of several items",[46] i.e. inseparable accidents are always present in that which constitutes difference. Since properties and accidents are always contained by species and difference, the five predicates can be reduced to three: genus, species and difference.

The unification of position and motion, and of mixture and difference in Maximus has similar results to Porphyry. The unification and combination of these two pairs leads to the understanding that all things subsist in terms of being, difference, and motion.

The further unification in Porphyry is between genus, species and difference. Genus contains species under it,[47] while also containing the difference potentially.[48] Differences are prior to their species,[49] but both of them are participated equally. The model with the genus on the top, followed by species differentiated on the basis of common property, and ending with particular individuals differentiated on the basis of accidents is known as the Porphyrian tree.[50] Porphyry substantiates this model with the following example:

---

[45] Porphyry, *Isagoge* 14, in *Porphyrii Isagoge et in Aristotelis Categorias commentarium*, ed. by A. P. Busse, Berlin, 1887 (*CAG* 4/1), p. 20,15–16 See also English translation of Johnathan Barnes in Porphyry, *Introduction*, Oxford, 2003, p. 17.

[46] Porphyry, *Isagoge* 13 (*CAG* 4/1, 19,15–17); Porphyry, *Introduction*, p. 17.

[47] Porphyry, *Isagoge* 8 (CAG 4/1, 15,23–24); Porphyry, *Introduction*, 14.

[48] Porphyry, *Isagoge* 7 (CAG 4/1, 14,21–23); Porphyry, *Introduction*, 13.

[49] Porphyry, *Isagoge* 11 (CAG 4/1, 18,23); Porphyry, *Introduction*, 13.

[50] See V. CVETKOVIĆ, "*Logoi*, Porphyrian Tree and Maximus the Confessor's Rethinking of Aristotelian Logic", in *Aristotle in Byzantium*, ed. by M. KNEŽEVIĆ, Alhambra, CA, 2020, pp. 149–173.

> Substance is itself a genus. Under it is body, and under body animate body, under which is animal; under animal is rational animal, under which is man; and under man are Socrates and Plato and particular men.[51]

Maximus is familiar with the Porphyrian tree as evident from *Ambiguum* 10.37, where he describes the movements of expansion (διαστολή) and contraction (συστολή) within substance. The process of expansion (διαστολή) is a downward movement from the most generic genus (γενικώτατον γένος), through more generic genera (γενικώτερα γένη), particular species (εἴδη) and most specific species (εἰδικώτατα εἴδη),[52] to the individuals (ἄτομα) and accidents (συμβεβηκότα). The process of contraction is the reverse movement directed upward, beginning from individuals, passing through generals and ending with the most general substance. Torstein Tollefsen rightly remarks that the movements of expansion and contraction do not only offer the solution to the problem of the relationship between universals and individuals, but they also establish an ontologically constitutive relation or an ontological arrangement.[53]

Maximus probably had in mind the Porphyrian tree when he structured five modes of natural contemplation in relation to God. However, Maximus replaces substance or being with God, who resides at the top of the hierarchy and is participated by lower realities.

Late antiquity knew three models of participation: Platonic, which allows differences in nature, or essence, between the participated and participating realities; Aristotelian, which allows participation only in beings that have the same nature or essence; and Neoplatonic, which represents a combination of these two models.[54] According to the Platonic

---

[51] Porphyry, *Isagoge* 2 (CAG 4/1, 4, 22–25); Porphyry, *Introduction*, 6.

[52] *Amb.Ioh.* 10,37 (*PG* 91, 1177BC; *supra*, p. 144).

[53] T. T. TOLLEFSEN, *The Christocentric Cosmology of St. Maximus the Confessor*, Oxford, 2008, p. 78.

[54] D. BIRIUKOV, "Hierarchies of Beings in the Patristic Thought: Maximus the Confessor, John of Damascus, and the Palamites", *Scrinium* 10 (2014), 281–304; D. BIRIUKOV, "Hierarchies of Beings in the Patristic Thought: Gregory of Nyssa and Dionysius the Areopagite", in *The Ways of Byzantine Philosophy*, ed. by M. KNEŽEVIĆ, Alhambra, CA, 2015, pp. 75–76. See also V. CVETKOVIĆ, "Maximus the Confessor's View on Participation Reconsidered", in *A Saint for East and West: Maximus the Confessor's Contribution to Eastern and Western Christian Theology*, ed. by D. HAYNES, Eugene, OR, 2019, pp. 231–244.

understanding of participation, there is the participation of the objects of the physical world in the ideas.[55] Thus, for example, the drawing of a house, the model of a house, the real house and the idea of a house have different ontological natures and stand in a hierarchical relationship. So the idea of the house is at the top of the hierarchy, followed by the real house as the image of the idea of the house. At the bottom of the hierarchy is a drawing or a model of the house as the image of the image, or as the shadow of the idea of house. In Aristotelianism, a model of hierarchy is established only between ontologically identical realities, as is the case with the Porphyrian tree.[56] Thus, different individuals like Socrates and Plato belong to a common human species which together with other animals or plants belongs to the genus of living beings. Hierarchy is set up in such a way that the most general or universal concepts, such as materiality, rationality or being itself, are at the top of the hierarchical ladder, while individuals, such as Plato or Socrates with their individual characteristics, e.g., their crooked nose, or eloquence, are at the very bottom of this ladder. The Neoplatonic, and especially the Proclean,[57] model of participation emerges as a combination of these two models and is based on the following triad: unparticipated, participated, and participating. The dialectical pair "unparticipated" – "participated" refers to beings of different essence or nature, while the pair "participated" – "participating" refers to beings of the same nature or essence. At the top of the hierarchical ladder in Proclus is the One, in which nothing participates, followed by a Being, which does not participate in anything but is participated by Life at the lower level. The levels of beings such as Life, Mind, Soul, as well as the material world, participate in higher realities even as lower realities participate in them. At the bottom of the ladder is matter that participates in the higher reality, but nothing participates in it.

Maximus navigates between the existing philosophical solutions of participation. Maximus does not employ the Neoplatonic model of participation, promulgated by Proclus and accepted by Dionysius the Areopagite. Instead, he makes God the participated reality, despite the fact that he is ontologically different from participating realities. How-

---

[55] Biriukov, "Hierarchies of Beings in the Patristic Thought", p. 284.
[56] Biriukov, "Hierarchies of Beings in the Patristic Thought", p. 284.
[57] Biriukov, "Hierarchies of Beings in the Patristic Thought", p. 284.

ever, this is not a direct participation, but rather participation which is approved by the participated reality. Let us see how this works.

In the five modes of contemplation, namely being, movement, difference, mixture and position, the first three modes pertain to the divine creative, providential and judging activities, while the last two relate to the human ability to unite the mind with the virtues, and to direct and fix such a virtuous mind in the good. Now, there are various combinations regarding how to proceed further up. For example, saints are capable of uniting position with motion, and mixture with difference. This means that they unite the fixedness of their virtuous minds in the good with the divine providence, i.e., the divine preservation of the universe in accordance with the *logoi* of which it consists. Moreover, saints unite mind and virtue with the divine judgement, or the preservation of the natural identity of beings and their conformity to the *logoi* according to which they were created. Simply put, the human mind permeated by the virtues simultaneously grasps the grand divine design of the universe and its purpose, as well as the purpose of each particular being in this divine plan. Therefore, the immediate gift of knowledge of God as the one who exists, the one who is wise and the one who is living, points to the Trinitarian nature of God, i.e. the Father as cause of divine being, the Son as the Wisdom of God in creation and the Holy Spirit as the giver of life. This is the most direct path that leads to God.

Maximus proposes another, less demanding, path. This path has the same trajectory as the first one, but contains a few more steps. If position is united with difference, or the fixedness of mind in the good with the divine judgement concerning the natural identity of each particular being constituted by its logos, then the five modes of contemplation are reduced to three; namely, ethical, natural and theological philosophy focused on earth, the beings between earth and heaven, and heaven respectively. If the whole creation is seen again from the perspective of difference, or divine judgement, all three aforementioned philosophies merge into a single philosophy, and earth and the beings between earth and heaven are contained by heaven. Thus, the three modes are reduced to two modes, namely philosophy (φιλοσοφία) and wisdom (σοφία). The task of philosophy is to unite all human intellectual and rational capacities such as character and choice, practice and contemplation, virtue and knowledge, and to direct them towards wisdom. Wisdom appears as the wise divine arrangement of the created universe consisting of the *logoi* of each particular being, as well as of the whole universe.

Finally, if the whole creation is considered from the perspective of mixture, i.e. from the perspective of the unity of mind and virtue, then the virtuous mind arrives at the Logos of God. However, Maximus points out that this is not a direct process, or direct participation of the mind in God, but a process facilitated by the Logos of God, who himself reduced the final two modes of contemplation into one mode. Thus, passing by way of a simple movement through the many *logoi* of being, the *logoi* of providence and judgment, as well as the *logoi* of the virtues, the mind arrives at the cause of these *logoi*, the Logos of God. Therefore, when Maximus explains the movement of the mind from contemplating the many *logoi* to contemplation of the one Logos, he does not employ the conventional Neoplatonic term of "return" or "reversion" (ἐπιστροφή); instead, he refers to "a converting and hand-leading offering and providence" (ἐπιστρεπτική καὶ χειραγωγικὴ ἀναφορά τε καὶ πρόνοια).[58] This means that the mind is brought, by a combination of its own virtuous life and activity and divine guidance and providence, to the level of offering itself to God. At this stage, it is God alone who acts, and who removes the ignorance (ἄγνοια) that distinguishes creation from God.[59]

Maximus portrays another Porphyrian tree in his *Mystagogia*, whose investigation may shed additional light on the contemplative upward movement in *Ambiguum* 10.19 and the role of wisdom in this movement. Like in *Ambiguum* 10.19, in the *Mystagogia* God resides at the top of the pyramid, or the tree.[60] Maximus first distinguishes between God and the Church in *Mystagogia* 1,[61] and then he divides the church building into nave and sanctuary in *Mystagogia* 2.[62] The nave corresponds to the visible cosmos, while the sanctuary corresponds

---

[58] *Amb.Ioh.* 7 (*PG* 91, 1081C; CONSTAS, 2014, 1, pp. 100–101). For more about Maximus' employment of these Neoplatonic terms see: V. CVETKOVIĆ, "The Transformation of the Neoplatonic Philosophical Notions of Procession (*proodos*) and Conversion (*epistrophe*) in the Thought of St. Maximus the Confessor", in *The Ways of Byzantine Philosophy*, ed. by M. KNEŽEVIĆ, Alhambra, CA, 2015, pp. 195–210.

[59] *Amb.Ioh.* 41 in CONSTAS, 2014, 2, pp. 106–107. See also *PG* 91, 1308A.

[60] Louth points to the hierarchy that Maximus explains in the first five chapters of *Mystagogia*. See LOUTH, "Sophia, the Wisdom of God, in St. Maximos the Confessor", pp. 257–258.

[61] *Mystagogia* (= *Myst.*) 1, in *CCSG* 69, pp. 10–11, 133–138.

[62] *Myst.* 2 (*CCSG* 69, pp. 14–15, 206–209).

to the invisible cosmos. In *Mystagogia* 3, Maximus divides the visible cosmos into heaven and earth, once again drawing a parallel between the sanctuary as heaven and the nave as earth.[63] Similar to *Ambiguum* 10.19, where the division between earth and heaven also includes what is between the two, Maximus introduces humanity as being between heaven and earth. In *Mystagogia* 4, he then draws a parallel between the church building and the human being. Thus, the nave corresponds to the body, the sanctuary to the soul and the altar to the mind (νοῦς).[64] Finally, in *Mystagogia* 5, Maximus explains how two faculties of the soul, the contemplative and the active pave the way to God.[65]

According to Maximus, the contemplative faculty of the soul is the faculty of mind, while the active faculty of the soul is the faculty of reason (λόγος). The mind as the contemplative faculty of the soul leads to God manifested in His essence as Truth, while reason as the active faculty of the soul leads to the divine activities manifested as the Good. Both movements pass through certain stages before attaining the final goal.

The mind (νοῦς) rests in wisdom (σοφία), since wisdom is the power (δύναμις) of mind and the mind is wisdom in potency. The habit (ἕξις) of mind is contemplation (θεωρία), while the act or activity (ἐνέργεια) of mind is knowledge (γνῶσις). Wisdom as the power of mind leads to contemplation, which becomes the habit of mind. By exercising contemplation as a habit, the mind acquires knowledge, which is its activity. One may perceive the three states of mind, i.e. wisdom, contemplation, and knowledge not necessarily as subsequent stages, but also as simultaneous and deeply interconnected, since the mind is led to the next level by its power (δύναμις), habit (ἕξις) and activity (ἐνέργεια). By actualizing its potency in wisdom, by discovering its habit in contemplation, and by performing its activity in knowledge, the mind ends in enduring, or abiding, knowledge (ἄληστος γνῶσις). The enduring knowledge is "the perpetual and unceasing movement" of wisdom, contemplation, and knowledge as potency, habit, and the activity of the mind around God as Truth (ἀλήθεια).[66]

---

[63] *Myst.* 3 (*CCSG 69*, pp. 17–18, 258–263).

[64] *Myst.* 3 (*CCSG 69*, pp. 18, 264–268).

[65] *Myst.* 3 (*CCSG 69*, pp. 19–20, 285–297).

[66] *Myst.* 3 (*CCSG 69*, 20–22, 298–336).

Several issues characterize this final stage, in which the mind experiences something completely new. Maximus introduces the reader into this new state by claiming that the mind moves toward "the knowable which transcends knowledge". Maximus moves beyond this "apophatic" figure, which denies the possibility of knowing God, by relying on the argument of Gregory of Nyssa regarding the divine infinity and the *adiastemic* nature of God. According to Maximus, the enduring and everlasting knowledge becomes circumscribed (περιγραφόμενος) as the ultimate knowable, or Truth. Since the mind, according to Maximus, gains knowledge about a certain object by recognizing the definition or circumscription of this object, one may expect that the knowledge of God is possible by circumscribing Him by the mind. For Maximus, however, although God is (in some sense!) knowable, He ultimately transcends knowledge. The knowledge of all created beings is possible due to their limited natures. Thus, in order to know a certain object, one must circumscribe it by the mind, or determine its borders, content, and purpose. However, when the mind passes from limited, created natures, to the unlimited nature of God, it cannot find any border in Him where to stop, so as to conclude something about His essence by distancing itself from Him. Therefore, the mind continues to move within the divine infinity and constantly gains knowledge of God, which is eternal, and which never ends or passes into memory. In this manner, God, who is knowable, at the same time transcends discursive knowledge. God as Truth is the final destination of the mind, and by this final truth the mind's essence, power, habit, and activity are determined.

The next intellectual activity is that of reason, which in similar fashion to the mind passes through several phases. The faculty of reason is not contemplative as is the case with the mind; rather, it is practical. Reason (λόγος) possesses its potency in prudence (φρόνησις), since the power of reason is prudence. The habit of reason is reflected in action (πρᾶξις), while the activity of reason is virtue (ἀρετή). The inward and unchangeable bond of prudence, action, and virtue, as the power (δύναμις), habit (ἕξις) and activity (ἐνέργεια) of reason, generates faith (πίστις). Faith leads reason further towards God as the Good (τὸ ἀγαθόν), where it finally comes to rest.[67]

Both mind and reason know God, but the former knows Him as the Truth, while the latter knows Him as the Good. However, the move-

---

[67] *Myst.* 3 (*CCSG 69*, 20–22,298–336).

ment of mind towards the divine essence, or Truth, and the movement of reason towards the divine activity, or the Good, are not two parallel unrelated processes. Already in *Ambiguum* 10.19, Maximus explains mixture as the unification of the mind with virtue, or as an unification of contemplative and practical philosophy leading to wisdom. He emphasizes that the practical aspects of philosophy such as character (ἦθος), activity (πρᾶξις) and virtue (ἀρετή) has to be united with the contemplative aspects of philosophy, such as inclination (γνώμη), contemplation (θεωρία) and knowledge (γνῶσις), in order to arrive at wisdom.[68] Therefore, the two upward movements, one of mind and the other of reason have to be united. This unification is not at the last level, i.e. the level of the essence and activity of God, which is naturally united and undivided, but on each lower level. The two separate realities became one by virtue of unification. The mind is united with reason as rational mind, wisdom is united with prudence as prudent wisdom, the contemplative activity is united with practical activity as active contemplation, knowledge is united with virtue as virtuous knowledge and, finally, enduring or abiding knowledge is united with faith as enduring knowledge which is faithful and unchangeable.

These unifications represent both mixture and position, to which Maximus refers in *Ambiguum* 10.19. Mixture is the mixture of natural opposites in the mean terms,[69] and position pertains to the mean terms, which maintain an equal distance from the extremes.[70] According to Maximus, divine providence secures the permanence of beings in their order, position and motion and "co-inherence through intermediaries of the extremes in them, which do not destroy each other when they are brought into combination with each other".[71]

The doctrine of "mean terms" and "extremes" derives from *Timaeus*, in which Plato introduces an intermediary bond in order to connect two extremes, and "the fairest bond [for Plato] is that which makes the most complete fusion of itself and the things which it combines, and proportion is best adapted to effect such a union".[72] Plato proposed

[68] *Amb.Ioh.* 10,19 (*PG* 91, 1136D; CONSTAS, 2014, I, pp. 210–211, *supra*, p. 80).

[69] *Amb.Th.*, Prolog (*PG* 91, 1032A; CONSTAS, 2014, I, pp. 2–3).

[70] *Amb.Ioh.* 71 (*PG* 91, 1412B; CONSTAS, 2014, I, pp. 318–319).

[71] *Amb.Ioh.* 10 (*PG* 91, 1188D; CONSTAS, 2014, I, pp. 310–311, *supra*, p. 162; Lollar, here, p. 163).

[72] Plato, *Timaeus*, 31c, in Plato, *Timaeus. Critias. Cleitophon. Menexenus. Epistles*, Cambridge, MA, 1929 (Loeb Classical Library 234). The English trans-

different kind of proportion, later defined by his Neoplatonic commentators as arithmetic (1:2 = 2:3), geometric (1:2 = 2:4) and harmonic (3:4 = 4:6).[73] Antoine Lévy points to Proclus as the most probable origin of the Platonic doctrine of "mean terms" in Maximus.[74] In his *Commentary on the First Book of Euclid's' Elements*, Proclus dealt with Euclid's definition of mean terms and extremes.[75] Euclid states that "a straight line is said to have been cut in extreme and mean ratio when, as the whole is to the greater segment, so is the greater to the less".[76] Maximus adopts the arithmetic proportion or 1:2 = 2:3 ratio. Departing from the Chalcedonian definition of perfect and unconfused divine and human natures in the person of Christ, Maximus understands the two natures as extremes and the person of Christ as the mean term.[77] However, the mean term does not imply a reduction of the specific differences of Christ's human and divine natures by fusing them together: for Maximus, this would be a form of monophysitism. It means, rather, that Christ's person as the mean term and his two natures as two extremes are structured in accordance with arithmetic proportion (1:2 = 2:3). Thus, Christ's hypostasis relates to Christ's divine nature in the same manner as Christ' divine nature relates to his human nature.[78] The same ratio is applicable to all kinds of mixtures, in which the position of the mean terms is equally, but asymmetrically, distant from the extremes.

lation in Plato, *Timaeus*, New York, 1959.

[73] D. J. O'MEARA, *Pythagoras Revived: Mathematics and Philosophy in Late Antiquity*, Oxford, 1989, p. 188.

[74] A. LÉVY, "Γωνια: Looking into Corners of St. Maximus' Cosmic Architecture", in *The Architecture of the Cosmos*, ed. by A. LÉVY et al., Helsinki, 2015, pp. 153–174: 164. See also V. CVETKOVIĆ, "The Towers of Jerusalem and Ontological Presuppositions of Creation: Exegesis and Philosophy in Maximus the Confessor's *Quaestiones ad Thalassium*", in *Greek and Byzantine Philosophical Exegesis*, ed. by A. DESPOTIS and J. BUCHANAN WALLACE, Paderborn, 2022, pp. 244–267: 260–262.

[75] *Procli Diadochi in primum Euclidis elementorum librum commentarii*, ed. by G. FRIEDLEIN, Lipsiae, 1873, I, 15.

[76] Euclid, *Elements of Euclid*, London – Edinburgh, 1975, VI, def. 3.

[77] *Amb.Th.* 5 (*PG* 91, 1056D; CONSTAS, 2014, I, pp. 50–51). See also CONSTAS, 2014, I, p. 476, n.19.

[78] LÉVY, "Γωνια", p. 165.

The rational mind, prudent wisdom, active contemplation, virtuous knowledge and enduring knowledge which is faithful and unchangeable, are the mean terms for Maximus, while mind and reason, wisdom and prudence, the contemplative activity and practical activity, knowledge and virtues, and finally, enduring knowledge and faith, are the extremes. Similarly, asymmetric mixtures or unions of mind, soul and body, or altar, sanctuary and nave (*Myst.* 4); heaven and earth, or sanctuary and nave (*Myst.* 3); visible and invisible cosmos, or nave and sanctuary (*Myst.* 2); and finally God and Church, as the union of Christ and his Body (*Myst.* 1), are also mean terms. In the last instance, the decade consisting of five pairs in *Mystagogia* 5, is reduced to the monad that is God. Similarly the ennead in *Mystagogia* 1-4, consisting of three pairs (*Myst.*1-3) and a triad (*Myst.* 4) is reduced to the monad. In Maximus' epistemological architecture of *Mystagogia* 5, wisdom again holds the prominent place. Wisdom is not the possession of mind;[79] rather, it constitutes the mind since, as the power of mind, it provides the possibility for contemplation to gain knowledge and enduring knowledge of God as Truth. Moreover, for Maximus the manifestation and act of wisdom is prudence,[80] and mind cannot attain wisdom if it is not united with prudence as prudent mind. Therefore, wisdom reveals the link that exists between God's being and his energy. Wisdom empowers the mind to discover the divine essence, and to acknowledge God as Truth. At the same time, wisdom manifested through prudence as the practice of the virtues, reveals God as the Good by acknowledging his creative, providential and judging energies.[81]

By way of conclusion, we would like to reassess the three above mentioned sophiological accounts in Maximus in light of our analysis of *Ambiguum* 10.19, as well as *Mystagogia* 5. Plested is right in his identification of wisdom with the divine energy of the Trinity, but an exclusive reduction of wisdom to divine energy may be problematic in two aspects. First, if wisdom is reduced to divine activity, then the human activities became irrelevant in gaining wisdom. Second, how to reconcile Plested's identification of wisdom with divine activity, with Maximus' association of wisdom with the potency of mind leading, not to divine activity or goodness, but to the divine essence or

---

[79] HARRINGTON, "Creation and Natural Contemplation", p. 208.
[80] *Myst.* 5 (*CCSG* 61, 28,437–438).
[81] *Myst.* 5 (*CCSG* 61, 22,329–336).

Truth.[82] Instead of identifying wisdom exclusively with divine activity, it should be perceived as the effect of the joint endeavor of the divine and human activities. This joint endeavor may be twofold, that is, at the level of practice of the virtues, and at the level of natural contemplation. Maximus refers to the former throughout his works.[83] Not only in *Ambiguum* 10.19, but also in *Ambiguum* 7, Maximus claims that by practicing virtue, human beings acquire the likeness of God in addition to the already inherent goodness of the divine image.[84] Divine creative and providential activity is here joined with the human activity of practicing the virtues, and both lead to goodness. This is also evident in the passage from *Ad Thalassium* 59,[85] where Maximus holds that there is no divine grace of knowledge without the receptive power of reason. Grace works through the already created channels, such as mind, reason or natural philanthropy as a response to the human endeavor to utilize its natural abilities properly. Thus, by working together with divine grace, human reason, whose proper or natural activity is virtue, leads to virtuous knowledge. In response to a second issue, Maximus makes it clear that wisdom is a potency of the human mind, whose habit is contemplation, and whose act is knowledge leading to the divine essence considered as Truth.[86] However, mind is not isolated from reason as prudence in potency, and only through the joint endeavor of practicing virtue and contemplation and gaining virtuous knowledge, can human beings reach both divine essence and divine activity. There is no divine grace without the receptive power of reason which, by exercising virtue as its proper or natural activity, leads to virtuous knowledge. Nor is there grace without the capacity of the mind to recognize the divine wisdom within the harmonious order of creation.

Paul Blowers rightly identifies wisdom with the activity of the Logos and Wisdom of God embodied in the structured order of creation as the one Logos and the many *logoi*, and realized in salvation as Christ's uniting the logos of nature with its proper mode, or tropos. This is also evident in *Ambiguum* 10.19, where the Logos of God, by his providence

---

[82]   *Myst.* 5 (*CCSG* 61, 22,323–327).

[83]   *Th.Oec.* I, 13; *Q.Thal.* 53 (*CCSG* 22, 435–437); *Amb.Ioh* 37 (*PG* 91, 1345D; CONSTAS, 2014, 2, pp. 180–181).

[84]   *Amb.Ioh.* 7 (*PG* 1084A; CONSTAS, 2014, 1, pp. 104–105).

[85]   *Q.Thal.* 59 (*CCSG* 22, 47–48, 55–64).

[86]   *Myst.* 5 (*CCSG* 61, 22,323–327).

and judgement, hand-leads (χειραγωγεῖ) human activities to united modes of natural contemplation with the virtues. Finally, the Logos of God is the one who helps creation to bridge the chasm of ignorance that divides God from creation, and to unite the love of wisdom with the state of divine wisdom as one. Although, "created" wisdom is not in Blowers' immediate focus, the comparative analyses of *Ambiguum* 10.19 and *Mystagogia* 5 prove that the wisdom embodied in Maximus's anthropology and psychology is perhaps even more transparent than in the wisdom embodied his cosmology.[87]

Finally, Andrew Louth is right in arguing that the ascetic struggle, which recovers the dispassion enabling us to practice natural contemplation, prevents the mode (*tropos*) from running counter to its fundamental *logos*.[88] The opposite is also true. The logos of contemplation (λόγος τῆς θεωρίας) is the basis for the virtues, and the development of the virtues necessitates contemplation as much as the virtuous life is a prerequisite for contemplation. In our opinion, Louth's significant contribution to the theme of Maximus' sophiology, lies in his observation that "the wise" (σοφοί) did not become wise through the rational knowledge of God, but through direct experience (πεῖρα) of God.[89] Therefore, he rightly locates the direct experience of the Logos of God as Wisdom in its proper settings, liturgical context and mystagogical progress.[90] However, the prerequisite for direct experience of divine wisdom in the Church and in the liturgy is the upward movement of mind and reason towards knowledge and faith. In order to transcend conceptual knowledge (νόησις) and intellectual contemplation (γνωστικὴ θεωρία), one needs to receive angelic understanding of sanctifying theology and to be adopted in the Spirit so as to become a son or daughter of God the Father in Jesus Christ.[91] The direct experience of God is the fruit, never earned, but always given, of natural contemplation and ascetic struggle.

---

[87] BLOWERS, *Maximus the Confessor*, p. 109.

[88] LOUTH, *Maximus*, pp. 57–58.

[89] *Q.Thal.* 60 (*CCSG* 22, 79–83).

[90] LOUTH, "Sophia, the Wisdom of God, in St. Maximos the Confessor", pp. 257–258.

[91] *Myst.* 12 (*CCSG* 61, 42, 683–687)

Christ before Christ

Some Observations on *Ambiguum* 10

Vukašin MILIĆEVIĆ

(*Belgrade*)

It is striking that St. Maximus in his *Ambiguum* 10, when he points to those who have managed to overcome the material dyad[1] and to reach the unity that is contemplated in Trinity, namely, to those *deified*, writes almost exclusively about the Old Testament personalities. Thus, it follows that the Old Testament saints not only knew the Mystery of Christ in a prophetic way, but that they actually and directly participated in it. In fact, the prophetic character of their personalities, of their works and words, should be considered precisely as the fruit of that participation. Among all those saints, a very special place is occupied by the mystical king and priest Melchizedek, to whom St. Maximus dedicates a series of contemplations in his *Ambiguum* 10.[2] The way in which St. Maximus

---

[1] As is well known, the *Ambiguum* 10 is meant to be a theological exegesis of a sentence from St. Gregory the Theologian's *Oratio* 21, dedicated to the memory of St. Athanasius of Alexandria. In Gregory's sermon St. Athanasius is considered as one among the saints who have managed to overcome "τὴν ὑλικήν δυάδα on account of the unity perceived in Trinity", cf. *Or.* 21.2; Grégoire de Nazianze, *Discours 20–23*, Paris, 1980 (*SC* 270), p. 114.

[2] G. Benevich comes to a very important insight regarding the broader historical and theological context of this use of Old Testament figures, especially Melchizedek, as paradigms of deification. Note here his observation that the insistence on the Old Testament personalities is by no means a matter of coincidence, but that it rather demonstrates a theological attitude: "For us, this place is interesting in two ways: on the one hand, it testifies that St. Gregory and, following him, St. Maximus speak about the equality of the Old Testament saints and those saints *after Christ*… without mutually distinguishing the exaltation of their knowledge of God when compared to one another", cf. Григорий B.

Ambiguum *10 of Maximus the Confessor in Modern Study: Papers Collected on the Occasion of the Budapest Colloquium on Saint Maximus, 3–4 February 2021*, ed. by Alexis LÉONAS & Vladimir CVETKOVIĆ, with the collaboration of Daniel HEIDE, Turnhout, 2025 (IPM 97), pp. 341–359
10.1484/M.IPM-EB.5.141868

describes Melchizedek's participation in the Mystery of Christ makes it entirely impossible to establish any difference in this respect between the Old and New Testaments. Namely, all those properties that Melchizedek acquires by grace, as the one "deemed worthy to transcend time and nature and to become like the Son of God",[3] signify the fullness of his participation in the divine life that cannot be surpassed.

> For it is said of him [Melchizedek] that he was *without father or mother or genealogy*,[4] which I understand to mean the complete setting aside of natural characteristics through the highest gift of grace in accordance with virtue. That *he has*, moreover, *neither beginning of days nor end of life*,[5] points both to knowledge that is not limited by the properties of time and the present age, and to contemplation that transcends all material and immaterial being.[6]

> More precisely, Melchizedek conquers the limitations of nature by virtue, and those of time through perfect contemplation. It is through virtue and contemplation, i.e. goodness and knowledge, that the divine likeness of man, created as the image of God, is manifested.[7]

> For those in whom inclination, by means of the virtues, has prevailed nobly against the unconquerable law of nature, and in whom the motion of the intellect, by means of knowledge, soars inviolate over the property of time and the age – these, I say, we should not characterize by the property of the things they have abandoned, but rather to name them from the magnificence of what they have assumed, for which and

Беневич, "Логос Мелхиседека. Экзегеза и парадигма обожения у прп. Максима Исповедника", *Вестник РХГА*, 12/1 (2011), p. 191.

[3] "...χρόνου καὶ φύσεως ὑπεράνω γενέσθαι, καὶ ὁμοιωθῆναι τῷ Υἱῷ τοῦ Θεοῦ κατηξιώθη...", *Amb.Ioh.* 10.20a. I will refer to the critical edition and English translation by Nicholas Constas (CONSTAS, 2014, 1 & 2).

[4] Hebr. 7.3.

[5] *Ibid.*

[6] *Amb.Ioh.* 10.20a, CONSTAS, 2014, 1, pp. 214–215. I would prefer to read the sentence "τὸ δὲ μήτε ἀρχὴν ἡμερῶν μήτε ζωῆς τέλος ἔχειν τὴν χρόνου παντὸς καὶ αἰῶνος ἰδιότητα περιγράφουσαν γνῶσιν καὶ πάσης ὑλικῆς καὶ ἀΰλου οὐσίας τὴν ὕπαρξιν ὑπερβαίνουσαν θεωρίαν μαρτυρεῖν..." in this way: "that *he has*, moreover, *neither beginning of days nor end of life* [Heb 7.3], points to the contemplation that transcends both knowledge that defines the properties of time and the present age and the existence of all material and immaterial being...".

[7] *Amb.Ioh.* 10.20a, CONSTAS, 2014, 1, pp. 214–215.

in which alone, henceforth, they exist and are known [...] If, then, he deliberately chose virtue over nature (and everything that comes with nature) through the noble acquisition of the dignity that lies within our reach, and by knowledge vaulted over every time and age, and cognitively through contemplation left behind all that comes after God, hurrying past whatever was marked by any kind of limit or boundary, the divine Melchizedek unfolded his intellect to the divine, beginningless, and immortal rays of God the Father, and was begotten of God through the Word in the Spirit by grace, so that he now bears within himself, unblemished and fully realized, the likeness of God the begetter, for birth creates identity between the begetter and the begotten, which is why Scripture says that *what is begotten of flesh is flesh, and what is begotten of the Spirit is spirit*,[8] from which it follows that he was not named from any natural or temporal properties – such as "father" and "mother", or "genealogy" or "beginning" and "end of days" – for he left these things behind and was completely released from them, and instead was named from those divine and blessed characteristics in the image of which he remade himself, and these cannot be touched by time, nature, reason, intellect, or by any being enclosed in a finite frame. Therefore the great Melchizedek is said to be *without father or mother or genealogy, having neither beginning of days nor end of life*, just as our God-bearing fathers have truly said, that is, not on account of his human nature, which was created out of nothing, and by virtue of which he had both a beginning and an end, but on account of divine and uncreated grace, which exists eternally and is beyond all nature and time, for it is the grace of the eternal God, and it was solely by this that he was begotten – wholly and willingly – and solely from this that he can now be known.[9]

It is especially important to notice now that the likeness to the *Son* and the *Logos* of God for St. Maximus has a very literal and direct *Christological* meaning. That is why the properties that Melchizedek acquires by being born from God, through the Logos in the Spirit, are *theandric*, i.e. properties of the incarnate Logos of God. In a supernatural way, therefore, through virtue and knowledge, through freedom, i.e. *by a good choice of the dignity intended for us*, Melchizedek overcame time and age and literally conformed himself to God. However, this means that:

---

[8] Io. 3:6.
[9] *Amb.Ioh.* 10.20a, CONSTAS, 2014, I, pp. 216–219.

> the great Melchizedek, having been imbued with divine virtue, was dee-
> med worthy to become an image of Christ God and His unutterable
> mysteries, for in Him all the saints converge as to an archetype, to the
> very cause of the manifestation of the Beautiful that is realized in each
> of them, and this is especially true of this saint, since he bears within
> himself more characteristics[10] of Christ than all the rest.[11]

Or even more directly:

> For alone, and in a way without any parallel whatsoever, our Lord and
> God, Jesus Christ, is by nature and in truth *without father, mother, or
> genealogy, having neither beginning of days nor end of life*. He is *without
> mother* according to His immaterial, bodiless, and utterly unknowable
> birth on high from the Father before the ages. He is *without father* ac-
> cording to His temporal and bodily birth on earth from His mother,
> in whose conception the seed of man did not take precedence. He is
> *without genealogy* because the manner of both of His births is wholly
> inaccessible and incomprehensible to all.[12]

Therefore, there is no doubt that Melchizedek more than anyone
manifests the reality of the incarnate Logos or, in other words, participates in the Mystery of Christ. Such full participation in the Mystery
of Christ implies not only that the perspective of infinity is open to
human existence but, more importantly, the perspective of *beginninglessness*. To the deified man, the man in Christ,

> absolutely no part of his existence will remain without a share in His
> presence, and thus he becomes without beginning or end, no longer
> bearing within himself the movement of life subject to time, which has
> a beginning and an end, and which is agitated by many passions, but
> possesses only the divine and eternal life of the Word dwelling within
> him.[13]

---

[10] I find that *prefigurations* for τὰς ὑποτυπώσεις here, as Constas puts it in
his otherwise excellent translation, is way too much *epexegetical*. Cf. LAMPE,
pp. 1463–1464.

[11] *Amb.Ioh.* 10.20a, CONSTAS, 2014, I, p. 220.

[12] *Amb.Ioh.* 10.20b, CONSTAS, pp. 220–223.

[13] *Amb.Ioh.* 10.20d, CONSTAS, 2014, I, pp. 224–225. Important reference to
this section may be found in St. Gregory Palamas, who speaks, contrary to his
opponents, about enhypostastic and therefore uncreated and unoriginate

Therefore, the state of being attained by Melchizedek cannot be relativized; it announces precisely and simultaneously God's original intention for creation and its final goal, one that will be fully realized in the eschatological perspective. Nevertheless, Melchizedek already participates fully in it. In the chapters that follow *contemplations* on Melchizedek, Maximus gives similar reflections on Abraham[14] and Moses,[15] although not as extensive and direct regarding the indicated problem. Explaining the ways in which the Old Testament saints experienced the reality of Christ, St. Maximus specifies that for them it was merely *figuratively* (τυπικῶς),[16] which, of course, echoes the words of St. Paul.[17] However, this broad formulation does not apply completely to what Maximus says about Melchizedek. For Melchizedek's participation in the divine reality is the participation of

> the one who has wisely understood how he ought to love God... [and of the one who] will pass by all sensible and intelligible objects, as well as all time, age, and place without establishing any relation to them; and finally, after having, in a manner beyond nature, stripped himself of every activity conforming to sensation, reason, and intellect, he will attain, ineffably and unknowably, the divine delight, which is beyond reason

character of the deifying gift: "But, as we have shown above, the saints clearly state that this adoption [υἱοθεσίαν καὶ τὴν θεοποιὸν δωρεὰν ταύτην], actualised by faith, is enhypostatic [ἐνυπόστατόν φασιν]. Nonetheless, our opponent affirms that the imitation of God, which he alone considers to be the thearchy and the deifying gift [θεοποιὸν δῶρον], is not enhypostatic. It is therefore something different from the deification [θέωσιν] which the Fathers possessed and knew. Yet the divine Maximus has not only taught that it is enhypostatic, but also that it is unoriginate (not only uncreated), indescribable and supratemporal [ἀλλὰ καὶ ἀγένητον, καὶ οὐκ ἄκτιστον μόνον, ἀλλὰ καὶ ἀπερίγραπτον καὶ ὑπέρχρονον]. Those who attain it become thereby uncreated, unoriginate and indescribable [ἀνάρχους καὶ ἀπεριγράπτους], although in their own nature, they derive from nothingness [ἐξ οὐκ ὄντων γεγονότας]" (English translation by Nicholas Gendle in Gregory Palamas, *The Triads*, Mohwah, NJ, 1983, p. 86; Greek text in Grégoire Palamas, *Défense des saints hésychastes*, Introduction, texte critique, traduction et notes par Jean Meyendorff, Louvain, ²1973, p. 617.

[14] *Amb.Ioh.* 10.21, CONSTAS, 2014, I, pp. 228–231.
[15] *Amb.Ioh.* 10.22, CONSTAS, pp. 230–237.
[16] *Amb.Ioh.* 10.23, CONSTAS, pp. 236–237.
[17] Cf. 1 Cor. 10.11.

and intellect, and he shall attain this in a mode and principle known to God who gives such grace, and to those who are worthy to receive it. Thus he no longer bears about with him anything natural or written,[18] since all that he could possibly say or know has been completely transcended and wrapped in silence.[19]

Obviously, there is nothing *figurative* about this account. Also, in addition to everything that has already been said, what St. Maximus writes in the rest of the text can be directly taken in support of the thesis regarding the eschatological character of Melchizedek's state of being. Connecting it with the Gospel story about the man who fell into the hands of robbers and the Good Samaritan,[20] Maximus says that the state of complete separation from created beings characteristic of the perfect, and the divine adoption of which the Gospel preaches, will be bestowed by the Lord when He comes again.[21]

---

[18] Bearing in mind that the *Ambiguum* 10 at large deals with the problem of natural and written law, *written* here may well apply to *scriptural*, so that the deified man goes far beyond the *letter* into the realm of Spirit.

[19] *Amb.Ioh.* 10.26, CONSTAS, 2014, 1, pp. 242–245.

[20] Cf. Lc. 10.30.

[21] *Amb.Ioh.* 10.27, CONSTAS, 2014, 1, pp. 244–246; Cf. Lc. 10.35. St. Maximus frequently writes about the complete overcoming of all the limitations of created nature, and this always implies the removal of all its properties. Here are a few relevant places that contain thoughts very close to those we encounter in the contemplation of Melchizedek: "...in order to become God by grace, he established himself beyond matter (as far as flesh was concerned) through ascetic practice, and beyond form (as far as intellect was concerned) through contemplation – for it is from matter and form that beings derive their existence – and to tell the whole of it, he became completely immaterial and formless through his state of virtue and knowledge, for the sake of God the Word, who for our sake took on matter and form, becoming as we are and truly one from among us, though by nature He is strictly immaterial and formless" [...ἵνα γένηται καὶ αὐτὸς χάριτι Θεός, ὑπὲρ τὴν ὕλην κατὰ σάρκα διὰ τῆς πράξεως, καὶ κατὰ νοῦν διὰ θεωρίας ὑπὲρ τὸ εἶδος, ἐξ ὧν ἡ τῶν ὄντων ὕπαρξις ὑφέστηκεν, ἑαυτὸν καταστήσας, καὶ τὸ ὅλον εἰπεῖν, κατὰ τὴν ἕξιν τῆς ἀρετῆς καὶ τῆς γνώσεως ἄϋλος καὶ ἀνείδεος πάντη γενόμενος, διὰ τὸν δι' ἡμᾶς ἐν ὕλῃ καὶ εἴδει καθ' ἡμᾶς ἀληθῶς ἐξ ἡμῶν γενόμενον Θεὸν Λόγον, τὸν κατὰ φύσιν κυρίως ἄϋλον καί ἀνείδεον...], *Amb.Ioh.* 30; CONSTAS, 2014, 2, pp. 36–39; "...as those who partake in God completely, and completely and in every aspect have become gods by grace, so much so that

Maximus' consideration of the relationship between natural and written law in *Ambiguum* 10,[22] as well as his contemplations on Melchizedek, show very clearly that for him not only separation but also a distinction between the pre-eternal Logos and the incarnate Son of God can hardly make any sense. If it were not so, the key premises of his system would collapse.

In the light of what has been said, several important questions need to be answered. First of all, starting from Maximus' text itself, we must ask ourselves how to explain his claim that Melchizedek, who is an Old Testament figure, reveals the image of Christ more than anyone else. Or, to put it more directly, how is it possible that Melchizedek, more than anyone else, participates in the Mystery of Christ when presumably he lived centuries prior to the incarnation of the Logos? Consequently, is it at all possible to talk about the Mystery of Christ as *historical*, as something that essentially has to do with time (both χρόνος and καιρός), or not? If not, then what does Maximus' unambiguous insistence that the Mystery of Christ is the mystery of the union of divinity and humanity in the hypostasis of Christ mean?[23] Does this

---

in every aspect we show ourselves to be another him, apart from the identity according to essence. Because that's what perfection is, that we don't have a single feature of this age in us at all..." [...ὅλου Θεοῦ χωρητικοὶ καὶ ὅλοι δι' ὅλου θεοὶ κατὰ χάριν γενώμεθα· τοσοῦτον, ὥστε ἄλλον αὐτὸν ἡμᾶς εἶναι διὰ πάντων νομίζεσθαι· χωρὶς τῆς πρὸς αὐτὸν κατ' οὐσίαν ταυτότητος· τοῦτο γὰρ ἡ τελείωσις, μηδὲν τὸ παράπαν ἐν ἡμῖν αὐτοῖς τοῦ αἰῶνος τούτου γνώρισμα φέροντες...], *Ep.* 1, *PG* 91, 376AB. Cf. *Th.Oec.* 1.54, *PG* 90, 1104AB; 1.68, *PG* 90, 1108C; 1.81, *PG* 90, 1116AB; 1.83, *PG* 90, 1117AC.

[22] This consideration, situated just before contemplations on Melchizedek, starts with the interpretation of the Gospel story about the Transfiguration of Christ (Mt. 17.1-9; Mc. 9.1-9; Lc. 9.28-36) and forms a considerable section of the *Amb.Ioh.* 10, cf. CONSTAS, 2014, 1, pp. 119-213.

[23] Cf. *Q.Thal.* 60: "In this passage of Scripture, the mystery of Christ is itself called *Christ*, and the great Apostle clearly bears witness to this when he says that *the mystery hidden from the ages and the generations has now been manifested* [Col. 1.26] identifying the *mystery of Christ* with *Christ* Himself. This mystery is obviously the ineffable and incomprehensible union according to hypostasis of divinity and humanity. This union brings humanity into perfect identity, in every way, with divinity, through the principle of the hypostasis, and from both humanity and divinity it completes the single composite hy-

mean that Christ's humanity preceded the temporal actualization of the Mystery, not just in a temporal sense, but in an absolutely atemporal sense as well? If so, then there seems to be no way to distinguish Christ's humanity from his divinity. In support of this position, one could also consider the fact that for St. Maximus, as we have seen, participation in the Mystery of Christ effects the complete overcoming of the limitations of body and material nature in general such that the participant acquires divine properties. As we have seen, Melchizedek did acquire *theandric* characteristics; the key consideration here, however, is that for Maximus this implies an ontological perspective that excludes *the beginning of existence*.

I believe that the answers to these questions are to be found in elaborating a concept or perspective that I would call *triadological-christological* analogy, and which is completely inspired by the ideas that we find in the Gospel of John. The simplest way to explain what this is would be to quote Io. 17.21: "...that they all may be one, as You, Father, are in Me, and I in You; that they also may be one in Us, that the world may believe that You sent Me".[24] Bearing in mind this New Testament perspective, it is possible to understand why, both at the level of form (i.e. terminological apparatus) and at the level of meaning, there is an *analogy* in the way that St. Maximus describes the reality of *intra-trinitarian* relations and the relation between the created (humanity) and the uncreated (divinity) in the Mystery of Christ, both in terms of what can be said (the fact of unity and difference) and what is ineffable (their nature).

---

postasis, without creating any diminishment due to the essential difference of the natures [...] the natures retained their integrity in every way, neither nature disowning anything properly its own because of the union" [Τὸ τοῦ Χριστοῦ μυστήριον Χριστὸν ὁ τῆς Γραφῆς ὠνόμασε λόγος, καὶ μαρτυρεῖ σαφῶς οὑτωσὶ φάσκων ὁ μέγας ἀπόστολος· τὸ μυστήριον τὸ ἀποκεκρυμμένον ἀπὸ τῶν αἰώνων καὶ ἀπὸ τῶν γενεῶν νῦν ἐφανερώθη, ταὐτὸν λέγων δηλαδὴ τῷ Χριστῷ τὸ κατὰ Χριστὸν μυστήριον. Τοῦτο προδήλως ἐστὶν ἄρρητός τε καὶ ἀπερινόητος θεότητός τε καὶ ἀνθρωπότητος καθ' ὑπόστασιν ἕνωσις, εἰς ταὐτὸν ἄγουσα τῇ θεότητι κατὰ πάντα τρόπον τῷ τῆς ὑποστάσεως λόγῳ τὴν ἀνθρωπότητα [...] τούτων ἀλώβητοι κατὰ πάντα τρόπον μεμενήκασιν αἱ φύσεις, μηδεμιᾶς τὸ σύνολον ἀρνησαμένης τὰ ἑαυτῆς διὰ τὴν ἕνωσιν], *CCSG* 22, pp. 73.5–13; 24–26; English translation: CONSTAS, 2018St. , pp. 427–428. Cf. also *Introduction* by Constas, pp. 49–51.

[24] Quoted according to *NKJV*.

First of all, it should be noted that in both cases (in both *Triadology* or Trinitarian theology and Christology) the main focus is on unity (of the hypostases of the Trinity in Triadology, of the uncreated and the created in Christology). Also, in both cases, it is crucial to emphasize the reality of difference without compromising unity. Ultimately, in both cases we come to the conclusion that the distinctions we use to understand both of these mysteries are actually ways to explain the unity. Namely, on the one hand, the Father cannot be a Father if he does not have a Son (and a Spirit) from eternity, so the one God cannot be one if the difference of hypostases is not preserved. On the other hand, Christ's divinity and humanity are inseparably united, which means that the distinction is possible only κατ' ἐπίνοιαν, so that the cognition of the one (through its adequate *energy*) implies the cognition of the energy of the other.[25] In the final perspective, we may say that difference and unity coincide: that by which we differentiate is also that by which we unite.[26]

In my opinion, one could go even further and say that in both cases (in Triadology and in Christology) the issue is about one and the same unity. That is, the unity of intra-trinitarian life is the very life that God in Christ bestows to his creation. Hence, the way that creation in Christ relates to God corresponds to the way in which the hypostases of the Trinity relate to each other. It is precisely this bestowal of intra-trinitar-

[25] This is precisely the logic by which St. Maximus explains his diathelite position. Cf. the metaphor of the incandescent sword (*D.P. PG* 91.337D–340A; *Op. PG* 91.85A), and the way in which Maximus explains the disputed expressions of St. Cyril of Alexandria (μίαν συγγενῆς δι' ἀμφοῖν ἐπιδεδειγμένον ἐνέργειαν) and Dionysius the Areopagite (καινήν τινα τήν θεανδρικήν ἐνέργειαν...), cf. *D.P. PG* 91.344A–348C. See also: D. BATHRELOS, *The Byzantine Christ: Person, Nature, and Will in the Christology of Saint Maximus the Confessor*, Oxford, 2004; A. NICHOLS, *Byzantine Gospel: Maximus the Confessor in Modern Scholarship*, Edinburgh, 1993, p. 63.

[26] I fully agree with the assessment made by V. Cvetković in this regard, namely, that the divine ὁμουσία is identical with ἑτερουποστασία, cf. V. CVETKOVIĆ, "The Oneness of God as Unity of Persons in the Thought of St. Maximus the Confessor", in *Maximus the Confessor as a European Philosopher*, ed. by S. MITRALEXIS, G. STEIRIS, M. PODBIELSKI, S. LALLA, Eugene – Oregon, 2017, p. 312. Cf. also: M. TÖRONEN, *Union and Distinction in the Thought of St. Maximus the Confessor*, Oxford, 2007, pp. 62–68.

ian life that is manifested in the dynamics of the identity of the *logoi* of being and God the Logos.

But what about the body? The Body of Christ is precisely the way in which God gives his life to creation. In a broader sense, the body may be understood as God's way of addressing creation. This *way* contains an incorporeal meaning or *logos* by which it is determined (in terms of ontology), but it always has the form of a body because the creation to whom God addresses Himself *is* a body.[27] One may see this

---

[27] One should recall here the St. Gregory of Nyssa's doctrine on creation ἐκ Θεοῦ. For St. Gregory, namely, the structure of the material world, taken as a whole, is actually *noetic*, since *the properties* that make it up, that by which the material world differs from that purely immaterial, noetic and uncreated – i.e. God, are all themselves concepts or, actually, the ideas of the Creator himself. Because these ideas are uncreated or divine by nature, what makes actual materiality – and this always means *actual bodies* – is their *concourse* or συνδρομή, which connotes a kind of *arbitrarity*. That is why Gregory says that an essence of a created being is ὕπαρξις of God's will (cf. "...ὅτι ἡ ὁρμὴ τῆς θείας προαιρέσεως, ὅταν ἐθέλει, πρᾶγμα γίνεται, καὶ οὐσιοῦται τὸ βούλευμα εὐθὺς ἡ φύσις γινόμενον, τῆς παντοδυνάμου ἐξουσίας, ὅπερ ἂν σοφῶς τε καὶ τεχνικῶς ἐθέλῃ, μὴ ἀνυπόστατον ποιούσης τὸ θέλημα. Ἡ δὲ τοῦ θελήματος ὕπαρξις οὐσία ἐστί", *De anima et resurrectione*, GNO III/3 93.10–14; cf. ibid. GNO III/3 94.12–15; cf. also: "...ἃ πάντα μὲν καθ' ἑαυτὰ ἔννοιαί ἐστι καὶ ψιλὰ νοήματα. Οὐ γάρ τι τούτων ἐφ' ἑαυτοῦ ὕλη ἐστὶν, ἀλλὰ συνδραμόντα πρὸς ἄλληλα, ὕλη γίνεται", *In Hexaemeron*, GNO IV/1 15.10–16.11; Cf. also: *De opificio hominis* 23, PG 44.212AC; Ibid. 24, PG 44.212D–213B. What we are talking about here is the immediate character of the act of God's creation, and this fully correlates with the later development that the doctrine of the *uncreatedness* of divine energies had in the works of St. Maximus and St. Gregory Palamas (cf. my paper in Serbian: В. Милићевић, "Св. Григорије Ниски и учење о нествореним енергијама", in *Исихазам у животу Цркве српских и поморских земаља: зборник радова са научног скупа поводом 800 година Цркве српских и поморских земаља и 630 година Манастира Тумане*, ур. З. Матић, Београд – Пожаревац, 2019, pp. 141–153). As I said, I find that St. Maximus' doctrine on creation and *logoi* largely depends on St. Gregory's doctrine. The frequency of use of the phrase ἐκ Θεοῦ in relation to God's creation in St. Maximus (cf. also E. D. PERL, *Methexis. Creation, Incarnation, Deification in St. Maximus*, Yale, 1991, p. 118, n. 14) bears witness to this very directly. In order to make it clearer, I will quote here only in Greek, so that the exact phrase might be visible easily:

clearly in Maximus' aforementioned treatment of the natural and written Law. Since it is always *bodily*, every manifestation of God implies
some kind of incarnation, and that's why it is never outside the frame
of Christology. St. Maximus occasionally writes about this with such
straightforwardness that it cannot be understood in any way if we try
to reduce this Christological character of God's manifestations to the
level of a metaphor.

Thus, St. Maximus sees every word of Scripture as an event of the
incarnation of the Logos:

> Our mind does not in this first encounter hold converse with the naked
> Word, but with the Word made flesh, certainly in a variety of languages;
> though he is the Word by nature he is flesh to the sight, so that many
> think they see flesh and not the Word even if he is truly the Word. For

"...καθ' ἣν πέφυκε πάντα τὰ ἐκ Θεοῦ γινόμενα εἰς Θεόν συνάγεσθαι μονίμως τε καὶ
ἀπαρατρέπτως... τῶν ἐκ Θεοῦ γενομένων νοητῶν τε καὶ αἰσθητῶν", *Amb.Ioh.* 7,
Constas, 2014, I, p. 80; "...λόγον παντός τῶν ἐκ Θεοῦ τὸ εἶναι λαβόντων", Ibid.,
p. 96; "πάντα γὰρ μετέχει διὰ τὸ ἐκ Θεοῦ γεγενῆσθαι...", Ibid., p. 96; "...ἐκ Θεοῦ
δεδωρημένην ταύτην μὴ εἶναι τὴν ζωήν...", *Amb.Ioh.* 10, Maximos the Confessor,
On Difficulties, p. 250; "ἢ τὰ μετὰ Θεὸν πάντα καὶ ἐκ Θεοῦ γεγονότα, τουτέστι
τὴν φύσιν τῶν ὄντων καὶ τὸν χρόνον...", Ibid., p. 262; "εἰ δὲ τοῦτο, πάντως ἐκ Θεοῦ
τὸ εἶναι τοῖς οὖσι καὶ τὸ εἶδος δεδώρηται... ἐκ Θεοῦ πᾶσα οὐσία", Ibid., p. 298; "...ἐκ
Θεοῦ τοῦ ἀεὶ ὄντος τὰ πάντα ἐκ τοῦ μὴ ὄντος γενέσθαι παντελῶς τε καὶ ὁλικῶς...",
Ibid., p. 308; "...πρόνοια γὰρ ἐστι κατὰ τοὺς θεοφόρους Πατέρας ἡ ἐκ Θεοῦ εἰς τὰ
ὄντα γινομένη ἐπιμέλεια...", Ibid., p. 310; "...τὰ μετὰ Θεόν ὄντα καὶ ἐκ Θεοῦ τὸ
εἶναι διὰ γενέσεως ἔχοντα...", *Amb.Ioh.* 41, Constas, 2014, 2, p. 114. P. Blowers
indicates that the idea of the creation *from God* appeared for the first time in
St. Irenaeus of Lyons, but it seems to me that he still overlooks the key importance which for its formulation had St. Gregory of Nyssa, the one who uses this
concept with a precisely defined meaning, cf. P.M. Blowers, "From Nonbeing
to Eternal Well-Being: Creation ex nihilo in the Cosmology and Soteriology of
Maximus the Confessor", in *Ancient Commentators in Dialogue and Debate on
the Origin of the World*, ed by G. Roskam, J. Verheyden, Tübingen, 2017,
p. 175. For more general assessment of St. Gregory's doctrine, see: R. Sorabji,
*Time, Creation and the Continuum: Theories in Antiquity and the Early Middle
Ages*, London, 1983, pp. 290–294; M. Edwards, "Christians against Matter:
A Bouquet for Bishop Berkeley", in *Gnosticism, Platonism and the Late Ancient
World: Essays in Honour of John D. Turner*, ed by K. Corrigan, T. Rasimus,
Leiden-Boston, 2013, pp. 577–578.

the understanding of Scripture is not what appears to the many but is otherwise than it appears. For the Word becomes flesh through each recorded word.[28]

Going back to the questions we asked earlier, we shall assert that, according to St. Maximus, the Mystery of Christ exists before all ages; it is *atemporal* or timeless in the absolute sense of the word since it is nothing other than the mystery of the unity of life which is God the Trinity. On the other hand, this mystery is both a fact and a way of creation's participation in this life which for it (creation) means its very existence. The unity of God and man, of God and his creature, in this sense is already contained in the unity of the life of the Triune God that is ὑπεράπειρον καὶ ἀπειράκις ἀπείρως[29] above all ages. The participation of creation adds nothing to this life since nothing can be added to that which is boundless. That is precisely why, I think, St. Maximus insists that the Mystery of Christ is the cause of everything, while it alone is caused by nothing other than itself.[30] On the other hand, this participation of the creation in the unity of life of the Triune God *adds* life to the creation, since it does not exist without it, because *participation* is its very existence. And since creation is a body, participation in the otherwise immaterial life of God always means for it participation in the Body of Christ.

But how, then, to understand the incarnation as an historical event? I find that it is impossible to conceive the Mystery of Christ as a purely historical event, as something constituted in time, in terms of ontology. It is rather an eschatological *intrusion from above*. But this *from*

[28] Κατὰ γὰρ τὴν πρώτην προσβολήν, οὐ γυμνῷ προσβάλλει Λόγῳ ὁ ἡμέτερος νοῦς· ἀλλὰ Λόγῳ σεσαρκωμένῳ· δηλαδὴ τῇ ποικιλίᾳ τῶν λέξεων· Λόγῳ μὲν ὄντι, τῇ φύσει· σαρκὶ δὲ τῇ ὄψει· ὥστε τοὺς πολλούς, σάρκα καὶ οὐ Λόγον ὁρᾶν δοκεῖν κἂν εἰ κατὰ ἀλήθειαν ἐστι Λόγος. Οὐ γὰρ ὅπερ δοκεῖ τοῖς πολλοῖς, τοῦτο τῆς Γραφῆς ἐστιν ὁ νοῦς, ἀλλ᾽ ἕτερον παρὰ τὸ δοκοῦν. Ὁ γὰρ Λόγος, δι᾽ ἑκάστου τῶν ἀναγεγραμμένων ῥημάτων γίνεται σάρξ, *Th.Oec.* 2.60, *PG* 90.1152A: English translation by George C. Berthold in Maximus Confessor, *Selected Writings*, New York, Mahwah: Paulist Press, 1985, p. 160. See this too: "[...] the Word, who for our sake became like us and came to us through the body, and likewise grew thick in syllables and letters, in both cases because of the senses [...]" *Amb. Ioh.* 10, CONSTAS, 2014, I, pp. 198–199.

[29] The phrase "a super-infinite plan infinitely pre-existing the ages an infinite number of times" is from the discourse on the Mystery of Christ in *Q.Thal.* 60, *CCSG* 22, p. 75.41–42; English translation in CONSTAS, 2018, p. 429.

[30] See section from *Q.Thal.* 60 referred above.

above, from the point of view of *time, age and what is in them*,[31] actually means *from the end*. Paradoxically, we may also assert that *from above* is at the same time *from below*, i.e. *from the beginning*, because the beginning and the end are identical in themselves. St. Maximus claims that what is both the beginning and the end are in no way similar to what is *the middle*.[32] This *middle* is nothing else but the *diastema* of time that *contains* history; the beginning and the end have *nothing* similar to this *diastema* to which they are limits on either side. Finally, we have to remember that, writing about the Mystery of Christ, St. Maximus says that it is precisely that which *limits* the ages (τὸ πάντας περιγράφον τοὺς αἰῶνας)[33] – so, the Mystery of Christ is both the end and the beginning.

---

[31] I've expounded my view on Maximus' *definition* of time and aion from *Amb.Ioh.* 10, CONSTAS, 2014, 1, p. 262) in V. MILIĆEVIĆ, "A Contribution to the Understanding of the Mutual Definition of the Aeon and Time in *Ambigua* 10", *Philotheos*, 17 (2017), pp. 66–71, and much more elaborately in my Ph.D. thesis (in Serbian): *The Aspects of the Problem of Time according to St. Maximus the Confessor* [Аспекти проблема времена код Св. Максима Исповедника], Belgrade, 2018. There are many aspects in which I don't agree fully with modern interpretations of Maximus' cosmology and particularly his *doctrine* on time.

[32] "The end [*the aim*] has altogether no resemblance to the middle, otherwise it would not be an end [*the aim*]. The middle is all that comes after the beginning and before the end [*the aim*]. Thus if all ages, times, and places and all that they include are after God who is the beginning without a beginning [*causeless cause*], and as they are much behind him as infinite end [*aim*], they do not differ in any way from the middle. Rather, God is the end [*aim*] of those who are saved, and no middle shall be contemplated by those who are saved when the ultimate end [*aim*] is reached" [Τὸ τέλος οὐδὲν τὸ παράπαν ἐμφερὲς ἔχει μεσότητα· ἐπεὶ οὐδὲ τέλος. Μεσότης δέ ἐστι, πάντα τὰ μετὰ τὴν ἀρχὴν κατόπιν ὄντα τοῦ τέλους. Εἰ τοίνυν πάντες οἱ αἰῶνες καὶ οἱ χρόνοι καὶ οἱ τόποι μετὰ τῶν συνεπινοουμένων αὐτοῖς ἁπάντων, μετὰ τὸν Θεόν εἰσιν, ἀρχὴν ἄναρχον ὄντα· καὶ ὡς ἀπείρου τέλους αὐτοῦ πολὺ κατόπιν ὑπάρχουσι, μεσότητος οὐδὲν διαφέρουσι· τέλος δὲ τῶν σωζομένων ἐστὶν ὁ Θεός, οὐδὲν ἔσται μεσότητος κατὰ τὸ ἀκρότατον τέλος γενομένοις τοῖς σωζομένοις συνθεωρούμενον], *Th.Oec.* 1.69, *PG* 90.1108CD; English translation by George C. Berthold (my insertions in brackets) in Maximus Confessor, *Selected Writings*, p. 140.

[33] *Q.Thal.* 60, *CCSG* 22, p. 75.40; English translation in CONSTAS, 2018, p. 429.

Consequently, the event and the reality of the incarnation cannot in any way be reduced to the limits of a historical phenomenon. In a way, this may well apply to all the *other* key events of the salvation history as well, which is evident, I find, on the basis of what we can read in the Gospel text. What I am pointing at is the fundamentally eschatological nature of these events, which is evident from the fact that the evangelists constantly refer, quoting Jesus himself, to the resurrection as a hermeneutical key for all other key events[34] and the Resurrection itself is by no means solely an historical event. Of course, it is clear that these quotes do not point to the Resurrection as something that bears *new information* that explains previous events, but rather a new order of reality.[35] Participation in this reality makes it possible to understand, or *to perfect* in an existential way, what has already been experienced by seeing (e.g. the event of Transfiguration or Christ's Passion). This is because all these events of the history of salvation are nothing but the manifestation of the one and only reality that the event of the Resurrection signifies, the reality of the Mystery of Christ. I feel the need to point out that this also applies to the death of Christ as well, which precisely because of this in itself becomes the victory over death, the ultimate manifestation of God's life in the realm of death.

It is important to pay attention to the fact that even the Gospel descriptions do not speak about the resurrection event in a way that makes it possible to understand it as solely historical. Thus, in Matthew's description historical and eschatological perspectives of the Resurrection literally coincide.[36] In Luke and John, the descriptions of Christ's appearances after the resurrection, with a subtle and constant insistence on their sacramental character focused on the Eucharist,[37]

---

[34] Cf. "Tell the vision to no one until the Son of Man is risen from the dead", Mt. 17.9 (*NKJV*).

[35] Cf. "Now as they came down from the mountain, He commanded them that they should tell no one the things they had seen, till the Son of Man had risen from the dead. So they kept this word to themselves, questioning what the rising from the dead meant", Mk. 9.9 (*NKJV*).

[36] Cf. Matt. 27.52–53, which is also very directly reflected in the iconography – I am referring to the traditional Byzantine depiction of the Resurrection or *the Descent into Hades*.

[37] Cf. O. CULLMANN, *Early Christian Worship*, London, 1953.

introduce fundamentally eschatological perspective in the events they describe.

If this eschatological-sacramental perspective is not taken into account, the description of Christ's ascension becomes absurd. Namely, if Heaven to which Christ ascends is not the eschatological fulfillment of God's creation,[38] it seems there remains nothing but to imagine that the body of Christ, being a body, now somehow sits or walks on some kind of solid heaven. On the other hand, if we interpret these descriptions in the sacramental key, bearing in mind that sacramental always means eschatological too, we arrive at a possible solution which I find easy to connect with some key aspects of Maximus' Christology, cosmology, and eschatology. Thus, *the place* where Christ *ascended* is an eschatological reality and this means, as we have seen, that in it the limitations of space and time are abolished. That is why Christ's ascended body can exist and be participated in time, but in a timeless way, and in space, but in a non-spatial way. Both of these characteristics refer to the way of being described by the concept of sacramentality. Following this line of thought, we can conclude that the only *place* and *time* in which Christ now exists is the eucharistic *kairos* which thus, becoming the event of the absolute unity of everything, i.e. of the Mystery of Christ, transcends and ceases to be both place and time. One might say quite literally that *now* there is no other body of Christ apart from the one being *broken but not sundered, always fed upon and never consumed*,[39] or, in other words, apart from the body that exists in a completely incorporeal way, with no perspectives, to paraphrase St. Maximus, of both beginning and end.[40]

---

[38] Cf. Apoc. 21:5.

[39] Cf. prayer before the Holy Communion from The Divine Liturgy of St. John Chrysostom, *The Divine Liturgy & the Sunday Gospels*, Athens, 1968, p. 45.

[40] Here I must draw attention to a very lucid insight of Paul Plass, which seems to me to support what has been said here: "...since there is a pattern of history, events separate in time are drawn together and superimposed on each other to make up a series all of whose moments coexist simultaneously. When the incarnation is set into this conception, the Logos – at once eternal and immanent – acts like a singularity bending and binding the historical environment to itself", P. Plass, "Transcendent Time in Maximus the Confessor", *The Thomist*, 44/2 (1980), p. 271.

But, again, how to explain the fundamentally orthodox belief that Christ's incarnation is the center of history? Could this be anything else but metaphor? I think that here we should pay attention to two concepts whose relevance, when it comes to the problem of temporality, is pointed out by Paul Plass with reason.[41] What I mean are the concepts of *systole* and *diastole*, of which St. Maximus writes in our *Ambiguum* 10 too. St. Maximus uses these two concepts to denote the structural movement of creation taken as a whole, which is designated as ἡ ἁπλῶς λεγομένη οὐσία, and which *moves* from the general level of being to the individual ones and vice versa. This movement is to be taken as proof of its contingency, i.e. its quality of being *created*.

> But even what is called "substance" in a simple sense – not just the substance of things subject to generation and corruption, which moves according to generation and corruption, but the substance of all beings – has been set in motion and continues to move according to the principle and mode of expansion and contraction.[42] For it is moved from the most generic genus through the more generic genera to particular species, through which and in which it is naturally divided, proceeding down to the most specific species, where its expansion comes to a limit, which circumscribes its being on the lower end of the scale; and once again it is gathered back from the most specific kinds of species, moving back through more and more general categories, until it is gathered up into the most generic genus, and there its contraction comes to an end, limiting its being on the uppermost end of the scale. Circumscribed thus from two directions, I mean from above and below, it plainly has a beginning and an end, and cannot possibly receive the definition of infinity. The same pattern is true for the category of quantity... The same holds true with respect to quality... Obviously, no intelligent person would say that something which by nature is alternately dispersed and gathered together – either in principle or actuality – can in any sense be without motion. And if it is not without motion, neither is it without beginning; and if it has a beginning, it is clear that it has been created at a moment in time, and just as such a person knows that whatever is moved had a beginning of its motion, so too does he also understand that whatever has come to be began coming into being, receiving both its

---

[41] Cf. PLASS, "Transcendent Time in Maximus the Confessor", pp. 262–263.

[42] [...] κατὰ διαστολὴν καὶ συστολὴν λόγῳ τε καὶ τρόπῳ.

being and being moved from that which alone is uncreated and unmoved. Thus, that which owes its existence to an act of coming into being cannot in any way be without a beginning.[43]

However, it is especially important to note that the concepts of *systole* and *diastole* are applied by St. Maximus directly to Christology, in a text that, I would say, summarizes almost everything that has been discussed in this paper. Namely:

> One could say that the Logos "becomes thick" in the sense that for our sake He ineffably concealed Himself in the logoi of beings, and is obliquely signified in proportion to each visible thing, as if through certain letters, being whole in whole things while simultaneously remaining utterly complete and fully present, whole, and without diminishment in each particular thing. He remains undifferentiated and always the same in beings marked by difference; simple and without composition in things that are compounded; without origin in things that have a beginning; invisible in things that are seen; and incapable of being touched in all that is palpable. Or one could say that the Logos "becomes thick" in the sense that, for the sake of our thick minds, He consented to be both embodied and expressed through letters, syllables, and sounds, so that from all these He might gradually gather those who follow Him to Himself, being united by the Spirit, and thus raise us up to the simple and unconditioned idea of Him, bringing us for His own sake into union with Himself by contraction to the same extent that He has for our sake expanded Himself according to the principle of condescension.[44]

---

[43] *Amb.Ioh.* 10.37, Constas, 2014, I, pp. 288–290.

[44] "[...] ἢ ὅτι τοῖς τῶν ὄντων ἑαυτὸν δι' ἡμᾶς ἀπορρήτως ἐγκρύψας λόγοις ἀναλόγως δι' ἑκάστου τῶν ὁρωμένων ὡς διά τινων γραμμάτων ὑποσημαίνεται, ὅλος ἐν ὅλοις ἅμα πληρέστατος, καὶ τὸ καθ' ἕκαστον ὁλόκληρος, ὅλος καί ἀνελάττωτος, ἐν τοῖς διαφόροις ὁ ἀδιάφορος καὶ ὡσαύτως ἀεί ἔχων, ἐν τοῖς συνθέτοις ὁ ἁπλοῦς καὶ ἀσύνθετος, καὶ ἐν τοῖς ὑπὸ ἀρχὴν ὁ ἄναρχος, καὶ ὁ ἀόρατος ἐν τοῖς ὁρωμένοις καὶ ἐν τοῖς ἁπτοῖς ὁ ἀναφής· ἢ ὅτι δι' ἡμᾶς, τοὺς παχεῖς τὴν διάνοιαν, σωματωθῆναί τε δι' ἡμᾶς καὶ γράμμασι καὶ συλλαβαῖς καὶ φωναῖς τυπωθῆναι κατεδέξατο, ἵνα ἐκ πάντων τούτων ἡμᾶς ἑπομένους αὐτῷ κατὰ βραχὺ πρὸς ἑαυτὸν συναγάγῃ, ἑνοποιηθέντος τῷ Πνεύματι, καὶ εἰς τὴν ἁπλῆν περὶ αὐτοῦ καὶ ἄσχετον ἔννοιαν ἀναγάγοι, τοσοῦτον ἡμᾶς δι' ἑαυτὸν πρὸς ἕνωσιν ἑαυτοῦ *συστείλας*, ὅσον αὐτὸς δι' ἡμᾶς ἑαυτὸν συγκαταβάσεως λόγῳ *διέστειλεν*", *Amb.Ioh.* 33, Constas, 2014, 2,

Following this, when it comes to the event of the incarnation seen as a *historical* reality, we might say that it represents the point of intersection of the *diastole* and the *systole* of the Logos. But the reality of the incarnation cannot be limited to this event alone. One could say, without hesitation, that the incarnation begins with creation itself since that is when the *diastole* of the Logos starts. Actually, the historical incarnation of the Logos is the ultimate limit of this *diastole*, the point at which it reaches its fullness. This is followed by the *contraction*, i.e. the ascension of the creation towards the Creator.[45]

Maximus' division of world history (*ages*) into two analogous parts (*two groups*) is directly related to what was said about the *systole* and *diastole* of the Logos, as well as about the event of the incarnation as the center of history. It also bears witness to the fact that Maximus' view of temporality and cosmology in general is fundamentally inseparable from his Christology, but also that the opposite may be equally true: Maximus' Christology is deeply cosmological. Therefore, we shall conclude this discussion with the text in which Maximus expounds his general vision of world history, seen simultaneously as the history of creation and salvation:

> He who brought all visible and invisible creation into being solely through the momentum of His will, had in His good counsel determined – before all the ages and even before the very genesis of created beings – an ineffably good plan for His creations. And this plan was for Him to be mingled, without change, with human nature through a true union according to hypostasis, uniting human nature, without alteration, to Himself, so that He would become man – in a manner known to Him – and at the same time make man God through union with Himself, and thus He wisely divided the ages, determining that

---

pp. 62–65. Since the concepts of *systole* and *diastole* are here in a verb form, I marked them by cursive. In *Amb.Ioh.* 33 Maximus comments on St. Gregory's *Oratio* 38.2 in which he says that "Logos becomes thick" [Ὁ Λόγος παχύνεται...], cf. *PG* 36, 313B.

[45] I fully agree with Eric David Perl's opinion 1) that creation and incarnation *are identical*, or that "the theophanic creation of the world *is* the incarnation of the Logos" (PERL, *Methexis*, p. 216) and 2) that this has to do with fundamentally (neo)platonic correspondence between *logic* and ontology, particularly evident *inter alia* in Maximus' appropriation of *systole* and *diastole* concepts (*Ibid.*, pp. 126–127).

some would be for the activity of His becoming man, and others for the activity of making man God [...] To state the matter briefly, of these ages, the former belong to God's descent to man, while the latter belong to man's ascent to God.[46]

[46] "Ὁ πάσης κτίσεως, ὁρατῆς τε καὶ ἀοράτου, κατὰ μόνην τοῦ θελήματος τὴν ῥοπὴν ὑποστήσας τὴν γένεσιν πρὸ πάντων τῶν αἰώνων καὶ αὐτῆς τῆς τῶν γεγονότων γενέσεως τὴν ἐπ' αὐτοῖς ἀφράστως ὑπεράγαθον εἶχε βουλήν· ἡ δὲ ἦν αὐτὸν μὲν ἀτρέπτως ἐγκραθῆναι τῇ φύσει τῶν ἀνθρώπων διὰ τῆς καθ' ὑπόστασιν ἀληθοῦς ἑνώσεως, ἑαυτῷ δὲ τὴν φύσιν ἀναλλοιώτως ἑνῶσαι τὴν ἀνθρωπίνην, ἵν' αὐτὸς μὲν ἄνθρωπος γένηται, καθὼς οἶδεν αὐτός, Θεὸν δὲ ποιήσειε τῇ πρὸς ἑαυτὸν ἑνώσει τὸν ἄνθρωπον, μερίσας δηλον ὅτι σοφῶς τοὺς αἰῶνας καὶ διορίσας, τοὺς μὲν ἐπ' ἐνεργείᾳ τοῦ αὐτὸν γενέσθαι ἄνθρωπον, τοὺς δὲ ἐπ' ἐνεργείᾳ τοῦ τὸν ἄνθρωπον ποιῆσαι Θεόν [...] Καὶ συντόμως εἰπεῖν, τῶν αἰώνων οἱ μὲν τῆς τοῦ Θεοῦ πρὸς ἀνθρώπους εἰσὶ καταβάσεως, οἱ δὲ τῆς τῶν ἀνθρώπων πρὸς Θεὸν ὑπάρχουσιν ἀναβάσεως[...]", Q.Thal. 22, CCSG 7, pp. 137.4–16; 139.54–56: English translation in CONSTAS, 2018, pp. 150–152.

The divinization of man according to the *Tenth Ambiguum* of Saint Maximus the Confessor

Dionysios SKLIRIS

(*Athens*)

The divinization of man is one of the most central themes in the theology of Saint Maximus the Confessor, considered tantamount to the profoundest goal of the creation of the world, and as explaining the very movement of beings. This chapter will observe how this subject is put in the Tenth *Ambiguum*, in which Saint Maximus synthesizes three diverse elements: i) an approach to divinization through the threefold schema "practical philosophy/purification" – "natural contemplation/illumination" – "mystical union/divinization". The passage from contemplation to divinization will be explored, raising the question whether there is an intellectualistic (as opposed to voluntarist) theory of divinization in the Tenth *Ambiguum*. ii) The ontological threefold schema "being" – "well-being" – "eternal well-being", in which divinization is considered as constituting the primordial existential goal of creation that confirms being itself. iii) The biblical theme of divinization by adoption, which prevents an excessively naturalistic account of divinization that would entail the loss of human natural particularity and personal otherness. After having examined these three dimensions of divinization, we shall observe how the intellectualist approach to divinization is integrated into a trinitarian structure which does justice to the uniquely Christian vision of man as image of the Trinity, through the Incarnation of the Son in the Spirit.

1. Divinization as the end of practical and natural philosophy

In the 10th *Ambiguum*, Saint Maximus employs a ternary schema concerning spiritual progress toward deification, beginning with "practical

Ambiguum *10 of Maximus the Confessor in Modern Study: Papers Collected on the Occasion of the Budapest Colloquium on Saint Maximus, 3–4 February 2021*, ed. by Alexis LÉONAS & Vladimir CVETKOVIĆ, with the collaboration of Daniel HEIDE, Turnhout, 2025 (IPM 97), pp. 361–380
   10.1484/M.IPM-EB.5.141869

philosophy"(πρακτικὴ φιλοσοφία),[1] i.e. the purification from passions. The latter is followed by the stage of the natural contemplation of beings, in which man discovers God's will after being illuminated. This entails the wisdom to discern the deeper meaning pertaining to the *logoi* of beings, pointing to the final causality of creation. For Saint Maximus, the *logoi* are both formal and volitional principles of beings. In other words, they constitute divine wills for the formation of beings and for their evolution toward their future fulfilment. Divinization comes as the final outcome of this process of purification and illumination: it means the mystical union with God as a result of grace. Saint Maximus considers that "the practical life is always joined to reason", since "it is the task of contemplation to choose to take hold of what must be thought and judged in a beautiful and intelligent way".[2] Through bodily practice, man discovers that God has become all things in everyone, and through all things is present to all,[3] the latter being the ground for divinization. It is to be noted, however, that the practical life has to be subjected to reason,[4] according to the relative subordination of the body to the mind. The practical virtues aid the wise man in proceeding to the knowledge of the *logoi* of beings, while the latter in turn help him to acquire virtues.[5] For Saint Maximus, the virtues are not a goal in themselves, but constitute a manifestation of the *logoi* of beings. Thus, the ascetic does not create the virtues within him, but simply exhibits the divine *logoi*,[6] i.e. the divine wills that stand for the relative virtues. However, the practice of the virtues helps in the process of discernment of the *logoi* of beings, since the latter requires a certain purification from the passions, which obscure the clarity of the divine will.

It is to be noted that the distinction between contemplation and praxis is not merely one between the soul and the body; it is also interior to the soul itself, since the latter has on the one hand the contemplative capacity of the intellect (νοῦς) and, on the other, that of the practical

---

[1] For the meaning of "practical philosophy" see also: *Amb.Ioh.* 58–60 in CONSTAS, 2014, 2, pp. 256–265: *PG* 91,1381D–1385A; *Q.Thal.*, CCSG 7, pp. 7,497,293–499,295, *PG* 90, 548B.

[2] CONSTAS, 2014, I, pp. 151–153, *PG* 91,1108A.

[3] *Amb.Ioh.* 10,1, CONSTAS, 2014, I, p. 153, *PG* 91,1108C.

[4] *Amb.Ioh.* 10,1, CONSTAS, 2014, I, p. 155, *PG* 91,1108D.

[5] *Amb.Ioh.* 10,1, CONSTAS, 2014, I, p. 157, *PG* 91,1109A.

[6] *Amb.Ioh.* 10,1, CONSTAS, 2014, I, p. 157, *PG* 91,1109B.

reason (λόγος), which defines the right use of beings according to the divine will discerned by the intellect. The human intellect thus has a priority over the human *logos*, but it is itself subjected to the divine *logos* that is contemplated by it. Saint Maximus insists that practical wisdom might be an indispensable step toward the perfection of divinization but, if the faithful remain at the practical level, this is a sign that they are not liberated from the attachment to material changeable things. There is a certain dialectic of *praxis* and *theoria*: If one takes the path of practical virtue to the extreme, one becomes such an intimate friend of God in contemplation that one is severed from any bond to what is perishable.[7]

The itinerary from practical wisdom to contemplation and then to divinization thus has a dialectical character: Praxis is indispensable, but only as a stage toward divinization; Illumination is not a goal in itself but only a union with the multiple *logoi* that is overshadowed when the union with the One *Logos* takes place. The final state of divinization is one in which the intellect is "freed completely from its motion in the midst of all of reality and is quieted even in its own natural activity".[8]

This final state of divinization is regarded by Saint Maximus as an intermingling with the whole of God through the Spirit. There is thus a Trinitarian structure in divinization. Divinization is the initial will of God the Father; it is achieved through the Incarnation of the Son which, according to Saint Maximus' expression, means that "God and man are paradigms of each other",[9] since man is deified due to the fact that God becomes man. The Holy Spirit is the One that brings this union to its eschatological fulfilment as mediator for our intermingling with God. God's incarnation in the Spirit conceived as basis for man's divinization is the ontological ground for the authentic spiritual life of the faithful, which consists in the incarnation of God in man through the virtues, this latter being the cause of man's divinization through the contemplative ascent.

This dialectic between the ascetic praxis, the intellectual contemplation and the mystic union with God is usually linked with the dialectic between the modes (τρόποι) of the virtues, the reasons (λόγοι) of beings

---

[7] *Amb.Ioh.* 10,1, CONSTAS, 2014, I, p. 159, *PG* 91,1109D.

[8] *Amb.Ioh.* 10,3, CONSTAS, 2014, I, p. 163, *PG* 91,1113B.

[9] Φασὶ γὰρ ἀλλήλων εἶναι παραδείγματα τὸν θεὸν καὶ τὸν ἄνθρωπον, *Amb.Ioh.* 10,3, CONSTAS, 2014, I, p. 165: *PG* 91,1113B.

and the end (τέλος) of divinization in the eschaton. The *tropoi* concern the first stage of the ascetic purification, which leads to the second stage of the natural contemplation of the *logoi*. The fact that Saint Maximus usually places the modes of virtue before the *logoi* is arguably linked to his more general view that the truth is the final cause of virtue and not the inverse.[10]

In general, in the work of Saint Maximus, this three-fold schema is formulated through characteristic terms, such as: "ethical, natural and theological philosophy" (ἠθικὴ καὶ φυσικὴ καὶ θεολογικὴ φιλοσοφία);[11] "virtue – knowledge – secret theology" (ἀρετή – γνῶσις – ἀπόρρητος θεολογία),[12] "practical philosophy – theoretical mystagogy" (πρακτικὴ φιλοσοφία – θεωρητικὴ μυσταγωγία),[13] "practical – natural – theological philosophy" (πρακτικὴ καὶ φυσικὴ καὶ θεολογικὴ φιλοσοφία),[14] "practical <philosophy> – natural contemplation – theological mystagogy" (πρακτικὴ – φυσικὴ θεωρία – θεολογικὴ μυσταγωγία).[15] In other contexts, one finds a double schema between the *tropoi* of praxis and the *logoi* of contemplation: "mode of ethical philosophy" – "*logos* and mode of the natural contemplation" – "mystery of the true vision" (τρόπος τῆς ἠθικῆς φιλοσοφίας – λόγος καὶ τρόπος τῆς φυσικῆς θεωρίας – μυστήριον τῆς ἀληθοῦς ἐποψίας);[16] "modes of virtues according to the practical philosophy" – "*logoi* of knowledge" (κατὰ τὴν πρακτικὴν φιλοσοφίαν τρόποι τῶν ἀρετῶν – λόγοι τῆς γνώσεως);[17] "modes according to virtue" – "*logoi* of knowledge according to contemplation" (κατ' ἀρετὴν τρόποι – κατὰ θεωρίαν γνωστικοὶ λόγοι – κατὰ τὴν χάριν μεταποίησις);[18] "modes of practical philosophy according to virtue" – "*logoi* of the gnostic contemplation" (κατ' ἀρετὴν πρακτικῆς φιλοσοφίας τρόποι – τῆς γνωστικῆς θεωρίας λόγοι);[19] "modes of the commandments" – "*logoi* of beings"

[10] *Q.Thal.* 30 CCSG 7, p. 219,18–20, *PG* 90, 369A.
[11] *Amb.Ioh.* 10,19, CONSTAS, 2014, 1, p. 208, *PG* 91, 1136C.
[12] *Q.Thal.* 35 CCSG 7, p. 239,25–26, *PG* 90, 377D.
[13] *Q.Thal.* 52 CCSG 7, p. 419,72–73, *PG* 90, 493A.
[14] *Div.Cap.* *PG* 90, 1172B.
[15] *Div.Cap.* *PG* 90, 1172B.
[16] *Amb.Ioh.* 31, CONSTAS, 2014, 2, p. 44, *PG* 91, 1277A.
[17] *Amb.Ioh.* 58, CONSTAS, 2014, 2, pp. 256–258, *PG* 91,1381D–1384A.
[18] *Amb.Ioh.* 65, CONSTAS, 2014, 2, p. 280, *PG* 91, 1393A.
[19] *Q.Thal.* 37, CCSG 7, p. 249,53–55, *PG* 90, 385B.

(τρόποι τῶν ἐντολῶν – λόγοι τῶν ὄντων);[20] "virtuous modes according to the action" – "gnostic visions according to contemplation" (κατὰ τὴν πρᾶξιν ἐνάρετοι τρόποι – κατὰ τὴν θεωρίαν γνωστικὰ θεωρήματα);[21] – "modes of honourable disposition" – "spiritual *logoi* of wisdom" (τρόποι ἀστείας ἀγωγῆς – σοφίας λόγοι πνευματικοί);[22] "modes toward virtue" – "spiritual *logoi* of gnosis" (πρὸς ἀρετὴν τρόποι – πνευματικοὶ τῆς γνώσεως λόγοι);[23] "modes of virtue according to the act" – "*logoi* of knowledge according to theory" (κατὰ τὴν πρᾶξιν τρόποι τῆς ἀρετῆς – κατὰ θεωρίαν λόγοι τῆς γνώσεως),[24] "modes according to act" – "*logoi* of knowledge that reside in true contemplation" (κατὰ πρᾶξιν τρόποι – τὴν ἀληθῆ θεωρίαν οἰκοῦντες λόγοι τῆς γνώσεως);[25] "modes of education" – "*logoi* of wisdom" (παιδείας τρόποι – σοφίας λόγοι);[26] "modes of virtue" – "*logoi* of knowledge" (ἀρετῆς τρόποι – γνώσεως λόγοι).[27] Another significant expression is "the modes of return and purification" (τρόποι ἐπιστροφῆς καὶ καθάρσεως),[28] which describes the first stage of the ascetic effort as the initiation of a process that leads to a return to God. This "return" is understood in the metaphysical context of the double movement of generation from God and return to Him.

In the entire Maximian corpus, there is a system of correspondences between this threefold process of divinization and other relative allegories or theories about the capacities of the souls: i) The modes of ascetic praxis are sometimes compared to the biblical theme of "Friday" as the day of preparation. Similarly, the contemplation of the *logoi* is regarded as the *Sabbath* of repose, while the mystical union of divinization is identified with Sunday as the eschatological eighth day of the Kingdom of God.[29] In other words, the biblical Friday means the preparation

---

[20] *Q.Thal.* 48, *CCSG* 7, p. 339,156–157, *PG* 90, 440B.

[21] *Q.Thal.* 50, *CCSG* 7, p. 383,94–95, *PG* 90, 469B.

[22] *Q.Thal.* 51, *CCSG* 7, p. 395,10–11, *PG* 90, 476C–477A.

[23] *Q.Thal.* 51, *CCSG* 7, p. 397,44–46, *PG* 90, 477A-B.

[24] *Q.Thal.* 52, *CCSG* 7, p. 427,200–202, *PG* 90, 497C.

[25] *Q.Thal.* 53, *CCSG* 7, p. 435,73–74, *PG* 90, 504C.

[26] *Q.Thal.* 54, *CCSG* 7, p. 457,240–241, *PG* 90, 517D.

[27] *Q.Thal.* 56, *CCSG* 22, p. 9, 100; *PG* 90, 581B.

[28] *Amb.Ioh.*17, CONSTAS, 2014, 1, p. 384, *PG* 91, 1125B.

[29] In *Amb.Ioh.* 65, CONSTAS, 2014, 2,, p. 280, *PG* 91, 1393A, the two first stages correspond to the biblical Sabbath, while the third one to the eighth eschatological day.

through the ascetic sacrifice of the body; the biblical Saturday entails the burying[30] of beings through their immobilization in the contemplation of their respective *logoi*;[31] while the biblical Sunday indicates the divinization that exceeds every mode and *logos* (while at the same time preserving them). ii) The virtues can also symbolize the body of Christ, the intellectual contemplation stands for His blood, while the secret theology of deification represents His bones.[32] iii) Practical philosophy corresponds to the Roman spirit, natural philosophy to the Hellenic one, and divinization to Judaic theology.[33] This is connected to the fact that the Cross of Christ bore an inscription in the language of Romans, Greeks and Jews. The way to divinization is thus paved with the accomplishments of the significant civilizations of Late Antiquity, such as Roman law, Greek philosophy and Jewish theology. The modes of virtues correspond to the Old Testament, while the knowledge of the *logos/logoi* corresponds to the New Testament.[34] In another allegorical consideration, praxis corresponds to the apostle Peter, while deifying knowledge corresponds to the apostle John.[35]

In order to understand the meaning of divinization according to this threefold Maximian schema, one should add that the characteristic natural traits of each stage are not abandoned. It might be true that, as pointed out earlier, the ascetic struggle and the contemplation of the *logoi* are overshadowed by the light of divinization; however, the human body is not abandoned during contemplation. In the same way, in the event of divinization, the particularity of the human nature is preserved, including all its operations, such as intellection, reason, will and corporeality. The modes and the *logoi* are two dialectical poles that are overshadowed yet preserved. Lars Thunberg remarks that this is the principal difference between the Maximian deifying ecstasy and the Evagrian ἐκδημία.[36] While in the Evagrian ἐκδημία, one abandons human elements like the body or even the passible part of the soul, in

[30] *Cap.Div.* PG 90, 1108B.
[31] *Cap.Div.* PG 90, 1097C.
[32] *Q.Thal.* 35 CCSG 7, p. 239, 25–26, PG 90, 377D.
[33] *Cap.Div.* PG 90, 1172B.
[34] *Q.Thal.* 63 CCSG 22, p. 165, 299–326, PG 90, 677B–D.
[35] *Q.Thal.* 3, CCSG 7,55,23–24, PG 90, 273B.
[36] L. THUNBERG, *Microcosm and Mediator: The Theological Anthropology of Saint Maximus the Confessor*, Chicago-La Salle, Illinois, ²1995, pp. 444–451.

the divinization as described by Saint Maximus the Confessor there is a preservation of all the transcended elements. One should add that the stages to divinization also describe different kinds of spirituality[37] that are equally legitimate. Not all ascetics achieve intellectual contemplation; ethical praxis should be sufficient for salvation. The *praktikos* reflects God's "thickening" (πάχυνσις) in the act of incarnation, whereas the *theoretikos* realizes the "refinement" of the return and ascension to God. Just as man refers to God the bread and the wine as two representative elements of creation, in the same way he refers the *tropoi* of ascesis and the *logoi* of creation, which are recollected through intellection.[38]

Thus, the meaning of the threefold path to divinization is, firstly, that man cannot achieve the contemplation of the *logoi*, if he is not purified.[39] Those who are subject to the passions cannot discern the *logoi*, i.e. God's will within creation. Besides, this passage from the *tropoi* to the *logoi* is sometimes described as a conception of the spiritual *logoi* that directs the modes of virtue[40] or the commandments.[41] The contemplation of the *logoi* of God is not a mere operation of the intellect. It is a much larger experience that includes the entire psycho-corporeal reality. The ultimate fruit of this progress is divinization through union with God. Later on in the Tenth *Ambiguum*, it is stated that similitude with God as basis for divinization is related to the intellectual vision that leads to a resemblance between the seer and what is seen:

> A person becomes god, for he has experienced divine existence and sees intellectually the full reflection of God's goodness coming from beings

---

[37] *Amb.Ioh .47*, CONSTAS, 2014, 2, pp. 206–211, *PG* 91, 1357D–1361A.

[38] *Q.Thal.* 51, *CCSG* 7, pp. 397–407, *PG* 90, 477A-485B.

[39] In *Q.Thal.* 54, *CCSG* 7, p. 463,336–357, *PG* 90, 524B, Saint Maximus describes the procedure through which man exercises virtue stating that only after such an exercise can he achieve the discernment through deliberation, science, knowledge of the *logoi*, prudence and, last but not least, the simplest theory of the truth of all beings. The chronological order is from the ascetic praxis to knowledge, but the teleological order is the inverse.

[40] In *Q.Thal.* 56, *CCSG* 22, p. 11,128–130, *PG* 90, 584A. In *Q.Thal.* 58, *CCSG* 22, p. 31,64–69, *PG* 90, 596A, the relation between the praxis and the contemplation is regarded as absolutely complementary: Contemplation is the ground for moral activity, whereas the latter is the manifestation of contemplation.

[41] Cf. *Myst.*, *CCSG* 69, p. 63, 1014–1026, *PG* 91, 709A.

and rationally gives shape in himself to this absolutely clear reflection. For they say that what the pure intellect sees naturally by means of pious knowledge, it is also able to experience and becomes that very thing by possessing it through virtue.[42]

This passage stresses that man doesn't become God by nature, but only through participation in His otherness. The latter is however related to the intellectual capacity of being oriented to God and transforming oneself according to the "object" of the orientation. The right intellectual vision is described later in the Tenth *Ambiguum* in the following way:

Finally, they understood creation in terms of mixture alone, that is, in terms of the harmonizing synthesis of the universe, and reflecting, by means of all the things that have been ineffably bound together with each other to form a complete single world upon the Word who alone is the fashioner who joins and binds the parts tightly to the whole and to each other, they closed the gap between the two to form one mode of contemplation. In this way, they conveyed the intellect to the cause approaching it simply through the essential ideas in existing things, and bound the intellect solely to the cause, since it gathers and attracts everything that comes from it. In this the intellect is no longer dispersed amongst the essential ideas of individual beings, because it has been, through a rigorous examination of beings, taken beyond them by being utterly convinced, that, in the end, God alone truly is and is the essence and motion of beings, the clear distinction of different things, the insoluble continuity of things that have been mixed together, and the immovable foundation of what has been established and that, in His simplicity He is the cause of every essence, motion, distinction, mixture and placement that can be thought in any way whatsoever.[43]

This passage is offering an insight into the relation between intellectual contemplation and divinization. For Saint Maximus, the human intellect constitutes a primordial capacity of orientation of the whole psycho-corporeal ensemble toward either God or the world, being assimilated to its "object". If the intellect is oriented toward the world, it becomes multiform and chaotic; however, if it is turned toward God, it can discern the presence of His will in beings through natural contemplation and, having been illuminated, it can be assimilated to the

[42] *Amb.Ioh.* 10,19, CONSTAS, 2014, I, p. 205, *PG* 91, 1333B.
[43] *Amb.Ioh.* 10,19, CONSTAS, 2014, I, p. 211, *PG* 91, 1136D–1137B.

divine energy. In this case, there is a smooth passage from purification to contemplation and then to divinization. During the latter, man becomes "the clearest of mirrors" for God the Word.[44]

In this sense, divinization is also considered as the transcendence of the duality of matter and form that brings man closer to the absolute divine simplicity.[45] Saint Maximus interprets the theology of divinization of Saint Gregory of Nazianzus in this way,[46] stating that divinization is an image of the Trinity that combines the absolute simplicity of the divine monad with the three persons, surpassing the dyad of "flesh" and "form" through which the material world is created. The transcendence by grace of the duality and split that is inherent in created being is thus a crucial aspect of divinization. In this sense, divinization also entails becoming without beginning and end,[47] the latter however taking place at the level of grace and not of nature. This means that the created nature of man is not annihilated as in Neoplatonist versions of divinization; it is saved, but participates by grace in the divine infinite timelessness and even beginninglessness. For Saint Maximus, however, unlike Neoplatonist philosophers, this is due to the presence of the Word in creation through the Incarnation, the *logoi* being divine volitions realized in the novel mode of existence through which Christ actualizes the created nature. The fact that divinization is by position and not by nature guarantees that the created beings will retain their proper natural difference during divinization, the latter being hypostatic in character.

In Saint Maximus' eschatology, divinization is defined as an ever-moving repose (ἀεικίνητος στάσις), a paradoxical concept that corrects the notion of *epektasis* in the theology of Saint Gregory of Nyssa. This Maximian antinomy expresses the tensions that we have observed in the Tenth *Ambiguum*, such as those between contemplation and mystical union, cataphatic and apophatic theology, etc. The deepest truth of these expressions is that we become human by becoming divine: The repose (στάσις) denotes the fact that human nature has reached and achieved its ontological goal. In other words, in the eschaton we will discover what humanity truly is, having become human

---

[44] *Amb.Ioh.* 10,19, CONSTAS, 2014, I, p. 213, *PG* 91, 1137B.

[45] *Amb.Ioh.* 10,20a, CONSTAS, 2014, I, p. 221, *PG* 91, 1141C.

[46] *Amb.Ioh.* 10,43, M. CONSTAS, 2014, I, p. 321, *PG* 91, 1193.

[47] *Amb.Ioh.* 10,20d, CONSTAS, 2014, I, p. 225, *PG* 91, 1144C.

in an absolutely authentic way. On the other hand, this occurs only through divinization, namely by suffering a passion that perpetually provokes a movement toward the unreachable God.[48] Thus, the antinomy of the ever-moving repose expresses the divine and human poles of divinization in a way that is more complete than the mere notion of dynamic *epektasis*, even though the latter shares the same existential goal. One could equally express this vision by remarking that in the eschaton the mystical union will show the profoundest truth of the contemplation of natures, while the dwelling within the darkness of the ungraspable God will confirm a cataphatic theology of the meaning of existence.

The threefold schema of spiritual progress toward divinization thus constitutes a movement of ascent, in which the ethical *tropoi* precede the *logoi*. In the Tenth *Ambiguum* it is complemented by an inverse movement of descent, in which the existential *tropoi* realize the primordial divine *logoi*. A similarly three-fold schema extensively employed in the Tenth *Ambiguum* is the distinction between being, well-being and eternal well-being, to which we shall now turn.

2. Divinization as the eternal well-being that confirms the being of creation and the well-being of ethics.

The second ternary schema that Saint Maximus introduces in the Tenth *Ambiguum*, in order to describe divinization, is that of being (εἶναι), well-being (εὖ εἶναι) and eternal being (ἀεὶ εἶναι). In general, this pattern is similar to a distinction between nature, virtue, and the grace of divinization; or between love as natural union, as ethical demand, and as deifying communion with God.[49] The relation of this ontological threefold structure with Maximus' favourite distinction between the *logos* of nature and the *tropos* of activity and, consequently, with the threefold structure of the spiritual path to divinization is not absolutely consistent throughout the Maximian corpus. However, one could make the following observations: i) In certain passages,[50] Saint Maximus consid-

---

[48] S. MITRALEXIS, *Ever-Moving Repose. A contemporary reading of Maximus the Confessor's theory of time*, Eugene, Oregon, 2017.

[49] *Q.Thal.* 64, *CCSG* 22, pp. 233,725–237,804, *PG* 90, 724C–728A.

[50] *Amb.Ioh.*7, CONSTAS, 2014, I, p. 104, *PG* 91,1084B; *Q.Thal.* 64, *CCSG* 22, p. 237,794–804: *PG* 90, 725D.

ers being, well-being and eternal well-being as three *logoi* that "pre-exist" in God,[51] according to the Pauline expression of Stoic inspiration "for in God we live and move and have our being" (*Act.* 17:28). One could note, however, that the order in Saint Maximus is the inverse, since it is the eternal being that constitutes real life, whereas the simple being refers merely to the initial given of existence. ii) In the 10th *Ambiguum*, however,[52] being, well-being, and eternal being, are considered as three different modes of the same more fundamental *logos*. Later in the *Ambigua*,[53] this *logos* is defined as "the *logos* of generation of rational essences", since it is evident that only the rational essences have the possibility to progress toward virtue and divinization. iii) One can equally find some passages,[54] in which well-being is opposed to ill-being, whereas inside the eternal-being one finds the two opposite modes of eternal well-being and eternal ill-being, among which only the eternal well-being could be identified with divinization proper. These passages raise the possibility of a distinction between resurrection and divinization, since the common resurrection of nature could be experienced by some persons as eternal ill-being. In other words, eternal being would denote the common resurrection of nature, while only the eternal well-being would denote divinization proper. iv) Finally, in some passages,[55] the *logos* is rather attributed to the first level of being, while *tropos* is restricted to the ethically contingent level of well-being. The eternal being of divinization is considered as an ineffable "mystery".

These variations are not necessarily contradictory: being, well-being, and eternal well-being, are divine wills for created being and, as such, constitute divine *logoi*. At the same time, one can consider that the ultimate divine will is the eternal being of creation, in which case the historical being and the well-being of virtue are specific modes of the wider *logos*, which will be manifested in the glory of the eternal well-being of the eschatological divinization. Ill-being and eternal ill-being would constitute in this case modes without foundation in a divine *logos*; that is, modes that are provoked by man's sinful response to the divine *logos*.

---

[51] *Amb.Ioh.* 7, CONSTAS, 2014, 1, p. 104, *PG* 91, 1084A–C.
[52] *Amb.Ioh.*10, CONSTAS, 2014, 1, p. 168, *PG* 91, 1116B.
[53] *Amb.Ioh.* 65, CONSTAS, 2014, 2, pp. 274–281, *PG* 91, 1392.
[54] *Ep.* 16, *PG* 91, 577D.
[55] *Cap.Div. PG* 90, 1104C; *Ep.* 16, *PG* 91 ,577D.

In the Tenth *Ambiguum*,[56] Saint Maximus considers being, well-being, and eternal-being, as three modes in a way similar to the more developed one employed later in the *Ambigua*.[57] Saint Maximus presents these modes as finalities by using the Dative "ἐφ ᾧ",[58] but he specifies that for the two extremes, namely the being of creation and the eternal being of divinization, God is the sole cause, whereas the middle, well-being, also depends on man's gnomic disposition and movement ("καὶ τῆς ἡμετέρας ἠρτημένον γνώμης τε καὶ κινήσεως"). But this middle constitutes a good connection ("εὖ συνημμένον") between the two extremes. The well-being thus contributes to the realization of the two other modes, which is obtained through their eternal movement toward God.

Due to the contingency of the use of human freedom, there is always the possibility of a mode according to the "misuse"[59] of the natural capacities, which is opposed to the "*logos* according to nature" that constitutes the authentic norm. The *logos* demonstrates the correct use of the natural capacities and operations, whereas the mode (*tropos*) designates the possibility of their misuse that can lead to their degradation, without however threatening the integrity of the divine *logos* that is always present within nature. One should always bear in mind that the *logos* is an uncreated divine will that cannot be corrupted and that is distinguished from the created being to which it refers and which can be altered, at least within the context of history. Saint Maximus employs the dramatic expression "from reason's own explicit crying out" ("αὐτοῦ βοῶντος τοῦ λόγου διαρρήδην ἀκούσαντες"),[60] which means that the saints are hearing the *logos* itself crying out for the necessity of the correct use of nature. One should probably consider here that it is the Logos with a capital "l" who cries out about the use of nature that would be according to His divine will. This accordance to the *logos* signifies receiving true being (ὄντως εἶναι) from God, having also received being (εἶναι) from the same source. One can thus conclude that being is considered in the perspective of true being, the latter being tantamount to the eschatological eternal being. In the Tenth *Ambigu-*

---

[56] *Amb.Ioh.* 10,3, CONSTAS, 2014, 1, pp. 167–171, *PG* 91, 1116.

[57] *Amb.Ioh.* 65, CONSTAS, 2014, 2, pp. 274–281, *PG* 91, 1392.

[58] *Amb.Ioh.* 10,3, CONSTAS, 2014, 1, p. 166, *PG* 91, 1116B.

[59] *Amb.Ioh.* 10,3, CONSTAS, 2014, 1, p. 169, *PG* 91, 1116C.

[60] *Amb.Ioh.* 10,3, CONSTAS, 2014, 1, p. 169, *PG* 91, 1116C.

um,[61] Maximus remarks that God is offering us the *logoi* of both. In *PG* 91,1116D, the term *logos* signifies the human psychic capacity, which interprets what is contemplated by the intellect.[62] This psychic faculty of the *logos* brings together with its universalizing capacity the unifying modes (ἐνοποιοὶ τρόποι), which are turned toward the intelligible realities. The "unifying modes" are ethical determinations which facilitate man's elevation to a greater level of universality. The ethical modes thus serve a goal that is similar to that of the intelligible *logoi*, namely that of a greater catholicity in view of the final union of divinization.

In conclusion, the divine *logos* of nature defines the correct use of the natural capacities[63] as it is realized in the Incarnate Logos. It is apprehended by the human faculty of the intellect and interpreted by the human faculty of the *logos*, or reason, the latter constituting an intermediary capacity between the intellect and sensation.[64] The *logos* in the first sense, namely that of a divine principle of created reality, is determined by the three modes of being, well-being, and eternal being. There is however one mode (τρόπος) that is provoked by human freedom, namely the mode of misuse of natural capacities against their logical norm. This mode is tantamount to what Saint Maximus usually terms "ill-being" (φεῦ εἶναι), the dilemma between well-being (εὖ εἶναι) and ill-being (φεῦ εἶναι) constituting what is at stake in the human response to the divine *logos* of being.[65] The ontological foundation of this question is that being must be approached from the perspective of divinized eternal being: being cannot be conceived in itself, but only from the perspective of its eternalization. This is confirmed in a significant passage of the *Quaestiones ad Thalassium*,[66] in which being and

[61] *Amb.Ioh.* 10,3, CONSTAS, 2014, 1, pp. 169–171, *PG* 91, 1116C–D.

[62] In general, the term *logos* presents a polysemy. It can signify the uncreated *logos*, i.e. the divine will that functions as an ontological principle; it can also mean the created faculty of human reason, which interprets the divine *logoi* as collected by the human intellect.

[63] *Amb.Ioh.* 10,3, CONSTAS, 2014, 1, p. 169, *PG* 91, 1116C.

[64] *Amb.Ioh.* 10,3,. CONSTAS, 2014, 1, p. 171, *PG* 91, 1116D.

[65] See also *Amb.Ioh.*7, CONSTAS, 2014, 1, p. 86, *PG* 91, 1073C, where Saint Maximus distinguishes between, on the one hand, the simple movement (ἁπλῶς κινεῖσθαι), which has its origin in God, and, on the other, the qualified movement ("πῶς κινεῖσθαι"), which is directed to God as its goal.

[66] *Q.Thal.* 60, *CCSG* 22, p. 79,117–120, *PG* 90, 624D.

eternal being are considered as two divine propositions to man that occur, respectively, within a protological and eschatological context. Man cannot alter the divine *logos*,[67] but he can determine his proper response, which Saint Maximus characterizes as a necessary intermediary "connection" between the two divine extremes.[68]

In general, Saint Maximus conceives of the divinization of the world as following a dialogue between God and man, in which the *logos* constitutes a divine proposition and the *tropos* man's response to this proposition. Saint Maximus similarly interprets the distinction between the image and the likeness of God.[69] The image concerns what is given by God; namely, being and eternal being, while the likeness concerns the contingent ethical struggle performed by man. For example, Saint Maximus considers that all men are rational according to their image. But only those who succeed in being virtuous and wise attain the likeness. In a similar way, later on in the *Ambigua*,[70] being, well-being, and eternal well-being, are considered as three modes identified with the three births of man; namely, the biological one, baptism, and resurrection. There is thus an ecclesiological dimension in man's movement toward well-being. The different modes signify distinct ontological modes of receiving existence. This is the deeper meaning of the one *logos* receiving three distinct ontological modes that we find in the Tenth *Ambiguum*. The one *logos* refers to the universality of the generation of all essences, whereas the *tropoi* concern the different personal modes of reception of the universality of the created and resurrected being as eternal well-being or eternal ill-being. Maximus' insight is that the being that is willed by God cannot be annulled: This is the meaning of the term *logos* in Maximian metaphysics. Its reception however can entail distinct personal modalities. In this sense, the resurrection concerns the divine *logos* of eternal being, while divinization requires the positive human response of the eternal well-being. Saint Maximus' eschatological vision consists in a divine presence that shines everywhere. However, according to the use made by the rational beings, this same presence can constitute an eternal well-being, that is tantamount to divinization for the saved ones, or an eternal ill-being for the non-

---

[67] *Amb.Ioh.* 10,3, CONSTAS, 2014, 1, pp. 169–171, *PG* 91, 1116C–D.
[68] *Amb.Ioh.* 10,3, CONSTAS, 2014, 1, p. 169, *PG* 91, 1116B.
[69] See, for example, *Car. PG* 90, 1024C.
[70] *Amb.Ioh.* 42, CONSTAS, 2014, 2, p. 143, *PG* 91, 1325B.

divinized persons. Divinization means the possibility to participate in the divine operation due to the right movement within history, whereas the lack of divinization entails an exterior knowledge of God's presence without participation. Divinization is also regarded as the "eighth day" of creation, which means the innovation of the world that was created on the sixth day.[71] However, this divinization in the eschaton constitutes the fulfilment of the existential demands of being as it was initially created. This is the deeper insight of the ontological threefold schema of being, well-being, and eternal being, employed in the Tenth *Ambiguum*.

3. Divinization as divine adoption by grace: The Christological synthesis of Saint Maximus

For a full rendering of the Maximian doctrine of divinization, one should consider its connection with the "honour of adoption",[72] bestowed upon man through the Son of God. In the Tenth *Ambiguum*, Saint Maximus combines, on the one hand, the intellectualist element of the likeness to God as an assimilation of the intellect to its "object" and, on the other hand, the biblical theme of divinization as divine adoption. It is the latter which truly guarantees that divinization is by position and not by nature: If one remained at the philosophical level of an intellectualist divinization, then the deified person would lose his or her natural difference. On the contrary, the biblical theme of adoption means that we are deified not as "natural sons", but as "adopted" ones. Hence, the natural difference is preserved. The originality of Saint Maximus' theory of divinization inside the patristic tradition lies in the fact that he shifts the emphasis from protology to eschatology in a decisive manner. For Saint Maximus, God's will for nature is a divine *logos* that both accounts for the creation of nature, and leads to its fulfilment in the future. In this sense, divinization is desired by the human nature according to its *logos*. But it is also something that transcends the *logos* of nature, i.e. its logical principle. Here lies a basic Maximian antinomy: The *logos* of human nature leads it toward its eschatological completion, which consists in the divinization in Christ. But at the same time, this goal is above the *logos* of nature since it is a product of grace.

---

[71] *Cap.Div. PG* 90, 1104C.

[72] *Amb.Ioh.* 10,20a, CONSTAS, 2014, I, p. 215, *PG* 91, 1140B.

The ontological ground of divinization is thus the deification of the human nature of Christ, the latter being a Trinitarian divine project[73] independent of the contingency of the human Fall.[74] For Saint Maximus, divinization is a cosmological project that refers to the whole of creation and not only to human beings. Man is the mediator between nature and God, since he constitutes a microcosm by integrating within himself representative natural properties.[75] Thus, while it is the human nature that is divinized in Christ, the consequences of this divinization encompass the whole of creation. Divinization is the limit of all beings existing in time as a unitary goal engulfing the whole of creation.[76] Saint Maximus follows an eschatological teleology[77] according to which the goal of the nature of each being consists in its participation in divine life which, however, transcends the natural capacities of these same natures. There is thus space for human freedom and cooperation in this metaphysical itinerary from the potentialities of human nature to their actualization, the utmost goal of nature standing beyond its capacities and only offered by grace. Humanity is divinized not in its very nature, but in the mode of existence of the latter.[78] It is thus not something that is acquired through an operation or actualization of human nature, but solely as a result of divine grace.[79]

The consequences of this divinization are offered to the faithful in the sacramental life of the Church, especially in the Eucharist. In the latter, we partake in the divine energies that deify human nature due to the holy communion that expresses our communication with

[73] J.-C. LARCHET, *La Divinisation de l'Homme selon Saint Maxime le Confesseur*, Paris, 1996, pp. 83–105.

[74] *Q.Thal.* 60, CCSG 22, pp. 73,5–79,120, *PG* 90, 620C–624D.

[75] Cf. L. THUNBERG, *Microcosm and Mediator*.

[76] *Q.Thal.* 59, CCSG 22, p. 53,141–146: *PG* 90,609A.

[77] I explain the antinomical notion of "eschatological teleology" in detail in D. SKLIRIS, "'Eschatological teleology', 'free dialectic', 'Metaphysics of the Resurrection': The three antinomies that make Maximus an alternative European philosopher", in *Maximus the Confessor as a European Philosopher*, ed. by S. MITRALEXIS, G. STEIRIS, M. PODBIELSKI, S. LALLA, Eugene, Oregon, 2017, pp. 3–23.

[78] P. SHERWOOD, *The Earlier* Ambigua *of Saint Maximus the Confessor and his Refutation of Origenism*, Rome, 1955, pp. 57–58.

[79] J.-C. LARCHET, "The Mode of Deification", in *OHMC*, p. 350.

the mystical body of Christ in a way that is both symbolical and real-istic.[80] The biblical ground of this ecclesiological participation is the relation between the Transfiguration, the Crucifixion and the Res-urrection of Christ. The Transfiguration manifests the divinization of Christ's human nature, as prefigured in the ascent of Moses to the divine darkness.[81] For Saint Maximus, Moses is the prophet of the goal of divinization for humankind, later reflected in Christ's transfigura-tion which consists in the revelation of the energy of the divine glory prior to the Passion. It is in this sense that the prophecy "He had neither form nor beauty", referring to the Crucifixion is synthesized with the prophecy that the Messiah is "fair in beauty beyond the sons of men".[82] Saint Maximus regards this antinomy as one between cataphatic and apophatic theology, both trying to convey the mystery of divinization as preserving both the incognoscibility of divine otherness and the sal-vation of the full human nature. The truth of the Transfiguration is confirmed in the Resurrection which, however, is necessarily medi-ated by the Crucifixion, the latter signifying the natural gap between humanity and divinity that is only bridged hypostatically by grace.

It is in this sense that we should understand divinization as a goal above nature, and not merely as its actualization: Man has to experience that the true end of his nature is something more than just its actuality. The human desire has the function of pointing to such a supernatu-ral fulfilment of nature's capacities and is thus crucial for divinization. Man's vocation lies in transforming his desire into divine eros, as well as in shaping the irascible part of his soul through divine love. This the-ology of desire also entails that man was not perfect in his pre-lapsarian state. He might have been sinless, but he was also immature and under the necessity of following a path to perfection. In this aspect, Saint Maximus is closer to the tradition of Irenaeus of Lyon and Clement of Alexandria who consider Adam as an immature child, rather than as an already perfect man.

Divinization is thus a participation of humanity in the divine energy, which allows human beings to be deified by grace without,

---

[80] J. D. Zizioulas, *Communion & Otherness. Further Studies in Personhood and the Church*, London-New York, 2006, pp. 286–306.

[81] *Amb.Ioh.* 10,4, Constas, 2014, I, p. 173: *PG* 91, 1117B.

[82] *Amb.Ioh.* 10, Constas, 2014, I, pp. 191–193: *PG* 91, 1128A.

however, becoming divine in their essence or nature.[83] This novel mode
of human nature in Christ is related to its new universality, connected
with the fact that Christ is subject neither to sexual reproduction,
which is connected to the fragmentation of nature, nor to the necessity
of death, His death being a "free passion". Besides, for Saint Maximus,
Christ does not have a gnomic will insofar as the latter pertains to the
post-lapsarian fragmentation of nature.[84] In this sense, the divinization of the human nature of Christ could be considered as equivalent
to its universality which reflects the divine mode of being of the Trinity. For Saint Maximus this is less a "restitution" of human nature as
in Gregory of Nyssa, and more a prolepsis of the eschatological state
of humanity which reflects the catholicity of the Trinity, the latter
being a philosophical way of articulating the revealed truth that God
is love. Instead of following a protological doctrine of double creation
as Saint Gregory of Nyssa, Saint Maximus changes the perspective: the
so-called "first creation" is rather the divine *logos*, i.e. a divine will for
the future of nature as it will be integrated in Christ and manifested
in the eschaton.[85] The novel mode of existence of the human nature of
Christ is due to His divine hypostasis[86] that is in eternal communion
with the Father and the Spirit. The fact that the basis for the divinization of the human nature is a hypostatic union with the divine means
that the human nature can be saved in its natural difference from God,
namely in its created character comprising both psychological and
corporeal properties. Divinization is thus a confirmation of human
nature insofar as it guarantees its survival, its flourishing and expansion
according to the divine plan of its characteristic *logos*.[87] The human
nature of Christ is also divinized in the sense that it is the universal
nature that knows no death, sexual reproduction and gnomic fragmen-

---

[83] J.-C. LARCHET, "The Mode of Deification", p. 351.

[84] I. MCFARLAND, "The Theology of the Will", in *OHMC,* pp. 516–532.

[85] For the relation of the notion of logos with universality and eschatology,
see: J. ZIZIOULAS, "Person and Nature in the Theology of St. Maximus the
Confessor", in *Knowing the purpose of creation through the resurrection. Proceedings of the Symposium on St. Maximus the Confessor. Belgrade, October 18–21,
2012,* ed. by M. VASILJEVIĆ, Alhambra, California – Belgrade, 2013, pp. 85–113.

[86] *Amb.Ioh.* 36, M. CONSTAS, 2014, 2, pp. 70–73: *PG* 91,1289C–D.

[87] L. THUNBERG, *Microcosm and Mediator,* 31–32; J. MEYENDORFF, *Le
Christ dans la théologie byzantine,* Paris, 1969, pp. 288–289.

tation. In this sense, Christ's divinized human nature is the *"aparche"* for the resurrection and divinization of the human nature of all of us in the eschaton following the Pauline theology (*Rom.* 11:16), according to which the totality of humanity is recapitulated in the human nature of Christ.

Conclusion

We have observed different ways in which the theme of divinization is developed in the Tenth *Ambiguum*:

i) Divinization is the conclusion in a movement of ascent in which man, after being purified from the erroneous perspective that is due to the vices, can discern the *logoi* of beings, i.e. God's wills for the future of creation. We have examined how natural theory signifies a turning of the human intellect to God and how this turning realizes its similitude to the Trinity. The biblical theme of the "likeness to God" has a certain intellectualist *penchant* in the Tenth *Ambiguum* in the sense that the intellect becomes what it sees. If the intellect is turned, not to the created beings themselves which are perishable by nature, but to their divine meaning, then it becomes deiform and can ascend to the mystical union with God's simplicity. The latter is also considered as transcending the split between matter and form that characterizes created being, since man can reach the level of the Trinity-in-Unity that is God. Saint Maximus, however, connects this intellectualist approach with biblical elements, such as the relation between the Transfiguration, the Crucifixion and the Resurrection of Christ, which fulfil the sixth, the seventh and the eighth day of creation.

ii) At the ontological level, divinization is equivalent to the eternal (well-)being that constitutes the eschatological confirmation of being. More precisely, the eternal-being is the resurrection that saves the being of created nature, whereas the personal divinization concerns the confirmation of the ethical well-being of history that survives after the final judgment of Christ, and which removes the sting of death from creation.

iii) Saint Maximus equally employs the biblical theme of "divine adoption" in order to show that the divinization is not by nature, but by grace and by "position", as having an hypostatic character such that we become "sons" of God through Christ in the Spirit. In the Maximian synthesis between metaphysics and biblical theology, the *logoi* of beings lead creation to the incarnated Logos who realizes the divinization of the created human nature in His flesh, and who then elevates the universal humanity to the life of the Trinity through the Spirit. The relation of the created human *logos* to the intellect in the spirit is thus an image of the Trinitarian life. But in order to achieve the authentic likeness of divinization, we have to incarnate the Word within ourselves through purification from the passions, contemplation of the divine *logoi* with our created intellect, and the reception of the grace of adoption through the Spirit leading us to the Father as members of the eschatological body of Christ. It is this synthesis of philosophical wisdom and theological soteriology that is arguably the most original trait in Saint Maximus' theory of divinization in the Tenth *Ambiguum*.

INDICES

Index of Maximus Citations

Index of Premodern Authors

Index of Philosophical and Theological Terms